COMMUNITIES OF VIOLENCE

COMMUNITIES OF VIOLENCE

PERSECUTION OF MINORITIES
IN THE MIDDLE AGES

David Nirenberg

with a new preface by the author

PRINCETON UNIVERSITY PRESS

PRINCETON AND OXFORD

Requests for permission to reproduce material from this work should be sent to
Permissions, Princeton University Press

press.princeton.edu

First printing, 1996
First paperback printing, 1998
New paperback edition, with a new preface by the author, 2015

Paper ISBN: 978-0-691-16576-9
Library of Congress Control Number: 2015930408

British Library Cataloging-in-Publication Data is available

This book has been composed in Bembo

Printed on acid-free paper. ∞

Printed in the United States of America

1 3 5 7 9 10 8 6 4 2

CONTENTS

PREFACE TO THE NEW PAPERBACK EDITION

I DID NOT have violence on my mind when I first entered the Archive of the Crown of Aragon in 1989. Relations between Muslims, Christians, and Jews in the Middle Ages were what I was looking for, and if I remember correctly I expected many of those relations to be loving, or at least sexual. My undergraduate studies had introduced me to a world of interfaith prostitution and occasional intermarriage in medieval Iberia, a world I hoped to explore and expand in a doctoral dissertation. My motives for that interest I cannot recollect. Perhaps I was searching for a potent and positive metaphor for the coexistence of the three faiths in the long ago and far away: an intimate medieval allegory for what seemed in 1989 (and still today) a religiously troubled present.

I say perhaps, but I doubt it. I was in my twenties when I researched and wrote *Communities of Violence*, the age at which rebellion against the comforting myths of childhood often takes its most aggressively intellectual form. From a lover of Andrew Lang and the Brothers Grimm I had turned into an (equally naïve?) foe of those who search for idylls in the past. Like the eighteenth century German philosopher Herder (who was also writing about medieval Iberia), I dismissed irenic accounts of medieval relations between Muslims, Christians, and Jews as *angenehmes Märchen*, "comfortable fairy tales."

Nor did I follow those who trafficked in nightmares, like the political scientist Samuel Huntington, whose *The Clash of Civilizations*, published in the same year (1996) as *Communities of Violence*, prophesied a new world order of increasingly religious confrontation in which geopolitical conflict would be structured along the fault lines between competing civilizational blocks, each unified by a shared religion and culture that would put them at odds with their neighbors. I had (and have) little confidence in such prophets, and least of all in their pretensions to quantify the relative capacity for violence of a given religion or civilization. "Islam has bloody borders," Huntington declared, blithely ignoring the beam in his own society's eye. To my mind, such projects were fairy tales as well, no less comforting for being terrifying.[1]

I did not read Huntington (or Herder) until many years after *Communities of Violence* appeared. But both the yearning to discover times and places of peaceful religious interaction, and to project blame for violence upon one faith or another, now seem to me symptoms of a *Zeitgeist* emerging in the time period in which I was studying and writing: an era in which religion began to occupy, in the world's attention, much of the space vacated by the receding ideological alignments of the Cold War. The topic of conflict between Muslims, Christians, and Jews was very much in the air (this was, after all, the period of the first Pal-

---

[1] Samuel Huntington, "The Clash of Civilizations?" *Foreign Affairs* 72, no. 3 (Summer 1993): 35. For "bloody borders," see Huntington, *The Clash of Civilizations and the Remaking of World Order* (New York: Simon & Schuster, 1996), 258.

estinian Intifada). All of us—whether as students, citizens, consumers of news or media, church- mosque- or synagogue-goers—imbibed various treatments of it more or less unconsciously in our intellectual water.

In short, although in retrospect I can propose a context, I cannot say exactly what impulses, hopes, and aspirations drove me up the stairs of Barcelona's Palau del Lloctinent, the mid-sixteenth century palace built by Charles V that had once provided offices to the Inquisition, and that housed (from 1836 to 1994) the Archive of the Crown of Aragon. What I do know is that a year's worth of bleary-eyed hours later I emerged from that palace with thousands of documents, some concerned with love and sex, to be sure; others with commerce, collaboration, even co-conspiracy; still others with riot, murder, and massacre. It seemed impossible to balance these archival registers through a polarized accounting: evidence of tolerance on one side of the ledger, of violence on the other.

On the contrary, the most intimate collaborations tended to surface in the archive only because accompanying violence had brought them to bureaucratic attention. The most regular acts of violence (such as annual riots by Christians against Jews during Holy Week) appeared, on account of that very regularity, to be part of a system of restraint that made coexistence possible. And even the bloodiest massacres (such as those that accompanied the arrival of the Shepherd's Crusade in 1320 or the Black Death in 1348) revealed not only the punctuating potential of exterminatory violence in these multi-faith communities, but also the power of those communities to recover, after such devastating ruptures, something like what today we might call a pluralist equilibrium.

This co-production of community and violence apparent in the sources is difficult for historians to tolerate, judging from my own reactions to this initially inchoate mass of documentation. Often enough we build our arguments for the tolerant virtues of a particular period or religious culture by neglecting episodes of violence, or setting them aside as aberrational, exceptional, non-systemic, unrevealing. In search of a heuristic golden age, we see nothing that isn't yellow. Conversely when we want to emphasize a given society, religion, or culture's propensity toward barbarity, it is violence that is structural, coexistence that is merely strategic or "situational," and history begins to look like a long list of cruelties, an endless tour of mass graves.

Such polarized histories are important. They articulate values (such as pluralism or toleration) by identifying heroes and villains and marking them with hats of the appropriate color, providing us with what we might call historicized morality tales. They can even make us more critically aware of our own prejudices and assumptions, as when a "golden age" (Herder's "fairy tale") of tolerance in medieval *Al-Andalus* (the Arabic name for Islamic Iberia) is today deployed to interrogate liberal Western claims to moral and political superiority over contemporary Islamic movements.

But precisely because these histories tend to divide the evidence, they tend to obscure the question that eventually came to interest me in *Communities of*

Violence, namely: what is it about a given multi-religious society that gives it the potential to produce both coexistence and violent intolerance, and what determines which of these potentials is actualized at a given time and place? Eleventh century Muslim Granada was simultaneously capable, within a generation, of elevating a Jew to the position of "prime minister" (*wazir*), and of massacring both Jewish vizier and Jewish community. We need to be capable of perceiving both these phenomena at once, rather than dismissing the importance of the one or the other. From this point of view neither histories of pluralism that ignore its failures, nor histories of persecution that overlook long periods of effective coexistence, are satisfactory.

What would a satisfactory history of a given society or religion's potential for coexistence and for violence look like? *Communities of Violence* was my own first attempt to engage this question, which I have not yet stopped asking. The question has no simple answer, not least because every history depends—as we are too well aware in our postmodern age—on countless very basic and always debatable decisions by the historian, decisions that can never be made fully independent of the historian's perspective. Every narration, even that of our own individual experience, requires selection so ruthless that we can compare it to mass violence: the recognition of a few voices as significant, and the consigning of untold others to oblivion. Sometimes we are conscious of the bases for our selective attention, often not.

But beyond such epistemological and psychological truisms, let me focus on just two very general types of decision that confront any historical inquiry into the capacities of Muslim, Christian, and Jewish communities for coexistence and for violence, and that I tried to interrogate in *Communities of Violence*. One has to do with historical time itself: how do we choose to divide or connect it? And the second has to do with our categories of analysis. How do we as historians decide what should be classified as evidence for or cause of violence, oppression, even extermination, and what as pointing toward toleration, coexistence, or religious freedom?

The first of these questions is acute for historians, who so often understand their *métier* as the study of change over time. Yet time does not come without a frame, and our choice of time frame—that is, our sense of what moments in the past are continuous with other moments in the future, or are relevant to our questions in the present—is always laden with commitments that are themselves historically conditioned. Some of these commitments are theoretical, others experiential, psychological, religious, political; some conscious, many not.

The same applies not only to the historian, but also to her sources. Like the nocturnal drunk from the old joke, looking for lost keys under the street-lamp because that is the only place where there is light, the historian's choice of what past to study is often conditioned by the survival of evidence over time. Our sense of time frame is therefore not independent of the motives, choices, and selections of those who produced and preserved these sources. Which is to say that as we look tipsily for our keys in the past, we must struggle to become conscious not only of our own choices, but also of those who built and maintained the lamp-posts.

Thanks in part to their precocious possession of paper mills conquered from their Muslim neighbors (paper is a much cheaper medium for writing than surfaces made of animal hides such as parchment or vellum), the archives of the kings of Aragon shed some of the brightest light on the medieval world. In *Communities of Violence,* I wanted to set the brilliantly lit world of this one fourteenth-century society in productive tension with some of the more influential time frames created by other historians. Many of these other time frames were oriented toward murderous twentieth-century futures, their goal to answer the governing question "when did Europe go wrong." For a number of great historians the answer to that question was in the Middle Ages. It was, for example, in Christian medieval myths of conspiracy (by Jews, lepers, and Muslims, among others), in medieval massacres and expulsions, that they sought Europe's "Warrant for Genocide," its origins as a persecuting society.

There is much to be learned from such Holocaust-oriented history. But my hoard of records suggested that something was also lost. Where many historians working on medieval France or Germany might have to make do with a few (if any) textual witnesses to large-scale episodes of violence, I had hundreds available for each of the events—such as the 1320 massacre of hundreds of Jews in the small mountain village of Montclus—I was encountering. These allowed me to ask questions about the different, often competing ways in which the participants in these events understood (or at least justified) their interactions, violent and non-violent, with their neighbors of different faiths.

Through these documents I tried to show how medieval Jews, Muslims, and Christians made sense of a world filled with many different possibilities for interaction, violent and non-violent; how and why they chose amongst those possibilities as they jostled their way toward a future; and how their choices changed the possibilities for that future. My goal was to restore some agency to the actors and some surprise to our sense of the relations between past and future, context and discourse, contingency and structure.

The second general question that concerns our decisions as historians is about the valence of the events we study. How do we choose between "positive" and "negative"? How do we classify actions and discourses as contributing to pluralism and coexistence, or intolerance, expulsion, and extermination? It may seem that the choice is easy and obvious, but if we transpose the question to our contemporary world some difficulties become clearer. There is today sharp disagreement about whether (for example) Western liberal democracy is a source of liberty or of crushing neo-colonial oppression; Islamism is a pluralist and anti-imperialist freedom struggle or a violent, sexist, and religiously intolerant terror movement; Israeli Zionism a tolerant and religiously plural democratic movement or a genocidal Jewish tyranny.

Powerful cases can be (and often are) made for each of these opposing choices and classifications, all of which can be supported by invocations of history. Each of these cases can, in turn, be offered as a source of geo-political explanation, moral certainty, and even cosmological comfort to communities in the present. Think here, for example, of Pope Benedict XVI's 2006 Regensburg address on "Faith, Reason, and the University," in which he explained why Islam was a religion of violence, and only Catholicism is capable of both truth and tolerance. Or conversely, consider article 31 of the Hamas Charter of 1988:

> The Islamic Resistance Movement is a humanistic movement. It takes care of human rights and is guided by Islamic tolerance when dealing with the followers of other religions. It does not antagonize anyone of them except if it is antagonized by it or stands in its way to hamper its moves and waste its efforts. Under the wing of Islam, it is possible for the followers of the three religions—Islam, Christianity and Judaism—to coexist in peace and quiet with each other. Peace and quiet would not be possible except under the wing of Islam. Past and present history are the best witness to that.[2]

I mention these claims simply as a reminder of the importance that these classifications of the past can still have in the politics of the present. Of course at some level we know, or ought to know, that these claims to classification are seldom innocent, and that the history of even our most cherished values and ideals is capable of being put to work in the production of horrors. Walter Benjamin's dictum that "there is never a document of civilization that is not at the same time a document of barbarism" is often quoted (even if often enough out of context). And at least in the case of European claims to progress and virtue, we have many works, like Horkheimer and Adorno's *Dialectics of Enlightenment*, exhorting us to speak of their histories with critical ambivalence.[3]

And yet, perhaps precisely because our various commitments in the present are so powerful, it has proven difficult to study the history of relations between Christians, Jews, and Muslims without splitting that history into two, violence on the one side, peace and tolerance on the other. I wanted to suggest something quite different, something I hoped to convey already in the nouns juxtaposed within the title *Communities of Violence*: namely, "the fundamental interdependence of violence and tolerance" (7) in the societies I was studying.

We can see this interdependence in multiple registers of society, both "high" and "low." Chapter five on "Sex and Violence between Majority and Minority" dwelt on prohibitions and anxieties in all three communities about interfaith sex. It traced the specific contours of those anxieties, showing how they tended

---

[2] Avalon.law.yale.edu/20th_century/hamas.asp. For a slightly different translation see http://www.palestinecenter.org/cpap/documents/charter.html.

[3] Benjamin, Walter. "Über den Begriff der Geschichte," Thesis VII. *Walter Benjamin Abhandlungen: Gesammelte Schriften*. 7 vols. Ed. Rolf Tiedemann and Hermann Schweppenhäuser. Frankfurt: Suhrkamp, 1991. Vol. I. 696.

to be contained in the bodies of prostitutes while ignoring other women. And it suggested that the violence provoked by those specific anxieties could simultaneously broaden the possibilities for interaction between members of different faiths, quarantining, so to speak, what might have been a highly generalizable fear by focusing it on specific agents. Those agents, that is, Christian prostitutes, were sensitive to their boundary-marking role, as were their Christian and non-Christian clients: a sensitivity that is not surprising, given that the penalty for intercourse between Christian and non-Christian was death. The study of how they played that role in their interfaith encounters provides a highly revealing and sometimes tragic illumination of both the range and the limits of negotiation in this multi-religious society.

"The Two Faces of Sacred Violence," chapter seven, on the other hand, took up a divine office, the annual stoning of Jews and Jewish quarters during Holy Week, in order to make a similar argument. These rituals both challenged and represented a venerable discourse legitimating the presence of Jews in Christian society. Their violence was ambivalent, simultaneously a gesture of inclusion and of seclusion, even potentially extermination. In important ways these riots, so strictly limited by the religious calendar, encouraged the toleration of Jews in Christian society for the rest of the year. But in equally important ways they articulated a messianic revolt against such compromises, and pointed toward an ideal world in which both toleration and the Jews would disappear.

Sex and ritual were only a few of the types of interaction emerging from the worm-eaten registers of the Aragonese kings to which I dedicated pages. Feuds and funeral processions, butcher shops and blacksmith guilds, even murder and marriage: these and many other less alliterative forms of relation brought people of all three faiths together in the Iberian Middle Ages, and also pushed them apart. My point here was not that there is no difference between violence and tolerance, coexistence and persecution. It was rather that, in these societies at least, coexistence was built out of the same types of conflict that could and would also destroy it.

Because books have fates and readers have rights, authors are the last who should opine about the reception of their works, except to express gratitude that others have found it useful to think with. I cannot know the many directions those thoughts have gone. But I would like to comment, first on what seems to me a road too seldom taken, and then on one perhaps too heavily travelled. The road not taken: *Communities of Violence* was, among other things, a manifesto for the interdependence of margin and center (to use a somewhat misleading metaphor), minority and majority, relative powerlessness and relative power. Among other things, it claimed to show the importance of the many "marginal" groups it studied—Muslims, Jews, lepers, converts, prostitutes, children, among others—to the articulation of the possibilities of existence, from the most stigmatized to the most ideal, in a given time and place.

In other words, this is not a book about the history of Jews, or Muslims, or lepers, or any other single minority group, although it did attempt to contribute to the history of all of these. It is a book about the dynamics of conflict and co-existence in a plural society. Many fine studies of Muslim or Jewish communities in Christian Europe (and of Jewish and Christian communities in the Islamic world) have since appeared. But few, to my knowledge, have attempted to treat multiple groups together. Even fewer have touched upon relations between minority groups (as I did in chapter six, "Minorities Confront Each Other"), a subject I still find fascinating not only for its own sake, but also because of the light it sheds upon the ways in which relations between Muslims and Jews in societies ruled by Christians can be shaped by the demands and the discourses of the dominant. And none (so far as I know) has taken up the more general suggestion, perhaps only implicit in *Communities of Violence*, that all of these groups and communities of faith, whether Muslim, Jewish, Christian or convert, produced and co-produced themselves through a process of simultaneous identification and dis-identification with their rival "siblings" and neighbors.

As for the roads too heavily travelled, all share a tendency to split ambivalences, rather than to explore their depths. For example, many historians today stress the importance of understanding the local contexts in which people in the past put their arguments and ideas to work. They seek (as I did) to trouble easy continuities between the medieval and the modern, between the massacres of the fourteenth century and the mass-murders of the twentieth. But my sense is that too often they try to cleave any continuity between the hatreds of the past and the present, rather than putting the two in productive tension with each other. My argument in *Communities of Violence* was not that continuities between past and present do not exist, but that context and contingency can offer us a testing ground for our projections of the future into the past, helping us become more critical of the continuities we create.

If we cut the past into small enough pieces—to paraphrase Montaigne and Seneca—every moment becomes unique and all continuity disappears. In this sense, context and contingency seem to promise a heady freedom from the gravity of history. But that freedom is just as false as the tyranny of deterministic histories. The past and the future can be (and will be) meaningfully related, even if the nature of that meaning cannot be fixed. The Holy Week riots of the thirteenth and early fourteenth centuries are not independent of the massacres, forced conversions, purity of blood statutes, and expulsions of the fifteenth and sixteenth centuries, which in turn have something to do with the possibilities of modernity. If historians abandon the struggle to determine just what this something is, there will be few critical voices left to hold the field of the past against the fantasies of the present.

Continuity vs. context: this was only one of the ambivalences fundamental to *Communities of Violence*. The interdependence between violence and tolerance, collective discourse and individual agency, contingency and structure: all of these have been split by scholars seeking relief from the burden of history. Some, for example, seize upon and generalize the pluralist potential of violence that I identified in fourteenth-century communities, ignoring what I showed was the equally present potential for the messianic extermination of difference. The result is a rose-tinted scapegoating theory, in which any act of violence can be interpreted as part of a system of tolerance, draining history of all its horrors.

In short, the years since the publication of *Communities of Violence* have impressed upon me the power of our yearning to "periodize through violence, to divide the... world into opposing categories of tolerance and intolerance, mutual interest versus mutual hostility, open society or closed," rather than accepting "the dependence of the one upon the other" (245). And above all, these years have surprised me by the tendency to find in this book authorization to dismiss the importance of the long history of ideas, prejudices, or theological and cultural discourses in shaping the possibilities for interaction between members of different religions. Though I had repeatedly written that "discourse and agency gain meaning only in relation to each other" (6), for many readers the book's appeal seems to reside in its distance from the long history of anti-Jewish and anti-Muslim discourses that we have so painfully learned to associate with Christianity and the West.

It was very much in reaction to that surprise that I wrote *Anti-Judaism: the Western Tradition* (2013). As its title implies, that book took a very long view. It traces the history of work done by ideas about Judaism in any number of societies, religions, and cultures, beginning with ancient Egypt and ending in the 1950s, in order to show how deeply these societies were shaped by thinking about Jews and Judaism, even when (as was often the case), there were no real Jews living within them.

Those readers and reviewers who have seen in *Anti-Judaism* a retraction of *Communities* have not, I think, quite understood either book. Both insist on the inseparability of discourse and agency, and explore the interaction of the accumulated choices and actions taken by people in the past (what we call history) with the choices and actions available and imaginable to people as they try to make their lives in their own present. In *Communities* the present was the fourteenth century, with the stress placed upon the creativity with which medieval people engaged with and transformed the historical structures in which they lived, because I believed that their previous historians had neglected that creativity.

But the opposite neglect—the neglect of the ways in which the past shapes our perception of and choices in the world—is just as dangerous. Over the past decade or two I have come to feel it to be the more pressing danger, not just in our writing of history, but also in our politics. So *Anti-Judaism* insists on the same creative interaction between what has been and what can be, but stresses the power of the past in constraining that creativity, showing how people in any number of contexts—ancient, medieval, and modern—transformed their worlds in ways that were not independent of the choices their predecessors had made. Every person makes their own history, but they do not make it as they please. With their different perspectives on this problem, both books tried to make the same point.

It is easy enough to feel that *Communities* pointed toward the positive, with its emphasis on the vast spaces of difference that separate medieval massacres from modern holocausts, whereas by encompassing all those differences within one narrative *Anti-Judaism* seems to threaten us with imminent disaster. But again, both books insisted that the positive and negative potentials are inseparable, that both have always been present in every gesture produced in the long history of these three religions, and that how we choose to classify those gestures often depends on what questions we feel most urgent, what futures we most fear.

Nevertheless I grant that the moods of the two books are very different. It was in part to make clearer the relationship between those moods, between optimism and pessimism, so to speak, that I wrote *Neighboring Faiths: Christianity, Islam, and Judaism Medieval and Modern* (2014). That book is something of a sequel to *Communities of Violence* in that it is built with the treasure of Iberian archives. But much more explicitly than the earlier book, it puts those archives into conversation with a long past and a long future. Its goal is to present a world in which the three religions are interdependent, bound together by a history of ideas as well as by an intimate sociology, creating and constantly transforming themselves by thinking about and (sometimes) living next to each other in a fundamentally ambivalent form of neighborliness.

Fundamentally ambivalent, because it is through this neighborliness that all three "sibling" communities of faith simultaneously recognize and deny their common claim to truth and divine love and truth. The visions of the world that result from this neighborliness can range from ecumenism to extermination. Often enough they include both at once (as in the messianic view that tolerates diversity as a necessary evil in this fallen world but eagerly anticipates its apocalyptic disappearance in an ideal future). But whether we consider them "positive" or "negative," these visions of the world are all co-productions, not only of Judaism, Christianity, and Islam, but also of past and present: the product of religious communities continuously constituting themselves by re-imagining the history of relations with each other. When I wrote *Communities of Violence* the need to understand the creative and destructive potentials produced by these three great faiths in their relations with each other seemed to me a most pressing question. Twenty years later I am still asking that same question, and it only seems more urgent.

ACKNOWLEDGMENTS

MANY OBLIGATIONS, material and spiritual, were incurred in the writing of this book. Financial support for the project came from a variety of institutions. The Andrew W. Mellon Foundation; the Ford and the William and Flora Hewlett Foundations under the auspices of the Social Science Research Council; the Fulbright-Hays/Spanish Government program; the Program for Cultural Cooperation between Spain's Ministry of Culture and American Universities; and the Mrs. Giles Whiting Foundation all made possible the dissertation from which the book has grown. The Dean of Humanities and the Center for the Study of Cultures at Rice University, as well as the National Endowment for the Humanities, supported that growth and revision.

I first began studying violence as a graduate student in the History Department at Princeton University, and I owe a great deal to its faculty, to the weekly *agon* of the Davis Seminar, and above all to my fellow graduate students there. The Department of History at Rice University, my home for the past three years, has proven equally hospitable and stimulating. The effect my colleagues here have had on my work will be evident to readers of footnotes. In Barcelona, the Archive of the Crown of Aragon provided both raw materials for my project and interlocutors with whom to hammer out their implications. The Director of the Archive, Rafael Conde y Delgado de Molina, and its staff were a constant source of help and knowledge. I would especially like to thank Jaume Riera i Sans, archivist of the Chancery section, who provided patient correction and wise advice. In addition to dispensing freely of his vast erudition, it was he who introduced me to the shepherds and led me to the slaughters of 1320, 1321, and 1348. Across the Ramblas and in the shadow of the medieval hospital, the Institució Milà i Fontanals (C.S.I.C., Barcelona) provided a congenial environment in which to read and learn. I would like to thank its director, Maria Teresa Ferrer i Mallol, for her hospitality, and for sharing so generously with me her monumental work on the Muslim populations of the Crown of Aragon.

For me, the pages that follow are crowded with the friends and colleagues on both sides of the Atlantic who contributed to their writing. I would like to acknowledge them all, though space allows me to recall only a few: Asunción Blasco Martínez, Dolors Bramon, Philippe Buc, Daniel Castro (who produced the maps), Lluís Cifuentes, David Cohen, Anna Domingo i Grabiel, María Echániz Sans, Gemma Escribà i Bonastre, Talya Fishman, Josep Fradera, Paul Freedman, Ben Glassman, Thomas Haskell, Sara Lipton, Elena Lourie, Michael Maas, Hilary Mackie, Michael McVaugh, Mark Meyerson, Kathryn Miller, Josefa Mutgé i Vives, Lauren Osborne, Carol Quillen, David Romano Ventura, Teófilo

Ruiz, Manuel Sánchez Martínez, Paula Sanders, Carmen Pi Sunyer, and Richard Wolin.

I can think of no way to adequately express my gratitude to my teachers. The late John Boswell introduced me to the minorities of the Crown of Aragon when I was an undergraduate, and somehow found the patience to laugh at the results of his matchmaking even in his final months. Peter Brown, Natalie Davis, and William Jordan taught me through their seminars, their writings, and their generous readings and critique. A part of my debt to them will be clear to anyone familiar with their work, but those many who have benefited as students from their sensitivity and rigor will realize how much goes unsaid. In particular Bill Jordan, my adviser, knows how much he has taught me by word and by example, though he would dismiss as sentiment any adequate expression of my gratitude, respect, and affection. Confronting these failures of language I limit myself to thanks, and hope that my teachers will accept this small gift in exchange for their great one.

Thus far my scholarly acknowledgments to the first edition of 1996. As for the more personal acknowledgements that followed, the intervening years have seen much change. Unmentioned then was my son Alexander, born shortly before the book, now grown into a writer himself and a creator of worlds, including my own. Such changes and so many others have only confirmed me in my last line, both then as now: it is to my family that I dedicate this book.

.   .   .   .   .

Portions of an earlier version of chapter 6 appeared in *Viator* 23 (1993) as "Muslim-Jewish Relations in the Fourteenth-Century Crown of Aragon," while an abbreviated translation of chapter 7 was published in *Annales: Histoire, Sciences Sociales* 50 (1995) as "Les juifs, la violence et le sacré."

ABBREVIATIONS

ACA	Arxiu de la Corona d'Aragó
C	Cancelleria Reial
cr.	cartes reials
MR	Mestre Racional
RP	Reial Patrimoni
ACB	Arxiu Capitular de Barcelona
ADG	Arxiu Diocesà de Girona
Adret	Solomon b. Abraham ibn Adret, *She'elot u-teshuvot (Responsa)*, 7 vols. (Jerusalem, 1965–1970).
AHCB	Arxiu Històric de la Ciutat de Barcelona
AHCG	Arxiu Històric de la Ciutat de Girona
AHM:LC	Arxiu Històric de Mallorca, Lletres comunes
AHPG	Arxiu Històric Provincial de Girona
AHPH Pr.	Archivo Histórico Provincial de Huesca, Protocolos
AHPT	Arxiu Històric Provincial de Tarragona
AM	Archivo Municipal
AMV	Archivo Municipal de Valencia
AMVil	Archivo Municipal de Vilareal
ARV	Archivo del Reino de Valencia
ASV	Archivo Secreto Vaticano
BN	Bibliothèque Nationale (Paris)
BNM	Biblioteca Nacional (Madrid)
CC	*Corpus Christianorum*, Series Latina
CoDoIn	Colección de Documentos Inéditos del Archivo de la Corona de Aragón
IMHB	Institut Municipal d'Història de Barcelona
Ll.M. *or* g³	Lletres Missives
MC	Manuals de Consells
MGH	*Monumenta Germaniae Historica*
NC	Notaria Capitular
PL	*Patrologia Latina*, ed. Migne.
RdÉJ	*Revue des Études Juives*
Régné	J. Régné, *History of the Jews in Aragon: Regesta and Documents (1213–1327)* (Jerusalem, 1978).

INTRODUCTION

THE TRUTH of the dictum that the present shapes the past is nowhere more evident than in the effects of World War II on historical writing about European minorities.[1] Before that war and its attendant horrors, Jewish history was by and large outside the mainstream of the historical profession, written by Jews and ignored by others (as in some ways it still is).[2] When mainstream historians did touch upon the history of Jews and other minorities, it was as part of confessional history. Protestants especially wrote about medieval violence and intolerance toward minorities (heretics, Moriscos, Jews, lepers, witches) in order to claim that Catholicism had benighted Europe and made its people brutal in the period between the fall of Rome and the birth of Luther.[3] For the most part, however, the study of "Medieval Society" writ large seldom intersected with the study of its minorities.

Since the Holocaust such a position has become untenable. Few today would argue, for example, that the study of Jews and attitudes toward Jews in Germany tells us little about the formation of modern German cultural and national identities. Nor, in the wake of current attacks on Muslims in the former Yugoslavia, on "foreigners" (often Muslim) in Germany, France, and Italy, or on Jews in Russia, is it possible to argue that episodes of violence against minorities are part of a primitive European past which modern societies have left behind. The study of medieval minorities has therefore acquired a new urgency, and it has been transformed by some into a search for the roots of modern evils. "When did Europe go wrong?" is a question that has been asked more and more frequently over the past fifty years.

A frequent answer, it seems, is "in the Middle Ages." As Norman Cohn put it in his book *Warrant for Genocide*,

> As I see it, the deadliest kind of antisemitism, the kind that results in massacre and attempted genocide, has little to do with real conflicts of interest between living people, or even with racial prejudice as such. At its heart lies the belief that Jews—all Jews everywhere—form a conspiratorial body set on ruining and then dominating the

---

[1] Cf. M. Bloch, *The Historian's Craft* (New York, 1953), pp. 43–47. Bloch wrote these words in hiding shortly before he himself was killed by the Nazis. I do not doubt that their articulation was itself a product of the war.

[2] See G. Langmuir, "Majority History and Postbiblical Jews," in *Toward a Definition of Antisemitism* (Berkeley and Los Angeles, 1990), pp. 21–41.

[3] G. G. Coulton is a salient example, most blatantly in his historical novel *The Friar's Lantern* (London, 1906). Such Protestant-Catholic polemics were particularly important in the early historiography on Muslims and Moriscos in the Iberian Peninsula.

rest of mankind. And this belief is simply a modernized, secularized version of the popular medieval view.[4]

The implications of Cohn's thesis are clear: the most dangerous attitudes toward minorities, or at least toward Jews, do not draw their strength from the interactions of individuals and groups within a society, but from collective beliefs, beliefs formed in the Middle Ages and transmitted to the present day.[5] Hence medievalists have written books like Cohn's *Europe's Inner Demons*, Robert Moore's *The Formation of a Persecuting Society*, and Carlo Ginzburg's *Ecstasies*[6]— books that are exercises in psychoanalysis, attempts to understand an assumed collective unconscious of modern Europeans.

There are different opinions, of course, as to when a "tolerant" European Middle Ages turned bad. Historians of Jews, Muslims, heretics, gay people, and lepers have all placed the shift at different dates, ranging from the First Crusade (which provoked a good deal of violence against European Jews) forward. Most recently Carlo Ginzburg has argued for a later date, claiming that there emerged in the first half of the fourteenth century (the period covered in the present work) an irrational fear of conspiracy which had previously been repressed in the European mentality: a belief that certain groups, whether Jews, lepers, or witches, were conspiring to destroy society. It was this irrational mentality, Ginzburg believes, that led to pogroms against the Jews, to accusations of well poisoning and ritual murder, and to the great witch hunts of the early modern period.

Regardless of their different periodizations, all these quests for the origins of European intolerance have much in common. All take the long view, seeking to establish a continuity between the hatreds of long ago and those of the here and now. This focus on the *longue durée* means that events are read less within their local contexts than according to a teleology leading, more or less explicitly,

---

[4] *Warrant for Genocide: The Myth of the Jewish World-Conspiracy and the "Protocols of the Elders of Zion"* (New York, 1967), p. 16. A similar passage from the same work is quoted approvingly and expanded by L. Rothkrug, "Peasant and Jew: Fears of Pollution and German Collective Perceptions," *Historical Reflections / Réflexions Historiques* 10 (1983): 59–77, here p. 60.

[5] There are, of course, historians with the opposite view. B. Blumenkranz, for example, writes that "the struggle of Christianity against Judaism is not inevitable, necessary, nor essential. Rather it is a product of general conditions emerging out of internal and external politics and sociological facts. In short, it is only contingent." Such pleas for contingency have had limited influence even upon those who quote them. Thus A. Cutler and H. Cutler, whose translation of Blumenkranz was just quoted, "could not agree more with these sentiments" but proceed on the same page to argue that "*Anti-Muslimism was the primary* . . . factor in the revival of anti-Semitism during the High Middle Ages (1000–1300), the effects of which have been felt in all subsequent centuries, including our own." *The Jew as Ally of the Muslim: Medieval Roots of Anti-Semitism* (Notre Dame, IN, 1986), p. 2, quoting from *Le juif medieval au miroir de l'art chrétien* (Paris, 1966), p. 136.

[6] (London, 1975); (Oxford, 1987); (New York, 1991). See also Léon Poliakov, *The Aryan Myth: A History of Racist and Nationalist Ideas in Europe* (New York, 1974); and Rothkrug's article cited above, n. 4.

to the Holocaust. Similarly, instead of emphasizing local or even individual opinions about minorities, they focus on collective images, representations, and stereotypes of the "other." The actions of groups or individuals are ignored in favor of structures of thought that are believed to govern those actions.[7] Historians therefore act as geologists, tracing the ancient processes by which collective anxieties accreted into a persecutory landscape that has changed little over the past millennium. The refutation of this widespread notion that we can best understand intolerance by stressing the fundamental continuity between collective systems of thought across historical time, or in this case across one thousand years, is an overarching goal of the present work.

The emphasis on continuity and collective systems of thought can be called "structuralist" without too much violence to that word.[8] Within the structuralist consensus in the historiography of persecution there are different methodologies. Two are especially common. The first links the rise of persecuting mentalities to other secular processes: the creation of a monetary economy or the rise of centralized monarchies, for example.[9] Exponents of this approach, such as Robert Moore, emphasize processes of historical change up to a point. They allow contingency during the gestation of intolerance, but after its birth the persecuting mentality seems to transcend particularities of time and place. The second methodology traces the pedigree of stereotypes and beliefs in order to establish the existence of a "discourse" about the "other" and fix its origins. It treats intolerance entirely as a problem in the migratory history of ideas, ignoring social, economic, political, or cultural variables. Thus Ginzburg follows the folkloric roots of the witches' Sabbath from eighth-century B.C. central Asia to Essex, England, 1645; while the author of another recent work traces the demonization and dehumanization of Jews from Alexandrian Egypt to high medieval Passion plays in order to understand "the daydreams of monks, the sermons of the preachers, the imagination of the artists, and the anxious psyche of Everyman."[10]

---

[7] These are, of course, relatives of very ancient dichotomies currently at the heart of theoretical debate about textual interpretation: subjectivism/objectivism, structure/agency, langue/parole, among others. Put most briefly and abstractly, the debate is over the degree of autonomy individuals have within the collective rules and institutions that structure their society. In the case of langue/parole, for example, langue refers to the background of rules by which language functions (the linguistics, so to speak), while parole refers to usage, to the ways in which individuals speak.

[8] Cf. P. Anderson, *In the Tracks of Historical Materialism* (Chicago, 1984), chap. 2, "Structure and Subject," esp. pp. 44 f.

[9] See, e.g., L. Little, *Religious Poverty and the Profit Economy in Medieval Europe* (Ithaca, NY, 1978), p. 42.

[10] Ginzburg, *Ecstasies* (though elsewhere he provides a very elegant formulation of the problem of continuity. See his *Myths, Emblems, Clues* [London, 1986], e.g., pp. vii–xiii); M. Lazar, "The Lamb and the Scapegoat: The Dehumanization of the Jews in Medieval Propaganda Imagery," in *Anti-Semitism in Times of Crisis*, ed. S. Gilman and S. Katz (New York, 1991), pp. 38–80, here p. 39. For a very different theoretical criticism of this methodology see M. Foucault, "Nietzsche, Genealogy, History," in *Language, Counter-Memory, Practice*, ed. D. Bouchard (Ithaca, NY, 1977), pp. 139–164.

"Everyman" makes out badly in such works. Often "irrational," at best the receptacle of external, inherited ideologies passively and uncritically absorbed, medieval people are presented as dominated by discourse, not as active participants in its shaping. I am not arguing that negative discourses about Jews, Muslims, women, or lepers did not exist, but that any inherited discourse about minorities acquired force only when people chose to find it meaningful and useful, and was itself reshaped by these choices. Briefly, discourse and agency gain meaning only in relation to each other.[11] Even thus delimited, the notion of a "persecuting discourse" requires qualification. Such a discourse about minorities was but one of those available, and its invocation in a given situation did not ensure its success or acceptance. The choice of language was an active one, made in order to achieve something, made within contexts of conflict and structures of domination, and often contested.[12] Thus when medieval people made statements about the consequences of religious difference, they were making claims, not expressing accomplished reality, and these claims were subject to barter and negotiation before they could achieve real force in any given situation.[13] This book is about these processes of barter and negotiation, not about the creation of a "persecuting discourse."

My approach also challenges the current emphasis on the *longue durée* in the periodization of the persecution of minorities. By showing how structures are transformed by the actions and choices of people working within them, it more readily explains change over time while relying less on an appeal to the irrational. We need no longer insist on continuities of meaning in claims about minorities wherever we find continuities in form, since we can see how the

[11] Here I am conflating Bourdieu's notion of "rule-governed creativity" (*Outline of a Theory of Practice* [Cambridge, 1977], pp. 15–17 and passim) with Sahlins's discussion of "historic agents" and their uses of cultural categories. See *Islands of History* (Chicago, 1985), pp. xiv, 125. A. Giddens has come to similar conclusions, albeit by different means. For the simplest exposition of his "structuration theory," see his "Hermeneutics and Social Theory," in *Hermeneutics: Questions and Prospects*, ed. G. Shapiro and A. Sica (Amherst, MA, 1984), pp. 215–231; and "Action, Subjectivity, and the Constitution of Meaning," in *The Aims of Representation: Subject/Text/History*, ed. M. Krieger (New York, 1987), pp. 159–174.

[12] A point made forcefully by S. Feierman, *Peasant Intellectuals: Anthropology and History in Tanzania* (Madison, WI, 1990), esp. pp. 1–35. The same can be said of the textual records of such choices, on which see G. Prakash, *Bonded Histories: Genealogies of Labor Servitude in Colonial India* (Cambridge, 1990), p. 39; R. Williams, *Marxism and Literature* (Oxford, 1977), pp. 36–42. This abstract point has practical implications for the medievalist. Compare M. Kriegel's claim—that royal documentation is compromised by interests, while municipal documentation represents "the reality of the perception of the Jew"—with my position that we have no disinterested sources, only sources with conflicting interests. For Kriegel, see his "Un trait de psychologie sociale dans les pays méditerranéens du bas moyen age: le juif comme intouchable," *Annales: ESC* 31 (1976): 326–330, here p. 327.

[13] An adaptation of L. Rosen, *Bargaining for Reality: The Construction of Social Relations in a Muslim Community* (Chicago, 1984), pp. 1–5, 47, 165–166, 180–192.

meanings of existing forms are altered by the work that they are asked to do, and by the uses to which they are put. This means that we can be more critical than we have previously been about attempts to link medieval and modern mentalities, medieval ritual murder accusations and modern genocide.

The problem of periodization is central in this attempt to disrupt a now almost orthodox view of the steady march of European intolerance across the centuries. Historians have assembled that view in large part by stringing together episodes of large-scale violence against minorities. In Jewish historiography, for example, scholars have drawn a line of mounting intolerance from the Rhineland massacres of the First Crusade, through the expulsions and massacres of the thirteenth, fourteenth, and fifteenth centuries, through German ritual murder trials and Russian pogroms, to Kristallnacht and the concentration camps. The first half of the present work challenges this view by choosing two massacres (of Jews, lepers, and Muslims) used in teleological narratives and placing them within their local social, political, and cultural contexts. The more we restore to those outbreaks of violence their own particularities, the less easy it is to assimilate them to our own concerns, as homogeneity and teleology are replaced by difference and contingency. The second half presents a very different, perhaps more provocative, criticism of the teleological model. Its argument is that by focusing on moments of cataclysmic violence and reading them with post-Holocaust eyes, the teleological model has overlooked the fundamental interdependence of violence and tolerance in the Middle Ages.

.   .   .   .   .

This last point may be the most controversial of my argument, in part because it is largely based on sources that come from a particular geographic area: the south of France and especially the Crown of Aragon (see chap. 1, n. 5). This will pose problems for some readers, since traditionally the history of minorities (especially Jews) to the south of the Pyrenees (i.e., in present-day Spain) has been treated as distinct from that to the north.[14] Such a distinction does not seem tenable to me, at least not in the fourteenth century, and not when applied to the lands of the Crown of Aragon, which moved as much in a Mediterranean orbit as in an Iberian one. Recent work, particularly that of Maurice Kriegel, has demonstrated that for the purposes of Jewish history the Crown of Aragon and the south of France can be treated as a coherent unit.[15] Each chapter in this

[14]See most recently K. Stow, *Alienated Minority: The Jews of Medieval Latin Europe* (Cambridge, MA, 1992), p. 1: "Most often, this history [of Spanish Jews] is a distinct one, as is the history of medieval Spain as a whole; it should be, and traditionally has been, treated as such."

[15]See especially his *Les juifs à la fin du Moyen Age dans l'Europe méditerranéenne* (Paris, 1979). See also, though much more generally, R. I. Burns, *Muslims, Christians, and Jews in the Crusader Kingdom of Valencia: Societies in Symbiosis* (Cambridge, 1984), pp. 6–7. On the increasingly close links within

book provides further evidence for this view, either because the events discussed occurred on both sides of the Pyrenees, or because, as in the case of Holy Week riots, they have analogues elsewhere in the Mediterranean. At a more abstract level, questions of periodization, of the continuity between past and present, of the relationship between violence and tolerance are all of broad (European, at least) relevance.

It is true, however, that reliance on Iberian documentation, and especially on an accompanying Iberian historiography even more sharply dichotomized about poles of violence and tolerance than is generally the case, has had the effect of heightening my perception of the need for synthesis. It is difficult to write about minorities in any of the regions that now constitute Spain without inserting oneself into long-standing debates within Spanish and Jewish history, particularly the debate over *convivencia*, a Spanish word meaning "living together" and one of the most contentious terms in Spanish historical writing. The term was coined by the philologist Américo Castro in his discussion of the effects upon Spanish culture of the coexistence of Christianity, Islam, and Judaism in the Iberian Peninsula.[16] Though there is no reason why *convivencia* need designate only harmonious coexistence, it has in fact acquired this meaning among certain historians who have romanticized the concept.[17] These historians present the Christian kingdoms of the Iberian Peninsula as uniquely tolerant of religious minorities until the expulsion of 1492. They minimize periods of violence and persecution, stress cultural cooperation, and talk frequently of a "golden age" of Jewish culture.[18]

At the opposite end of the spectrum are certain schools of Jewish historical interpretation, particularly the so-called lachrymose and Jerusalem schools. The

---

Jewish cultural circles between Iberian and northern French communities, see B. Septimus, *Hispano-Jewish Culture in Transition: The Career and Controversies of Ramah* (Cambridge, MA, 1982).

[16] See his *España en su historia: cristianos, moros, y judíos*, 2d ed. (Barcelona, 1983), pp. 200–209. Castro's position was attacked by C. Sánchez-Albornoz in his *España: un enigma histórico*, 2 vols. (Buenos Aires, 1956), precipitating a bitter and long-running debate within Spanish historiography. For an analysis of the debate, see T. Glick, *Islamic and Christian Spain in the Early Middle Ages: Comparative Perspectives on Social and Cultural Formation* (Princeton, 1979), pp. 6–13.

[17] E.g., N. Roth, "The Jews of Spain and the Expulsion of 1492," *Historian* 55, no. 1 (Fall 1992): 17–30, here pp. 19–20.

[18] Perhaps the most extremely optimistic of these historians is N. Roth, who does "not like to talk about a particular 'golden age' of Jewish culture in medieval Spain, for the whole history of that civilization was a golden age for the Jews." The quotation is from his "The Jews in Spain at the Time of Maimonides," in *Moses Maimonides and His Times*, Studies in Philosophy and the History of Philosophy 19, ed. E. L. Ormsby (Washington, DC, 1989), pp. 1–20, here pp. 1–2. Roth has also defended Ferdinand and Isabel, the issuers of the edict of expulsion, from charges of intolerance and has argued that Christian religious attitudes were "rarely if ever" hostile to Jews (as opposed to the Jewish religion) in the Middle Ages. See, in addition to "The Jews of Spain and the Expulsion of 1492," his "1992 and Its Mythology: A Warning," *Jewish Spectator* 55, no. 4 (Spring 1991): 26–30, here p. 26; and most recently, *Jews, Visigoths, and Muslims in Medieval Spain: Cooperation and Conflict* (Leiden, 1994), p. 2: "The true story [of *convivencia*] is nothing short of amazing."

lachrymose school, which dates back to medieval chronicle traditions, sees the history of Judaism since the fall of Jerusalem as a vale of tears, a progression of tragedies. It is in part an eschatological vision, with each disaster increasing in magnitude until the last and greatest disaster precipitates the coming of the Messiah and redemption. The Jerusalem school of Jewish history is in some ways a post-Holocaust, secularized version of the lachrymose school. Though its messianism is more muted, it shares with its predecessor a teleological vision in which each incident of persecution foreshadows greater persecutions to come. Within the field of Sephardic Jewish studies the Jerusalem school has been very influential, owing in large part to the work of Yitzhak Baer, whose two-volume *History of the Jews in Christian Spain* remains the standard reference.[19]

The present work argues against both these positions, against a rose-tinted haven of tolerance and a darkening valley of tears, but it also borrows from both. For example, it agrees with the lachrymose school in recognizing the existence of long-standing vocabularies of hatred, although it rejects the lachrymose interpretation of the meaning, function, or virulence of these vocabularies. In this it agrees with the "optimists," and yet it questions the very existence of an age of peaceful and idyllic *convivencia*, whether long or short. Far from arguing for peaceful *convivencia*, Part Two of this book demonstrates that violence was a central and systemic aspect of the coexistence of majority and minorities in medieval Spain, and even suggests that coexistence was in part predicated on such violence.

This dependence is more important than it seems. The central dichotomy in modern studies of the treatment of medieval minorities is that between tolerance and intolerance.[20] Thus polarized, violence, hostility, and competition can be seen only as destructive breakdowns of social relations, the antithesis of associative action. The identification of a constructive relationship between conflict and coexistence suggests that such a dichotomy is untenable. We should not be surprised that such a constructive relationship does exist: it is virtually a commonplace of post-Enlightenment political philosophy that violence and aggres-

[19](Philadelphia, 1978). It is worth noting that the same polarization between "golden age" and vale of tears occurs in Italian Jewish historiography, on which see R. Bonfil, *Jewish Life in Renaissance Italy* (Berkeley, 1994), pp. 6–9. For more on Baer's position, see below, end of chap. 3. On the Jerusalem school in general, see D. Myers, " 'From Zion will go forth Torah': Jewish Scholarship and the Zionist Return to History" (Ph.D. diss., Columbia University, 1991). For Myers's treatment of Baer, see pp. 219–258.

[20]Cf. Bonfil, *Jewish Life in Renaissance Italy*, pp. 7–9. An example of the continuing importance of this dichotomy is the current debate over the status of Jews in Arab lands between "neo-lachrymose" historians who emphasize persecution and those who emphasize toleration. See M. Cohen, "Islam and the Jews: Myth, Counter-Myth, History," *Jerusalem Quarterly* 38 (1986): 125–137, and the preface to his *Under Crescent and Cross: The Jews in the Middle Ages* (Princeton, 1994). See also the exchange in *Tikkun* 6, no. 3 (May–June 1991) between Cohen ("The Neo-Lachrymose Conception of Jewish-Arab History," pp. 55–60) and N. Stillman ("Myth, Counter-myth, and Distortion," pp. 60–64).

sion are forms of association. According to this point of view, capitalism and bourgeois society are built upon the hostile competition of individuals. Even wars, unless they are wars of obliteration, are forms of interaction that seek to establish relations, not destroy them.[21] As Georg Simmel put it: "In contrast to . . . pure negativity, conflict contains something positive. Its positive and negative aspects, however, are integrated; they can be separated conceptually, but not empirically." Or, in the words of an African proverb: "They are our enemies; we marry them."[22]

.   .   .   .   .

As a historian, I am not equipped to represent this empirically inseparable fusion of polarities with the analytical clarity of a philosopher or the revelatory opacity of a speaker of proverbs. Instead, I have tried to build it into the structure of the book by writing across sources (e.g., administrative and cultural), topics (e.g., Muslim, Jews, lepers; sex, markets, liturgy), analytical categories (e.g., violence and tolerance), and theoretical positions (e.g., structuralist and subjectivist) that are normally kept separate or posed against one another. The result is that the two parts of this book, and indeed each of the chapters themselves, are heterogeneous. In that each attacks a different aspect of the role of violence in the medieval toleration of minorities, they can be read individually and stand alone. Their full effect, however, is intended to be cumulative, and it is only in aggregate that they sustain the larger claims presented in these prefatory pages.

Chapter 1, "The Historical Background," is meant as a general introduction to the place of minorities and of violence in fourteenth-century Europe and particularly in the Crown. It is explicitly comparative, contrasting the differing places Jews and Muslims occupied in Christian society, and the different kinds of violence each group was subject to.[23] Because several later arguments depend

[21]See, as one example among many, Kant's "Idea for a Universal History with a Cosmopolitan Purpose," seventh proposition (ed. H. Reiss, in *Kant's Political Writings* [Cambridge, 1970], pp. 41–53, here p. 47): "Nature has thus again employed the unsociableness of men, and even of the large societies and states which human beings construct, as a means of arriving at a condition of calm and security through their inevitable *antagonism*" (emphasis in original). See also his "On the Common Saying: 'This May Be True in Theory, But It Does Not Apply in Practice,'" in ibid., pp. 61–92, here p. 91; and, for the trust that must exist in all wars except those of extermination, "Perpetual Peace: A Philosophical Sketch," in ibid., pp. 93–130, here p. 96.

[22]See Simmel's "Conflict," in *"Conflict" and "The Web of Group-Affiliation,"* trans. K. Wolff (London, 1955), pp. 11–123, here p. 14 (but see also pp. 18, 23 f., 26, 32 f., 61 f.). For the proverb, see M. Gluckman, *Custom and Conflict in Africa* (Oxford, 1956), pp. 12–13.

[23]Muslims and Jews living in Christian lands are rarely treated in comparative perspective. For pioneering efforts in this regard, see E. Lourie, "Anatomy of Ambivalence: Muslims under the Crown of Aragon in the Late Thirteenth Century," in her *Crusade and Colonisation: Muslims, Christians and Jews in Medieval Aragon*, Variorum Collected Studies 317 (Aldershot, 1990); and M. Meyerson, "Comparative Perspectives on Muslims and Jews in Christian Spain" (paper presented at the Midwest Medieval History Conference, Ohio State University, October 1990).

on an understanding of these differences, its principal aim is to be descriptive. Its conclusions are unsurprising, though too easily forgotten: the types of violence and articulations of hatred minority groups are subject to are not independent of the roles those groups play in society.

The critique of the teleological treatment of violence begins in earnest with chapters 2, 3, and 4, which constitute Part One. These chapters focus on two collective and cataclysmic acts of violence by Christians against Jews, lepers, and Muslims: the "Shepherds' Crusade" of 1320, which began as a Crusade against Islam but quickly focused instead on Jews; and what one chronicler later called the "Cowherds' Crusade," which began by attacking lepers in 1321 but also came to encompass Jews and Muslims. These events have been chosen because they are frequently invoked in support of the circular argument that the steady decline of European tolerance for minorities was mirrored by outbreaks of violence which grew progressively more brutal. Each of these events began in France before crossing into the Crown of Aragon, and each took very different forms on either side of the Pyrenees. This fact in itself forces a comparative approach, even when the comparison is between a place that experienced extensive violence (e.g., France in 1320) and another that did not (the Crown of Aragon in the same year).[24] Such comparisons have one considerable value: they make us ask why two areas that share a common stock of stereotypes and attitudes toward minorities nevertheless respond so differently to accusations drawn from that stock. In short, they force us to move from the collective to the local and back again.

Chapter 2, "France, Source of the Troubles," has two broad goals. First, because the violence of 1320 and 1321 spread from France to the Crown of Aragon, the chapter provides necessary French background and a useful point of comparison to events in the Crown. Its second aim is to situate attacks on Jews and lepers within the context of conflicts over taxation, the proper role of kings, and the health of the body politic in order to argue that violence against minorities cannot be understood in isolation from the political, economic, and cultural structures within which it occurs. It emphasizes (as does each of the other chapters in the book) that violence against minorities is not *only* about minorities. By providing these attacks with multiple senses and contexts, it highlights the price we pay in loss of meaning when we categorize them only as "irrational" and restrict their interpretation to a persecutory *longue durée*.

The two remaining chapters of Part One engage as well in the search for local context and plural meaning, though differences in the sources available for Aragon result in differences in the questions asked.[25] Chapter 3, "Crusade and

[24]E. P. Thompson recently urged this type of comparison. See "The Moral Economy Reviewed," in his *Customs in Common* (London, 1991), pp. 262–263: "Comparative study of food riots has been, inevitably, into the history of nations which *had* riots" (emphasis in original).

[25]Much less material survives from France: most of it has been published, more of the sources are narrative (e.g., chronicles), and fewer are royal. In Aragon, on the other hand, the events of 1320–

Massacre in Aragon," for example, contrasts several competing narratives of one massacre that occurred in the mountain village of Montclus: those of villagers, royal bureaucrats, sixteenth-century Jewish chroniclers, and modern historians, each with their own agenda and their own version of history. It shows how royal bureaucrats put together accounts of violence in order to justify extortionate fiscality, and discusses the role these bureaucratic narratives played in creating the violence they claimed merely to describe. For contemporaries, administrative representations of violence against minorities gave such violence new motives, meanings, and potential uses. For modern historians, they have provided a deceivingly univocal source for analysis. The chapter ends by tracing the creation of a narrative about the Shepherds' Crusade in one strand of a later Jewish historiographical tradition, a tradition that sought for prophetic prefigurations of more recent acts of violence in medieval ones.

Chapter 4, "Lepers, Jews, Muslims, and Poison in the Crown," describes the struggle that took place among people throughout the Crown (including the king), all of whom sought to gain control of a new "persecutory discourse" of poisoning in order to make it meet their own particular needs. It is as concerned as the previous chapters with the interplay between languages of hate and local contexts, but its rhetorical focus is slightly different. More explicitly than its predecessors, it confronts the argument that Europe grew progressively more intolerant because its people were increasingly governed by an irrational and paranoid "collective unconscious," a shift manifested in outbreaks of violence. By emphasizing the degree to which people in the Crown of Aragon manipulated the accusations against lepers, Jews, and Muslims in 1321, the chapter shows the limitations of the irrational in illuminating how cognitive structures affected the actions of individuals toward minorities. And by studying the past and the future of these accusations, it challenges progressive models of intolerance.

The explicit juxtaposition of case studies with different outcomes on either side of the Pyrenees suggests a rather obvious, though neglected, conclusion: that ideas about minorities function within and are contingent upon a host of other structures and ideas, many of which have quite local meanings (ideas about monarchy, fiscality, the body, or the weather, to name some of those put forth in these chapters). The study of these local meanings, their historicization, contextualizes any broader discourse about minorities and challenges attempts to impose teleologies. This does not mean that in our attempt to understand collective violence we should replace structural or teleological history with local history, or embrace a naive rationalism in our haste to escape the irrational.

1321 are less studied, and the surviving (primarily royal and fiscal) documentation is extensive but almost entirely unpublished. Even more important, there is for France the historiography necessary for a cultural contextualization of these events (for example, on the ideology of kingship or the place of lepers in society). In the Crown of Aragon, this historiography is lacking. There is virtually no work on lepers and leper houses, studies of royal fiscality are only just beginning to appear, and the theory and theology of kingship is practically unstudied.

Such an approach would have its own dangers, as the current debate in Germany over *Alltagsgeschichte* (history of the everyday) and the history of the Holocaust makes clear.[26] But it does suggest that this polarization of methodologies is itself impoverishing, and it reinforces the importance of a more integrated approach.

．　．　．　．　．

An unintended consequence of this attempt to identify agency in the face of cataclysm is that the constraining effects of rules and culture are minimized, so that actors sometimes float weightlessly in a world without the gravity of history. Part One stresses the contingent because it seeks to question the centrality of collective mentalities and cataclysmic events in existing historical narratives about tolerance for minorities. Part Two moves in the opposite direction. It focuses not on rare moments of mass murder, but on more common types of violence emerging from competition between groups. Each chapter in this latter half arbitrates between the rules (cultural, religious, social, and economic) that structured conflict and the ability of individuals to manipulate and change these. It is through such arbitration, I suggest, that we can best understand how violence stabilized relations between groups and why, when mass violence occurred, it took the forms that it did.

There were many ways in which individuals could invoke collective anxieties in order to attack minorities with whom they found themselves in conflict. Chapter 5, "Sex and Violence between Majority and Minority," studies one of particular resonance for North American readers: accusations and violence caused by allegations of sexual interaction between members of different religious groups. Because (as they have in many multiethnic societies) claims about group difference in the Crown of Aragon clustered in specific ways around issues of miscegenation, the study of violence caused by allegations of sexual liaisons provides an entry into contemporary ideas about religion and race, gender and group identity, acculturation and social purity at the collective level. But arguments about miscegenation served a multitude of strategic purposes as well and were marshaled by individuals to further their interests in a wide variety of day-to-day situations. Within religious communities such arguments and the violence they legitimized could reinforce communal boundaries; within

---

[26] *Alltagsgeschichte* has been criticized as trivializing the Nazi past and ignoring structural explanations for the actions of the Third Reich. The debate is part of the broader *Historikerstreit* controversy that erupted in Germany in 1986. On this controversy, see *Reworking the Past: Hitler, the Holocaust, and the Historians' Debate*, ed. P. Baldwin (Boston, 1990). For the *Alltagsgeschichte* debate in particular, see M. Broszat et al., *Alltagsgeschichte der NS-Zeit: Neue Perspektive oder Trivialisierung?* (Munich, 1984). Martin Jay has suggested that *Alltagsgeschichte* be pursued not as an antithesis to structuralist historiography, but as its dialectical complement, a position that I would take. See his "Force Fields. Songs of Experience: Reflections on the Debate over *Alltagsgeschichte*," *Salmagundi* 81 (1989): 29–41.

families they could be used to support or to challenge male control of women; and at an individual level they could play an important role in countless situations, ranging from extortion to conversion. By exploring the relationship between the collective and the strategic in the particular case of violence arising from sexual interaction, the chapter demonstrates both the range and the limits of negotiation in medieval social relations.

Chapter 5 moves from an anxiety arising at a particular religious boundary, in this case the sexual one, to the strategic deployment of that anxiety in a competitive world and shows how this interaction between discourse and context limits the potential of miscegenation anxiety to provoke violence. Chapter 6, "Minorities Confront Each Other," takes the opposite tack, asking how particular and contingent historical situations encourage the emergence of "intolerant" religious discourses and give them strength, a question approached in this case through the study of Muslim-Jewish relations in the Crown. Muslims and Jews not only acted and argued out their conflicts in their own religious languages but also sought access to explicitly Christian discourses. Their competitive interactions were structured by Christian institutions (economic, political, judicial, and the like) and the religious ideologies that supported these. The need to function within such institutions forced non-Christians to participate in their logic and to adopt those modes of argument that were most effective within them. To demonstrate this, the chapter begins with structural situations of Muslim-Jewish conflict (moneylending, meat markets, sex) and ends with the violent consequences of Muslim accusations that the Jews were the killers of Christ.

This charge of deicide against the Jews has often been invoked as the clearest example of the destructive powers of persecutory narratives. For this reason, chapter 7, "The Two Faces of Sacred Violence," studies the explicitly religious annual riots against Jews during Holy Week. These riots, largely ignored by modern historians, were in fact ancient rituals carried out by clerics and children that reenacted through stylized violence the conquest of Jerusalem by the Romans in 70 A.D. Contemporaries described these actions as a "divine office" and performed them as ritual sacrifice, a sacrifice that, once a year, reemphasized the boundary between Christian and Jew. These were complex rituals whose manifold meanings bear on a number of arguments. For example, the ways in which Holy Week riots represented notions of the divide between secular and clerical power through battles between clerics and local secular elites served to criticize the distribution of power within the Crown. For this reason their analysis has implications that reach beyond questions of tolerance and minorities and toward what the French call historical political anthropology. But it is in terms of the narrower question of the relationship between violence and tolerance that these riots are most significant. As regular calendrical events they suggest an episodic model of religious intolerance, not a continuous or evolutionary one.[27] Perhaps

[27] Of course calendrical rites are also partly linear: they are performed at a particular historical moment and draw meaning from contemporary events. But at the same time, they impose rhythm

more important, these violent rituals reiterated a discourse legitimating the presence of Jews in Christian society at the same time that they challenged it. Within their particular recounting of sacred history, their violence was simultaneously a gesture of inclusion and one of seclusion. We are nowhere closer to the marriage of enemies.

The epilogue, "The Black Death and Beyond," recounts the advent of the plague and the so-called pogroms of 1348, not because these are the end of any story, but because it is here, at the earliest moment when fears about social purity emerge with startling and ferocious clarity in the Crown of Aragon, that we can best see how tightly cataclysm and massacre are related to the more systemic and stabilizing violences of the everyday. By focusing on a discrete event of extraordinary brutality, while analyzing it within the context of a variety of types of strategic and ritualized violence, the conclusion integrates the themes and methodologies of the two parts of the book. In the process, it represents an effort to express (at least metaphorically) the difficulties involved in narrating in a continuous fashion a history punctuated by events so violent that they seem to bear no immediate relation to their future or their past.

. . . . .

In this work I situate myself of necessity in minority historiography, but I want to reiterate that I am nevertheless not writing a history of minorities or marginal groups. My aim is not to reconstruct the experiences of Jews, lepers, or Muslims as they encountered violence (though at times I do so), but to explore the functions and meanings of such violence within medieval societies, even when this requires an emphasis on the view of the victimizers rather than of the victimized. Paradoxical as it may seem, this approach maximizes the importance of ideas about minorities within medieval culture and calls into question the notion of their marginality.

The importance of ideas about minorities is heightened through a demonstration of their relationship to issues conventionally regarded as more central to medieval society: kingship, fiscality, money, disease, sex, and theology, to name some of those discussed in the pages that follow. Others could easily be added. Feudalism, for example, was deeply influenced in the Crown of Aragon by notions about the differences between Muslim and Christian. The mythical origins of certain types of lordship like the *ius maletractandi*, the "right to abuse" serfs in Catalonia, were predicated on such differences. Lords argued that the peasants had incurred such serfdom because their ancestors had refused to help Charlemagne repel the Muslim invaders and had instead apostasized to Islam. The penalty for such cowardice was perpetual servitude.

---

upon those events. See H. Hubert and M. Mauss, "Étude sommaire de la représentation du temps dans la religion et la magie," in idem, *Mélanges d'histoire des religions* (Paris, 1929), pp. 189–229.

But feudalism could be resisted, as well as legitimated, by arguments about religious difference. A particularly delightful example is the claim by Catalan serfs that they were descended from Muslims. Their ancestors were not apostates, they argued, but converts to Christianity from Islam, and should not therefore be punished by servitude.[28] The claim may have been purely strategic, but it is nevertheless astounding to watch Christian peasants ascribe to themselves a status so insulting that its imputation by anyone else would have demanded vengeance.[29] Armed rebellion against the seigneurial order could also be justified with arguments about minorities. In Valencia, for example, the *Germanías* (brotherhoods) revolted against the fiscal and judicial administration of their lords by using Crusade ideology and rumors of Turkish invasion to justify attacks on Muslims, who made up an important part of the seigneurial labor force and of seigneurial private armies.[30]

The point, in short, is that the study of minorities and attitudes toward them is not the study of society's margins, and that the terms "margin" and "center" are of little relevance in the effort to understand the place of minorities in medieval society. This will not be surprising for historians in disciplines where it has become increasingly difficult to conceive of political, social, or cultural histories that pay no attention to questions of race, class, or gender. Some medievalists, however, still resist such a view, as Norman Cantor made clear in his recent polemical survey of the field.[31] One of the goals of this work, therefore, is to demonstrate the importance of minorities in the construction of medieval worlds.

.   .   .   .   .

It is never easy to think or write about violence, however meaningful one believes it to be. Throughout the writing of this book I have tried to find sense in horrors, to place acts of violence in cultural and social contexts that would give them meanings beyond the literal ones which emerge with such visceral force. To some readers this search for context may seem to trivialize or mini-

---

[28]For these arguments over the *ius maletractandi*, see P. Freedman, "Cowardice, Heroism and the Legendary Origins of Catalonia," *Past and Present* 121 (1988): 3–28; idem, *The Origins of Peasant Servitude in Medieval Catalonia* (Cambridge, 1991), pp. 191–192, 199–200.

[29]Calling a Christian "Saracen" or "son of a Saracen" was an insult punishable by law. See chap. 4, n. 32.

[30]For references to violence against Valencian Muslims by the antiseigneurial *Germanías* in 1521, see M. Meyerson, *The Muslims of Valencia in the Age of Fernando and Isabel: Between Coexistence and Crusade* (Berkeley, 1991), pp. 89–90; and R. García Cárcel, *Las Germanías de Valencia* (Barcelona, 1975), pp. 208–216. Compare B. Wyatt-Brown, *Southern Honor: Ethics and Behavior in the Old South* (New York, 1982), pp. 422, 433, where the author comes close to suggesting that poor whites in the southern United States created rumors of slave insurrection as a pretext for attacking plantation owners' slaves.

[31]*Inventing the Middle Ages: The Lives, Works, and Ideas of the Great Medievalists of the Twentieth Century* (New York, 1991), pp. 375 f.

mize the violence that is its subject matter.[32] Nothing could be further from my intent. The midsummer killing of 337 Jews in the castle of Montclus may have been symbolically meaningful, but none of these meanings attenuates the brutality of the event, and the same is true of the other acts of violence described in the pages that follow.[33] I hope that readers will not find violence against persons, past or present, less appalling for having read this book, even as they leave it with a sense of how rare and strange a similarity the nightmares of a distant past bear to our own.

[32]See, for example, n. 26 above, for some criticisms of *Alltagsgeschichte* on these grounds.

[33]I am reacting here to the position sometimes taken vis-à-vis the Holocaust. See, for example, B. Lang's call for a literal language in his *Act and Idea in the Nazi Genocide* (Chicago, 1990), pp. 144–145; and the critique of Lang's position (to my mind convincing on this point) in H. White, "Historical Emplotment and the Problem of Truth," in *Probing the Limits of Representation: Nazism and the "Final Solution,"* ed. S. Friedlander (Cambridge, MA, 1992), pp. 37–53, here 43–49.

Chapter 1

THE HISTORICAL BACKGROUND

IN MODERN TEXTS the words "fourteenth century" are often accompanied by others such as "calamitous" and "crisis." To demographers at least, this must surely be the bleakest of medieval centuries. The previous three hundred years had been expansive ones during which European plows conquered new territories, agricultural productivity increased, trade recovered, and the population grew. By 1300, however, with little fertile earth left to find, agricultural yields (always appallingly low by modern standards) began to fall. A civilization that in the previous century had effortlessly raised new cities, new cathedrals, new governments, came to weigh more and more heavily on its countryside. The result was famine. In 1315–1318, for example, bad weather and bad harvests resulted in "the great" famine that affected most of northern Europe. Hunger and its attendant diseases reduced the population of some areas (like Essex in England) by as much as 15 percent. The Mediterranean basin, spared in 1315–1318, suffered similar dearth in the early 1330s culminating in 1333, a year that Catalans would later call, with hindsight, "the first bad year."[1] These were reminders, if any were needed, that medieval society was walking a knife-edge. Premodern demography is scarcely an exact science, but it appears that the population of Europe grew very little, and perhaps fell slightly, between 1300 and 1347.

Nevertheless, it was not famine but the arrival of the bacillus *Yersinia pestis* in 1348 that definitively awarded the fourteenth century the title of "calamitous." No precise demographic instruments are needed to measure the effect on the European population of the arrival of the Black Death: whether the death toll was 25 or 50 percent, it was a disaster. The epilogue discusses some of the initial reactions to this disaster and their importance for the treatment of minorities. Here it is sufficient to point out that the fourteenth century pivoted on a mortality so massive, so widespread, and so unexpected that it has few parallels in any age.[2]

[1] For the famine of 1315–1318, see, inter alia, H. S. Lucas, "The Great European Famine of 1315, 1316 and 1317," *Speculum* 5 (1930): 341–377, reprinted in *Essays in Economic History*, ed. E. M. Carus-Wilson, 3 vols. (London (1954–1966), 2:49–72; I. Kershaw, "The Great Famine and Agrarian Crisis in England, 1315–1322," *Past and Present* 59 (1973): 3–50; and more generally C. Dyer, *Standards of Living in the Later Middle Ages* (Cambridge, 1989), pp. 258–273. For famines in Catalonia see A. Curto i Homedes, *La intervenció municipal en l'abastament de blat d'una ciutat catalana: Tortosa, segle XIV* (Barcelona, 1988), pp. 209–221; in Languedoc, M. Larenaudie, "Les famines en Languedoc aux XIVème et XVème siècles," *Annales du Midi*, 1952, pp. 27–39; and in Italy, G. Pinto, *Il libro del biadaiolo: Carestia e annona a Firenze della metà del '200 al 1348* (Florence, 1978).

[2] For the literature on the plague see the epilogue.

Hunger and plague might be attributed to divine wrath. War was a more immediately human failing, and an increasingly expensive one. The fourteenth century was a century of war. It opened with Philip the Fair's wars against England in Aquitaine (1294–1303) and against Flanders (1302–1305), and closed in the midst of the so-called Hundred Years War (1337–1453). Besides destroying people and property, these conflicts further depressed economies already fragile. Even the most bloodless of these wars, like the one in Aquitaine, proved extraordinarily expensive. Armies, then as today, needed to be paid, and kings paid them with funds raised by taxes. The machinery of royal fiscality therefore grew more oppressive at the same time as resources were diminishing, producing conflict.[3]

Some of this conflict occurred between kings and their subjects. If in the thirteenth century kings tended to claim and exercise greater and greater power, these claims were increasingly, sometimes violently, challenged in the fourteenth. Baronial rebellions and tax revolts against monarchs occurred throughout Europe, the deposition and murder of England's Edward II (1327) and of Castile's Peter the Cruel (1369) being the most dramatic examples. But many other social relations were also polarized: between urban elites and laborers, city dwellers and countryfolk, peasants and seigneurs.[4]

Relations between minorities and majority suffered as well. The history of minorities can easily be made to parallel the cataclysms of the fourteenth century. Jews, for example, were expelled from England in 1290; from France in 1306, 1322 (or 1327), and 1394. They were massacred in Germany in 1298, 1336–1338, and 1348; in France in 1320 and 1321. Lepers were attacked, imprisoned, or burned in France in 1321; witches were pursued more or less everywhere after 1348. For minorities, the fourteenth was among the most violent of centuries.

.   .   .   .   .

Within this general European context the Crown of Aragon was in some ways exceptional, in others not.[5] Like the rest of Europe, the Crown suffered from

---

[3] On the costs of Philip the Fair's wars, see J. Strayer, "The Costs and Profits of War: The Anglo-French Conflict of 1294–1303," in *The Medieval City*, ed. H. Miskimin, D. Herlihy, and A. Udovitch (New Haven, 1977), pp. 269–291; and his *The Reign of Philip the Fair* (Princeton, 1980), pp. 314–346. On the social effects of the Hundred Years War see C. Allmand, *The Hundred Years War: England and France at War c. 1300–c. 1450* (Cambridge, 1988), pp. 120–135. On taxation and resistance to it, see J. Henneman, *Royal Taxation in Fourteenth Century France: The Development of War Financing 1322–1356* (Princeton, 1971).

[4] See, for example, M. Mollat and P. Wolff, *Ongles bleus, Jacques et Ciompi: les révolutions populaires en Europe aux XIVe et XVe siècles* (Paris, 1970). For a recent regional study, see W. TeBrake, *A Plague of Insurrection: Popular Politics and Peasant Revolt in Flanders, 1323–1328* (Philadelphia, 1993).

[5] The term "Crown of Aragon" refers to the polity constituted by the union of the counties of Catalonia with the kingdoms of Aragon and Valencia (and sometimes also including Majorca, Sardinia, and Sicily, as well as other areas). These diverse areas constituted one polity in the sense

food shortages and famine (e.g., the "first bad year" of 1333, the "year of the great hunger" in 1347, the "bad year" of 1374), from plague, and from war. Some of these wars, like the eternal campaigns against Sardinia, were at least fought away from home. Others—for example, the long "War of the Two Peters," which broke out in 1356 between Peter the Ceremonious (1336–1387) of Catalonia-Aragon and Peter the Cruel (1350–1369) of Castile—were bloody and destructive affairs from which the Crown's economy took decades to recover.[6] All these wars had one thing in common: they were expensive.

Like other European monarchs, the kings of Catalonia-Aragon found their attempts to extend the reach of royal power increasingly resisted by barons and burghers alike. In the Crown of Aragon this resistance sporadically took the form of "unions," sworn confederations of nobles and municipalities mobilized to assert their privileges against the monarchy.[7] In this they were more successful than elites in other countries. At times, and particularly in 1347–1348, the conflict between king and unions was indistinguishable from civil war. In 1347 King Peter was forced to ratify the Aragonese Union's demands to avoid being taken prisoner. For the next year he waged war against the nobles and cities of two of his kingdoms, Aragon and Valencia, and lost. Only the arrival of the plague allowed the defeated king to escape imprisonment in Valencia and reconquer his territories. The bitterness of the conflict is apparent in the king's professed desire after his victory to raze the city of Valencia and sow it with salt. When his advisers counseled against this, he contented himself with beheading and drowning some rebels, as well as forcing others to drink the molten metal of the bell that they had forged to call their cohort to arms.[8]

In all these categories of calamity Europe and the Crown of Aragon were more or less congruent. But there were also more structural similarities in areas

---

that they were ruled by one person, but each had its distinctive laws, privileges, and institutions. Before the conquests of the thirteenth century the term "Catalonia-Aragon" is nearly synonymous with "Crown of Aragon," since it encompasses both parties in the original confederation. Similarly, the monarchs of the Crown are sometimes referred to as "count-kings," counts of the Catalan territories, kings of Aragon. These hyphenated terms, though slightly anachronistic, will occasionally be used here.

[6] Henceforth, rulers of the Crown of Aragon are referred to with anglicized names and Aragonese numeration. The names of popes and other foreign rulers are also anglicized, as are country names (Aragon, Catalonia, Majorca, etc.). Other proper names (with some exceptions) are given in Catalan for Catalans, Aragonese for Aragonese, and so forth. The names of Muslims and Jews in Latin or Romance documents are generally given as they appear in those documents. No attempt has been made to convert them into Arabic or Hebrew form. Toponyms are generally given in the language of the region in which they occur. (To avoid confusion, both Valencia kingdom and Valencia city are unaccented.)

[7] For the unions of 1283, 1286, and 1301 see L. González Antón, *Las Uniones aragonesas y las Cortes del reino (1283–1301)*, 2 vols. (Zaragoza, 1975).

[8] Unfortunately, no monograph has yet been published on the unions of 1347–1348. For King Peter's point of view see bk. 4 of his chronicle, in *Pere III of Catalonia (Pedro IV of Aragón): Chronicle*, trans. M. Hillgarth, ed. J. Hillgarth, 2 vols. (Toronto, 1980), pp. 391–453.

that specifically affected the treatment of minorities. For example, virtually the same general legal and ethical principles justified to Christians the existence of Jews throughout Christian Europe. It is tempting to argue that the Islamic concept of *dhimmī* status survived in Spain even after that land was reconquered from the Muslims. This status allowed "Peoples of the Book" (i.e., Christians and Jews) living in Islamic states to practice their religion privately in relative freedom, though burdened by higher taxes and some restrictions on dress and social interaction. Yet one searches in vain for such a general principle of toleration in the Christian Crown of Aragon.[9] What religious and legal arguments there were for permitting the existence of religious minorities were those current in the rest of Europe. Christians since the time of Augustine had argued that Jews should be tolerated in Christian society as abject witnesses to the truth and triumph of Christianity, and they did so in Iberia as well. The great law code of the Castilian king Alfonso X "the Wise" proclaimed that

> the reason the Church, emperors, kings, and other princes permitted the Jews to reside among Christians is this: that they might live forever as in captivity and serve as a reminder to mankind that they are descended from those who crucified Our Lord Jesus Christ.[10]

Similarly, the protection that Muslims and Jews enjoyed at law in the Crown of Aragon stemmed from the same legal fiction that legitimated the protection of Jews in France, England, or Germany: that all Jews (and Muslims) were slaves of the king's chamber, his royal treasure, and therefore not to be harmed by anyone except, of course, the king himself.[11]

Yet there were important differences between the Iberian countries and the rest of Europe. The most obviously relevant difference is in the demographic weight of minority populations. Most European countries had (at some point in time) small minorities of non-Christians, usually Jews, living among them, but none of these populations approached the number of non-Christians, most of them Muslims, who dwelled in the Crown of Aragon. The sheer numbers of non-Christians in Iberia rendered them less exotic. No Iberian writer fantasized,

[9] R. I. Burns touches cautiously on the issue of the relation between *dhimmī* traditions and Christian provisions in *Islam under the Crusaders: Colonial Survival in the Thirteenth-Century Kingdom of Valencia* (Princeton, 1973), p. 157. On the *dhimmī* tradition, see A. Fattal, *Le statut légal des non-musulmans en pays d'Islam* (Beirut, 1958); and B. Lewis, *The Jews of Islam* (Princeton, 1984), chap. 1.

[10] *Siete Partidas* 7.24.1, translated in D. Carpenter, *Alfonso X and the Jews: An Edition and Commentary on* Siete Partidas *7.24 "De los judíos"* (Berkeley, 1986), p. 28. On Augustine and the Augustinian attitude toward Jews see B. Blumenkranz, "Augustin et les juifs, Augustin et le judaïsme," *Recherches Augustiniennes* 1 (1958): 225–241; *Die Judenpredigt Augustins: Ein Beitrag zur Geschichte der jüdisch-christlichen Beziehungen in den ersten Jahrhunderten* (Basel, 1946).

[11] The "serfdom" of Jews is addressed more fully in chap. 7. For Muslims, see J. Boswell, *The Royal Treasure: Muslim Communities under the Crown of Aragon in the Fourteenth Century* (New Haven, 1977), pp. 30–37; *Los Fueros de Aragón según el manuscrito 458 de la biblioteca Nacional de Madrid*, ed. G. Tilander (Lund, 1937), pp. 164–165.

as the German Wolfram von Eschenbach did, that the offspring of a Christian-Muslim couple would be mottled white and black: they knew better.[12]

The distribution of minority populations in the Crown affects many aspects of minority-majority relations. This is especially true in the case of Mudejars (a word commonly used by historians to designate Muslims living in Christian Iberian lands),[13] whose condition in the Crown of Aragon cannot be separated from the pace of the Christian reconquest. The Muslim invasion of Spain in 711 had confined the Christian polities to a few counties clustered in and about the Pyrenees. The future kingdom of Aragon was limited to the six hundred square kilometers of valleys above the river Aragón. Further east the future Catalan counties stretched from Girona to a bit beyond Barcelona. Until roughly the year 1000, these were the frontiers delimiting what we might call for the sake of convenience Old Catalonia and Old Aragon. Because these regions had never been firmly controlled by the Muslims and were reconquered so early, very few Mudejars would live there in the fourteenth century.[14]

Following the collapse of the Islamic caliphate of Córdoba in 1031, both the kingdom of Aragon and the Catalan counties began to expand at the expense of the Muslims.[15] By the mid-twelfth century, Aragon had conquered the Muslim kingdom of Huesca (1096) and Zaragoza (1118), as well as the dry lands beyond the Ebro River: Calatayud, Soria, Daroca. Aragon had expanded to roughly its present-day borders. Catalonia, too, extended its borders beyond the ancient frontier of the river Llobregat, past Tortosa (1148) and Lleida (1149), forming an area called New Catalonia whose frontier with the Muslim kingdom of Valencia was south of the river Ebro.[16]

These were considerable conquests. They needed to be populated with laborers if they were to be productive, and with Christians if they were to be defended against Islam. The conquerors therefore encouraged the immigration of Christians from their older territories and beyond (e.g., from France) into the

---

[12] *Wolfram von Eschenbach: Parzival: Studienausgabe*, ed. K. Lachmann (Berlin, 1965), 57:18–22, p. 25. On this aspect of Wolfram's *Parzival*, see S. C. Van D'Elden, "Black and White: Contact with the Mediterranean World in Medieval German Narrative," in *The Medieval Mediterranean: Cross-Cultural Contacts*, ed. M. Chiat and K. Reyerson, Medieval Studies at Minnesota 3 (St. Cloud, MN, 1988), pp. 112–118.

[13] The word "Mudejar" will be used here in this sense, though the usage is controversial. On this issue see, most recently, L. P. Harvey, *Islamic Spain, 1250 to 1500* (Chicago, 1990), pp. 1–5.

[14] This is not to say that the fourteenth-century residents of Old Catalonia were unfamiliar with Muslims. Muslim slaves and visiting Muslim traders were common in many Catalan cities, and even a city like Girona, squarely in the middle of the ancient Frankish march, could boast at least one Mudejar household. For the large Muslim population in Barcelona, see D. Romano, "Musulmanes residentes y emigrantes en la Barcelona de los siglos XIV–XV," *Al-Andalus* 41 (1976): 49–88. See the amusing ACA:C cr. Jaume II, box 40, no. 4947 for Girona.

[15] For recent general overviews of the Muslim polities in Aragon and Catalonia, see respectively M. Viguera, *Aragón Musulman: La presencia del Islam en el Valle del Ebro* (Zaragoza, 1988); P. Balañà i Abadia, *Els Musulmans a Catalunya (713–1153)* (Barcelona, 1993).

[16] For a survey of early Aragonese and Catalan expansion, see T. Bisson, *The Medieval Crown of Aragon: A Short History* (Oxford, 1986), pp. 8–30.

newly conquered areas. Because this immigration was not always large enough to satisfy labor demands, they also permitted some of the old agricultural labor force to remain in place. They granted peace treaties to the Muslims they conquered so that those Muslims would continue to work their traditional holdings. These treaties stipulated the terms of surrender for the defeated Muslims, but they also guaranteed extensive privileges for those who chose to remain: among others, the right to continue practicing Islam and the right to govern their own communities according to Islamic law.[17]

As a result, both Aragon and New Catalonia had extensive Muslim populations. There were roughly 6,000 Mudejars in Catalonia circa 1250, for example, with most of these concentrated around the Ebro River. In Aragon the number of Mudejars was much greater: perhaps as much as 35 percent of a total population of approximately 200,000 was Muslim. Every major town in that kingdom had witnessed continuous Mudejar habitation in the centuries since its reconquest, and in some rural areas Muslims constituted a majority of the population.[18]

The gradual extension of the Aragonese and Catalan frontiers had taken centuries. The most spectacular expansion of the Crown, however, took place within the lifetime of one monarch: James the Conqueror. When the adolescent James I assumed the throne in 1213, he could sign himself king of Aragon, count of Barcelona, and lord of Montpellier. Within some thirty years he tripled the number of his crowns, adding the kingdoms of Mallorca and Valencia to the list. The subjugation of the Muslim polities of Majorca, Minorca, and Valencia was dramatically rapid. King James defeated the *wālī* of Majorca in 1229–1232 and reduced the much larger kingdom of Valencia in a series of campaigns between 1237 and 1245. Thanks to these campaigns the Crown of Aragon almost doubled in area, while the population of Muslims within its borders more than tripled (see map 1). The kingdom of Majorca was relatively small, and its resettlement was accomplished without the granting of substantial rights to the conquered Muslims.[19] The opposite is true of Valencia. There Muslim numerical dominance of the countryside was the rule, not the exception, and an

[17]See, for example, J. M. Font Rius, "La carta de seguridad de Ramon Berenguer IV a las morerías de Ascó y Ribera del Ebro (siglo XII)," in idem, *Estudis sobre els drets i institucions locals en la Catalunya medieval* (Barcelona, 1985), pp. 561–576. The treaty granted the Muslims of Tortosa is published by P. Bofarull y Mascaró, CoDoIn, 4:130–135.

[18]For a brief summary of Mudejar settlement patterns in Aragon, see J. M. Lacarra, "Introducción al estudio de los mudéjares aragoneses," in *Actas del I Simposio Internacional de Mudejarismo* (Madrid-Teruel, 1981), pp. 17–28. J. Utrilla Utrilla and J. C. Esco Samperiz, "La población mudejar en la Hoya de Huesca (siglos XII y XIII)," in *Actas del III Simposio Internacional de Mudejarismo* (Teruel, 1986), pp. 187–208, make clear how widespread Mudejar settlement was within one particular area.

[19]The fate of Muslims in the Balearics is unclear. See E. Lourie, "Free Moslems in the Balearics under Christian Rule in the Thirteenth Century," *Speculum* 45 (1970): 624–649 (reprinted in idem, *Crusade and Colonisation*); and, most recently, D. Abulafia, *A Mediterranean Emporium: The Catalan Kingdom of Majorca* (Cambridge, 1994), pp. 56–72.

Map 1. The Crown of Aragon and its environs

Islamic population of well over 100,000 outnumbered Christian settlers by more than three to one at the time of the Conqueror's death in 1276.[20]

This immensely variable distribution of the Muslim population meant that Muslims in different parts of the Crown experienced minority-majority relations differently, as a comparison of Muslim status in the kingdoms of Aragon and Valencia makes clear.[21] The Muslims in Aragon had lived in a Christian polity for centuries. They had watched the frontiers with their coreligionists recede further into the distant south with every passing year. Some, among them many members of the intellectual and military elites, had followed the frontier, emigrating to Muslim lands. Those who remained developed allegiances to their new lords. In Valencia, on the other hand, the reconquest had been recent and the frontier with Granada was both close by and easy to cross. Further, in Valencia the Muslim military and intellectual leadership was to some extent still intact. As late as 1317, for example, there was still a Muslim *ra'īs* ruling over Crevillent, albeit as vassal of a Christian king.[22] Equally important, in Valencia Muslims were for many years following the reconquest a numerical majority, overwhelmingly so in the countryside, whereas in Aragon they remained a minority.

Variations in demographic weight, date of conquest, and proximity to Muslim Granada also affected the cultural development of Mudejars in Valencia and Aragon. In Valencia, the large Mudejar population could isolate itself from contact with Christians, especially in the countryside.[23] Muslims could live in villages with other Muslims, pay taxes to Muslim (and sometimes Jewish) tax collectors who kept the tax rolls in Arabic, shop only in Muslim stores, and so forth. It seems, in fact, that a large proportion of the Valencian Mudejar population could not even speak the language of its conquerors, preserving Arabic and refusing to learn Romance.[24]

---

[20] All population figures for the thirteenth and fourteenth centuries should be understood as highly approximate, since they are in large part extrapolated from later sources. See, inter alia, H. Lapeyre, *Géographie de l'Espagne morisque* (Paris, 1959), pp. 96–99; J. Reglá Campistrol, *Estudios sobre los moriscos*, 3d ed. (Valencia, 1974). Burns summarizes the data and discusses its limitations in *Islam under the Crusaders*, pp. 72–81. See also A. Domínguez Ortiz and B. Vincent, *Historia de los moriscos* (Madrid, 1978), p. 77, and Meyerson, *Muslims of Valencia*, p. 14.

[21] Even within each of these kingdoms there was a wide range of "climates" for Muslims. What follows is therefore very generalized.

[22] P. Guichard, "Un seigneur musulman dans l'Espagne chrétienne: le 'rais' de Crevillente (1243–1318)," *Melanges de la Casa de Velázquez* 9 (1973): 283–334.

[23] A part of the process of Christian settlement and Muslim resettlement that effected this segregation is studied by J. Torró, "Sobre ordenament feudal del territori i trasbalsaments del poblament mudèjar: La Montanea Valencie (1286–1291)," *Afers* 7 (1988–1989): 95–124.

[24] The language of Valencian Muslims, like many of the other issues adumbrated in this chapter, has a vexed and contentious bibliography. See R. I. Burns, "The Language Barrier: The Problem of Bilingualism and Muslim-Christian Interchange in the Medieval Kingdom of Valencia," in *Contributions to Mediterranean Studies*, ed. M. Vassallo (Malta, 1977), pp. 116–136, and the similar chapter in his *Muslims, Christians, and Jews in the Crusader Kingdom of Valencia*, pp. 172–192; M. Barceló Torres, *Minoría islámicas en el país valenciano* (Valencia, 1984), esp. pp. 121–151.

In Aragon and Catalonia, on the other hand, where a smaller Muslim population had been incorporated piecemeal over centuries, Muslims tended to live cheek by jowl with Christians. Even when Mudejars were assigned a specific quarter for their habitation, as often happened in the larger towns, effective segregation was seldom achieved and Muslims could be found living in Christian neighborhoods as well. In the countryside there were some villages populated entirely by Muslims, but many others had mixed populations. In such villages Muslims and Christians jointly paid taxes, fought rival villages, tended sheep, and even governed each other.[25] Such a setting encouraged acculturation, at least in language. Nearly all Muslims in the north spoke Romance. It has even become commonplace to state that, because of assimilation and the emigration of elites, many Muslims in Aragon and Catalonia forgot much of their Islamic culture, including Arabic.[26] This position seems overstated, since it makes little sense of, for example, the existence of a Mudejar medical school in Zaragoza in 1494, or the petition in 1385 by the Muslim aljama (corporate municipal body) of Fraga that it be allowed to conduct all of its legal business in Arabic.[27] It nevertheless remains true that the Muslims of Aragon and Catalonia were much more integrated into the majority Christian society than those of Valencia.

.   .   .   .   .

The distribution of the Jewish population in the Crown is in some ways the inverse of the Muslim. First, there were far fewer Jews in the Crown than Muslims. Estimates range from a maximum of 20,000 Jews in Aragon, 25,000 in

[25] The Aragonese village of Pedrola, for example, had a town council made up of both Muslims and Christians, as is evident from a "salva de infanzonía" taken in 1332 that mentions "nos Johan Ferrelleyo & Hamet Avencecri, jurados del dito lugar . . . & todo el sobredito concellyo, xristianos & moros, del dito lugar." (My thanks to E. Lourie for this reference.) In Naval, Muslims paid a third of the taxes and appointed one Muslim *jurado* (representative on the village council), while the Christians paid two-thirds and appointed two Christian ones. See ACA:C 371:235r (1322/11/18). See also n. 56, below. For Christian violence against the Muslims of Naval, see chap. 3, below.

[26] See J. Mutgé i Vives, *L'aljama sarraïna de Lleida a l'edat mitjana: aproximació a la seva història* (Barcelona, 1992), p. 61, who treats this as proven and cites Burns, *Islam under the Crusaders*, pp. 413 ff. (who was writing, however, about Valencia, not the north). Boswell, *Royal Treasure*, pp. 381 ff., provides some evidence for this position.

[27] For the *madrasa* in Zaragoza, see J. Ribera y Tarragó, "La enseñanza entre los musulmanes españoles," in idem, *Disertaciones y opúsculos*, vol. 1 (Madrid, 1928), pp. 229–359, here pp. 248–249, 352–354. For Fraga, see ACA:C 1690:196 (1385/12/14), confirming a privilege first granted in 1362. The document is published in J. Salarrullana de Dios, "Estudios históricos acerca de la ciudad de Fraga: la aljama de moros de Fraga," *Revista de Archivos, Bibliotecas y Museos*, 3ª epoca, año 26 (1921), 42:361–381, 491–512, and 43:19–44, 197–234, 354–374, here 42:498–499. A. Blasco Martínez agrees with those who portray Aragonese Arabic culture as vanishing, but also provides evidence of the continued use of Arabic in Zaragozan notarial documents. See her "Notarios mudéjares de Aragón (siglos XIV–XV)," in *Aragón en la Edad Media* (*Homenaje a la profesora emérita María Luisa Ledesma Rubio*) 10–11 (1993): 109–133.

Catalonia, and 10,000 in Valencia to a minimum of perhaps half that, or between 6 and 2 percent of the population of the Crown.[28] Further, unlike Muslims, Jews had greater demographic weight in urban areas than in the country as a whole.[29] For instance, cities like Barcelona or Girona in Catalonia and Huesca in Aragon probably had populations that were more than 10 percent Jewish. Some smaller provincial towns also had relatively large Jewish populations. Santa Coloma de Queralt, a town of roughly 150 houses, had some fifty Jewish families in the early fourteenth century, and in the village of Montclus in Aragon Jews may even have constituted a majority. Though there may have been scores of rural villages like Sarrion in Aragon with one or two Jewish inhabitants, these Jews did not make up an important (or at least not a measurable) fraction of the Jewish population.[30]

Just as Jews were more urban than Muslims, they were also more acculturated. One obvious index of this acculturation is language. Jews entered the Crown in a variety of ways: some emigrated from Muslim lands, others were conquered by Christian armies along with the Muslims, and still others came from elsewhere in Europe. Regardless of their provenance, however, all Jews in the Crown spoke the local Romance dialect as their language of everyday life, even if many retained Hebrew and Arabic as languages of religion and learning. Jewish social structure also approximated Christian models more than the Muslim one did. Jews, for example, modeled their society on the Christian division into upper, middle, and lower classes, and conflict among these classes was an important source of social unrest. Mudejar society, on the other hand, was relatively horizontal, and internal Mudejar conflict stemmed from lineage group feuds, from ʿaṣabīya (solidarity between agnates), not from class struggle.[31]

---

[28] See J. Hillgarth, *The Spanish Kingdoms*, vol. 1 (Oxford, 1976), pp. 30–32; J. Vicens Vives, *Manual de história económica de España*, 4th ed. (Barcelona, 1965), p. 163; Baer, *The Jews*, 1:193–196. See also J. Riera i Sans, "La Catalunya jueva del segle XIV," *L'Avenç* 25 (March 1980): 52–55.

[29] The distribution of Jewish population in the Crown of Aragon is thus very similar to that in the south of France. Of the approximately 70,000 Jews in royal France ca. 1300, the great majority lived in commercial cities and towns along the Mediterranean coast. See W. Jordan, *The French Monarchy and the Jews: From Philip Augustus to the Last Capetians* (Philadelphia, 1989), pp. 112–114. The figure of 70,000 is but one of many estimates ranging as high as 140,000.

[30] For the demographics of Santa Coloma see Y. T. Assis's *The Jews of Santa Coloma de Queralt* (Jerusalem, 1988), pp. 22–25. See also G. Secall i Güell, *La comunitat hebrea de Santa Coloma de Queralt* (Tarragona, 1986). For Montclus, see chap. 3, and on Sarrion, chap. 4. For the existence of small towns with Jewish populations see Assis, *Jews of Santa Coloma*, p. 16, who cites, among other sources, the responsum of Solomon ibn Adret about "a town in which there are not ten [Jewish] men for the wedding benedictions." Because Jews in such communities might be vassals of lords other than the king, and often paid taxes together with their Christian neighbors, they rarely surface in royal documentation.

[31] This "flatness" of Mudejar society is due in part to the early emigration of its intellectual, military, economic, and religious elites, and in part to the survival of pre-reconquest social structures. See Meyerson, *Muslims of Valencia*, esp. chap. 6, e.g., p. 247. On Jewish class stratification, see A. Blasco Martínez, "Los judíos de Zaragoza en el siglo XIV: su evolución social," in *Minorités et*

Another difference between Jews and Muslims, one that parallels the divide between urban and rural, is that between royal and seigneurial dependence. Though there were some great lords who were allowed by the king to have Jewish vassals, the great majority of Jews depended directly on the king. This resulted in a close relationship between Crown and Jews. Jews paid the king taxes, taxes that came to represent an important fraction of the funds available to him.[32] Jews also served the royal court as administrators, physicians, ambassadors, translators, as well as in a variety of other capacities. In exchange, they were closely subject to the jurisdiction of royal officials and depended on royal authority for protection. In some ways this close relationship to the monarchy resulted in increased acculturation, since participation in royal service involved a number of Jews in Christian social and political structures.[33] But it also isolated the Jews, since it forced them to depend almost entirely on the king, who was but one among several competing powers in the Crown. The costs of this dependence were most obvious when royal power was at a low ebb. In 1283, for example, when a *Unión* rose up against King Peter III "the Great," it attacked royal administration by demanding that the king not appoint Jews as officials in his realms, a petition that the king was forced to grant in perpetuity.[34]

Muslims were in a very different position. In theory, the king claimed ultimate jurisdiction over all Muslims in his realms. Like the Jews, Muslims were "the royal treasure"; that is, they had a special relationship of dependence to the Crown and this relationship brought them special rights.[35] But in fact, the great majority of Mudejars were direct vassals of lay and ecclesiastical lords rather than of the king. By the fourteenth century, the king directly controlled most urban Muslim communities, as well as Muslim tenants on royal lands, but he rarely

---

marginaux en France méridionale et dans la péninsule Ibérique (VIIe–XVIIIe siècles) (Actes du colloque de Pau, 27–29 mai, 1984) Paris, 1986), pp. 177–201.

[32]See M. Sánchez Martínez, "La fiscalidad real y las aljamas catalano-aragonesas en el primer tercio del siglo XIV," *Acta Historica et Archaeologica Mediaevalia* 3 (1982): 93–142.

[33]These Jews are sometimes called "court Jews." Their access to royal authority (and their wealth) gave them a great deal of power in Jewish society, though by the fourteenth century this power was considerably diminished. See B. Septimus, "Piety and Power in Thirteenth Century Catalonia," in *Studies in Medieval Jewish History and Literature,* ed. I. Twersky (Cambridge, MA, 1979), pp. 197–230. See p. 214 for the suggestion that the famous thirteenth-century Rabbi Naḥmanides thought of royal service as acculturative and corrupting of Jewish spirituality. For a general analysis of the relations between diaspora Jews and the monarchs in whose realms they lived, see D. Biale, *Power and Powerlessness in Jewish History* (New York, 1986), pp. 34–86.

[34]On the *Unión* of 1283, see González, *Las Uniones aragonesas.* On the ban against Jewish royal officials and its effects on Jewish participation in administration, see D. Romano, *Judíos al servicio de Pedro el Grande de Aragón (1276–1285)* (Barcelona, 1983), esp. pp. 175–178.

[35]For example, unlike Christian serfs, Muslim peasants could not legally be maltreated or forced by a lord to remain tied to that lord's lands, since they were theoretically part of "the royal treasure." See E Hinojosa, "Mezquinos y exaricos," in *Homenaje a Codera* (Zaragoza, 1904), pp. 523–531, here 529 f. Cf. also Lourie, "Anatomy of Ambivalence," pp. 15, 43.

interfered in the affairs of the many Muslims working seigneurial lands. This meant that in addition to the king, all the landowning oligarchies of the Crown also had an interest in protecting the Mudejars, since in New Catalonia and especially in Aragon and Valencia, Muslims constituted an important part of the agricultural labor force.

Lords depended on Mudejars not only because they were numerous, but also because they were relatively cheap. There are few unequivocal data, but it seems that Muslim vassals paid their lords slightly higher rents and higher taxes, and in turn received smaller plots of land, than their Christian counterparts.[36] Perhaps as a result of this, Muslims came to symbolize peasant status in the eyes of some Christians, and to represent subjection to exploitative lordship: hence complaints like that of an Aragonese Christian in 1323 that he and his fellows were treated "worse than Muslims" by their lord, or popular sayings like "He who has no Muslim has no money."[37] It is difficult to say for a prestatistical age precisely how important a role Mudejars played in seigneurial economies, but it is clear that the nobility believed their prosperity depended on them. After the coming of the Black Death, when shortages of agricultural labor became endemic, the nobility successfully pressured the Crown to restrict the traditional right of Mudejars to purchase licenses for emigration to Muslim lands. Similarly in the fifteenth century, whenever an expulsion or forced conversion of Mudejars was rumored, lords would petition the monarchy against it in apocalyptic terms, arguing that such a policy would ruin the kingdom. Later events suggest that they were exaggerating only slightly. When the Moriscos (Mudejars converted to Christianity) were expelled from Spain in 1609, the result was a sharp economic depression in Aragon and Valencia.[38]

Not only were the king and the nobility agreed on the importance of Muslims, they actually competed for Mudejar services. Because of shortages of agri-

[36] For examples, see Lourie, "Anatomy of Ambivalence," pp. 15–17; A. Gargallo Moya, "La carta-puebla concedida por el Temple a los moros de Villastar (1267)," in *Actas del III Simposio Internacional de Mudejarismo* (Madrid, 1986), pp. 209–220; and the articles collected in *Actas del V Simposio Internacional de Mudejarismo* (Teruel, 1991). Under the Alfonsine jurisdiction promulgated by Alfonso the Benign, a landlord need have only seven Muslim tenants in order to claim seigneurial jurisdiction over them, whereas if the tenants were Christian he needed fifteen. On Alfonsine jurisdiction, see S. Romeu Alfaro, "Los fueros de Valencia y los fueros de Aragón: jurisdicción Alfonsina," in *Anuario de Historia del Derecho Español* 42 (1972): 75–115, here pp. 96 f.

[37] ACA Salva de Infanzonía no. 69 (1323), testimony of Felipe Eximin of Laupes, a reference kindly provided to me by E. Lourie. For "quien no tiene moro, no tiene oro," see R. I. Burns, "Muslims in the Thirteenth Century Realms of Aragon: Interaction and Reaction," in *Muslims under Latin Rule: 1100–1300*, ed. J. M. Powell (Princeton, 1990), pp. 57–102, here p. 65.

[38] For post-1348 restrictions on emigration, see especially M. T. Ferrer i Mallol, *Els sarraïns de la Corona Catalano Aragonesa en el segle XIV: segregació i discriminació* (Barcelona, 1987), pp. 162–183. For the nobility's arguments in the fifteenth century see Meyerson, *Muslims of Valencia*, p. 143. For the consequences of the expulsion, see Reglá, *Estudios sobre los moriscos*, pp. 41–152, 219–243; and J. I. Gomez Zorraquino, "Consecuencias económicas de la expulsión de los moriscos aragoneses: los censales," *Actas del III Simposio Internacional de Mudejarismo* (Teruel, 1986), pp. 269–275.

cultural labor, landowners were forced to offer incentives to attract Muslim peasants. The Mudejars voted with their feet: the lands of less generous lords were gradually depopulated. As a result Mudejars secured greater autonomy and greater religious freedom. For example, lords attracted many Muslims by ignoring church-inspired edicts that imposed distinctions on Muslims or restricted their religious practice, or by paying the king for exemptions to these laws.[39] These increased privileges, then, were an additional benefit of Muslim dependence on a wide variety of oligarchical interests.

.   .   .   .   .

How did this historical background affect the general types of religious violence to which Muslims and Jews were subject? Before we address this question, it is important to remember that violence was a common and often acceptable way of settling disputes in medieval Iberia, although in our society it is considered aberrant, a sign only of a breakdown in social relations.[40] In Valencian law, for example, physical action (*guerra*: war, feud) was explicitly permitted if one's opponent refused to render legal satisfaction. In all three communities, Christian, Muslim, and Jewish, violence was a normal way of pursuing goals within (conflictive) relationships.[41] And not all acts of violence were directly physical. Accusations at law, attempts to mobilize the "state" (judge, torturer, executioner) against an individual, were forms of violence that did not involve direct physical action on the part of the attacker.[42] When Jucef, a Jew of Calatayud,

[39] Consider the case of laws stipulating that Muslims wear a particular hairstyle to distinguish them from Christians. (See also below.) As well as differentiating between Muslims and Christians, these laws were designed to raise revenues for the Crown, since infractions were subject to a monetary penalty. Seigneurs could ignore these laws, or they could pay the king to secure exemptions from them. On obligatory distinctions of dress and hairstyle for Muslims see Ferrer, *Els sarraïns*, pp. 41–60. For an example of nobles paying the king to secure exemptions from such rules for their Muslims, see ACA:C 1979:7v–8r (1391/1/21), published in ibid., pp. 335–336.

[40] D. Riches warns of the limitations of modern Anglo-Saxon understandings of violence in "The Phenomenon of Violence," in *The Anthropology of Violence*, ed. D. Riches (Oxford, 1986), pp. 1–27.

[41] *Fori Antiqui Valentiae*, ed. M. Dualde Serrano (Valencia, 1967), cxx.16: "Facimus forum novum, quod nullus nobilis vir, nec miles, nec aliquis alius possit alicui guerram facere, ex quo paratus est iuri parere." On feud in Christian communities see, most recently, R. Narbona Vizcaíno, "Violencias feudales en la ciudad de Valencia," in *Violència i marginació en la societat medieval* (= *Revista d'Història Medieval* 1 [1990]), pp. 59–86. For Muslims, see Meyerson, *Muslims of Valencia*, pp. 232–254; and for Jews, see E. Lourie, "Mafiosi and Malsines: Violence, Fear and Faction in the Jewish Aljamas of Valencia in the Fourteenth Century," in *Actas del IV Congreso Internacional "Encuentro de las Tres Culturas,"* ed. C. Carrete Parrondo (Toledo, 1988), pp. 69–102 (reprinted in her *Crusade and Colonisation*).

[42] A. Radcliffe-Brown drew a distinction between physical force employed by the state, which might be termed government, and that by private individuals and groups, which is violence. Such distinctions were not so sharp in the Middle Ages. See his preface to *African Political Systems*, ed. M. Fortes and E. Evans-Pritchard (London, 1940), p. xiv.

lost all his money and his clothes gambling in the house of the Christian Dominic del Gan and infuriated his fellow gamblers by refusing to go into debt and continue gambling, the angry players made a choice about how to proceed. They did not beat him up. Instead, "as he waited, totally naked, for the shades of night to fall so that he could [discreetly] leave the house . . . the said Dominic falsely accused him of entering into the house to commit adultery with his wife, . . . so that he had to flee the town." Words, not deeds, but violent nonetheless in intent and effect.[43]

Just as the violence in these actions is not always apparent to the modern eye, so also their religious nature is sometimes obscure. The term "religious violence" as used throughout this book means simply violence between members of different religious groups, though such a definition may seem naive to modern readers. In cases where members of a particular group are attacked today, we (as jury members, journalists, members of the public) tend to engage in a process of skeptical categorization. Was it a "bias crime," or simply a robbery; random violence, or an act of insanity? When a man carrying a Bible broke into a home for elderly Jews two days before Christmas 1990 in Dallas, Texas, and attacked six residents, "officials discounted bigotry as a motive." "The police said the assailant made no anti-Semitic comments in the attack, and a local Jewish leader said the man simply appeared to be deranged."[44]

In the medieval Crown of Aragon, however, all violence between members of different religious groups was argued, or could potentially be argued, in explicitly religious terms. This is because religious status determined legal status, and both together determined what kinds of violence were appropriate and how such violence would be treated by the courts. Thus, although feud and private violence were a perfectly legitimate way of settling differences between Christians, Jews and Muslims were specifically exempted from such activities

---

[43] ACA:C 174:153v (1322/3/18): ". . . ibique remanens totaliter denudatus noctis tenebras ut inde exire posset expectando . . . , idem Dominicus false diffamavit Jucefum predictum quod domum intraverat ut cum uxore sua adulterium comitteret." Physical violence did not, of course, exclude the concurrent use of accusations, as when a Christian beat up a Muslim and then, when the Muslim sued, accused him of having had sex with a Christian woman. See ACA:C 175:264v (1322/7/21). Violent eruptions among gamblers were extremely common. For detailed accounts of such violence, see the trial transcripts preserved as ACA:C Procesos, no. 22/5 (1324–1326) (provisional numeration) and ACA:C Procesos, no. 26/20 (1302) (provisional numeration. Old reference no. 502/5). For Castilian legislation against it, D. Carpenter, "Fickle Fortune: Gambling in Medieval Spain," *Studies in Philology* 85 (1988): 267–278.

[44] *New York Times*, Dec. 24, 1990, p. A-10. This example is chosen as extreme. Compare the case in Manresa in 1320, where the Jews complained that a man was roaming the roads pretending to be insane, insulting Jews and hitting them. Royal officials had refused to act, they said, because they claimed that the man was attacking these people not because they were Jews, but because he was mad. The king ordered that whether the man was detained as a lunatic or arrested as an assaulter of Jews, he should be locked up in either case. ACA:C 364:190v (1320/6/7). On the legal immunity of the insane in the medieval Crown of Aragon see, for example, *Fori Antiqui Valentiae*, cxvii.10 and cxx.30.

and placed under the king's protection, since their religious status made them "serfs of the king's chamber."[45] The motives of participants, then, were not the most important factor in determining whether or not a given act of violence was "religious": their religious identity was. This is true of even the most "interested" attacks. Armed robbery of travelers, for example, was frequent and ecumenical. One robber, the noble Pere Zapata of Morvedre, once killed three Jewish merchants on the royal highway, robbing them of 2,000 sous; attacked three Christian merchants from Provence, killing one while making off with 5,000 sous; and despoiled three Muslim merchants of 3,000 sous.[46] Certainly no contemporary was blind to the worldly motives of robbers. Nevertheless, when attempting to mobilize justice on their own behalf, Jewish and Muslim victims appealed on the basis of their religious, hence juridical, identity. After a Jewish woman of Agramunt was injured by two Christians, the aljama urged the king to act: "Because the Jews are your subjects and serfs, it is feared that if this deed is not punished with a great and worthy vengeance," others would begin to attack the Jews, who could then not collect *terces* and *fadiges* (i.e., taxes) on the king's behalf, which would be to the great detriment of the Crown. The letter continued: "The said Jews live beneath . . . your name and your highness." If the Christians were not daunted by fear of the king, wrote the Jews, nothing would restrain them, for the Christians knew "that the said Jews cannot wreak any vengeance upon them." In this way Jewish legal status transformed what we might call "random violence" against an individual into an issue of religious status and identity affecting an entire group.[47] Religious violence, therefore, is here defined as violence across religious boundaries. I believe such violence was relatively rare. The majority of altercations took place within religious communities, not across them.[48]

[45] For a discussion of the laws limiting violence between religious groups see A. Guallart de Viala, *El derecho penal histórico de Aragón* (Zaragoza, 1977), pp. 136–142.

[46] Pere was accused of more than twenty serious crimes, including the kidnapping and murder of the justice of Algezira, the kidnapping of the bailiff of Albau, the murder of a female trader ("corredora") of Valencia, and the hiring of a female Muslim converted to Christianity to poison one of his enemies. His career is detailed in ACA:C cr. Jaume II, box 108, no. 13,481 (no date).

[47] ACA:C cr. Jaume II, box 135, no. 369 (no date) addressed to Prince Alfonso, from the Jews of Agramunt.

[48] Only a handful of Jews appear as murder victims, for example, in the royal archives. A survey of the following account books of local officials reinforces my impression that assaults were rare across religious boundaries, common within them: *Llibre del batlle reial de Barcelona Berenguer Morey (1375–1378)*, ed. J. M. Casas Homs (Barcelona, 1976); C. Orcástegui and E. Sarasa, "El libro-registro de Miguel Royo, merino de Zaragoza en 1301: una fuente para el estudio de la sociedad y economía zaragozanas a comienzos del siglo XIV," in *Aragón en la Edad Media* 4 (1981): 87–156; idem, "Miguel Palacín, merino de Zaragoza en el siglo XIV," in *Aragón en la Edad Media* 1 (1977):51–131; L. Ledesma Rubio, "El libro de cuentas del merinado de Jaca (años 1387–1399)," in *Aragón en la Edad Media* 1 (1977): 133–174; M. de Bofarull, *El registro del merino de Zaragoza el caballero don Gil Tarín, 1291–1312* (Zaragoza, 1889); P. Bertran i Roigé, "El llibre del batlle reial de Lleida Ramon de Carcassona (1366–1369)," in *Miscel.lània Homenatge al Professor Salvador Roca i Lletjós* (Lleida,

What forms of religious violence did occur, however, were deeply affected by the historical context described above. Consider the position of the Muslims in Valencia. Because they lived close to the border with the Muslim kingdom of Granada, which was often at war with the Crown, because they were so numerous, and because they were largely unassimilated, they were feared by Christians as possible rebels, a "fifth column."[49] Such fears were used to legitimate anti-Muslim riots, most notoriously in 1276 and 1455: in 1455 a mob in Valencia city yelled, "The Moors are coming, the Moors are coming," as they sacked Muslim homes.[50] In times of war with Granada tensions generally rose, and rumors became accusations. During the disastrous (for the Christians, at any rate) Crusade of 1329–1334, when Granadan forces struck across the frontier and burned the Valencian town of Guardamar, many people "spoke mad and disordered words against the Muslims living in the said kingdom [of Valencia]," and the king had to order his procurator to protect the Muslims from violence.[51] Christians in Aragon did not fear Muslims in this way, nor did they participate in this type of violence. It seems that their confidence was not misplaced. During the "War of the Two Peters," for example, when the Crown of Aragon battled Castile, the Mudejars of Aragon fought actively on behalf of the Crown, while some Valencian Mudejars defected to the enemy.[52]

The ongoing war with Islam also put Valencian Muslims at risk of illegal

---

1981), pp. 157–186; idem, "Els jueus en els llibres de batlle i cort de Cervera (1354–1357)," *Ilerda* 44 (1983): 189–205; idem, "Conflictes socials a Cervera segons el llibre del batlle Antoni de Cabrera (1356–1357)," *Miscel.lània Cerverina* 6 (1988): 53–70.

[49] Mudejar revolts did in fact occur, especially in the half century immediately following the conquest (the most extensive of these took some two years to repress, in 1276–1277). See R. I. Burns, "The Crusade against Al-Azraq: A Thirteenth-Century Mudejar Revolt in International Perspective," *American Historical Review* 93 (1988): 80–106; idem, *Islam under the Crusaders*, pp. 323–352. Though Christian anxieties were less justified in the sixteenth century, they continued to be voiced. See Meyerson, *Muslims of Valencia*, pp. 61–98.

[50] On anti-Muslim riots in the 1270s, see R. I. Burns, "Social Riots on the Christian-Moslem Frontier: Thirteenth-Century Valencia," *American Historical Review* 66 (1961): 378–400. For later anti-Muslim riots in Valencia, see Boswell, *Royal Treasure*, pp. 372–400; M. T. Ferrer i Mallol, *La frontera amb l'Islam en el segle XIV: Cristians i sarraïns al país valencià* (Barcelona, 1988), pp. 21–29, 41–43. On the attack of 1455, see M. Gual Camarena, "Los mudéjares valencianos en la época del Magnánimo," in *IV Congreso de Historia de la Corona de Aragón*, vol. 1 (1959), pp. 467–494; and especially M. Ruzafa García, " 'Façen-se Cristians los moros o muyren!' " in *Violència i marginació en la societat medieval* (= *Revista d'Història Medieval* 1 [1990]), 87–110.

[51] The quotation is from ACA:C 541:182r–v (1331/11/9), "Per rahó de la entrada que.ls moros han feta en lo regne de València . . . persones han dites e dien paraules desordenades e folles contra los moros habitans en lo dit regne," transcribed in M. Sánchez Martínez, "La Corona de Aragón y el Reino Nazarí de Granada durante el siglo XVI: Las bases materiales y humanas de la cruzada de Alfonso IV (1329–1335)," (Ph.D. diss., University of Barcelona, 1974), appendix of documents, no. 74. On the nature of the frontier and its effect on Christian-Muslim relations in Valencia, see Ferrer, *La frontera*, and idem, *Organització i defensa d'un territori fronterer: La governació d'Oriola en el segle XIV* (Barcelona, 1990).

[52] Boswell, *Royal Treasure*, pp. 391 ff.

enslavement. A Muslim captured in war, "de bona guerra" (or conversely, a Christian captured by Muslims), could be legally enslaved. There was an international trade in such captives, and special religious orders and confraternities were set up to help mediate their ransoming.[53] But the trade in captives was lucrative and hard to control, so that peaceful Muslim residents of the Crown were sometimes kidnapped and sold as war captives. Though such kidnappings of Mudejars were illegal and were often harshly prosecuted, they were not infrequent.[54] Conversely, when Muslim raiders crossed the frontier and kidnapped Christians to sell as captives in Granada, Valencian Muslims might be accused of complicity in the abduction, and these accusations could lead to violence.[55] These were forms of violence to which Muslims in Valencia, but not Muslims in Aragon, were subject.

When interreligious violence did occur, it is my impression that it involved Muslims and Christians more frequently than Jews. The vast majority of Jews belonged to the Crown, were vigorously defended by it, and had institutions of government separate from Christians and Muslims. Muslims, on the other hand, were often seigneurial vassals, shared institutions with Christians, and participated in the feuds and conflicts that arose within these institutions. Muslims were bound to be involved when one lord fought against another, or when villages clashed over pasture lands. As a result, and despite the theoretical royal protection extended over all Muslims, Mudejars participated both willingly and unwillingly in a variety of types of violence.[56]

[53]On religious orders established for the redemption of captives, see J. Brodman, *Ransoming Captives in Crusader Spain: The Order of Merced on the Christian-Islamic Frontier* (Philadelphia, 1986). For local confraternities of Muslims and Christians, see J. Torres Fontes, "La hermandad de moros y cristianos para el rescate de cautivos," in *Actas del I Simposio de Mudejarismo* (Teruel, 1981), pp. 499–508; A. Nieto Fernández, "Hermandad entre las aljamas de moros y las villas de la gobernación de Orihuela en el siglo XV," *Primer Congreso de Historia del País Valenciano*, vol. 2 (Valencia, 1980), pp. 749–760; Ferrer, *La frontera*, pp. 187–222.

[54]ACA:C Proceso 28/7 (1320–1327) (6 fols.) provides a detailed narrative of an attack upon a fortified Muslim farm near Oriola by such kidnappers, and of the ensuing manhunt by police officials who tracked the perpetrators into Castile, where they had gone to sell the Muslims. Some of the kidnappers were captured and hanged.

[55]For a variant of this type of accusation, see M. P. Gil García, "Conflictos sociales y oposición étnica: La comunidad mudéjar de Crevillente, 1420," in *Actas del III Simposio Internacional de Mudejarismo* (Teruel, 1986), pp. 305–312. Nevertheless, contemporaries realized that violence by Christian and Muslim raiders (called "almugavers") was fairly ecumenical. See, for example, ACA:C 519:73r–v (1328/4/6).

[56]For examples of town councils on seigneurial lands jointly staffed by Christians and Muslims, see C. Contel Barea, *El císter zaragozano en los siglos XIII y XIV: Abadía de Nuestra Señora de Rueda de Ebro*, 2 vols. (Zaragoza, 1977), here vol. 2, documents nos. 198, 206, pp. 193–195, 202–205. Compare the case of Naval, where royal Muslims paid taxes jointly with Christians (Muslims paid one-third of the burden), elected one out of three councilmen, and shared revenue from judicial fines (see ACA:C 371:235r [1322/11/18]; ACA:C 455:268r [1332/8/3)]). For one example among many of Muslim participation with Christians in intermunicipal raids, see ACA:C 520:270v (1329/2/14). On the preponderance of seigneurial Muslims see Lacarra, "Introducción al estudio de los mudéjares aragoneses," pp. 7–22.

One case best summarizes this tension between theory and practice. On a February night in 1322 a Muslim called Jucef was arrested for taking part in an attack on a mill and was taken to the bailiff of Daroca's prison. Sancho de Ravanera, a Christian of the town, rode up to the gates of the prison with a gang of thugs ("comitiva") and demanded that the bailiff set bail. The bailiff refused, since it was late and he did not know of what crimes the Muslim stood accused. Then Sancho, "puffed up with pride, put one hand to his sword and grabbed the Saracen with the other hand. . . . And when the bailiff said to him that he did wrong by including Our [i.e., the king's] Muslims in his gang, the said Sancho Ravanera answered that he would form factions with Muslims as well as Jews, to the displeasure of anyone who said otherwise," and took off with the Muslim.[57] Sancho and Jucef insisted that religion could not prevent them from making common and violent cause, although an alternative argument based on religious identity existed, and this was the argument that the bailiff made in his complaint.

We might contrast the account of Sancho and the Muslim Jucef given above with one of the few surviving documents concerning Jewish-Christian feuding. In 1343 some men of Alcañiz rode into town in the night and affixed a notarized challenge against the Jews to various doors in the town, and in all public meeting places. The document proclaimed that in ten days (the waiting period stipulated by law) they would proceed violently against the Jews "as if against enemies" unless their complaints were redressed. The Jews appealed promptly to the king, who forbade such a challenge on the grounds that it was against the *fuero* (local law) and custom of Aragon.[58]

Unlike Muslims and Christians, who persisted in their violent "cooperation" despite official attempts to fortify the juridical boundary between them, Jews tended to invoke that boundary as a way of escaping the obligations inherent in an economy of violence. Both Jews and the Crown insisted that disputes with Jews should be settled only in royal courts and not by force.[59] Muslims, on the other hand, frequently subject to nonroyal jurisdictions, tended not to make such claims except in special cases, and the Crown was careful about invoking its theoretical rights over all Muslims in the face of seigneurial resistance. In

---

[57] ACA:C 247:52r–v (1322/4/1): ". . . dictus Sanccius . . . elevatus in superbiam posuit manum ad gladium et cepit cum manu altera sarracenum. . . . Et cum dictus baiulus dixisset eidem Sanccio quod male faciebat de faciendo bando cum sarracenis nostris dictus Sanccius Ravanera respondit quod ipse faceret bandum cum sarracenis atque judeis ad displicentiam contrarium asserentium."

[58] ACA:C 627:31r–32r (1343/3/17): "De nocte . . . posuerunt seu confixerunt aliqua instrumenta publica et alias scripturas privatas difidamentorum adversus aliamam judeorum predictorum et singulares ex eis in portis sive hostiis domorum aliquorum vicinorum ipsius ville [sic] . . . in quibus instrumentis et scripturis difidamentorum inter cetera dicitur contineri quod . . . elapsis decem diebus . . . procedent contra personas et bona dictorum judeorum et singularium [sic] ex eis ad captionem vel aliter tanquam contra inimicos."

[59] Perhaps because of this, when the word *jueu* ("Jew") was used as an insult in medieval Catalan, it meant a coward who refuses to take vengeance, not a cheat, as it sometimes does today. For several instances of such usage see the sermons of St. Vincent Ferrer.

short, Jews were more or less effectively isolated from physical violence as a form of dispute resolution, Muslims less so.[60]

These boundaries, porous as they were, are full of implications for any study of religious violence. First, they orient the surviving documentation, especially by directing it toward attacks on Jews. Violence involving Jews interested the royal bureaucracy more than other types because it represented an opportunity for relatively effective bureaucratic action. Further, the recognition that violence against Jews and Muslims touched upon Crown interests structured the arguments of contemporaries about such events. We have already seen examples of the types of arguments Jews used in order to mobilize royal vengeance and protection. Christians, too, might borrow these strategies, even in situations seemingly unrelated to religious issues. In 1327, the location of the official weighing station for grain in the city of Xàtiva was under dispute, with rival interest groups coming to blows in their support for particular locations. In the thick of this debate Pere Fuster, a native of the city, wrote to the royal councillor Vidal de Vilanova hoping to enlist Vidal's intercession in favor of his preferred location. First, Pere warned that if Vidal did not intercede, the violence would escalate so that two or three hundred men might easily die in a day. He then turned to more subtle arguments. Moving the weights to the "canto de sancta Maria" would be prejudicial to the king's interests, because

> Jews and Muslims have much to do all day long at the scales . . . , and the scales would be close to the cemetery, and the clergy do not cease all day long . . . to go with crosses about the tombs to carry out the divine offices which a Christian deserves, and the ordinance of the Church is such that if Jews or Muslims do not . . . bend their knees in front of the cleric who passes with the cross, the students and clerics who are escorting the cross beat them harshly with sticks.

In this case, arguments about religious violence, here only anticipated, served to lobby the Crown in a conflict over "urban development."[61]

---

[60]The extreme dependence of Jews on the courts meant that violence against Jews also involved violence against the representatives of justice, as in ACA:C 529:44v–45r, where a Jew and a lower court official (*sagione*) were killed trying to collect the Jew's debts. Lourie discusses the comparative vulnerability of Muslims and Jews to violence in "Anatomy of Ambivalence," pp. 51–69, reaching different conclusions from mine. On pp. 66–67, Lourie briefly mentions the susceptibility of Muslims to feudal violence, though not their frequent participation in it.

[61]ACA:C cr. Jaume II, box 134, no. 233 (1327/7/7): ". . . com jueues e moros que han molt a fer tot dia en lo pes e en l'almodi e que l'almodi e el pes fosen atinent del fosar e los clergues que tot dia no cesen ne poden cesar danar . . . ab cru[cifix] sobre les foses de fer los altres divinals oficis que xristia mereix, e la ordinacio de la ecclesia es aytal que si lo juheu o moro no fogira davant lo clergue que va ab la cru[cifix] o no ficara els genolls los escolers o clergues que van ab la cru[cifix] donen de grans bastonades a aquells." Interestingly, the letter goes on to state that the Jews earn their livelihood exclusively at the grain market. On the career of Vidal de Vilanova, named commander of Montalbán a month after the date of this letter, see R. Sáinz de la Maza, *La orden de Santiago en la Corona de Aragón (II): La encomienda de Montalbán bajo Vidal de Vilanova (1327–1357)* (Zaragoza, 1988).

Finally, the same legal structures which allowed Jews (and sometimes Muslims) to argue that they were exempt from private violence also made them especially vulnerable to state, or official, violence. The claim that Jews were "royal serfs" could induce royal officials to treat the king's property as their own; the king indeed had to forbid royal officials to extort ransoms from Jewish travelers.[62] More often, however, it meant that people in conflict with Jews would tap into the judicial monopoly on violence against Jews by taking judicial action. We have already seen how, rather than attacking Jucef through (illegal) physical violence, his fellow gamblers accused him of attempting to have sex with a Christian. The accusation of miscegenation was one of the most commonly used against Jews and Muslims, perhaps because it was particularly effective at bringing the judicial apparatus unpleasantly to bear upon the accused.[63] Thus, for example, a Christian debtor's complaint about a loan might begin with charges of usury, move to the unfair seizure of goods as security by the Jewish creditor, and end with the charge that the creditor tried to rape the debtor's daughter.[64]

Christians were not the only ones to bring such accusations. Members of minority communities themselves tried frequently to use the judicial apparatus against their enemies. Jewish aljamas complained constantly of lower-class Jews' bringing such accusations against wealthy ones and attempted to prohibit accusations by Jews against other Jews in Christian courts. Hence the extensive and largely ineffectual Jewish legislation against *malshins* (informers, i.e., accusers in Christian courts), a type of legislation that was explicitly imitated by Muslim communities by the end of the fourteenth century.[65]

Put briefly and at its most abstract, in an economy of violence fragmented by boundaries of religious and legal status the Crown was more successful in controlling violence against Jews and defining the channels within which such violence flowed than it was in the case of Muslims or Christians.[66] To say this is not

---

[62] ACA:C 449:269v (1332/1/16).

[63] For a detailed analysis of this subject see chap. 5.

[64] In ACA:C 365:188v–189r (1320/12/13), Pedro Domingo de Ayneto made such complaints against his creditor, Jucef Abutarda of Daroca, though Pedro claimed that Jucef's son Jaco, not Jucef himself, had tried to seduce his daughter and wrongfully seized some chickens. For more on this vulnerability of Muslims and Jews to certain types of accusations, see chap. 5. For more on Jaco's career, see below.

[65] One example of a complaint: ACA:C 519:111r–v, where a poor Jew is accused of extorting money from rich ones by threatening to accuse them of heresy or miscegenation. On the issue of *malshins* in Jewish communities, see Lourie, "Mafiosi and Malsines"; F. de Bofarull, "Los judíos malsines," *Boletín de la Real Academia de Buenas Letras de Barcelona* 6 (1911): 207–216. On the Muslim adoption of laws about *malshins*, see ACA:C 1905:233v–234v (1393/12/18), granting the Muslim aljama of Huesca the right to put to death "sarracenus aliquis . . . per vos repertus fuerit accusator, qui hebraice malsini et agarenice namem vulgariter nuncupatur." Each such execution would cost the aljama a fee of one thousand sous of Jaca. The document is published in M. B. Basañez, *La aljama sarracena de Huesca en el siglo XIV* (Barcelona, 1989), doc. no. 96, pp. 235–237.

[66] Compare L. Pospisil, *The Ethnology of Law*, 2d ed. (Menlo Park, CA, 1978), pp. 52–60; M. Weber, *Law in Economy and Society* (New York, 1967).

to say that any of these groups was more susceptible to violence than another, only that the kinds of violence which each group encountered or used differed. Nor should we doubt that contemporaries were experts in navigating these dangerous waters, as I hope the rest of this book will make clear.

.   .   .   .   .

The chapters that follow all focus on particular aspects of the economy of violence described above. This emphasis should not be allowed to obscure the fact that relations between Christians and non-Christians in the medieval Crown of Aragon were largely nonviolent. It is fitting, therefore, to end with an emphasis upon one form of such relations: what Mark Meyerson has called "the economic foundations of *convivencia*." For Meyerson (writing about Muslims in fifteenth-century Valencia), face-to-face interaction in the work- and marketplace created a web of economic relations between individuals that lent stability to Muslim-Christian *convivencia*.[67] Several factors account for this stability. Jews and Muslims sometimes concentrated in trades where they came to exercise a near monopoly. Muslim blacksmiths, for example, virtually controlled that industry in some Aragonese towns, and in modern Aragon the survival of Mudejar-style buildings like the Aljafería in Zaragoza testifies to another Muslim-dominated industry: the building trades.[68] The social utility of minorities in such trades was obvious, and towns even competed to attract a Jewish physician, or a Muslim master builder.[69] At a more general level, town councils recognized that the presence of minorities had a significant effect on their economic well-being, and often spoke openly about the benefits of minority immigration and the dangers of the reverse. This recognition of the economic utility of minorities is important, but it should be emphasized that such recognition did not preclude violence. At the same time that the town council of Oriola was attempting to attract Muslims to settle there in the 1420s, for example, it sent an armed mob to attack the Muslims of neighboring Crevillent, whom it accused of having abducted some local Christians.[70]

[67] Meyerson, *Muslims of Valencia*, p. 271.

[68] In Daroca, a Muslim blacksmith even had a monopoly on the unloading and sale of iron in the town. His privilege, granted by James II, was frequently challenged and frequently upheld. See, inter alia, ACA:C 433:216r; 434:157v–158r; 442:143r–v; 447:168v–169r; 476:164v–165r; 485:251v–252r. For the Muslim dominance of the building trades in Aragon, see Boswell, *Royal Treasure*, p. 57. In 1492 Aragonese Mudejars were even sent to Granada to carry out repairs on the Alhambra, on which see L. Piles Ros, *Estudio documental sobre el Bayle General de Valencia* (Valencia, 1970), p. 314 (also cited by Boswell).

[69] As when the council of Jaca promised a Jewish physician an annual stipend in wheat if he would move to the town (ACA:C 471:108r–v, 1335/3/7).

[70] Municipal councils often urged the king to reduce tax assessments on the local minority communities, arguing that their depopulation through emigration would harm the town. See, e.g., ACA:C cr. Jaume II, box 76, no. 9262, where the sworn men of Alzira write on behalf of the

In other cases, minorities might occupy particular niches within an industry. Muslim leatherworkers in Valencia, for example, specialized in shoemaking and depended on Christian tanners for their supplies of cured leather. Conversely, Christian tanners depended on Muslim shoemakers as a market for their goods. Within the cloth trade, a Jew might provide a Christian silk-weaver with raw materials, and the weaver might sell his goods to a Jewish tailor whose clothes would dress a Christian burgher: a system of specialization and interdependence that attenuated competition.[71]

Even direct economic competition among Muslims, Jews, and Christians could result in forms of cooperation. The same Christian blacksmiths of Teruel who tried to limit the workweek of Muslim colleagues by petitioning the king to silence their hammers on Sundays were members of the Confraternity of St. Eloy, a union of Muslim and Christian smiths who jointly donated a candle to the Virgin Mary each week.[72] And despite the fact that the meat trade was one of the most conflictual areas of commercial relations between Christians and Jews, Jewish and Christian butchers formed business associations for the joint purchase and pasturage of animals.[73]

As a result of these relations, individuals of all three faiths found themselves economically dependent upon one another, a dependence even more striking when viewed at a more general level. King and seigneurs, of course, depended

---

Muslims of the town; or ACA:C cr. Jaume II, box 134, no. 170, on behalf of the Jews and Muslims of Oriola. For Oriola in the 1420s, see Gil, "Conflictos sociales y oposición étnica," pp. 305–312.

[71] On Muslim leatherworkers see Meyerson, *Muslims of Valencia*, pp. 129–132. Some of the few Christian shoemakers even worked in Muslim shops. The example of the silk trade is a loose one, based on documents like ACB, NC, Bernat Vilarrúbia 1338, 179r–v (1338/9/2), where Agnès, the wife of Guillem de Tortosa and a silk-weaver of Barcelona, buys raw silk from Maymó Vidal, Jew of Barcelona. But Jews did not specialize in or control any one aspect of the silk industry, and plenty of Jewish weavers bought raw silk from Christian merchants. Jews do seem to have controlled trades like dice making (e.g., ACB, NC, Nicolau de Fàbrega 1389–1390 [1389/10/8]), perhaps because the trade was considered sordid by Christian moralists. For the opinion of one such on dice makers, see J. Hernando i Delgado, "Realidades socioeconómicas en el *Libro de las Confesiones* de Martín Perez: usura, justo precio y profesión," *Acta Historica et Archaeologica Mediaevalia* 2 (1981): 93–106, here p. 102.

[72] See ACA:C 442:236r–v (1331/3/5), in which Andreas Boson, a servant of Domingo Martin, the confraternity's majordomo, complains that when he went to collect the weekly denarius for the confraternity's candles from Hazan Alguar, Hazan's wife and son attacked him. Although such bireligious professional organizations have not previously been documented in Aragon, there are examples elsewhere. In Segovia the Cofradia de San Eloy was founded in 1484 as a confraternity of Muslim and Christian blacksmiths dedicated to "Sancta Maria . . . et todos los sanctos et sanctas de la corte del cielo." Each incoming member took an oath according to his particular religious law and contributed one hundred maravedis, but only Christians were expected to give a pound of wax for the saints' candles. On Segovia, see the Marqués de Lozoya, *La morería de Segovia* (Madrid, 1967), p. 10. Such examples qualify, though they do not invalidate, D. Bramon's thesis about the function of guild religious barriers in economic competition. See her *Contra moros y judíos* (Barcelona, 1986), pp. 108–113.

[73] On conflict and cooperation in the meat trade, see chap. 6.

on peasant labor, whether Muslim or Christian, for their rents and taxes. But urban bankers and rentiers depended on these same peasants to produce the surplus that would allow the seigneurs to pay the interest on the sums they had borrowed from the bankers. These same bankers and rentiers lent their money to Jews, who used it to pay their taxes to the king, as capital for their retail and artisanal activities, and to finance the small loans they made to Christian and Muslim peasants. The peasants, in turn, used the funds to tide them over until harvesttime, buy seed, or pay taxes to their lords. This was an economic chain with many links.[74]

None of these relations need preclude violence or hatred. If anything, post-Enlightenment social theorists have been too sanguine about the integratory potential of economic relations. As Durkheim put it: "Interests never unite men but for a few moments, contracts are mere truces in a continuing antagonism. Nothing is less constant than interest. Today it unites me to you; tomorrow, it will make me your enemy."[75] Nevertheless, these "economic foundations of *convivencia*" should remind us that the violence detailed in the following chapters was not directed at strangers or at economically marginal groups occupying insignificant niches in local economies. Attacker and victim alike were tightly bound in a wide variety of relations that enmeshed moments of violence and gave them meaning.

[74]The full documentation of this chain would require another book (at least), but one for which there is abundant documentation. See, e.g., ACB, NC, Bernat Vilarrúbia 1335 (2), 51r–57r (1335/11/24), where the Jewish aljama of Barcelona borrows 7,000 sous from Geralda, wife of the jurist Ramon Vinater. Such loans would ultimately be repaid by the Jews from interest produced by their relending of the principal. But debtors to the Jews might pay off their Jewish creditors with the proceeds of other loans made by the same Christian financial elites that funded Jewish moneylending, as in ACB, NC, Guillem Borrell 1332 (4), where the village of "Les Borgetes" and the castle and village of Arbeca borrow 7,000 sous from Arnau de Bastida, a merchant of Barcelona, in order to repay their debts to the Jews. In short, the flow of money was very complex, and only one stage of this process, Jewish lending, has received adequate attention. On this stage see, e.g., I. Ollich i Castanyer, "Aspects econòmics de l'activitat dels jueus de Vic, segons els *Libri iudeorum* (1266–1278)," in *Miscel.lània de Textos Medievals* 3 (1985): 1–118; and M. Casas i Nadal, "El *Liber iudeorum* de Cardona (1330–1334)," in ibid., pp. 121–345.

[75]See his *The Division of Labour in Society* (New York, 1964) (translation of *De la division du travail social: études sur l'organization des sociétés supérieures* [Paris, 1893]), pp. 203 f., and pp. 114, 211. Consider, too, his insistence that "tout dans le contrat n'est pas contractuel."

PART ONE

Cataclysmic Violence: France

and the Crown of Aragon

Chapter 2

FRANCE, SOURCE OF THE TROUBLES: SHEPHERDS'
CRUSADE AND LEPERS' PLOT (1320, 1321)

W
HEN ARGUING for the irrational, even hysterical nature of acts of violence against minorities, medievalists often invoke both the Shepherds' Crusade of 1320, which attacked Jews, and the attacks on lepers and Jews of the following year. These are held up as examples of a "tradition of emotional and irrational action by the inarticulate . . . masses," and as evidence for the increasing virulence of persecutory fantasies in the fourteenth century.[1] The danger here is that words such as "irrational" suppress analysis. If violence against minorities is without reason, then there is no need to study the contexts within which the violence occurred or look for conflicts that might have caused it: the interpretative landscape becomes monotonously flat.

One way to demonstrate the costs of the "irrationalist" approach is to pursue its (admittedly equally overstated) polar opposite, an "intentionalist" interpretation. How would it affect our understanding of the events of 1320 and 1321 if we assumed that the killers had motives, that their actions had meaning, and that this meaning is decipherable from context? Such is the strategy of this chapter, as it argues that violence against minorities, however motivated by irrational hatred of them as it may have been, only gained meaning and usefulness for contemporaries in the context of much broader social conflicts, ideologies, and discourses.

Let us begin where the shepherds began, with a vision:

In Spain, a young boy, seventeen years of age, said that a dove had appeared to him one afternoon and had alternately alighted on his shoulder and on his head; that then the Holy Ghost, as they call it, had begun to visit him. When he tried to take the dove in his hand, an exceedingly beautiful maiden appeared to him and said, "I now make you a shepherd on the earth. You shall go forth to fight with the Moors. And here is the sign of what you have seen with your eyes." When the lad took a look at himself, they say he found the account of this event written on his arm. At the same time, another man came forward who announced that the lad had discovered the sign of the cross inscribed on his shoulder. People said, however, that he had only dreamt all this while sleeping near a fountain.

But, however it may have happened, the meek dove turned into a venomous scorpion for me, and the dream became a true and disastrous reality; for when the nobles

[1] For these interpretations, see below.

of the land heard the news, they all became excited, treated the boy like a saint, and conferred solemn honors upon him. When the masses saw this, a large rabble attached itself to the lad and followed his call to conquer the Kingdom of Granada. But woe is me: although the people were only against the Moors, Heaven had secretly decreed that a cruel blow be struck against the Jews. And when the Devil, our Enemy, gave an Israelite a chance to scoff at this miracle, the people were filled with bitter hatred against me.[2]

With Samuel Usque, the sixteenth-century Jewish chronicler and author of these words, we shall set aside the question of whether or not the vision actually occurred: if it did not, yet it could have done. So we may believe that the Shepherds' Crusade of 1320 began with a young boy's vision, a vision steeped in the symbolism of Crusade against Islam. The geographic origins of the Crusade are more obscure. Although Usque, Ha-Kohen, and Ibn Verga, writing some two centuries after the fact, placed the initial vision somewhere in Spain, archival documentation stresses that the crusaders came from France.[3]

Fortunately, contemporary French chroniclers were very interested in the shepherds.[4] According to Jean de Saint-Victor, they began to assemble in early 1320, and the *Chronique parisienne* adds that this occurred in May, in Normandy.[5] All the chroniclers agree that the multitudes of "shepherds" were poor,

[2]Samuel Usque, *Consolation for the Tribulations of Israel*, trans. M. Cohen (Philadelphia, 1965), pp. 186–187, translating *Consolaçam as Tribulaçoes de Israel* (Ferrara, 1552) no. 16, fols. 180–183. Compare Joseph Ha-Kohen, *ʿEmeq ha-Bakha*, ed. M. Letteris and S. Luzzatto (Cracow, 1895), no. 78, translated and annotated by P. Leon Tello in *Emeq Ha-Bakha de Yosef Ha-Kohen* (Madrid, 1964), here p. 137. On the events of 1320 Ha-Kohen parallels Usque's account, which itself parallels Solomon Ibn Verga, *Shevet Yehudah* (Jerusalem, 1947), no. 6, p. 22 (translated by F. Cantera Burgos as *Chébet Jehuda (La vara de Judá) de Salomón Ben Verga* [Granada, 1927]). Whether these accounts draw on a source contemporary with the events is not known. For more on the Jewish chronicle accounts of 1320, see below.

[3]See the following chapter for Aragonese documentation stressing the French provenance of the crusaders.

[4]The bibliography on the pastoureaux in France is nevertheless short. See C. Devic and J. Vaissete, *Histoire générale de Languedoc*, ed. A. Molinier (Toulouse, 1885), 9:402–406; P. Lehugeur, *Histoire de Philippe le Long, roi de France (1316–22)* (Paris, 1897), pp. 416–422; J.-M. Vidal, "L'Émeute des pastoureaux en 1320: Lettres du pape Jean XXII; déposition du Juif Barac devant l'Inquisition de Pamiers," *Annales de Saint-Louis-des-Français: Publication trimestrielle des études et travaux des chapelains* 3 (1898): 121–174; P. Alphandéry, "Les croisades des enfants," *Revue de l'histoire des religions* 73 (1916): 259–282; P. Alphandéry and A. Dupront, *La chrétienté et l'idée de croisade* (Paris, 1959), 2:257–264; N. Cohn, *The Pursuit of the Millennium*, rev. ed. (New York, 1970), pp. 102–104; J. Weakland, "Pastorelli, Pope, and Persecution: A Tragic Episode in 1320," *Jewish Social Studies* 38 (1976): 73–76; and especially M. Barber, "The Pastoureaux of 1320," *Journal of Ecclesiastical History* 32 (1981): 143–166.

[5]Jean de Saint-Victor, *Prima vita Joannis XXII*, in E. Baluze, *Vitae paparum avenionensium*, ed. G. Mollat (Paris, 1914), 1:128–130; *Chronique parisienne anonyme de 1316 à 1339 précédée d'additions à la chronique française dite de Guillaume de Nangis (1206–1316)*, in *Mémoires de la Société de l'Histoire de Paris et de l'Ile-de-France* 11 (1884): 46–48. There is no discrepancy in dating between May and the beginning of the year, since the year began at Easter.

many adolescents, who had a rudimentary organization if any, and who sub-
sisted largely on alms from the Christian faithful.[6] But the movement had other
adherents as well: papal and Aragonese documentation calls attention to the
presence of women, married couples, clerics, and minor nobles.[7] By early May,
after storming various prisons, some ten thousand shepherds (or so the chronicles claim) had reached Paris, where they called upon the king to lead them on
Crusade, asserting that the necessity for this had been revealed to them by an
angel. The king refused to meet them. After storming the prison of the Châtelet, seat of the *prévôté* of Paris and a symbol of royal authority, they left Paris and
marched south into Aquitaine, perhaps intending to reach Mediterranean ports
such as Aigues-Mortes whence they could embark for the Holy Land.[8]

As the shepherds moved south they attacked royal castles,[9] royal and seigneurial officials—and clerics, an activity that prompted a good deal of papal
concern.[10] Bernard Gui stated that "they struck terror and dread of their name
in the communities of the towns and castles, and in the rectors and leaders of
them, and among the princes and prelates and rich persons." Then too "there
was afterwards found through some of them that they had arranged to rise up
against the clergy and monks having riches and to seize their goods."[11]

The shepherds came to focus most spectacularly on the Jews, converting or
killing Jews at Saintes, Verdun on the Garonne, and in the dioceses and cities of
Cahors, Toulouse, and Albi (the massacre in Toulouse occurred on June 12).
Massacres are also recorded at Castelsarrasin, Grenade, Lézat, Auch, Rabastens,
Montguyard, and Gaillac. In many of these places townsfolk and municipal
officials may have been sympathetic to the pastoureaux, even complicit in their
atrocities. Thus Pope John XXII wrote to the archbishop of Toulouse, ordering
him to convince by any means at his disposal the "populares" of that city to
withdraw their support from the shepherds. The archbishop hesitated to take

---

[6]Add to the above *Chronique latine de Guillaume de Nangis de 1113 à 1300 avec les continuations de
cette chronique de 1300 à 1368*, ed. H. Géraud (Paris, 1843), 2:25–28; Bernard Gui, *Tertia vita Joannis
XXII*, and Amalric Auger, *Septima vita Joannis XXII*, both in E. Baluze, *Vitae paparum avenionensium*,
ed. G. Mollat (Paris, 1914), 1:161–163 and 191–193.

[7]For Pope John XXII's description, see ASV, Reg. Vat. 70, fol. 27r–v; 110A, fols. 50v–51r;
published most recently by S. Simonsohn, *The Apostolic See and the Jews. Documents: 492–1404*
(Toronto, 1988), no. 302, pp. 313–315, with bibliography. For the relevant Aragonese documentation, see the following chapter.

[8]Following Barber, "The Pastoureaux," pp. 145–146, 157. On the Châtelet as a symbol of royal
authority, see the general comments of C. de Mérindol, "Mouvements sociaux et troubles politiques à la fin du Moyen Age: essai sur la symbolique des villes," in *Actes du 114e Congrès National des
Sociétés Savantes* (Paris, 1989), pp. 291–293. On Aigues-Mortes as a crusader port, see W. C. Jordan,
Louis IX and the Challenge of the Crusade (Princeton, 1979), pp. 71–76.

[9]An inquest held in Albi in 1324 stated that they attacked "royal castles, . . . Jews, and some
others." See C. Compayré, *Études historiques et documents inédits sur l'Albigeois, le Castrais et l'ancien
diocèse de Lavaur* (Albi, 1841), p. 253.

[10]See Simonsohn, *Apostolic See*, p. 314.

[11]Translation by Barber, "The Pastoureaux," p. 147. See also Cohn, *Millennium*, pp. 103–104.

providing it had not already been collected by the Crown, and two-thirds of whatever they collected was to be paid to the Crown.[26] By 1317 Philip V, Louis X's successor, was ordering royal officials to help the Jews collect their loans from Christian debtors. Some officials apparently went so far as to make the king the heir of the Jews. According to them, though not to the king, the Jews were *mainmortable*, so that their property reverted to the king when they died.[27] In the light of such actions by royal officials, no debtor could have failed to believe that the Jews were representatives of state fiscality, protected by the Crown as such.

Thus when the shepherds attacked the Jews in 1320, they were both attacking a much-resented aspect of administrative kingship and dramatizing the state's inability to protect its agents, the Jews. This is why the king called the shepherds "notorious enemies of the royal majesty." The Shepherds' Crusade was not merely the product of the naive literalism of the masses, confused by a court discourse of Crusade (though this was doubtless true for some). It was also a rebellion against royal fiscality, camouflaged with the very language of sacred monarchy and Crusade that had helped to legitimize the fiscality under attack.[28]

This needs elaboration. While it is true that the Jews in France were considered fiscal agents of the monarchy, occasionally serfs of the king, it is also true that royal action against the Jews played an integral part in the Crown's self-presentation as a sacred monarchy: expulsions, for example, were portrayed as a royal defense of the faith.[29] Jews in France were often used as a foil against which to define the king as the most Christian of monarchs: *rex christianissimus*. There was a tension, then, between the role of Jews within administrative kingship and their role within sacral kingship, and this is the tension that the shepherds and their supporters exploited in order to legitimize their rebellion against a hated aspect of state fiscality. By attacking the Jews they could claim that their intention was not to challenge the monarchy, but to restore to it the purity the

[26]Jordan, *French Monarchy*, p. 240; R. Chazan, *Medieval Jewry in Northern France: A Political and Social History* (Baltimore, 1973), pp. 202–203; Saige, *Les juifs*, pp. 330–331, no. 57; Barber, "The Pastoureaux," pp. 163–165. *Ordonnances*, 1:596, chap. 4.

[27]Jordan, *French Monarchy*, pp. 242–243; *Ordonnances*, 1:645–647, chaps. 3, 5, 10. Chap. 5 forbade the treatment of Jews as *mainmortable*.

[28]On Crusade as a fiscal device see Barber, "The Pastoureaux," pp. 160–161. The phrase "notorious enemies" is from an investigation held in 1324 by the king's officials against the town council of Albi, charged with cooperating with the shepherds. The townsmen defended themselves in that trial by, among other arguments, claiming that they believed they were helping the Crusade by supporting the shepherds. The document is published in Compayré, *Études historiques*, pp. 252–255.

[29]See, for example, J. Baldwin, *The Government of Philip Augustus* (Berkeley, 1986), pp. 50–52, 379–380, on chronicle representations of Philip Augustus after his expulsion of the Jews. For the use of expulsions as a "propaganda device," see M. Kriegel, "Mobilisation politique et modernisation organique: les expulsions des juifs au bas moyen âge," *Archives des sciences sociales et des religions* 46 (1978): 5–20.

monarchy itself claimed to desire.[30] The point here is simple: context matters. Surely the shepherds disliked the Jews, but it was the particular ways in which royal fiscality and power were legitimated in France that turned this hatred into a useful and meaningful way to pursue grievances against the powerful and to articulate complaints that could otherwise never be uttered without danger.

It does not much matter here whether the shepherds believed or did not believe in the Crown's self-presentation as a sacred monarchy. If they accepted the reigning ideology in its idealized version, this does not mean that violent conflict could not erupt over its real implementation. The shepherds could claim, for example, that the toleration and exploitation of Jews polluted the monarchy, without questioning the sacral nature of the monarchy itself.[31] If they did not accept the ideology of the dominant, they would nevertheless justify their revolt so far as possible in terms of that ideology in order to minimize resistance to their claims.[32] Whenever a ruling group elaborates an ideology to justify its claim to power, it opens itself to the criticism of failing to live up to that ideology. This is what James Scott has called "critiques within the hegemony."[33] It may prove impossible to determine whether or not the shepherds believed the sacral claims of their monarchy. What we should not doubt is that when they invoked it, they did so in what they perceived to be their own interests.[34]

.   .   .   .   .

Whatever the rebellious intentions of the Shepherds' Crusade, they failed. The shepherds were eventually crushed, or they disbanded or passed into foreign lands where attacks on Jews had other meanings, and the Jews remained in France. Ironically, the revolt provided the Crown with yet another opportunity for extortion. The state mobilized its fiscal machinery and moved to fine many of the localities where Jews had been massacred, an action that prompted further resistance to the Crown and deeper resentment of the Jews, who were once again seen as providing the point of entry for exploitative royal "justice."[35] It

[30]"Ruling groups can be called upon . . . to live up to their own idealized presentation of themselves to their subordinates." See J. Scott, *Domination and the Arts of Resistance: The Hidden Transcript* (New Haven, 1990), p. 54.

[31]See B. Kapferer, *Legends of People, Myths of State: Violence, Intolerance, and Political Culture in Sri Lanka and Australia* (Washington, DC, 1988), pp. 101–112, on the possibilities for rebellion when an ideology is shared by both the dominant and the subordinate. See also Scott, *Domination*, p. 74.

[32]Scott, *Domination*, pp. 90–96.

[33]Ibid., pp. 103–107. See also B. Moore Jr., *Injustice: The Social Bases of Obedience and Revolt* (White Plains, NY, 1987), p. 84; Bourdieu, *Outline of a Theory of Practice*, pp. 193–194.

[34]D. Field, *Rebels in the Name of the Tsar* (Boston, 1976), p. 209: "Naive or not, the peasants professed their faith in the Tsar in forms, *and only in those forms*, that corresponded to their interests. Peasant leaders, finding the myth ready to hand in its folkloric expressions, used it to arouse, galvanize, and unify other peasants."

[35]The municipality of Toulouse petitioned the king, apparently successfully, to stop his inquiries

was these areas where the pastoureaux had been active that would again rebel in 1321, this time by attacking the lepers first and then the Jews, whom they accused of conspiring to destroy Christendom.

In about 1350, a chronicler writing in Montpellier tried to claim an obvious continuity between the events of 1320 and 1321 by stating that the Shepherds' Crusade of 1320 was followed by the "Cowherds' Crusade" of 1321. This pastoral theme was in fact a complete fabrication. The protagonists of 1321 were drawn from a much more urban cast of characters than those of 1320, though they may have been inspired by their rustic cousins in their choice of victims, since the pastoureaux had already begun to attack leprosaria. In July of 1320 the lieutenant of the *prévôt* of Sauveterre-de-Guyenne had public record made of the fact that he had forbidden the torching of the leprosarium of Sauveterre, an action that was blamed on the pastoureaux. The chronicle of Raymond-Bernard de La Mote, bishop of Bazas, stated that some pastoureaux who were later hanged for their crimes had found some barrels full of rotting bread while pillaging the leprosarium of a certain town (perhaps Mas-d'Agenais). The lepers, it was said, had planned to use the bread in the preparation of some poisons with which to contaminate the wells.[36] A striking charge, and an uncommon one this early in the fourteenth century.[37]

This last rumor may help explain another interesting precedent to the violence of 1321, the bishop of Dax's move to arrest all the lepers of his diocese in December of 1320. The bishop was acting to preserve his jurisdiction over the lepers from encroachments by the sire d'Albret. The latter had burned a leper accused of an unstipulated crime, one in which other lepers were implicated.

---

against them on several matters, including complicity in the Shepherds' Crusade. On June 22, 1321, Philip V ordered his officials not to inquire against Toulouse "pro secretis informacionibus aut aliis processibus racione Pastorellorum, vsurarum seu feodorum nobilium acquisitorum factis." Toulouse, Archives municipales, AA 34, no. 87, published in E.A.R. Brown, "Philip V, Charles IV, and the Jews of France: The Alleged Expulsion of 1322," *Speculum* 66 (1991): 294–329, here p. 309. The petition presented by the citizens of Toulouse was probably similar to that of various communities from the seneschalsy of Carcassonne, which opened by protesting against the investigations carried out by royal officials and ended by demanding the expulsion of the Jews. For the document, see Compayré, *Études historiques*, pp. 255–257. Albi paid a fine of eight hundred pounds for its complicity in 1320, ibid., p. 255. On the fines collected by the Crown in the affair of the pastoureaux, see Barber, "The Pastoureaux," pp. 148, 153–156; Jordan, *French Monarchy*, p. 244. The fines continued to be collected years later. See *Les Journaux de Trésor de Charles IV*, ed. J. Viard (Paris, 1917), no. 3668, cited in Brown, "Philip V," p. 319n.81.

[36] These three texts are analyzed in F. Bériac's "La persécution des lépreux dans la France Méridionale en 1321," *Le Moyen Age* 93, no. 2 (1987): 203–221, here p. 207. Ginzburg does not address these events in *Ecstasies*, chap. 1.

[37] The accusation against lepers or Jews of mass poisoning was practically unknown before 1321, though given the future of the charge, especially following the plague, this is easy to forget. Accusations of Host desecration and ritual murder had much longer pedigrees. See Little, *Religious Poverty*, p. 52.

The ensuing jurisdictional conflict involved a large number of ducal, episcopal, and even papal officials. Rumors of the accusations against the lepers of the diocese of Dax could well have contributed to the charges brought against lepers in the spring of 1321.[38]

Whatever the precedents, it is clear that before February of 1321, communities in the areas of Toulouse, Albi, and Carcassonne were petitioning the French monarchy to expel the Jews from France and to segregate the lepers. The petitioners generously declared themselves willing to administer all the revenues and pious donations that had accrued to the lepers, and in exchange to provide for the lepers' maintenance. Segregation was necessary, they claimed, because the lepers intended to infect the whole country with their illness by poison and sorcery. The lepers also provided Jews with consecrated Hosts, which the Jews desecrated. Moreover, Jews had sex with the wives of their Christian debtors and committed other horrible crimes, all of which merited their expulsion.

These accusations should not be read in isolation from the rest of the petition. The consuls' primary complaints were about royal justice. Royal officials were claiming jurisdiction over cases that should have been heard by local courts. They were inquiring unjustly on charges of usury against Christians, as well as on charges of complicity with the pastoureaux. Not only were the consuls trying to gain jurisdiction over the autonomous property of the lepers, but they were also resisting extortionate royal justice and attempting to limit the range of inquisitorial procedure, an attempt triggered, at least in part, by vigorous inquisitional activity against Christians on charges of attacking Jews during the Shepherds' Crusade.[39]

In short, well before widespread attacks on the lepers began, a broad coalition of forces was agitating against them and against the properties and rights of the charitable foundations that cared for them. Even in these early attacks, issues of jurisdiction were coming to the fore. Thus the bishop of Dax arrested his lepers in order to protect his rights over them from encroachment by a local nobleman, while the municipalities were attempting to use rumors of leper poison in order to appropriate resources currently outside of their control.

The municipal petition to the king was not received favorably (if indeed it was received at all), so municipal officials took matters into their own hands. During Holy Week, 1321, the mayor of Périgueux ordered the lepers arrested. Rumors of crimes committed by the lepers had been circulating since earlier in

---

[38]H. M. Fay, *Histoire de la lèpre en France: lépreux et cagots du Sud-Ouest* (Paris, 1910), pp. 520–526; J. B. Marquette, "Les Albret: le rôle politique," *Cahiers du Bazadais* 41 (1978): 445 f.; cited in Bériac, "La persécution," p. 208.

[39]For the text of the Albi petition, see Compayré, *Études historiques*, pp. 255–257, briefly discussed by Ginzburg, *Ecstasies*, p. 37 and n. 14. For the suggestion that the communities of Toulouse presented a similar petition, see Brown, "Philip V," p. 309n.41.

the spring, but now the lepers were seized and tortured by judicial officials. Many confessed and were burned.[40]

Few of these early confessions survive.[41] Most probably resembled the confession of the leper Johan de Bosco before officials of the town of "Regale ville" (France).[42] Johan was from Alterque, and on the 16th of May he appeared before the officials "free of all jail chains" and stated on oath that three weeks before, brother Geraldus, leper, "preceptor" of the leprosarium of Alterque, had brought two bags full of a "pessimam" powder and ordered Johan to put this powder in the fountains, waters, and rivers of diverse areas. The powder would poison the waters so that anyone who drank from them would either die or turn leprous. Geraldus then gave Johan twenty sous as payment, and ten sous for expenses. The rest of the confession lists the dozens of villages Johan visited, poisoning wells and rivers in each place. According to Johan, he was caught in "locum Regalis ville" when he was seen leaving a well he had just poisoned. Johan claimed not to know the recipe for the powder, but he believed that anyone who drank it would turn leprous or die within two months.[43]

Perhaps in response to confessions like this one, officials in towns throughout the region began arresting, condemning, and executing lepers on charges of poisoning.[44] Unlike the Shepherds' Crusade, the attack on the lepers was carried out by municipal authorities, not mobs of rioters. The violence was therefore judicial in form, though nevertheless extralegal, since such actions on the part of the municipalities were a clear usurpation of royal judicial prerogatives. Royal officers were unable to intervene effectively, and municipal authorities notified the king of their actions only after the fact.[45] Municipal officials were

[40]M. Barber, "Lepers, Jews and Moslems: The Plot to Overthrow Christendom in 1321," *History* 66 (1981): 1–17, here p. 2; Bériac, "La persécution," p. 208; both based on G. Lavergne, "La persécution et la spoliation des lépreux à Périgueux en 1321," in *Recueil de Travaux offerts à M. Clovis Brunel* (Paris, 1955), 2:107–112.

[41]For confessions of lepers from Archignac and Salignac, see Bériac, "La persécution," p. 204, citing BN, Coll. Périgord, 92, fols. 86–87; J. M. Maubourguet, *Le Périgord méridional des origines à l'an 1370* (Cahors, 1926), p. 271.

[42]Curiously, the confession is preserved in the Museum of Montblanc (Catalonia): uncataloged manuscript, dated "primo die sabbati post festum Translationis sancti Nicholay," 1321. A transcription of this document was kindly provided me by Jaume Felip of Montblanc, who is preparing an edition. The officials were: "Guillermo de Cayraco, locum tenentem Andree de Mercato bauili regii dicti loci [Regalem villam] necnon, et coram Matheo de Condomio et Amelio de Rechas, consules eiusdem loci."

[43]A more peripatetic poisoner is hard to imagine. He confessed to visiting and poisoning the waters at some twenty-eight villages and cities in the modern French departments of Aveyron, Tarn, and Tarn et Garonne.

[44]For partial lists of towns where lepers were arrested, see Bériac, "La persécution," p. 205–206, 209–210. Only a few of these are included in map 2.

[45]For the powerlessness of royal officials, Bériac, "La persécution," pp. 210–211. For the late notification of the king, see Lavergne, "La persécution," pp. 108–109; Barber, "Plot," p. 2. There is only one documented case of effective royal action, at Castelnau-de-Montmirail. Ginzburg was apparently not aware of the limited extent of royal intervention. See *Ecstasies*, p. 34.

well aware that their actions constituted a direct challenge to royal authority. Hence in 1342 the town council of Périgueux found it politic to rewrite the history of 1321 and stressed its role as defender of the monarchy: "Since the plague-stricken mob of lepers had rebelled . . . against the royal magnificence . . . the infamy and the odious crime discovered, with our lord the king notified of them as quickly as possible . . . the said consuls, like true champions of justice. . . ." In 1321, however, they and their colleagues persisted in what could only be called open rebellion.[46]

King Philip V was in Poitiers presiding over an assembly of southern towns when messengers reached him from those places that were acting against the lepers. Upon receiving the news, the king took immediate action.[47] On the 21st of June, he issued an edict ordering the burning of any leper who confessed to having poisoned the waters. Torture should be used against those who did not confess spontaneously. Those lepers who were innocent, and any under fourteen years of age, were to be imprisoned in their places of origin. Most ominously, the crime of the lepers was declared one of lèse-majesté. All their goods therefore reverted to the Crown, and jurisdiction over their crimes belonged exclusively to the king, not to any temporal lords.[48]

The king was cloaking the municipalities' public break with royal authority by claiming that those actions already under way had been undertaken at his command. It was not in the interests of the monarchy to let it be known that royal jurisdiction had been successfully breached. At the same time, Philip insisted that henceforth there should be no infraction of regalian rights. He publicly declared that any contravention of his claim to the lepers' goods would be considered treasonous, since their crime was one against his person. Here too he was successfully defied and forced to back down. By August 18, confronted by the bishop of Albi (whose men had arrested, imprisoned, and condemned many lepers), the king admitted to some doubt as to whether the crime was one of lèse-majesté. Philip, perhaps borrowing from the arguments made by those who had opposed him, stated that in matters of such urgency, where it was imperative to punish the guilty as quickly as possible, the Crown should not insist on its prerogatives.[49]

[46] The quotation is from Archives Municipales de Périgueux, FF 52, art. 282, as cited in Bériac, "La persécution," p. 216.

[47] For the path taken by messages to the king, see the map provided by Bériac, "La persécution," p. 209. For more on the assembly, see below.

[48] The edict is published in H. Duplès-Agier, "Ordonnance de Philippe le Long contre les lépreux (21 juin 1321)," *Bibliothèque de l'Ecole des chartes*, 4th ser., 3 (1857): 270–271. For further references, see Brown, "Philip V," pp. 309–310n.43.

[49] For the edict of August 18, see *Ordonnances*, vol. 11 (Paris, 1769), pp. 481–482. Municipal officials, secular and ecclesiastical lords alike, all resisted this assertion of royal authority, and in Narbonne, Carcassonne, and Toulouse the king was forced to release the lepers' property to rival claimants. The best treatment of the resistance to the king's decrees is that of Bériac, "La persécution," pp. 210–211, 214–217. See also Barber, "Plot," p. 4; Ginzburg, *Ecstasies*, p. 34.

In the case of the lepers, ambiguity of jurisdictional status may have contributed to the rapidity of their arrest and the confiscation of their property. Crown, municipality, lay lords, abbeys, and bishoprics might all have some claims on leper houses. The accusation of poisoning gave competing claimants a powerful excuse to extend their jurisdiction. In 1321, it was wise to strike first, rather than leave one's claims to the courts. Those town councils who were slow in seizing their local leper house found that establishing their rights later in royal courts took years.[50]

. . . . .

Earlier we asked what it was about the position of Jews that made attacks upon them a meaningful way of attacking the monarchy, and we need to ask the same about the lepers.[51] Attacks upon lepers were rebellious in some obvious ways. The most obvious is jurisdictional. If the attacks against lepers were presented as nonjudicial, they were an illegal breach of the peace and a violation of royal authority. If they were presented as judicial, they were a usurpation of royal jurisdiction. Certainly once the king declared his sole right to judge the lepers (June 21), further actions against them were considered acts of lèse-majesté. Moreover, leper houses were privileged, endowed institutions: some of them were royal foundations; others received annual donations from the Crown; many were under royal protection.[52] To the extent that attacks on these houses infringed upon rights of the Crown, or protections extended by it, those attacks could be termed "antimonarchical" in some sense.[53]

But violence against the lepers (like violence against the Jews) took place in a context that was much more than merely juridical or jurisdictional. Lepers and monarch both played related roles in what one might call the "moral economy" of the kingdom: a belief that the moral management of the body (social, political, individual) was manifest in the physical condition of that body, a condition most often described through metaphors of illness, infection, or corruption.[54] The events of 1321 must be understood within this economy.

[50]See above for the bishop of Dax. For the experience of several towns forced to resort to the courts, see Bériac, "La persécution," p. 217.

[51]Given the current state of our understanding of the cultural meaning of leprosy in the Middle Ages, or of the social and juridical status of lepers, this question cannot be conclusively answered. What follows is meant to be suggestive.

[52]A more conclusive statement of this point would require careful documentation of the privileges and status of each leper house attacked in 1321. For examples of one monarch's relations with lepers and leper houses, see Jordan, *Louis IX and the Challenge of the Crusade*, p. 128.

[53]F.-O. Touati, "Histoire des maladies, histoire totale?" *Sources. Travaux historiques* 13 (1988): 3–14, here p. 11, believes that royal foundations may have been spared the brunt of the violence, but is tentative and gives no evidence.

[54]My use of the phrase is therefore quite different from E. P. Thompson's famous coinage. See his "The Moral Economy of the English Crowd in the Eighteenth Century" and "The Moral Economy Reviewed" in *Customs in Common* (London, 1991), pp. 185–351, here p. 188. On the

Leprosy was a disease of the soul, brought on by moral corruption and sin. Leprosy thus served as a sign of sin. The leper was a heretic or an unrepentant sinner and should be separated from communion with society: "Whoever has been corrupted by the disease of spiritual leprosy, as either by the offense of faithlessness or because of depravity of morals, should be sequestered from association with the faithful."[55] What distinction there was between "spiritual" and "physical" leprosy was easily obscured in popular moral tradition, where physical leprosy was invariably a punishment for spiritual sin.[56] Then too, moral corruption, like the disease that was its physical manifestation, was believed to be highly infectious. In the words of a Catalan complaint against a neighbor accused of immorality, "one sick sheep infects the whole flock." These were the metaphors of illness—moral and medical—that underlay the ritual and physical isolation of lepers from society.[57]

The charges of poisoning made against the lepers functioned within this moral context, but they were abstracted from the body of the individual to the body social. The use of images of leprosy and leprous venom to illustrate infection and the vulnerability of the flesh to sin was standard practice of preachers and sermon writers. In the *Gesta Romanorum*, a collection of moralizing stories intended for use by preachers, for example, the image is elaborated at the level of the individual body and the family. Once upon a time, when the noble knight Iosias was sleeping, his wife went out and forgot to lock the door. A bear came into the house and bathed in the well, infecting it with venom. When Iosias and his household drank the water, they were poisoned with "sinful leprosy." The story was meant to illustrate that even the flesh of good Christians was open to the devil, who, by putting venom into the well of mercy, can infect the flesh.[58] It emphasized that leprosy, like the sin which caused it, was unrestricted by group identity, but was rather the somatization within individuals of God's punishment of sins that, to a greater or lesser degree, affected all people.

---

language of disease as "a comprehensive and systematic model" for heresy, see R. I. Moore, "Heresy as Disease," in *The Concept of Heresy in the Middle Ages (Eleventh–Thirteenth C.)*, ed. W. Lourdaux and D. Verhelst (The Hague, 1976), pp. 1–11, here p. 9.

[55] Radulphus Flaviacensis (mid–twelfth century), cited in S. Brody, *The Disease of the Soul: Leprosy in Medieval Literature* (Ithaca, NY, 1974), pp. 133–134.

[56] Brody, *Disease of the Soul*, p. 142. See also P. Diepgen, *Die Theologie und der ärztliche Stand*, vol. 1 (Berlin, 1922), pp. 48–58; and G. Pichon, "La lèpre et le péché: étude d'une représentation médiévale," *Nouvelle revue de Psychanalyse* 38 (1988): 147–157.

[57] ACA:C 668:89r–90r (1351/8/24): ". . . qui semel malus semper presumitur esse malus, et etiam quia una ovis morbida inficit omne pecus." The phrase was used by the neighbors of Allemanda, a married woman of Barcelona, accused of "perverse conversation," infamy, and sexual transgressions. Her presence represented a danger to honest people, her neighbors argued.

[58] Taken here from *The Early English Version of the Gesta Romanorum*, ed. Sidney J. H. Herrtage, Early English Text Society, e.s., no. 33 (London, 1879), "LXII. Solemius a Wyse Emperore," pp. 263–268, cited in Brody, *Disease of the Soul*, p. 141.

The accusations of 1321 may have drawn from stories like those contained in the *Gesta Romanorum*, though now the lepers took the place of the bear and the body social took the place of the individual. By infecting the healthy, lepers sought to reduce all Christians to the same corrupt and sinful state in which they found themselves: "If all [people] were the same," the lepers were thought to have said, "no one would despise another."[59] The attack on the lepers was thus framed in interrelated idioms of infection and corruption, identity and difference, idioms which were meant to represent that society was in a moral, hence physical, crisis. The seclusion of lepers no longer sufficed: removal of the source of infection was required.

If the French realm was in a state of moral and physical illness symbolized by the threat of universal leprosy, then the French monarch was its obvious physician. The Capetian kings of France were thaumaturges and healers. Each year, hundreds of people afflicted by diseases, especially skin diseases, came to the king to be healed by his touch.[60] It is easy to overlook the significance of this fact for the lepers, since we know that by the fifteenth century the *mal le roi*, the disease cured by kings, was scrofula, not leprosy. It was then that sufferers from other diseases were barred from coming to the king for cures, though even at such a late date the reaction of some who were disqualified suggests that this specialization of practice did not sit well with popular expectations. When the king's officials refused to allow Henri Payot's sister to approach the king in 1454 because they ruled that her disease was not scrofula, Henri "called down the curse of God upon his sovereign and the queen."[61]

Despite this later specialization, leprosy had once occupied an important place among the diseases Henri Payot's ancestors would have expected the king to heal.[62] The first wonder-working Capetian, Robert the Pious, was a healer

---

[59] *Chronique latine de Guillaume de Nangis*, 2:34: "Vel omnes uniformiter leprosi efficerentur, et sic, cum omnes essent uniformes, nullus ab alio despiceretur."

[60] The classic study of Capetian thaumaturgic powers is that of M. Bloch, *The Royal Touch: Sacred Monarchy and Scrofula in England and France*, trans. J. E. Anderson (London, 1973). More recently, see J. Le Goff, "Le mal royal au moyen âge: du roi malade au roi guérisseur," *Mediaevistik* 1 (1988): 101–109; and P. Buc, "David's Adultery with Bathsheba and the Healing Power of the Capetian Kings," *Viator* 24 (1993): 101–120. For a later period, see J. Merrick, *The Desacralization of the French Monarchy in the Eighteenth Century* (Baton Rouge, LA, 1990). For a comparative case, see Kapferer, *Legends of Peoples*, p. 13, writing about leprosy, which in Sri Lanka was "the king's disease." Kapferer writes of the ceremony of the touch in both France and Sri Lanka: "By this act the bodies of royal subjects were made whole, ordered once again, through their incorporation into the body of the king."

[61] On the gradual specialization of the king, see Bloch, *Royal Touch*, pp. 19–20, 55. The quotation is from p. 55, citing a letter of remission, Arch. Nat., JJ. 187, fol. 113v, dated October 23. 1454.

[62] The history of this specialization is extensively treated in Le Goff, "Le mal royal au moyen âge," an article that came late to my attention and is therefore not fully engaged here. Le Goff believes that a shift occurred in the definition of *morbus regius* from leprosy to scrofula late in the thirteenth century (p. 104), after which leprosy was at most an object of special royal devotion. But see n. 82, below.

of lepers: "The divine virtue granted to this perfect man a very great grace, to wit, the power of healing men's bodies; for by touching with his most pious hand the sores of suffering and signing them with the holy cross, he was wont to deliver them from their pains and diseases."[63] Indeed, the two diseases, scrofula and leprosy, were closely connected. Leprosy was thought to afflict pigs, while scrofula derives from *scrofa*, "sow," believed to be prone to the disease. Du-Cange, writing in the eighteenth century, defined *morbus regius*, "king's disease," as jaundice among recent authors, leprosy of old.[64]

Then too, miraculous cures of leprosy were central to medieval conceptions of divine healing. Christ had cured lepers, readmitting in his person those who typified ritual impurity. Writing in 1081, either unaware of or ignoring early Capetian claims to thaumaturgy, Gregory VII stressed the inferiority of kings to priests: "What emperor or king has ever . . . restored health to the lepers. . . ?" Only clerics, who shared supernatural grace, could work such miracles, according to Gregory. But even as Gregory wrote, kings in France were presenting themselves as participants in such grace, whether (as in the popular mind) through their anointment and consecration, or whether (as later propagandists would emphasize) through some inherited grace of God.[65] Whatever the mechanism, "through the king's hands, God most evidently performs miracles on behalf of the sick," as Nogaret and Plaisians wrote in 1310 of Philip the Fair.[66] It would not be surprising if people in early-fourteenth-century France believed that the sick whom God could heal through the hands of the king included lepers.[67]

In 1321, however, the people, not the king, "healed" the kingdom by attacking the lepers. They did so, I would argue, because they viewed the king himself as a source of the corruption, rather than the cure. The loss of the "royal touch" by unclean kings was not unprecedented. Guibert of Nogent wrote that Philip I (1060–1108) had lost the power to touch because he had committed

[63] The account is by the monk Helgaud of Fleury, translated in Bloch, *Royal Touch*, p. 19, citing from *PL* 141.931. For a more modern edition, see Helgaud de Fleury, *Vie de Robert le Pieux*, ed. R.-H. Bautier and G. Labory, *Sources d'histoire médiévale* 1 (Paris, 1965), p. 128.

[64] "Porco leproso" comes up most often in injunctions against selling "leprous" pork. See W. Jordan, "Problems of the Meat-Market of Beziers 1240–1247: A Question of Anti-Semitism," *RdÉJ* 135 (1976): 36n.23. For the authors, *recentioribus* and *antiquioribus*, cited by DuCange, see his *Glossarium ad scriptores mediae et infimae latinitatis*, vol. 4 (Paris, 1733), col. 1037. Hansen's disease (i.e., leprosy) does not in fact infect pigs, but "leprous" pork was believed by medieval doctors to be an infectious agent. Cf. F. Bériac, *Histoire des lépreux au Moyen Age* (Paris, 1988), p. 21. Jewish tradition associated pigs with leprosy as well. See *Liqqute ha-Pardes*, attributed to Rashi, extracted in C. Horowitz, *Tosefta ʿAtiqta*, pt. 5 (Frankfurt, 1890), pp. 57–61. Rashi cites b. *Oid.* 49b on the ten types of skin diseases that entered the world, nine of which were taken by pigs. Compare b. *Shab.* 129b on pigs as infectious agents of leprosy. My thanks to M. Swartz for the reference to Horowitz.

[65] See Bloch, *Royal Touch*, pp. 71–91.

[66] Ibid., pp. 63–64.

[67] On the conflation of leprosy and scrofula see also F. Barlow, "The King's Evil," *English Historical Review* 95 (1980): 3–27, here pp. 9–13; Buc, "David's Adultery with Bathsheba," pp. 104 and 105–106n.15; and Le Goff, "Le mal royal au moyen âge."

sins. These sins doubtless included the adulterous union between Philip and Bertrade de Montfort, for which he was excommunicated and (according to contemporaries) stricken by divine wrath with various "shameful" diseases.[68] But in what ways was Philip V corrupt?

Here we must turn to the political events of 1321, and especially to that ill-omened assembly at Poitiers where news first reached Philip of the attacks against the lepers. Early in the year, before the first accusations against the lepers, Philip had summoned representatives of the southern towns to meet him in Poitiers in June to ratify his plans for fiscal reform and increased centralization.[69] Modern historians have unanimously seen these reforms as administratively sound and well intentioned, but contemporaries seem not to have agreed. Rumor about the assembly's purpose ran wild, with the populace suspecting what one historian has called "a plot revealing human sin and corruption."[70] Throughout the south, it was said, "the king wished to extort a grave, even intolerable, extortion." "Among the populace," the king was believed to be demanding one-fifth of his subjects' goods. The chronicles discreetly claimed that the king was moved by bad council, though he himself was "benign." Nevertheless, they confessed that many feared "lest because of this rebellion erupt against the king." His subjects were cursing him, praying for his death, and saying, "Better that one man die for the populace, than that so many people be subjected to so much danger."[71] Outside the chronicle tradition, the danger that Philip's avarice was believed to bring upon his kingdom was expressed through the lepers' plot. It was the king's avarice that would allow the plotters another chance to poison Christendom, according to a forged letter purportedly written by a Jew to the king of Granada (see below).

Philip continued to pursue his proposals despite extensive resistance until early August, when he was struck with a double illness. When the king fell gravely ill, he was forced to suspend his plans, and the people came to believe that the illness had been sent by God as punishment for his corruption and in answer to their prayers. Many said that "he had fallen into this illness because of

---

[68]Bloch, *Royal Touch*, p. 13, citing Guibert of Nogent and Orderic Vitalis.

[69]Narbonne, for example, was summoned on March 30, 1321. See *Histoire générale de Languedoc*, ed. A. Molinier (Toulouse, 1872–1893), vol. 10, *preuves* 612–613, no. 221; E.A.R. Brown, "Subsidy and Reform in 1321: The Accounts of Najac and the Policies of Philip V," *Traditio* 27 (1971): 399–430, here p. 405.

[70]The quotation is from C. Taylor, "French Assemblies and Subsidy in 1321," *Speculum* 43 (1968): 217–244, here pp. 242 f. For the chronicle sources, see Jean de Saint-Victor, in *Recueil des historiens des Gaules et de la France* (Paris, 1840, 1855), 21:674–675; the *Chroniques de Saint Denis* in ibid., 20:705; and ibid., 20:630, 21:57; Taylor, "French Assemblies," p. 240n.157.

[71]Jean de Saint-Victor, in *Recueil des historiens*, 21:674–675: "Ad quarum instinctum, ut creditur, rex gravem extorsionem et quasi intolerabilem volebat a suis subditis extorquere." Ibid., p. 675: ". . . fuit a pluribus formidatum ne propter hoc surgeret rebellio contra regem, unde tot mala evenirent quod vix per hominem aliquem sedarentur." Again on the same page: "Quare forte aliquibus fuit visum quod expediebat ut unus homo moreretur pro populo, et non tanta gens tanto periculo subjaceret." Compare John 11:49–51.

the curses of the people under his regime," who were angered by the unheard-of extortion he imposed upon them.[72] When, after a brief remission, the king died, some said he was poisoned. Many felt relieved. The king had been demoted from thaumaturge to sacrificial victim, from healer to source of corruption. The continuator of Guillaum de Nangis put the following words in the king's mouth as he lay dying: "I recognize that I was cured by the merits and prayers of St. Denis, and by the evil of my regime I fell again into that sickness."[73]

Through the politic language of these royalist chronicles we can hear faint echoes of a popular conception—one that Marc Bloch took considerable pains to suppress—about the infectious and demonic potential of royalty. James Frazer, writes Bloch, had presented monarchs as both agents and doctors of disease. Their power was two-sided. But while this might have been true in Frazer's Polynesian examples, Bloch argued that it was not true of Europe, where the royal "magic" was only beneficent.[74] Yet it seems that in 1321 some people believed that the king was not ruling rightly in the defense of his people, a violation of his coronation oath.[75] As a result, he lost not only his sacral healing power but also the health of his body and his kingdom.[76] Like the lepers

---

[72]Jean de Saint-Victor, in *Recueil des historiens*, 21:675: "Aliorum autem erat opinio quod propter maledictiones populi formidantis ne sic notabiliter gravaretur, et mortem regis a Domino requirentis, cito de medio sit sublatus." Similarly in *Chronique latine de Guillaume de Nangis*, 2:37.

[73]*Chronique latine de Guillaume de Nangis*, 2:38: "Scio me meritis et precibus beati Dionysii curatum fuisse, et malo meo regimine iterum in eandem aegritudinem incidisse." The use of the word *regimine* here is a pun. Here it means both "regimen," as in health care, and "regime," as in government. It was in this latter sense that the author had just used the word: ". . . propter maledictiones populi sub ejus regimine constituti." See also *Chronicon Girardi de Fracheto*, in *Recueil des historiens*, 21:57. Compare Feierman's argument that peasants in the Shambaa kingdom of Tanzania rejected royal claims to be able to bring rain and "heal the land" when kings became uncustomarily extortionate, in *Peasant Intellectuals*, pp. 112–119. For a wide-ranging and comparative exposition of the notion that the prosperity of the kingdom depends on the behavior of the king, see A. M. Hocart, *Kings and Councillors: An Essay in the Comparative Anatomy of Human Society*, ed. R. Needham (Chicago, 1970), pp. 133–137, 143f.

[74]Bloch, *Royal Touch*, pp. 28–30. Bloch does, however, discuss the double-edged potential of other agents of the sacred, namely, priests. See Jacques de Vitry, *Exempla ex sermonibus vulgaribus*, ed. Crane (London, 1890), p. 112, no. 268, cited by Bloch, p. 42. Though Bloch does not mention it, this tradition was already ancient in Jacques de Vitry's time. See *Sermo de sacrilegia*, PL, Supplementum, 4.969–973, here 970–971: "Et qui clericum vel monachum de mane aut quacumque hora videns aut ouians, abominosum sibi esse credet, iste non solum paganus, sed demoniacus est, qui christi militem abominatur."

[75]On the king's coronation oath and its relationship to sacral kingship, see A. Graboïs, "La royauté sacrée au xiie siècle: manifestation de propagande royale," in *Idéologie et propagande en France*, ed. M. Yardeni (Paris, 1984), pp. 31–41, here p. 35. For the opinion of commentators like Peter the Chanter and Stephen Langton that rulers tainted by sin lost judicial power over their subjects, see Buc, "David's Adultery with Bathsheba," p. 113.

[76]My analysis highlights the ambivalence of sacrality and thaumaturgy, not their rejection. It should be noted, however, that such a line of attack was available as well. Using biblical commentaries, Buc has well shown how "in the thirteenth century, acceptance (or refusal) of the miracle [of healing], of royal legislative supremacy, and of royal taxation go hand in hand." See his "David's Adultery with Bathsheba," passim and p. 118.

(and the Jews, as we shall see), the king had to be sacrificed to prevent his disordering power from corrupting society.[77]

I would not claim that by attacking the lepers in 1321, French royal subjects were making an explicit statement about the king's avarice and moral corruption. But it is true that ideas about pollution, avarice, and the "king's disease" were closely related.[78] Sometime about the mid–thirteenth century, for example, the Anglo-Norman poet Walter of Wimborne wrote a poem called "Of Simony and Avarice." The poem opens with the paradigmatic avaricious act, the betrayal of Jesus by Judas in exchange for a bag of coins. But when Judas hanged himself, his guts poured forth their excrement and polluted the land of Judea (and hence the Jews).[79] His feces (the poet uses several synonyms) were a *virus*, a slimy, stinking liquid poison, that infected first the homeland (*patria*) and then the Church (*ecclesia*) with avarice. This corruption, this stench, could be comprehended only in juxtaposition to the proverbially putrid odor of the leper:

> Of old, when Judas died by hanging,
> the flow from his guts polluted Judah.
> Today, an effusion of shit more fetid stinks
> than the smell of a sufferer from the king's disease.[80]

[77] Against Bloch's view there is an abundance of material in Western monarchical theory concerning the notion that the right rule of a king brings about victory, good weather, fertility, and the health of a people, and that, conversely, bad rule brings about their opposites. One example is the seventh-century Irish tract "De duodecim abusiuis saeculi" (The twelve abuses of the world), ed. by S. Hellmann in *Texte und Untersuchungen zur Geschichte der altchristlichen Literatur*, ser. 3, vol. 4 (Leipzig, 1909), pp. 1–62, where bad kingship is "the ninth class of perversion." According to M. Laistner (*Thought and Letters in Western Europe, A.D. 500–900* [New York, 1931], pp. 111–112), this text influenced a variety of Carolingian and post-Carolingian theorists of kingship such as Hincmar, Sedulius Scotus, Jonas of Orléans, and Kathvulf. To his list I would add Alcuin: see *Alcuini epistolae*, ed E. Dümmler, *MGH, Ep. Karolini*, vol. 2 (1895), no. 18, p. 51. Later echoes of this· tradition exist, as in the argument of *De glorioso rege Ludovico filio* concerning the evils that would afflict the realm if kings failed to wield their *potestas protectionis* justly. (See *De glorioso rege Ludovico Ludovici filio*, in *Vie de Louis le Gros par Suger, suivie de l'histoire du roi Louis VII: collection des textes pour servir à l'étude et à l'enseignement de l'histoire*, ed. A. Molinier [Paris, 1887], p. 171, cited and discussed in G. Spiegel, "'Defense of the Realm': Evolution of a Capetian Propaganda Slogan," *Journal of Medieval History* 3 [1977]: 115–133.) Arnau de Vilanova, a near contemporary of the events of 1320–1321, wrote a treatise on kingship for Frederick III of Sicily in which he stated explicitly that kings who overtax their subjects, debase the coinage, and commit other misdeeds inflict illnesses (including sterility) on themselves and their kingdoms, while good kings bring prosperity, health, and fertility. See his *Allocutio christiani*, discussed in chap. 4, n. 81.

[78] On the relationship between leprosy and avarice, see Brody, *Disease of the Soul*, pp. 127–128, 136–137. Brody does not, however, cite the poem that follows, or draw a connection with Jews.

[79] Judas hanged with his moneybag personified avarice, as in the tympanum at Conques. He also served as a symbol of all Jews. As Othlon de Saint-Emmeran put it, "these things that have been said concerning Judas the traitor extend to the entire Jewish people." In the *tenebrae* services of Holy Thursday he was referred to as "that most vile of merchants." See Little, *Religious Poverty*, p. 53. The allusion to the land of Judea would also have been understood to refer to all Jews. See L. Poliakov, *The History of Anti-Semitism* (London, 1965), p. 24.

[80] "De Symonia et Avaritia," in *The Poems of Walter of Wimborne*, ed. A. G. Rigg (Toronto, 1978).

From Judas had sprung an avarice that had infected all the Jews, an avarice most evident among Christians in its dermatological manifestation as leprosy. Only the king could tame the virulence of this disease, but he himself seemed infected.[81] Such is the nexus of ideas that in 1321 provided the context for both the attack upon the lepers and the curses of French subjects against their king.[82]

. . . . .

It is not surprising, then, that the attack on lepers in 1321 was followed by an attack on Jews, especially when we recollect that a king's ability to heal was believed to be proportional to the zeal with which he persecuted Jews. Precisely this logic is implicit in a later (1491) poem in honor of King Charles VIII (1470–1498) inserted by Anthoine Vérard in his version of Eustache Marcadé's *La Vengance Jhesucrist*. Here praise for Charles's anti-Jewish zeal and for his healing touch are juxtaposed in the context of a drama in which the Roman emperor Vespasian is cured of leprosy by a relic of the Crucifixion and out of gratitude avenges Christ's death by destroying the Jewish capital of Jerusalem. (For a more detailed analysis of such "Vengeance of Our Savior" stories see

---

Stanzas 1–20 (pp. 113–115) are relevant, especially stanzas 17–18: "Judas antiquitus quando nephariam / uentris nepharii fudit spurciciam, / unam tantomodo fedauit patriam; / nunc totam turpiter fedat ecclesiam. // Quondam cum periit Judas suspendio, / Judeam polluit uentris profluuio; / nunc fimi fedior fetet effusio / quam sentit quilibet in morbo regio." Rigg, citing DuCange, equates "morbo regio" here with leprosy. For an earlier example of the connections among avarice, leprosy, and Judas, see Caesarius of Arles, *Sermones*, ed. G. Morin (Maretioli, 1937), sermon 129, p. 509. For stereotypes about the stench of lepers, see Moore, *Persecuting Society*, pp. 61–65. The stench of lepers was cited as an aid in diagnosis by doctors as eminent as Arnau de Vilanova. See his *Compendium medicine*, bk. 2, chap. 46, translated by Bériac, *Histoire des lépreux*, pp. 36 f. The leper's stinking breath was also believed by some to be the infectious agent of leprosy: ibid., p. 25. Florimond de Raemond noted in 1599 that "le peuple" believed *cagots* (best described as hereditary "lepers": see chap. 4) to be tainted with leprosy, so that their breath and bodies stank, like the Jews. See B. Bauchau, "Science et racisme: les juifs, la lèpre et la peste," *Stanford French Review* 13 (1989): 21–35, here pp. 27–28.

[81]Contemporaries would not have had to look very far for examples of "good kings" who successfully stopped the spread of the poison of Jewish avarice. One frequently invoked was St. Louis. See, e.g., Guillaume de Chartres, *De vita et miraculis sancti Ludovici*, in *Recueil des historiens*, vol. 20 (Paris, 1840), p. 34: "Ad me vero pertinet de Judaeis, qui jugo servitutis mihi subjecti sunt; ne scilicet per usuras christianos opprimant, et sub umbra protectionis meae talia permittatur ut exerceant, et veneno suo inficiant terram meam." Similarly there were examples ready to hand of bad kings who ruined their kingdoms and contracted leprosy: literary in *Le Roman de Perceval*, ed. W. Roach (Geneva, 1956), ll. 4670–4683; ecclesiastical in papal reaction to the leprosy of King Baldwin of Jerusalem, on which see M. Pegg, "Le corps et l'autorité: la lèpre de Baudouin IV," *Annales: ESC* 45 (1990): 265–287.

[82]This reading suggests a softening of Le Goff's conclusion that, parallel to the shift of *morbus regio* from leprosy to scrofula, there occurred a shift in the ideology of kingship from an ideal of a healing and ordering king to one of a suffering king ("Le mal royal au moyen âge," p. 107). The two ideals coexist in some tension over time, and though the balance between the two is doubtless shifting, how we quantify this balance at any one time depends a good deal on what sorts of evidence we use.

chapter 7.) The moral of the poem was not meant to be obscure: killing or expelling Jews was good medicine.[83]

"Medicinal" judicial and mob violence against the Jews seems to have been almost concurrent with violence against the lepers in some towns, but the extent and timing of the violence is not easy to document. Later Jewish chroniclers, for example, mention no spontaneous local massacres of Jews. According to Samuel Usque, the Jews were arrested when a strange disease broke out in France. Suspected of poisoning the Christians with the help of the lepers, the Jews were imprisoned for nine months. Finally, the French "sentenced five thousand souls to death *as a sacrifice*, while the rest were freed." Offered the choice between baptism and death, the five thousand chose death and were burned.[84]

French chronicle accounts, on the other hand, suggest that a good deal of local violence did take place against the Jews. One chronicler mentioned the burning of 160 Jews in a large pit at Chinon. Nobles were said to have been present, and the massacre was probably "judicial."[85] He also stated that in some areas Jews were burned indiscriminately, especially in Aquitaine, that is, in the same area where most lepers were killed. Other chroniclers reported that forty imprisoned Jews committed suicide.[86] In Tours the Jews were arrested by municipal officials on the 11th of June on suspicion of poisoning.[87] The burning of Jews in various towns, presumably with the support of municipal authorities, is documented indirectly in the Vatican Archives. In 1335, for example, Benedict XII granted dispensation to a cleric who, at the age of fifteen, had carried wood to help burn the Jews in the town of Arbois, diocese of Besançon. In 1332 John XXII absolved the Cistercian monk Peter of a similar crime. Moved by a "naive zeal for the faith," Peter had thrown two sticks that he was carrying onto the pyre upon which the Jews of Nuits-Saint-Georges were burning.[88]

In contrast to the previous year, the king seems to have maintained a studied silence with respect to these attacks against his Jews. Perhaps this was because

---

[83]For the text and translation of this poem, see S. Wright, *The Vengeance of Our Lord: Medieval Dramatizations of the Destruction of Jerusalem* (Toronto, 1989), p. 126. Vérard was relating Vespasian's conquest of Jerusalem and forced exile of the Jews with Charles's expulsion of the Jews from Provence: "Celluy bon roy, second Vaspasien, / A tant hay les juifs et déboutés, / Qui'il est nommé le roy très chrétien, / Qui de son pais les Juifs a hors boutés."

[84]*Consolation*, pp. 190–191 (emphasis added: for more on sacrifice, see chap. 7 and the epilogue). Ha-Kohen gives much the same account (perhaps based on common sources), though he adds a report of forty Jews who committed suicide (presumably the Jews of Vitry mentioned by French chroniclers: see following) without connecting it to the poison accusations. Ha-Kohen does state that the Jews were massacred by the populace in France in 1322, but gives no reasons.

[85]*Chronique latine de Guillaume de Nangis*, 2:35.

[86]Ibid., p. 336; *Chroniques de Saint-Denis*, p. 704; *Chronicon Girardi de Fracheto*, p. 57; all cited in Barber, "Plot," p. 5.

[87]L. Lazard, "Les juifs de Touraine," *RdÉJ* 17 (1888): 210–234, here 232–234.

[88]ASV, Reg. Vat. 119, fol. 250v; ASV, Reg. Vat. 103, fol. 485v; ASV, Reg. Aven. 42, fol. 166r. The documents are published in Simonsohn, *Apostolic See*, pp. 366–368.

Philip recognized that he was in a precarious position, unable to protest the attacks openly without incurring more direct rebellion. Similarly, the Crown delayed for months before acknowledging the accusations that had been made against the Jews as justification for the violence against them. According to the chroniclers, "it was generally said" that the Jews had been approached by the Muslim king of Granada, who planned, together with the lepers, to poison Christendom. The king of Granada wanted the Jews to do the poisoning themselves, but they refused to do so, since the Christians already suspected them, and instead convinced the lepers to carry out the plot.[89] The king of Mallorca wrote to the king of Aragon about the Jews' complicity on June 2, yet the edict issued by Philip V at Poitiers on the 21st of that month continued to state that the lepers alone were involved.[90] Philip maintained this position throughout the attacks on the Jews, although chroniclers state that he was presented with "evidence" of their guilt. The lord of Parthenay, it was said, had sent the king the confession of a leper that implicated the Jews.[91]

No confessions by lepers that implicated the Jews survive, though the most famous of these confessions, that of Guillaume Agasse before the Inquisition of Pamiers, stated that the lepers abjured the Christian faith and agreed to spread the poison at the behest of two Muslim monarchs, the king of Granada and the "sultan of Babylon" (i.e., the Mamluk sultan of Cairo).[92] Nevertheless, a variety of groups undertook elaborate attempts to convince the king to take action against his Jews, and some of these "proofs" survive.

In late June Philip, count of Anjou (later Philip VI of France) wrote to Pope John XXII (and perhaps also to the king?). On the 26th of June, he wrote, there had been a solar eclipse in the counties of Touraine and Anjou, and later the sun had run red with blood. Other portents followed. On the 27th, the people had attacked the Jews. During the looting a letter had been found addressed to a number of exotically named Muslim monarchs by the Jew Bananias. In this letter it was revealed that, because of a series of miracles, all the Muslims wished to be circumcised and convert to Judaism. The Muslims would return Jerusalem to the Jews, but first the Jews had to give the Muslims the city of Paris and the kingdom of France. To carry this out, the Jews seduced the lepers into poisoning the wells. Unfortunately, the lepers were captured, and their accusations

---

[89]See Barber, "Plot," p. 10, for the various chronicles that carried this account.

[90]The letter from the king of Mallorca is translated in chap. 4.

[91]The involvement of the lord of Parthenay is preserved only by chroniclers, for which see Barber, "Plot," p. 2. There is some irony here, since Jean Larchevêque, lord of Parthenay, would shortly be accused of practicing sorcery, and the Jew Abraham of Perpignan, now converted and called Johannes de Foresio, would testify against him. Johannes is summoned to testify in ASV, Reg. Vat. 113, fol. 1r (1324/9/13), published in Simonsohn, *Apostolic See*, p. 342. Jean was accused toward the end of 1322 or the beginning of 1323. See J.-M. Vidal, "Le messire de Parthenay et l'Inquisition (1323–1325)," *Bulletin historique et philologique*, 1913, pp. 414–434.

[92]Guillaume's various confessions are published in *Le registre de l'Inquisition de Jacques Fournier*, 3:135–147.

against the Jews had led to the martyrdom of many. If the Muslims would only send the Jews money, the Jews would buy off the Christians and try again, and the world would be united under one Law and one God. The pope seems to have accepted the proof and recirculated the letter in an encyclical exhorting the faithful to Crusade.[93]

So at least one great noble, the count of Anjou, was willing to lend his weight to the accusations against the Jews, though it should be stressed that his motives for doing so and the constraints under which he was acting are completely unknown. Other surviving "proofs" have a much more "municipal" air about them. On the 2d of July, a group of local officials from the town of Mâcon attested to the existence of two letters written in Arabic. The witnesses included the keeper of the commune's seal, several notaries, a local canon, and an archdeacon, as well as the local bailiff.

The letters were purportedly sent by the king of Granada and the king of Tunis, and stated that the Jews, lepers, and Muslims had met the previous Easter week and agreed to the plot. The king of Granada repeated his promise to return the Holy Land to the Jews and enclosed some additional poison, to be put in the drinking water of the king of France. The king of Tunis alluded to the theme of conversion: "We are brothers in the same law." If the letters were a "municipal" forgery, they were clearly intended for a royal audience. The crime, it was argued, was one against the king. Just as the Jews and lepers poisoned France, so too they poisoned the Crown in its physical manifestation.[94]

This type of evidence was intended to provide an ideological context within which the monarchy could accede to "popular" demands without losing face: municipal councils and urban mobs were attacking the king's Jews in order to save the king, not challenge him. This is not to say that the proofs did not contain implicit criticism of the king. Bananias's letter, for example, made obvious reference to royal fiscal oppression when it stated that because of the greed of the Christians (i.e., the king), the Jews would have another chance to poison France. But whatever the criticisms, these proofs of Jewish perfidy cloaked what could be construed as an attack upon the king's Jews and jurisdiction by presenting it as defense of the king and his realms. On a date traditionally given as

---

[93]Ginzburg gives an extensive paraphrase of Philip of Anjou's letter in *Ecstasies*, pp. 45–47. The document itself is available in a later papal recirculation published by G. D. Mansi, *Sacrorum oecumenicorum conciliorum nova et amplissima collectio*, vol. 25 (Venice, 1782), pp. 569–572. Ginzburg points out that an eclipse of the sun visible throughout France did occur on June 26, 1321. See also Bériac, "La persécution," p. 211. Surprisingly, these events are not discussed in Cutler and Cutler, *The Jew as Ally of the Muslim*.

[94]The letters are summarized in Barber, "Plot," pp. 9–10; Ginzburg, *Ecstasies*, pp. 47–48. They are published in J.-M. Vidal, "La poursuite des lépreux en 1321 d'après des documents nouveaux," *Annales de Saint-Louis-des-Français: publication trimestrielle des études et travaux des chapelains* 4 (1900): 419–478, here pp. 459–461; See also H. Chrétien, *La prétendu complot des juifs et lépreux en 1321* (Châteauroux, 1887), pp. 15–16; V. Rivière-Chalan, *La marque infâme des lepreux et des christians, sous l'Ancien Régime* (Paris, 1978), pp. 41–42.

July 26, but perhaps as much as two weeks earlier, the king capitulated. The Jews were "coupables et suspecionnez," guilty and suspected, of collaborating with the lepers. They were to be arrested, those under serious suspicion tortured. Most important, their property was to be secured for the Crown.[95]

Events following the arrest are unclear.[96] Historians are virtually unanimous in declaring that the Jews were expelled from France, at least in part because of their "crime." Contemporary chroniclers were more ambiguous. Jean de Saint-Victor provides the most detail:

> Since many Jews have been found guilty, in various parts of the kingdom all have been burned without distinction, but in Paris only the guilty; and all others have been condemned to perpetual exile, certain rich ones having been reserved until they have recovered [or will have recovered] what was owed to all and have paid [or will have paid] 150,000 l. to the treasury, and afterwards they will be perpetually exiled from the kingdom.[97]

Chroniclers celebrated the exile of the Jews but were unsure whether it had really occurred. Jews left France, but they were apparently never compelled by a royal edict of expulsion. Philip V seems to have done his best to ignore the charges against the Jews and seems to have accepted them only in the face of armed rebellion. That the king may not have officially expelled the Jews is evidence that the impulse for their departure did not come from him: it is best for rulers to conceal the fact that they have been successfully defied.

For the first time in France, the departure of the Jews was achieved by "popular," that is, nonroyal, violence. The events of 1321 in France were not a royal scheme to seize the property of the lepers, as Brody believed. Nor were they a conspiracy of "deliberate and coordinated actions," orchestrated from above, "intended to guide a series of pre-existing tensions in a predetermined direction," as Ginzburg would have it. Finally, attributing the accusations to irrational hysteria, as Barber does, simply elides whatever conflict underlay the violence.[98]

---

[95] The edict of July 26 is published in C.-V. Langlois, "Registres perdus des archives de la Chambre des comptes de Paris," *Notices et extraits des manuscrits de la Bibliothèque nationale et autres bibliothèques* 40 (1917): 33–399, here pp. 253–255. On the edict and its effects, see especially Brown, "Philip V," pp. 311–312. Evidence from the ACA suggests that the king may actually have ordered the Jews arrested earlier. On July 15, 1321, the king of Aragon wrote to the *sénéchal* of Carcassonne complaining that the *sénéchal* had arrested a Catalan Jew in Montpellier. The Jew, Bendit Deulogar, a physician, had been in Montpellier consulting with other doctors about the illness of the viscount of Castronovo and was arrested when the king of France ordered the arrest of the Jews. See ACA:C 173:195r.

[96] What follows is based on the review of the evidence carried out by Brown, "Philip V." Because many of the arguments are quite technical, only a general summary is provided here.

[97] The translation is from ibid., p. 303, and n. 22.

[98] Brody, *Disease of the Soul*, pp. 92–93; Ginzburg, *Ecstasies*, pp. 49–50; Barber, "Plot," pp. 1, 11, 17.

Behind the atrocities of 1320–1321 in France we should not see the eruption of monolithic "collective mentalities," but rather social conflict expressed through and justified by competing interpretations of a variety of discourses about kingship, bodies, Jews, and the nature of evil in a Christian society.[99] Until violent action against minorities is placed within these various contexts, it resists interpretation. Once contextualized, however, its meaning can no longer be reduced to that of a simple measurement of hatred. Nor should we forget that this is as true of violence in the Crown of Aragon as in France, despite the fact that cultural contexts in the former realms remain much more obscure, and that events across the Pyrenees took a quite different turn.

[99] Compare Moore, *Persecuting Society*, p. 107; and S. Lukes and A. Scull, *Durkheim and the Law* (Oxford, 1984), p. 4 (also cited by Moore).

Chapter 3

CRUSADE AND MASSACRE IN ARAGON (1320)

> In the year of our Lord M.CCCXX there arose those vulgarly called
> the pastorelli, without head or leader, and especially in the
> Basque region and in Toulouse with an indiscreet fervor of faith
> they killed all the Jews they could find in cities, towns, and
> other places, and some of them came to Montclus, in the
> diocese of Lleida.
>
> *(Chronicle of G. Mascaró, Catalan, late fourteenth century)*

THUS WROTE the only chronicler in the Crown of Aragon to note the crusaders' entry into the kingdom and their massacre of Jews in the tiny village of Montclus. Mascaró appears loquacious next to a Catalan chronicle entry that mentions neither the massacre at Montclus nor the responsibility of the shepherds: "In the year MCCCXX there was the death of the Jews of Toulouse."[1] It is a silence that deepens over time. The great sixteenth-century historian Jeronimo Zurita found space in his massive history of Aragon for shocked indignation that the Jews of Barcelona had dared to insult some retainers of the queen of Aragon on Easter of 1318, but he somehow failed to notice the massacre of hundreds of Jews by the shepherds two years later.[2] If the Christian chronicle tradition bears true witness, the events of 1320 in Aragon were of no moment.

But Christian chronicles are not the only witnesses, and others saw things quite differently. Royal officials and their scribes, for example, spent a great deal of time and ink documenting the massacre. In the best tradition of medieval administrative kingship, they extended the massacre's implications as widely as they could in order to justify judicial extortion through the widespread imposition of fines. We might call the records they produced the bureaucratic version of the massacre. Some contemporary Jews and, more important, later Jewish chroniclers saw prophetic significance in the event, treating it as a foreshadowing of escalating tragedies to come. Finally, modern historians have seen in Montclus a telling sign of an "era of decline" for the tolerance of Jews in fourteenth-century Iberia. We have, then, at least four narratives for the same

---

[1] From a mid-fourteenth-century manuscript of a chronicle redacted probably in Tortosa, excerpted by J. Villanueva, *Viaje literario a las Iglesias de España* (Madrid, 1803–1852), 5:236. Mascaró is excerpted in 18:9. The manuscript of his chronicle, as yet unedited, may be consulted at the Biblioteca de Catalunya, MS no. 485. For biographical data on Mascaró, see J. Cabestany Fort, "El cronicó de Guillem Mascaró: l'autor i l'obra," *Estudís Universitaris Catalans* 24 (1980): 115–122.

[2] *Anales de la Corona de Aragón*, ed. A. Canellas López (Zaragoza, 1978), 3:141.

that anyone who struck or insulted a Jew or Muslim would be hanged without remission. The decree was against customary law and would be revoked after the danger abated, but it underscores the extent of official concern that the violence might spread.[13]

Wherever they entered, their first act of consequence was the slaughtering of 337 Jews in the royal castle of Montclus.[14] This act spurred King James to take stern measures against the shepherds, and to commission Infant Alfonso, the heir to the throne, to travel to Barbastro to crush the invasion. The *sobrejuntero* of Ribagorza, Sobrarbe, and Valles, the official traditionally charged with raising local military forces, was ordered to collect as many men as possible and have them ready for the prince's arrival. In the meantime, the *sobrejuntero* was to guard the passes to prevent the entry of more pastoureaux, and to kill any who attempted to enter by force.[15]

Some attempts were made to negotiate with the crusaders. Infant Alfonso sent two of his most trusted officials to contact the shepherds, together with a letter urging the pastoureaux to obey whatever the bearers of the letter told them on his behalf. This is the only surviving letter directed to the pastoureaux themselves.[16] Unfortunately for the shepherds, it was on this same day, shortly after his ambassadors had departed, that the infant heard of the events at Montclus, and he wrote again to his ambassadors, ordering them to abandon their diplomatic mission and join the *sobrejuntero* in ejecting the pastoureaux by force from the Crown of Aragon.[17] He then turned his attention to raising an army.[18]

At this point the shepherds disappear from the documentation for almost a week, though their movements can be partially reconstructed from later sources. From Montclus, they seem to have moved toward Naval, where the Muslim quarter was assaulted and pillaged with the help of local Christians. The

---

[13]James II's edict is ACA:C 246:45v (1320/7/6). Infant Alfonso reissued it under his own name the next day, ACA:C 364:211r. King James instructs Infant Alfonso to revoke his order in a letter dated August 24, 1320. The leading men of Valencia had complained that the order was against *fur*, and since "nunc cessat ratio" (i.e., fear of the pastoureaux), the edict should be revoked. ACA:C 170:129r.

[14]The toll of the dead has escaped previous mention because it does not appear in the king's correspondence. It is given by the Infant Alfonso in ACA:C 406:93v–94r (1320/7/28). The first mention of the violence occurs in ACA:C 246:45r (1320/7/6): ". . . pastorellos cum transitum facerent per terminos castri nostri Montisclusi dicentes se ad partes frontarie [*sic*] regni Granate pro Dei servicio acessuros propia [*sic*] ducti temeritate temptaverunt absidere dictum castrum et de judeis ville castri ipsius in non parvo numero occidere presumpserunt, ob quod ad partes illas mittimus infantem."

[15]On the *sobrejuntero*, see A. Ubieto, *Historia de Aragón*, vol. 1, *Divisiones Administrativas* (Zaragoza, 1983), pp. 132–137. The office was only about half a century old in 1320. For King James's order, ACA:C 246:45v (1320/7/7). For more on the raising of the militia, see below.

[16]ACA:C 406:82v (1320/7/7), addressed to "universis et singulis dictis pastorellis." ACA:C 406:83r is similar, but addressed to all officials.

[17]ACA:C 406:84r–v.

[18]See, e.g., ACA:C 406:84r (1320/7/7).

bands of shepherds presented a moving target. When the men of Pertusa were summoned by the lieutenant of the *sobrejuntero* of Huesca and Jaca to fight the pastoureaux, they were first called to Naval. As they passed through Ponzano, however, they were met by that official, who told them that the shepherds had veered off toward Barbastro and would probably pass through Pertusa. The men returned to Pertusa to protect it, and indeed forty pastoureaux who had participated in the attack on Montclus were captured there before July 18, and another twenty-six were captured in Cellas.[19] Arnaldo Coloni, a merchant from Barbastro on his way to Ainsa, had met a band of pastoureaux as they marched from Montclus along the Sierra de Arp to Naval.[20] Pastoureaux were also reported in Ainsa and Barbastro,[21] and with the help of some local clerics they robbed the Jewish aljama in Ruesta, putting it to the torch.[22] While the group of crusaders who attacked Montclus and Naval was defeated by the *sobrejuntero* of Ribagorza before the 13th of July, by the 17th pastoureaux were reported in the environs of virtually every major city in Aragon as far south as the Ebro. King James ordered authorities in these regions to deny the shepherds entry to the cities in their jurisdictions, to forbid the sale of provisions to them, and to expel any who remained in the country after the date of departure given them as an ultimatum, the last day of July.[23] No atrocities against Muslims or Jews were reported from any of these cities or their hinterlands.

Fear of the pastoureaux traveled even more widely than the pastoureaux themselves. Letters were sent to officials all over Catalonia.[24] In Valencia, cities as far away as Oriola on Valencia's southern border received vigorous commands to counter the shepherds.[25] Some of these places were so far removed

[19]ACA:C 170:89v (1320/8/7). The men of Pertusa complain that they were afterwards accused of not appearing at Naval as ordered and fined ten sous of Jaca per household, when in fact the lieutenant had sent them back to defend their own town. In ACA:C 246:54r (1320/7/18), King James orders the *sobrejuntero* of Huesca and Jaca to guard closely those forty pastoureaux captured in Pertusa and the twenty-six captured in "locum de las Cellas." Published in Masiá, "Aportaciones," p. 21.

[20]ACA:C 370:96v (1322/5/3).

[21]See ACA:C 364:217v, ordering the municipality of Barbastro to protect the Jews living there against the pastoureaux; ACA:C 406:85r–86r, (1320/7/13), in which pastoureaux are reported as having entered Barbastro, Ainsa, and Naval.

[22]ACA:C 383:61v (1320/9/29): Remission to the men of Ruesta, for an illegible price, because they "conçensisse invasioni, raubarie et subpositioni ignis facte judarie dicti loci de Ruesta per pastorellos." For the complicity of the clerics, see ACA:C 170:92r (1320/8/9): "Nos etiam prout petiistis scribimus episcopo p[a]mpilonen[sis] ut procedat adversus clericos illos qui in predictis culpam comiserunt." Defensive forces were also mustered at Bierge (see ACA:C 170:100r–v [1320/8/16]) and probably in many other villages as well.

[23]Several documents in ACA:C 246:54v–55r (1320/7/17) mention pastoureaux in the regions of Zaragoza, Tarazona, Huesca, Jaca, Sobrarbe, Ribagorza, Ejea, Castro Leon, Uncastillo, Ainsa, Tamarite de Litera, Sarinena, and Pertusa.

[24]See the several documents in ACA:C 246:58v–60r (1320/7/17), to Vic, Berga, and Tortosa; 246:59v to Girona, Besalú, Barcelona, Manresa, Vilafranca, Montblanc, Cervera, Tàrrega, Lleida, Tarragona, Figueras, and Urgell.

[25]ACA:C 246:61v (1320/7/17) to Valencia, Morella, Castelló del Camp de Burriana, Burriana;

from the itinerary of the pastoureaux that the authorities there were puzzled. King James had to answer an anxious letter from the municipality of Morvedre and explain that it was not anger at anything they had done that had motivated his fierce letter about protecting the Jews, but the fact that a group called the pastoureaux had massacred three hundred Jews at Montclus.[26] Even in places that the shepherds never reached, officials took these orders seriously, sometimes too seriously. King James, answering a letter from Bernat Sanou, bailiff general of Valencia, had to explain that he did not intend for all the Jews to be moved into royal fortresses for safekeeping. They should instead be adequately defended in the cities where they lived.[27]

In Barcelona, the pastoureaux were a source of real concern. The bishop of Barcelona wrote to warn King James of the danger they posed, as did the councillors of the city.[28] The Jewish aljama also sent messengers to the king, believing itself to be in imminent peril: two years later one messenger complained that the hurried trip had cost him his mule.[29] Perhaps most revealing is the fact that Christian creditors of the Jews in Barcelona, worried by rumors about the pastoureaux, began to demand sureties from their Jewish debtors, even though such sureties were not stipulated in the contracts.[30] All of this suggests that the shepherds traveled within the Crown of Aragon as they entered it, in separate bands. In this, and in its insistence on the wide dispersal of the pastoureaux throughout the Crown of Aragon, the Jewish chronicle tradition was not far off the mark. It is all the more amazing, given the wide dispersion of these troops of shepherds, that actual incidents of violence against the Jews and Muslims were so few. Outside the immediate area of Montclus, in fact, there is no record whatsoever of violence committed by the pastoureaux.

The fate of the crusaders is as unclear as their itinerary. Some, like A. G. de Armanyach, G. A. de Pomeres, and Bertrand de Cacus, all from the diocese of Auch in the south of France, had come with a "familia" of several hundred men each to fight for Prince Alfonso in a Crusade against Granada. When they were informed that plans for the Crusade had been canceled, they asked the prince for safe-conducts to return to France.[31] Men such as these were not described as

ACA:C 246:62r (1320/7/17) to Alacant; ACA:C 246:61r to Morvedre, Alzira, and Xàtiva; ACA:C 246:62v to Elx and Oriola.

[26] ACA:C 246:90v (1320/8/21).

[27] ACA:C 246:79v, dated 1320/7/18.

[28] For the bishop, ACA:C 246:58r (1320/7/19), in answer to his letter. The council wrote several letters, answered in ACA:C 246:63r (1320/7/22) and ACA:C 246:58v (1320/7/19).

[29] ACA:C 172:280r (1322/1/22), where Astrug Saltelli, Jew of Barcelona, complains that the Jewish aljama of Barcelona refused to reimburse the expenses he incurred in traveling to the king's court.

[30] ACA:C 170:57v–58r (1320/7/20): ". . . moti propter rumorem pastorellorum . . . inquietant et inquietare et molestare intendunt dictos judeos . . . ad tradendum ipsis creditoribus pignora pro debitis supradictis."

[31] See, for example, ACA:C 364:214r (1320/7/12), where Infant Alfonso writes to the guards

"pastorellos." They had been attracted by the same rumors of Crusade that had brought the shepherds into Aragon, but they came from higher up the social scale, probably nobility looking for employment as mercenaries. The presence of such men in Aragon suggests, however, that the Crusade fervor which brought diverse classes of Frenchmen across the Pyrenees was not some popular frenzy, or a search for a few more prosperous Jewish aljamas to sack once those at home were destroyed, but a concrete belief that the Muslims of Granada were about to attack the Crown of Aragon.[32] In fact, Prince Alfonso had been planning a defensive Crusade against the kingdom of Granada, whose invasion of Valencia was believed imminent.[33] It was only in early July that the danger of Muslim invasion had lessened to a point where the state of alert could be ended.[34]

More humble people, clearly identified as pastoureaux in the documentation but judged innocent of any crimes against Jews or Muslims, followed men such as Bertrand de Cacus peaceably home. The documents that provide for their safe-conduct are the only ones preserving the names of pastoureaux, and they reveal artisans and married couples, as well as the young male shepherds traditionally associated with the movement.[35] Others, like Gilote de Pontesa, a stonecutter cleared of criminal charges, chose to remain in Aragon and received the prince's permission to do so.[36]

Not all the shepherds were so lucky. Prince Alfonso had decided before the 16th of July to have a number of the pastoureaux who attacked Montclus, as well as those Aragonese natives who helped them, put to death as an example.[37]

---

posted at the Pyrenean borders: ". . . cum Bertrandus de Cacus, Auchitanense diocise, intellecto nos esse in Dei servicio in frontaria regni Granate, venerit pro serviendo Deo et nobis in dicta fronteria. Et nunc scito nos ad praesens non intendere citra dicta negotia, velit redire ad terram suam cum familia quam ducebat . . . qui sunt ut intelleximus centum viginti homines."

[32]Miret ("Le massacre des juifs") suggested that the pastoureaux had only wandered across Montclus on their way to Navarre, where they had heard there were some rich Jewish communities to attack. Cohn, *Millennium*, p. 104, says only that "they crossed the Pyrenees to kill more Jews, which they did until the son of the King of Aragon led a force against them and dispersed them."

[33]See ACA:C cr. Jaume II, box 52, no. 6,439; box 52, no. 6,433; box 148, no. 438; transcribed in A. Masiá, *Jaume II: Aragó, Granada i Marroc* (Barcelona, 1989), pp. 508–513. Unfortunately Masiá missed the documentation concerning the border crisis and preparations for the defense of Valencia, and so provides only the following comment on the year 1320: "The activities that took place in [this year] were very few."

[34]There are many documents relating to the border crisis, for example, ACA:C 406:81v (1320/7/4), addressed to the noble Eiximen de Foncibus: "Recepta et visa vestra litera super facto vestri adventus ad nos ratione defensionis regni Valentie contra sarracenos Granate." Not until July 28 did James II write to Pere de Queralt, the lieutenant of the procurator in Valencia, informing him that it appeared that the Muslims of Granada were not going to invade (ACA:C 246:79r–v).

[35]ACA:C 364:231v (1320/7/31). Pope John XXII had already noted that there were women among the pastoureaux. See *Jean XXII (1316–34). Lettres secrètes et curiales relatives à la France*, ed. A. Coulon (Paris, 1906), vol. 2, no. 1104, pp. 936–938, letter from John XXII to the archbishop of Narbonne.

[36]ACA:C 365:3r–v (1320/8/8).

[37]ACA:C 246:52r (1320/7/16), where James II approves of Alfonso's plan.

The *sobrejuntero* of Ribagorza had captured several hundred prisoners by the 18th of that month, among them some subjects of the Crown: Pedro Sanchez de Lacano, "who guided the pastorellos," and Juan de Pisa, who called himself a royal lieutenant and had been complicit, along with five associates, in the attack on the Jews.[38] This was not the sum total of the prisoners: other officials had captured more.[39] The prisoners were judged in mass trials so large that normal procedures had to be suspended. Torture was used, according to a complaint by the municipality of Barbastro, in an illegal fashion. Those declared innocent were freed, those claiming clerical privilege were held until the question of their status could be addressed, and forty of the guilty were ordered hanged in diverse places throughout the county.[40] In view of the fact that twenty-seven shepherds had already been killed in fighting with the *sobrejuntero* (compare the figure of two thousand in the Jewish chronicle tradition), the prince recommended mercy for the rest, who were freed and expelled from the kingdom on the 6th of August.[41]

Bernard Gui had said of the pastoureaux in France that they were favored by "weighty persons," although he did stress that the shepherds also terrorized the upper classes.[42] In France, however, no record of this upper-class complicity survives. In Aragon, it appears that the pastoureaux were led by one Pedro Sanchez de Lacano, son of an Aragonese knight. His status was a matter of concern because, unlike the vulgar among the guilty, he could not be hanged. He was decapitated in the market of Barbastro.[43] Four others described as "generosos" met the same fate. Juan de Pisa, Rodrigo del Bien, Lup de Burgassa, and Martin de Co[. . .]ielle were found guilty of violence against the Jews and were ordered decapitated in Montclus. The prince was concerned that because Montclus was remote and now depopulated, the executions would be insufficiently public, so he ordered the beheadings to take place in the market of Barbastro.[44] While these five were not exactly "weighty persons," neither were they the poor rustics from whom the movement drew its name.

With these executions and expulsions, we hear nothing more of the pastoureaux in Aragon. The remaining documentation is concerned with exacting

[38] ACA:C 246:54r (1320/7/18). I have not been able to determine what office Juan de Pisa claimed to hold.

[39] Cf. ACA:C 246:54r (1320/7/18), concerning the sixty-six prisoners of the *sobrejuntero* of Huesca, mentioned above.

[40] ACA:C 406:95v–96r (1320/7/30): ". . . ordinaverimus XL ex ipsis culpabilibus per diversa loca huius comarche tradi mortis suspendio."

[41] For the recommendation of mercy, ACA:C 406:95v–96r (1320/7/30). For the release and expulsion, ACA:C 364:239v (1320/8/6).

[42] The contradiction (if there is one) is pointed out by Barber, "The Pastoureaux," p. 148.

[43] ACA:C 406:95v–96r (1320/7/30): ". . . contra Petro Sanccii de Lacano, qui guidavit dictos pastorellos . . . quia filius est militis, decapitari mandavimus publice in Barbastre." See also ACA:C 246:54r (1320/7/18).

[44] ACA:C 406:99r–v (1320/8/6): ". . . huiusmodi exequtionem iustitie magis [in] Barbastro fore publicam quam in dicto loco de Montecluso, qui depopulatus est et in remotis constitutus."

fines from the local population, enforcing royal rights, reconstructing destroyed documentation of debts, and dealing with the claims of surviving Jews and Muslims as well as those of forced converts to Catholicism. It was through such issues that royal power turned a local massacre perpetrated almost entirely by foreigners into an affair of state of general concern to natives of all three faiths. But before we address those important issues, it is appropriate to ask what happened in those places where violence against the Jews and Muslims did break out.

.　.　.　.　.

The fact is that until now we knew virtually nothing about what occurred in Montclus during the massacre: not even the number of the dead had been established. The king's edicts, upon which previous work has been based, give nothing but the most general information about the attack. The documentation pertaining to the infant on this subject, which I have utilized here, is much more voluminous, but volume is not always informative. Of the five hundred or so documents concerned with the affair of the pastoureaux, perhaps five contain some detail about the massacre itself. Still, something of a coherent picture of the tragedy emerges.

The castle of Montclus was in large part financed by the Jews, and the castellan's salary was paid by them.[45] It is therefore no surprise that the advent of the pastoureaux drove the Jews into the protection of the castle and its keeper. How many sought refuge there is unknown, though the number is probably about 400, since 337 were killed and there were a number of survivors. With the alcalde of the castle absent,[46] the task of protecting the Jews fell to his lieutenant, García Bardaji. It is impossible to know what resources this official had at his disposal when he confronted the pastoureaux: perhaps only a handful of men and weapons, since only he, his "squire,"⋅ and one guard are named in the later denunciations.[47]

We know nothing of the steps taken to defend the castle, except that, with the pastoureaux storming the gates,[48] García convinced the Jews to give their loan documents to the besiegers in the hopes that this would satisfy them.[49]

---

[45] In 1288 the aljama paid eight hundred sous a year to Pedro de Huesca, castellan of the castle at Montclus. See ACA:C 78:45r (= Régné no. 1939). For a similar arrangement in 1295, see Miret "Le massacre des juifs," p. 257. J. Boix Pociello, "Montclús: una aljama jueva a la capçalera del Cinca," *Occidens* 1 (1985) (*Homenatge a J. Lladonosa*), pp. 19–23, offers a cursory survey of the history of the aljama.

[46] He was in the region of Huesca: ACA:C 406:94v–95r (1320/7/30).

[47] ACA:C 406:91r (1320/7/28).

[48] According to BN, *Collection Doat*, cix. 73, cited in Barber, "The Pastoureaux," p. 153, the shepherds were armed with "swords, large knives, lances, spears, shields and helmets, among other weapons" when they entered Lézat.

[49] ACA:C 365:89v (1320/10/14): ". . . eo tempore quo pastorelli predictum locum invaserunt,

Many of the later charges, particularly those against García, against the notary of Montclus, and those involving debt documents, probably stemmed from this action.[50] Whether or not García acted in this manner to protect the Jews, he failed: somehow the pastoureaux took over the castle and began to massacre and to convert.[51]

No narrative source such as that left by Baruch l'Allemand for Toulouse describes the scene at Montclus.[52] Put dryly and bureaucratically, in the manner of our sources, 337 Jews were killed by the pastoureaux. Children seem to have been spared and forcibly converted, or at least this occurred often enough to bring the issue of the education of child converts before the royal court.[53] Some adults too, both men and women, were converted: the financial problems occasioned by their conversions are well attested in the documentation.[54] A few Jews seem to have been spared without converting.[55]

---

alcaydus qui erat tunc dicti loci et alii xristiani qui tunc aderant, metum mortis predictis judeis incurientes [sic], coegerunt eosdem ad faciendum ipsis xristianis de debitis in quibus prefatis judeis tenebantur apochas de soluto. Verum cum negotia gesta [occasione?] metus qui viri constantis mentem incuraret ut pote mortis ad occulum imminentis cum eo tunc, ut asseritur, alii judei dicti loci a prefatis pastorellis crucidi passin [sic] ac rabide necarentur, nullius momenti debeant judicari." Full text in D. Nirenberg, "Violence and the Persecution of Minorities in the Crown of Aragon: Jews, Lepers and Muslims before the Black Death" (Ph.D. diss., Princeton University, 1992), pp. 338–339.

[50] The pastoureaux had demanded Jewish documents from notaries in France as well. See Barber, "The Pastoureaux," p. 153.

[51] The castle's defenses seem to have been destroyed by the pastoureaux, judging from the extensive rebuilding necessary in the aftermath of the massacre. See ACA:C 220:55v (1321/7/7). In Usque's narration of the massacre in Jaca (by which he presumably meant Montclus, since no massacre occurred in Jaca), he stated that the Jews took refuge "up on the wall," and that "only ten escaped into the castle" (Consolation, p. 188). In fact, the Jews had all taken refuge within the castle at Montclus.

[52] For bibliography on Baruch's deposition, see chap. 2, n. 15, above. Baruch had been dragged to the Church of Saint-Etienne in Toulouse and offered the choice of baptism or death, a choice made stark by the bodies of Jews lying about, and by the crowd beginning to strike at him as he vacillated.

[53] For the conversion of children, see among other examples ACA:C 365:5v (1320/8/9?), where Salema Abenadret is reported killed in Montclus while his child "Bernard" and his other children "ad fidem catholicam sunt conversi." Adult converts could be guardians to such children. Thus Johan de Montalt, convert, was guardian of Bernardini, the converted son of Lup de Morcat, who was killed in Montclus (ACA:C 365:15v–16r [1320/8/12]). Nevertheless, these children were not to live among Jews: "Illi pueri ex judeis dicte ville qui tempore ruine judarie eiusdem ad instantiam pastorellorum babtitzati fuerunt non sint seu habitent in judaria dicte ville nec inter judeos" (ACA:C 220:55v [1321/7/7]).

[54] See, for example, the dowry dispute occasioned by the conversion of Guallarde, whose husband Jucef Avadia was killed in Montclus, in ACA:C 170:156v–157r (1320/9/13).

[55] The categories are best summarized in Infant Alfonso's instructions for the handling of debt documents pillaged from Montclus by the pastoureaux but later recovered. He ordered the documents divided into three parts: those that "sunt xristianorum qui judei fuerunt de Montiscluso" were to be brought to the neophytes. Those that "sunt judeorum qui vivi sunt" were to be given to these survivors, and those belonging to dead Jews were to be taken to the justice of Ribagorza on behalf of the Crown. See ACA:C 364:235v (1320/8/1).

Elsewhere events were less violent. In Naval, for example, the Muslim quarter was pillaged and robbed, but no Muslims were injured or killed. In Ruesta, the Jewish quarter was likewise robbed, and perhaps partly burned, again with no reports of injury. In both these cases, it is possible that the Jews and Muslims had fled before the arrival of the pastoureaux, preventing bloodshed.

Flight was not, however, without its dangers. When the Muslims of Cillas left their homes and marched toward Estadella, where they had been promised protection against the shepherds, the citizens of Cuscullola robbed them of the goods they were carrying.[56] Some unidentified Jews of Aragon took refuge in the village of Lus (I have not been able to locate this village). After the pastoureaux had been destroyed, these Jews hired a group of Christians to escort them back to their homes. Instead, the Christians murdered them on the road and stole their goods.[57] This account is not specific, nor is the event mentioned again. Perhaps the infant had heard a confused rumor of the following crime, which he prosecuted three months later.

In May of 1321, the infant wrote to Pedro de Canellis, justice of Ribagorza. The prince had recently heard that, during the time when the pastoureaux were attacking Jews in France and in the Crown of Aragon, Augerio de Lus, of "Vasconia" (i.e., not part of the Crown of Aragon) and G. Sorrosal promised to protect 120 French Jews who wished to flee to Aragon.

> Once within the confines of the aforesaid kingdom [of Aragon], having seized the great quantity of money, jewels, and goods that [the Jews] were carrying, against the safe-conduct and good faith they had promised them, they killed all of these Jews.

Because the murders had taken place in the king's domains, and because the prince had heard that some royal subjects of the valley of Breoto (not located) participated in the massacre, the officials were to collect the fines for homicide.[58]

Such violence against Jewish refugees from France may have been more

---

[56] ACA:C 365:20r–v (1320/8/16): ". . . homines loci [sic] de Cuscullola per cuius terminos dicti sarraceni transitum faciebant abstulerant eisdem res et utensalia quod ferebant."

[57] ACA:C 384:18r–v (1321/2/11): "Infans etc. dilecto suo bajulo de Lus etc. Ad nostrum auditum noveritis pervenisse quod, cum aliqui judei regni Aragonum ob timorem pastorellorum ad loca bajulie vestre confugerent, et post tempus lapsum ipsis pastorellis per nos preeunte justicia a regio dominio ex[tirpatis?], cum ipsi judei ad lares proprios vellent redire, receperunt guidaticum a quibusdam christianis [r]eg[alis] ac nostri dominii [sic], ut ipsos ad has partes secure conducerent . . . , qui quidam christiani . . . in eos[dem] judeos in itinere publico pergentes eos sub fide inhumaniter occiderunt, auferendo eis bona."

[58] ACA:C 384:141r–v (1321/5/12): ". . . cum iam eos usque ad terram regiam duxissent constituti citra regnorum predictorum confines, ablatis eis moneta, jocalibus et aliis rebus que et quas in magnis quantitatibus deferebant, omnes ipsos judeos contra securitatem jamdictam et fidem eis prestitam occiderunt." See also ACA:C 384:141v–142r, 173v–174r. In October of 1321, the prince authorized the justice of Ribagorza to agree on a fine for G. de Sorrosal and others involved in the "attack on French Jews." If these men refused to pay a fine, the justice was to prosecute them with the understanding that they could expect no grace or remission from the prince. See ACA:C 384:227v–228r.

common than we know. The massacre described above took over a year to come to the infant's attention: others may have gone unnoticed.[59] It is certain, however, that in 1320 Aragon was flooded with refugees from the violence in France. We know that in the wake of the well-poisoning scare of 1321 the king ordered inquests throughout the Crown to ascertain which Jews had immigrated in 1320: those identified were to be expelled.[60] It is possible that some of these refugees had sought sanctuary in the castle of Montclus, swelling the ranks of the unnamed dead.[61] On the road with their fortunes on their backs, with no claim on the protection of local officials, these refugees were especially vulnerable.

.   .   .   .   .

Thus far, I have concentrated on the shepherds and the violence they left in their wake. Given the fragmentary nature of the evidence, most of my conclusions are negative. Unlike France, the violence in Aragon was limited to tiny villages over a very small area. With the tragic exception of Montclus, Aragonese Jews seem to have been spared fatal violence. In villages such as Ainsa and in larger towns such as Barbastro, both places accused of sympathy for the pastoureaux, local Jewish and Muslim populations seem to have been protected. Despite the extensive dispersal of the shepherds in the Crown of Aragon, violence against religious minorities does not seem to have been widespread.

How then are we to transform a local event, precipitated by "foreign" invasion, into a metaphor of Christian-Jewish (or Christian-Muslim) relations? Here, modern historians (of Russian pogroms, for example) have generally turned to the question of "complicity" in order to extrapolate broad social attitudes from a discrete event, and to rise from the local to the general, from the individual to the state. Did government officials participate in the pogroms? What did local leaders do? Did nonparticipants intervene on behalf of the Jews? Was the pogrom instigated by foreigners? Were national political parties involved? By linking crowd action to official and institutional action, historians attempt to move from the messy anonymity of riot to issues deemed of greater consequence: popular anti-Semitic mentalities, elite attitudes, high politics, and the state.[62]

[59] The murder of two Jews by the men of Samitier in 1320 may have been one such occasion. See ACA:C 384:146r (1321/5/18).

[60] For the original order, see ACA:C 246:239r (1321/7/13): "Cum a tempore citra quo contra illos qui aquas nituntur inficere rumor invaluit nonnulli judei extranei terram nostram ingressi fuerint et adhuc ingredi non cessent. Nosque ad tollendam omnem suspicionem eosdem a terra nostra eici velimus." ACA:C 246:261r (1321/8/18) stipulates "illorum judeorum qui ab uno anno citra terram nostram introierunt." For more detail see chap. 4.

[61] A suggestion first made to me by J. Riera i Sans.

[62] The questionnaire distributed by the Londoner Zionistischen Hilfsfonds in the wake of the October 1905 pogroms in Russia raised these questions explicitly. See *Die Judenpogrome in Russland* (Cologne, 1910), 1:6–10.

Historians of the pastoureaux have asked these same questions with the same intent.[63] In the case of Aragon, we are lured to these questions by the sources. King James and Prince Alfonso seem to have been concerned with these very issues in their investigation. Throughout, royal agents strove to establish the complicity of royal officials, municipal councils, and villagers along the path of the pastoureaux.[64] The records of these investigations have led their few students to assert the general complicity of the populace and of local officials. But we should not lose sight of the obvious. The king raised the question of complicity not to learn about attitudes toward Jews in the communities where violence occurred, but to broaden the opportunities for fiscal intervention and the assertion of regalian rights. "Complicity" served as the point of entry for the royal extraction of fines and extraordinary revenues. This does not mean that there is nothing to be learned about the broader issues of social relations among Muslims, Jews, and Christians from the records produced by royal investigators in the wake of the Shepherds' Crusade. It does mean that these records should not be used as transparent windows into the failures of *convivencia*. And it suggests that we should ask how this royal construction of complicity, this bureaucratic representation of the effects of violence against minorities, affected the ways in which contemporaries, let alone later historians dependent on these sources, thought about such violence.

By complicity, royal officials meant a variety of things. The surviving Jews of Montclus, for example charged that

> some people, both officials and other subjects of the king's and our realm . . . participated without fear in the [crimes] perpetrated recently against the Jews of Montclus by those who call themselves the shepherds, giving their consent and aid to the crimes perpetrated by the said shepherds against the said Jews and also to the robbery committed by the same shepherds against the Jews' goods. . . . Some officials and others also participated in the robbery of the goods of the Muslim aljama of Naval or consented to it. And the officials and communities of Barbastro, Ainsa, and Naval, as well as some other places, seeing the public auction carried out in those places of the aforesaid stolen goods, made no attempt to seize, retain, or capture the said murderers or robbers present there. Further, they consented to the auction and supported it, giving favor and aid to the robbers and murderers. And some of these officials and others [thrust] their hands into this robbery, [. . .], and others bought goods from these spoils. Also some officials and others who had received written commands from Us or by command of the *sobrejuntero* to capture shepherds guilty in the aforesaid, let them go free, merely keeping for themselves the goods and money that [the prisoners] carried. And many within the militia zone refused to follow the *sobrejuntero* when he commanded them to pursue the aforesaid malefactors, and some offered violence and

---

[63]Barber, "The Pastoureaux," pp. 148, 153–155, 159–166. For Aragon see Masiá, "Aportaciones," pp. 12–13.

[64]That French royal officials did the same should be evident from chap. 2, n. 35.

insult against the men of the *sobrejuntero* who were transporting some captive shepherds.[65]

Participation in the murder of Jews, participation in the robbery of property from Jews and Muslims, the purchase of goods stolen from Jews and Muslims, the harboring of pastoureaux, the refusal to join royal militias summoned to march against the pastoureaux, failure to adequately defend against the shepherds—all these fell under the charge of complicity.

It is hard to know what to make of these charges, beyond the fact that, stated thus narrowly, they were undoubtedly true. Six Aragonese, some of noble birth, had helped guide the pastoureaux.[66] At least one Aragonese Christian, according to a letter from the king to the prince, played a direct role in the death of a Jew of Montclus: "As to the affair of the trial that you carried out against our subjects who were inculpated in the massacre of the pastoureaux, and especially against that [subject] who found a Jew hiding in the castle and brought him to the pastoureaux to have his throat slit, we respond to you that we are very pleased by what you have done in the aforesaid case."[67] Domingo de na Gracia, a Christian of Ainsa and the only person specifically accused of sheltering participants in the robbery at Montclus in his home without denouncing them, was absolved in September 1320.[68] Two men of Saint Peter of Ayna were assessed a 250-sou fine for having purchased a spade and other minor articles stolen from the Jews of Montclus by the pastoureaux.[69] The lieutenant of the justice of Jaca

[65] ACA:C 406:85r–86r (1320/07/13): ". . . non nulli tam officiales quam alii subditi domini regis et nostri . . . prestiterunt tractatum et consensum ac dederunt consilium super necibus perpetratis per dictos pastorellos in judeos predictos ac super raubaria per eosdem pastorellos facta de bonis judeorum ipsorum. . . . etiam. . . aliqui . . . tractaverunt raubariam factam de bonis aljiame sarracenorum de Nabal ac consenserunt eidem. Quodquae officiales et universitates Barbastri, Aynse et de Nabal ac quorumdam aliorum locorum videntes encantum fieri publicum in dictis locis de bonis et rebus predictis raubatis non curaverunt ea [et] emperare nec retinere seu capere interfectores seu raubatores predictos inibi existentes. Immo consensientes encanto [sic] predicto ac sustinentes ipsum fieri favorem et auxilium prefatis raubatoribus et interfectoribus prestiterunt. Et quod non nulli etiam tam ex officialibus quam aliis in raubariis predictis manus prohicien[t]es plura ex dictis bonis raubatis [penes] se d[eti]nent et q[ua]dam alii de eisdem raubatis bonis emerunt. Quodque etiam aliqui officiales et alii qui ex literatorio mandato nos[tro] seu ex mandato superiunctariorum ceperant pastorellos in premissis obnoxios dimiserunt eos ab[i]re, retinentes penes se [. . .] [sibi] ipsis aplicantes res et pecuniam quas ferebant. Et plures etiam infra junctas degentes ad mandatum superiunctariorum noluerunt sequi superiunctarios ad persequendum malefactores predictos, et aliqui violencias et iniurias i[rr]ogaverunt hominibus superiunctariorum captos ducentibus aliquos ex pastorellis predictis." Full text in Nirenberg, "Violence," pp. 347–351.

[66] See ACA:C 246:54r (1320/7/18) and ACA:C 406:95v–96r, discussed above.

[67] ACA:C 246:85r–v (1320/8/13): "Quantum ad negotium procesuum quod fecistis contra subditos nostros in strage pastorellorum obnoxios et specialiter contra illum qui quendam judeum qui in castro se recollegerat pastorellis iugulandum tradidit, respondemus quod placet nobis vehementer quidquid per vos actum est in premissis." This is the only explicit account of an Aragonese native's direct involvement in the massacre at Montclus.

[68] ACA:C 383:52r (1320/9/10). The absolution does not mean that he was innocent. He may simply have paid a fine.

[69] ACA:C 219:310r (1321/5/4).

and four lower police officials of Jaca were absolved of having allowed the escape of some captured pastoureaux.[70] And of course the royal officials in charge of Montclus were prosecuted by the Crown: the lieutenant of the castellan for "consenting to the injury and robbery of the Jews," and the castellan (who had been away during the massacre) for failing to arrest his lieutenant and obstructing justice.[71] In short, specific examples, though few, can be found for all of the accusations of complicity made above. But royal officials made much more sweeping accusations than these, accusations that had more substantial implications for Christian-Jewish relations.

The broader activities of royal officials fall into three general categories: fining individuals accused of complicity, fining those who failed to answer the royal call to arms, and enforcing debts for which documents were stolen or destroyed by the pastoureaux and their accomplices. The first of these is hardest to define. Some 70 Christians, 7 from Montclus and the remainder from neighboring villages, were accused of participating in the crimes against the Jews of Montclus, though the precise crime is never specified.[72] Did they kill Jews? The unique mention of an Aragonese who found a Jew hiding in the castle and dragged him to the pastoureaux to be killed suggests that they did not. More probably they formed part of the mob that looted the homes of the Jews during or after the massacre, though there is no way of knowing with certainty. We do not even know how many of the accused were found guilty, nor of what their punishment consisted. But we do have a record of their socioeconomic status, or at least that of 28 of the defendants: the men from Ainsa.

On the 1st of August, 1320, the town crier of Ainsa announced that the movable and immovable property of these 28 men would be sold at auction to pay fines for the homicide of 337 Jews in Montclus. The next day it was noted

[70]ACA:C 383:60r (1320/9/13). It should be kept in mind, however, that the Crown generally accused police officials of complicity whenever a prisoner of any type escaped, in order to generate fine income.

[71]For the general charge against García Bardaji, the castellan's lieutenant, see 406:91r. García seems to have fled the country for a time. He was absolved in 487:191v (1333/9/23) (partially transcribed in Miret, "Le massacre des juifs," pp. 259–260, without archival reference). The charge, brought by the Jews of Montclus, provides few details but seems to concern the robbery of their goods and loan documents, not the massacre (pace Miret's "Il est presque certain que Garcia Bardaji . . . favorisa le massacre et le pillage," p. 259). The general charge of "consenting to the injury and robbery of the Jews" should not be taken to mean complicity in any strict sense, as the charges against the absent castellan (García Lop de Ançano) make clear. The document detailing these begins with the general formula, but the issues themselves are much more limited. First, the castellan failed to arrest his lieutenant and the lieutenant's assistant. Second, when the *sobrejuntero* rode up to the gates of the castle demanding that they be turned over to him, the castellan told him that they had gone out for victuals and were not in the castle. He may also have been held responsible for the fact that the castle was deemed insufficiently stocked with weapons, food, and other necessities. See 406:94v–95r (1320/7/30). Again, such charges of malfeasance against Crown officials were not uncommon, since the Crown treated them as a source of fine income.

[72]For the list of those accused, see ACA:C 406:91r–92r and 93v–94r, both dated 1320/7/28. The latter document, better preserved, is transcribed in full in Nirenberg, "Violence," pp. 351–354.

that no one was willing to bid on any of the movable goods of the accused, and a commission was assigned to assess the value of these goods and sell them, half the assessed price going to the Crown.[73] The records of this commission survive as our only source for the economic status of the accused. Not unexpectedly, the majority of the accused were very poor. Only 4 of the 28 possessed 50 sous or more in movable goods, 8 possessed no movable goods at all, and the balance owned nothing but the crudest of household objects. More surprising is the presence of some men of substance on the list. Berenguer de Portolas, by far the wealthiest, had 242 sous in movable goods, was owed 680 sous, including 500 sous owed him by the notary of the town, possessed houses worth at least 1,200 sous (the price officials obtained for them), and owned other property that gave him an annual rent of 300 sous. This was not fabulous wealth, but it was more than the great majority of his contemporaries.[74]

His fine, too, was larger. Berenguer paid more than 1,000 sous (how much more is not known) as penalty for his participation in the homicides.[75] Ferrer Daura, who we are told had only 16 sous in movable goods, was fined 200 sous, and managed to pay 70 of them,[76] while Johan d'Aran, who owned nothing, paid no fine because of his "poverty and old age."[77] Despite the survival of this type of detail, it is impossible to arrive at a total amount paid to the Crown in fines by those people accused of complicity in the massacre of the Jews. The process of collecting the fines, however, was enough to keep three experienced royal officials busy for at least two years.[78]

In the case of Montclus, some seventy accusations were made against, and fines extracted from, individuals. Other charges, less serious, were made at the collective level. The men of Muro and Tarantona (I have not been able to

[73]The refusal to bid competitively may have represented a form of resistance against royal officials, or a strategy to keep prices as low as possible. Such a strategy is documented in the southern United States. See S. Hahn, *The Roots of Southern Populism* (Oxford, 1983), pp. 81–84. It need not, however, be taken as a sign of sympathy for the pastoureaux.

[74]The commission's report is preserved in ACA:RP Apendice General no. 1044 (uncataloged), transcribed in full in Nirenberg, "Violence," pp. 300–312. Assessing relative wealth six hundred years after the fact is never easy. For some sense of scale, see D. Romano, "Prorrata de contribuyentes judíos de Jaca en 1377," *Sefarad* 42 (1982): 3–39, esp. p. 23; and José Camarena Mahiques, *Colección de documentos para la historia de Gandía y su comarca* (Gandía, 1959–1961), pp. 46–47. Even the phrase "non habet bona" is problematic. Guillermo de Binyech, who was described in ACA:RP Apendice General no. 1044 as having no goods and absent in "Gasconia," nevertheless owned sufficient property to satisfy his fine of 1,500 sous in the affair of Montclus. See ACA:C 384:142v–143r (1321/5/12).

[75]The fines of Berenguer de Portolas, Pedro Portolas de la Sala, Pedro Portolas de Castillione, and Ferran de Castilione, together totaled 2,600 sous. See ACA:C 386:32r (1322/7/10).

[76]For the fine, see ACA:C 384:77v (1321/4/5).

[77]For the remission granted Johan d'Aran, see ACA:C 384:54r (1321/3/10). Jacob, son of Garçia el Metge, received a similar remission for poverty. See ACA:C 384:50r (1321/3/6).

[78]From July of 1320 until August of 1322, when the remaining cases were suspended. See ACA:C 371:12v (1322/7/21) and ACA:C 386:90r–v (1322/8/14) for the suspensions.

CRUSADE AND MASSACRE IN ARAGON

locate the latter) paid 500 sous to be absolved of the charge of having consented to the robbery of the Jews of Montclus. In September of 1320, the town of Ruesta (more accurately, its *universitas*) was absolved of the charge that it had permitted the pastoureaux to torch and rob the Jewish aljama of the town. The town of Naval was given the opportunity to defend itself collectively against charges of robbing the goods of the Muslims of Naval, though fines were also paid by individuals.[79] These fines were substantial enough to have an effect on the local economy. Thus King James wrote to his son asking him to keep in mind when he set his fines that the area was very poor, since depopulation might result if the fines were too high.[80]

While it was a common bargaining ploy for taxpayers to warn that residents would flee if tax rates were set too high, the threat of depopulation seems not to have been an idle one in this case of judicial revenue extraction. The vassals of the Hospital in the mountains of Ayna, for example, fled their lands because they feared accusations of having participated in the affair at Montclus.[81] When Infant Alfonso absolved all those not actually imprisoned on charges of complicity in the massacre at Montclus, he stated that this absolution was necessitated by the destitution which royal justice had inflicted on the region.[82] Accusations of complicity had repercussions that reached far beyond the defendant. In case after case, the lords, wives, creditors, business associates, and family members of the accused complained of the Crown's seizing goods that did not belong to the accused.[83] Once mobilized, royal justice cut a very wide swath.

The Crown found an even broader basis for the exaction of fines in the charge of failing to appear when summoned to arms by royal officers. When the pastoureaux advanced through Aragon, the *sobrejunteros* of Huesca, Jaca, and Ribagorza had called the inhabitants of many villages in the region, both royal and seigneurial, to arms (*exercitum*). A substantial number must have answered the call, since the officials and their militias successfully defeated the pastoureaux. Of the townsmen and villagers who came when summoned we have no further notice: they were not of financial interest to the Crown. Those who

---

[79] For Muro and Tarantona, see ACA:C 383:46r (1320/8/11): "Consensisse raubarie bonorum." For Ruesta, ACA:C 383:61v (1320/9/29): ". . . conensisse [*sic*] invasioni, raubarie et subpositioni ignis factae judarie dicti loci [*sic*] de Ruesta per pastorellos." The price of the remission is unfortunately illegible. For permission granted to the municipality of Naval to appoint procurators to defend itself, see ACA:C 365:9r (1320/8/9). One individual chose to purchase his own remission. See ACA:C 383:51v (1320/9/10).

[80] ACA:C 219:256r (1321/3/13), referring to the region of Muntayna. In ACA:C 246:87r (1320/8/16), the king asked Alfonso to temper his asperity in setting monetary fines against people accused of complicity in the affair at Montclus, because many of these people were very poor.

[81] ACA:C 170:102v (1320/8/18). The commander of Barbastro complained that his rents were diminished by this depopulation. Officials were ordered to allow these vassals to return to their lands, so long as they gave surety of standing trial.

[82] ACA:C 386:90r–v (1322/8/14?).

[83] E.g., ACA:C 365:5v; 11r; 14v; 14r–v; 20v; all from August 1320.

did not, or whose compliance was inadequately noted by officials, are abundantly recorded in the Archive of the Crown of Aragon.

Almost as soon as the call to arms was issued, the investigation into noncompliance began.[84] Officials were ordered to account for every village under their jurisdiction, while appeals by seigneurs on behalf of their vassals were almost uniformly ignored. When a noble intervened on behalf of the men of Turres (belonging to the monastery of St. Victor), the prince replied that he would like to act mercifully, but that he could not do so because the king had ordered the fining of all who did not follow his officials. Other nobles, the prince stated, had made the same request, to which the prince wished he could accede.[85] Many villages claimed that they had been excused from taking up arms by royal officials themselves, or that they had attended but had not been given credit. In some cases, at least, this proved to be true. The *sobrejuntero* of Ribagorza, for example, assured the prince that he had personally excused the men of the village of "Vall de Gescau," so that proceedings against them should be halted.[86] Many others alleged that they could not be fined, because they were exempt by status, privilege, or custom from such duties. Nevertheless, the Crown collected large sums in fines from a number of villages and towns. The village of Gradilo paid 2,000 sous in fines. A partial list of fines paid by villages in the district of Boltaña alone totals approximately 5,450 sous.[87]

It is tempting to extrapolate the level of popular sympathy for the pastoureaux, as well as antipathy toward the Jews, from the extent of nonparticipation in the call to arms. Such an extrapolation would be problematic. To begin with, we have no way of knowing how many people did respond to the call to arms, or whether that call was represented as in defense of the Jews. All the surviving documentation concerns those places that, for fiscal reasons, were alleged not to have participated. Second, there is ample evidence that royal summonses for militia duty were routinely resisted, no matter what the occasion.[88] Both nobles and municipalities found objectionable the Crown's claim

---

[84]Orders to carry out investigations of those who did not respond to the call to arms are contained in ACA:C 406:93r (1320/7/28); ACA:C 406:95r (1320/7/29).

[85]ACA:C 407:2r (1320/8/16).

[86]ACA:C 365:17r (1320/8/16).

[87]For Gradilo see 384:118r (1321/4/26). For a listing of towns and villages in the district of Boltaña, together with their fines, see ACA:C 383:46v–47r (1320/8/16): Besine, 200 sous of Jaca (sj); Puertolas, 300 sj; Tella, 300 sj; Liguerre de Cinca, 100 sj; Revilla, 100 sj; Trillo, 300 sj; Delson, 400 sj; Boyl, 300 sj; Arcusa, 300 sj; Castejón de Sobrarbe, 500 sj; Montclus, Mediano, Alazans, Plan, and Palauelo, 450 sj; Naval, 500 sj; Ainsa, 1,000 sj; Boltaña, 700 sj. The remissions for Ainsa and Naval are repeated on 48r, dated the following day, but this time including the charges of complicity in the attack on the Jews of Montclus and the robbery of the Muslims of Naval. I have not been able to locate some of the places on the list.

[88]Two contemporary examples: the men of Cervera were fined 8,000 sous of Barcelona (sb) for failing to report to a muster against the rebellious noble B. Fulc: ACA:C 384:118r (1321/4/26). Proceedings were begun against the men of Manresa on the same account. They were to be fined 100 sb for each member of the upper class (*mayoribus*), 50 sb for the middle, and 20 sb for the

that it was owed military service (or a fine in lieu of service) on demand. Their objections to this practice formed part of the platform of the unions that repeatedly took up arms against the monarchy.[89] In such a conflictual context, it is impossible to tell whether the lack of response to royal summons signifies hatred of the Jews, sympathy for the pastoureaux, resistance to regalian rights perceived as arbitrary, or simply a preference for redeeming military service with cash fines (which could sometimes be evaded) rather than in person.

In at least one case, the Crown attempted to move from charges of failure to appear when called to the more general charge of failure to adequately resist the pastoureaux. Infant Alfonso, angry that the municipal council of Barbastro had apparently permitted pastoureaux to sell goods stolen from their victims, tried to take members of the council hostage in order to secure a large fine. The action was extreme, and it was protested as such. By mid-August, the charges had been dismissed as against the privilege and custom of Aragon.[90]

The third sphere of widespread "state" activity in the wake of the pastoureaux was the collection and enforcement of loans made by Jews to Christians. As the documentation constantly reminds us, during the sack of Montclus the Jews' documents were burned, looted, and dispersed throughout the countryside.[91] A box of documents was found in Barbastro, and other documents appeared in the homes of Christians of Montclus; the vast majority were doubtless lost.[92] Not all of these documents concerned debts. Christian squatters, for example, took advantage of the destruction of property deeds by occupying

---

minoribus. See ACA:C 384:120r (1321/4/23). A decade later King Alfonso's Crusade against Granada would be frustrated by the same nobiliary and municipal resistance. See Sánchez, "La Corona de Aragón y el Reino Nazarí de Granada durante el siglo XIV."

[89] See C. Laliena Corbera, "La adhesión de las ciudades a la Unión: poder real y conflictividad social en Aragón a fines del XIII," in *Aragón en la Edad Media* 8 (1989): 402, 411–412; A. Wolf, "Los *Fori Aragonum* de 1247 y el Vidal Mayor," in *Anuario de Historia del Derecho Español* 53 (1983): 197–201; González, *Las Uniones aragonesas*, 1:397–398.

[90] I use the word "apparently" because no specific allegations survive, other than those listed against officials of various municipalities in ACA:C 406:85r–86r (1320/7/13). In ACA:C 170:98r–v (1320/8/15), King James informs Alfonso that the University of Barbastro has protested that the prince was acting against the *fuero* of Aragon. The prince, charging that the sworn men of Barbastro "in resistendo pastorellis qui terram nostram intraverunt fuerant negligentes," had seized the men "tanquam capti" until they pledged adequate guarantees ("fidancias"). The king ordered Alfonso to drop the charges because they were indeed against *fuero*, which he did in ACA:C 365:21v (1320/8/19). Barbastro had both a Muslim and a Jewish community, neither of which was reported to have been attacked by the pastoureaux.

[91] ACA:C 171:261r (1321/4/3), James II to Infant Alfonso: ". . . bene scitis quod quando gentes pastorells [*sic*] vocate ad castrum Montisclus venerunt et interfecerunt quamplures judeos habitantes in ipso loco, fuerunt barrigiata instrumenta debitorum quae debebantur eisdem super quibus reficiendis in notis fuit facta provisio quam vos scitis." ACA:C 430:172v (1328/12/30), ACA:C 173:197v (1321/7/7), and ACA:C 170:58v (1320/7/22) are among many other documents that allude to the event.

[92] For the box found in Barbastro, see ACA:C 364:235v (1320/8/1). For documents found in the houses of Christians of Montclus, see ACA:C 384:227v–228r (1321/10/6).

Jewish lands illegally.[93] Nevertheless, Montclus had been a center of credit activity, lending (and borrowing) sums both large and small all over the surrounding countryside and in surrounding towns; those involved in these transactions included nobles and peasants, clergy and laity.[94] The reconstruction and exploitation of this credit network became a primary concern of the Crown, as heir to the loans made by those Jews who had died without issue.

The Crown began by ordering the reconstruction of the documentation. Notaries in the towns where the Jews of Montclus did business were to make their record books available to royal officials so that documents whose original no longer existed could be reproduced.[95] This procedure was not cheap, and the cost seems to have been divided between the Crown, as heir to the dead Jews of Montclus, and the surviving Jews of the town.[96] Once the documents were reconstructed, the real conflict began. In normal times, a borrower's possession of the original promissory note constituted proof that the debt had been repaid.[97] But since so many original notes were stolen during the sack of Montclus, royal officials refused to acknowledge such notes as proof of payment. In town after town, debtors complained that they were being forced to repay loans they had already paid. The inhabitants of Boyl, for example, complained that the burden of double payment was so great that it was causing the depopulation of the town.[98]

---

[93]ACA:C 173:197v (1321/7/7): ". . . cum ad nostrum pervenerit auditum quod a tempore citra quo judaria dicti loci Montisclusi destruita extitit per pastorellos et alios aliqui tam clerici quam laici occupaverunt auctoritate propria et sibi apropiaverunt de terris seu possessionibus judeorum predictorum easque sibi retinere conantur ex eo videlicet si sciunt instrumenta dictarum terrarum seu possessionem non appere(?) cum fuerint amissa seu combusta tempore destructionis predictae."

[94]Without notarial records it is impossible to reconstruct the credit activity of the Jews of Montclus in any detail. For an idea of the size of some loans, see ACA:C 385:185v–186r (1322/5/9), which concerns the debts of a knight owed to deceased Jews of Montclus. The cash debts alone (a large amount of grain was also owed) totaled 1,300 sj. Bonaffos, Jucef, and Vidal Gallipapa, perhaps the most prominent lenders in Montclus, lent the noble Thomas Pedro de Foces 1,300 sous (s), but forfeited the principal, an equal amount in interest, and an additional 1,000 s in fines when the borrower charged them with illegal usury. See ACA:C 220:65r (1321/8/2). Much smaller loans are also documented, and some Jews of Montclus operated pawnshops, on which see ACA:C 364:240r–v (1320/8/6). For an example of a loan of 500 s made by a Christian of Estadella to two Jews of Montclus, see ACA:C 365:11r (1320/8/11).

[95]See, among many possible examples, ACA:C 170:58v (1320/7/22); ACA:C 384:29r–v (1321/2/20).

[96]ACA:C 384:23r (1321/2/11) stipulates such a divided payment to Raimundo de Alagon, notary of Ainsa. As late as 1328 Pedro de Canelles, the officer in charge of debt reconstruction from February of 1321 on, had still not been paid his salary by the Jews of Montclus: ACA:C 430:172v (1328/12/30).

[97]Joseph Shatzmiller details the niceties of loan documentation in his *Shylock Reconsidered: Jews, Moneylending, and Medieval Society* (Berkeley, 1990), chap. 1, here p. 14.

[98]For the complaints from Boyl, see ACA:C 174:195v–196r (1322/4/4), from King James II to the Infant Alfonso; and ACA:C 370:91v (1322/4/30), from Infant Alfonso to Pedro de Canelles, the official in charge of debt collection. The inhabitants of Montclus had also complained of double

Charges of complicity, evasion of military service, and nonpayment of debts were the means by which the Crown linked the population at large to the actions of the shepherds and their handful of native accomplices, and all three evoked cries of destitution and depopulation from inhabitants of the area around Montclus. For the vast majority of that area's residents who were never accused of any direct participation in the crimes of the pastoureaux, the events of 1320 constituted an object lesson: Jews and their affairs had brought the judicial and fiscal apparatus of the state to bear upon their towns and villages. We have little evidence of local hatred of the Jews before the entry of the pastoureaux, but plenty after the trials began. Already in August of 1320 the king wrote to the town councils of Barbastro, Ainsa, and Naval. The surviving Jews of Montclus had complained that many people hated them because of the inquisitions being carried out by Infant Alfonso, and the king wanted the Jews protected.[99] By July of 1321 relations had deteriorated to such a point that violence was expected:

> Because of the inquests carried out against those who participated in or abetted the invasion and destruction of the Jewish aljama of Montclus committed by the pastoureaux, we have heard that some people of that region hate the Jews living there. . . . Therefore we desire and command you to defend strongly each and every [Jew] of the said town of Montclus against anyone perpetrating . . . any violence or injury against them . . . admitting the Jews, if necessary, within the walls of the said castle for their protection, security, and well-being, and exhibiting the customary diligence in the custody of the castle.[100]

Crown, Jews, and locals alike understood that the state's activities of extortion and retribution in the wake of the pastoureaux had had a greater impact on Christian-Jewish relations in the region than the presence of the shepherds themselves. Violence and fiscality marched hand in hand. In Aragon, unlike France, the story of the Shepherds' Crusade was written by bureaucrats, not chroniclers.

. . . . .

---

payment but lost their appeal. For the complaint, ACA:C 384:209r (1321/8/23). The appeal is denied in ACA:C 384:227v–228r (1321/10/6). There are many more examples, but these are chosen as representative.

[99]ACA:C 170:125v–126r, 126r (1320/8/21).

[100]ACA:C 173:197v (1321/7/7): "Cum ratione processus facti [sic] adversus eos qui interfuerunt vel operam prestituerunt invasioni et destructioni aliame judeorum Montisclusi facte per pastorellos, aliqui de partibus illis ut intelleximus odio habeant judeos inibi habitantes et eis etiam cominentur. Idcirco volumus vobisque dicimus et mandamus quatenus universos et singulos dictae villae Montisclusi manuteneatis et viriliter deffendatis adversus quoscumque inferentes seu inferre conantes eis violentiam aut iniuriam aliquam vel gravamen, nec permitatis ipsos a quoquam indebite molestari, admitendo etiam judeos ipsos si necesse fuerit infra ambitum murorum dicti castri pro tuitione, securitate et salutate ipsorum, sollitam tamen circa custodiam ipsius castri diligentiam adhibendo." The document is transcribed in full in Nirenberg, "Violence," p. 321.

If the activities of the shepherds in Aragon were indeed so limited and tell us so little about the position of the Jews, why have they been infused with such significance by historians? Yitzhak Baer, for example, in his incomparable *History of the Jews in Christian Spain*, placed 1320 squarely in the trajectory of cataclysmic events that defined the "era of decline": 1306 (the expulsion of the Jews from France), 1320, 1321, and 1348. These events, for Baer, both symbolized and caused what he saw as the deteriorating position of Iberian Jews in the fourteenth century.

Some contemporaries agreed with Baer. The anonymous mystic of Zaragoza, who lived through some of these events, connected them without hesitation:

> And behold, fourteen years after the banishment of 5066 [1306], in the year of wrath and anger the Shepherds came and slew about eight thousand men of Israel. . . . And concerning this matter I preached to the multitude on the verse "for the hand of the Lord hath not waxed short for salvation [Is. 59.1]"—meaning salvation from the Shepherds—"nor is his ear dull from hearing"—meaning from hearing the libellous accusations made against us of having poisoned the waters, on account of which they slew most holy ones in France.[101]

But the anonymous mystic was, like all good prophets, in a distinct minority. His tract went on to attack the elites of the Jewish aljama of Zaragoza who, like those cosmopolitan Jews described by R. Kalonymos in his *Even Boḥan*, were unperturbed by this chain of disasters.[102]

Not until after the expulsion of the Jews from Spain in 1492 would the mystic's prophecies find a sympathetic ear. To Joseph Ha-Kohen, Samuel Usque, Salomon Ibn Verga, and the other Spanish exiles collectively known as the "lachrymose school" writing history in the sixteenth century, 1320 was another landmark in a vale of tears. History for them was an accounting of the tribulations of Israel that climaxed in the Spanish expulsion, a narrative so terrible in retrospect that it suggested the imminence of redemption. It was this teleology that they strove to convey in their chronicles, which until recently provided our only memory of the pastoureaux. However, the events they narrated did not "derive their significance . . . from any intrinsic links they might have to one another, but from [the] conviction that these events [were] fulfillments of biblical prophecies that predicted what would happen to the Jewish people in exile."[103]

This proved a narrative of extraordinary force for Jewish historians writing in the aftermath of a disaster greater than Ha-Kohen could ever have imagined.

---

[101] Baer, *The Jews*, 2:20, translating and discussing *Livnath ha-Sapir* (Jerusalem, 1913), fols. 9b, 25–26, 38b. See in general vol. 2, chap. 8, "The Era of Decline in Aragon."

[102] *Even Boḥan* (Lemberg, 1865), pp. 24 f., 35 f., discussed by Baer, *The Jews*, p. 19.

[103] See Y. Yerushalmi, *Zakhor: Jewish History and Jewish Memory* (Seattle, 1982), pp. 57–65, here p. 64; idem, "Messianic Impulses in Joseph ha-Cohen," in *Jewish Thought in the Sixteenth Century*, ed. D. Cooperman (Cambridge, MA, 1983), pp. 460–487.

Yitzhak Baer was among the most eloquent of these historians. Whereas in his early work Baer had argued against the view of earlier historians that the period of Jewish life in Christian Spain was an era of decline, by the late 1930s he was insisting that "Jewish history in the Middle Ages was a relentless series of persecutions."[104] Baer concluded *Galut*, his somber study of the diaspora first published in Nazi Berlin, by severing the Jewish experience from historical context: "There is a power that lifts the Jewish people out of the realm of causal history." And in 1955 he wrote, "Every episode in the long history of our people, every significant point in our historical existence, contains within it the secret of all previous and subsequent generations." History, including that of the massacre at Montclus, was prophecy.[105]

Epilogue

Throughout the preceding pages little has been said of contemporary Jewish reactions to the massacre at Montclus because little is known. But the royal bureaucracy did memorialize one action of the Jews, an act of violence. In the days following the slaughter, many of the Jewish communities of Aragon sent delegations to Montclus to help with the burial of the dead. Once there, the Jews rioted. They allegedly cut down trees, destroyed the bridge of the town, insulted local Christians, and smashed the doors of some houses belonging to murdered Jews. It was, the king would later agree, an understandable outburst of anger and sorrow. It was also, like any other act of violence involving Jews, an opportunity for state intervention. Immediately the fiscal apparatus was set in motion. In the only intrusion of emotion into our documentation, the king urged moderation upon the prince because of the great sorrow that must have afflicted the Jews when they saw the devastation at Montclus. This argument was quickly followed by a more important consideration: the Jews were paying the king a large subsidy for the conquest of Sardinia and the purchase of the county of Urgell, and he did not wish the flow of money to be interrupted. Nevertheless, the fines were substantial. The aljama of Fraga was fined 5,000 sous, Monzón 8,000 sous, Barbastro a similar amount. Jews of Lleida who had participated in the violence fled their homes, fearing the prince's justice. In its reaction to events at Montclus the royal fisc was ecumenical as well as thorough.

---

[104]Baer criticized the notion of decline in *Die Juden im christlichen Spanien* (Berlin, 1936; reprint, London, 1970), vol. 2, "Kastilien/Inquisitionakten," p. xxiv. The quotation about persecution is from his review of S. Baron's *A Social and Religious History of the Jews* (New York, 1937), published in *Zion* 3 (1938): 290–291, and cited in Myers, " 'From Zion will go forth Torah,' " p. 240.

[105]Y. Baer, *Galut*, trans. R. Warshow (Lanham, MD, 1988), p. 120; idem, *Yisrael ba-ʿamim* (Hebrew) (Jerusalem, 1955), p. 117, cited in Myers, " 'From Zion will go forth Torah,' " p. 255, and in E. Shmueli, *Seven Jewish Cultures: A Reinterpretation of Jewish History and Thought* (New York, 1990), p. 225. For Shmueli's general critique of the "Jerusalem School" of Jewish history, see pp. 217–233.

Thanks to its bureaucracy we have record of the violent tribute paid by the Jews of Aragon to their fallen coreligionists.[106]

[106]Record of the event is preserved in ACA:C 170:93r, 101v–102r; ACA:C 219:176r (published in Baer, *Die Juden*, 1:222–223, no. 176/2); ACA:C 246:89v–90r; ACA:C 364:236r–v; ACA:C 365:15r, 22r; ACA:C 383:45v–46r, 63r; ACA:C 384:27v, 31r–v, 37r–v; ACA:C 406:98r; ACA:C 407:6v–7r.

Chapter 4

LEPERS, JEWS, MUSLIMS, AND POISON

IN THE CROWN (1321)

I N FRANCE, I suggested earlier, the accusations of 1321 against Jews, lepers, and Muslims, drawn from an ancient hoard of stereotypes as they may have been, were used in novel ways to resist evolving royal power and to further jurisdictional conflicts. Within a French context, this strategic adaptation and adoption of vocabularies of hatred is easily overlooked both because the magnitude of the violence numbs analysis and because we lack the volume of archival evidence necessary to demonstrate how these accusations worked in practice, how their usefulness was negotiated case by case. Herein lies the value of the Aragonese comparison. Violence was extensive within the Crown in 1321, but because we do not have the narrative sources for the burning and torture that exist for France, our visceral sense of horror is suspended. Conversely, because in Catalonia-Aragon the great majority of surviving sources were produced by attempts to appropriate, limit, or redirect the violence, these heighten our sense of the strategic value of the accusations. Much of this chapter is a narration of these transformations and negotiations as reflected in Aragonese documentation. Intended as an extended example of the dynamic relationship between collective anxieties and individual actions, it serves as well as a base from which to ask why the same accusation had such different effects in France and the Crown of Aragon.

News of the French accusations spread quickly to other monarchies. On June 2, 1321, King Sancho of Mallorca wrote a letter to his cousin and overlord, James II of Aragon. The letter included details of what Sancho had learned from his procurator at the papal court in Avignon:

> Know also, lord, that lepers have been captured in Avignon and subjected to torture, and it is said that they have confessed that they were to poison all the waters of wells and fountains that were outside of houses, and that this is to be presumed. It has already been decreed in Avignon that no one should use water from outside fountains. And it is said that Jews consented to all this. We are notifying Your Serenity of this so that you may take precautions that from this or similar deeds no harm come to your people. In order to have greater certainty of the aforesaid, we have sent one of our couriers to . . . the Roman Curia, so that he might fully inform himself of the aforesaid and of all that is to be done in the aforesaid, and [. . .] write to us fully

afterwards. And if it seems that what he writes to us is significant for you, we will write to Your Serenity.[1]

After nearly a week of consideration, James ordered the borders patrolled. In a letter to officials throughout Catalonia and Aragon, the king explained that he had been informed by people of repute that the king of France had ordered the lepers arrested because they had planned to infect the people and had formed factions against the public good. The lepers, seeking to escape "the lash of justice," were crossing the borders clandestinely into the Crown of Aragon. The king's order was consciously restrained: officials were to bar entry into the kingdom to any lepers. Those who had already entered were to be captured. Nonleprous travelers from France were not to be harassed. Jews were not mentioned.[2]

Given such caution, the king's subsequent actions seem remarkable. On the 27th of June, he wrote again to officials throughout the Crown. From inquests and confessions he knew for certain, the king informed them, that foreigners, both lepers and nonlepers, wished to make his people leprous by poisoning their water. Many of these malefactors had fled other lands and had come to Aragon to perpetrate their crimes. The king recalled that he had written his officials on this subject earlier, but now, "since it is difficult, truly even impossible, to recognize such [lepers] and identify them," the king was choosing a path of more stringent caution. Officials were to arrest all foreigners, male and female, who were not specifically and obviously above suspicion. Those found to be lepers (and other guilty persons) were to be tried immediately and punished. Nonlepers were to be escorted to the borders and ejected from the Crown. Finally, native lepers who did not live in leprosaria were to be imprisoned so

---

[1] ACA:C cr. Jaume II (1321/6/2), published without further archival reference by H. Finke, *Acta Aragonensia*, vol. 3 (Berlin, 1922), pp. 390–391, no. 178/1. James replied to this letter three days later, requesting that Sancho keep him informed of developments so that he could decide on the best course of action. See ACA:C 246:223r (1321/6/5). Lepers were burned in Avignon in 1321. See Bériac, "La persécution," p. 213.

[2] ACA:C 246:227r (1321/6/10): ". . . didiscerimus quod illustris rex francorum mandavit capi universos et singulos leprosos in suis regnis et terris positos pro exequenda justicia in eisdem pro eo videlicet quia ut asseritur predicti leprosi nituntur et nisi sunt certis excogitatis modis gentes alias regnorum predictorum morbo inficere quo preniuntur inter se aliasque illicitas factiones etiam contra rem publicam inhierunt [*sic*]. Et non nulli ex dictis leprosis, laqueum justitiae evadere cupientes [. . .], ad terras et regna nostra clandestine se transferunt, ex quorum praesencia posset nostre rei publice et gentibus terre nostre grande periculum invenere [*sic*]. Idcirco . . . vos in jurisdictione vobis comissa faciatis publice praeconitzari ne aliquis de dictis leprosis sub pena corporis terras nostras ingredi audeant, quodque siqui post dictam praeconitzationem ausi fuerint ingredi illos protinus capiatis et captos teneatis donec a nobis aliud receperitis in mandatis. Verum ex praesenti nostra provisione non intendimus ut aliis subditis regis francie ingressus ad terras nostras aliquatenus interdicatur." The document is transcribed in full in Nirenberg, "Violence," pp. 327 f.

that they could not travel about. They were to be told that if they left their place of imprisonment, they would be executed without mercy.[3]

It may seem odd to the modern reader that King James treated leprosy as something hard to identify, rather than as a disease with clearly recognizable symptoms. Yet in the Middle Ages leprosy was difficult to diagnose. *Mycobacterium leprae*, the infectious agent of leprosy (Hansen's disease in more modern terminology) can cause a multitude of symptoms in infected individuals.[4] Medieval doctors, aware of the difficulties of diagnosis and of the legal disabilities attached to officially diagnosed lepers, but believing leprosy to be a highly infectious disease that needed to be isolated early, worked to develop a set of diagnostic techniques. Some of these, such as pricking extremities to detect loss of sensation and looking for facial deformations, were effective in identifying advanced forms of lepromatous leprosy. Others, like placing a drop of the patient's blood in his urine and observing the mixture, were not. The frustration of doctors at the difficulties of diagnosis they encountered are evident in the *Lilium medicine*, a diagnostic manual written by Bernard de Gordon, eminent physician of Montpellier, in 1303. Bernard included a chapter called "De lepra" because he felt that leprosy was not well diagnosed in his day, concluding with an

---

[3] ACA:C 246:232r–v (1321/6/27): "Cum pro certo sciverimus . . . quod aliqui de partibus alienis tam leprosi quam alii non leprosi tractatu et assensu dictorum leprosorum volentes inficere gentes nostras venenis et aliis poculis mortiferis nisi sunt aquas corrumpere, ut ex eis bibentes interficerentur aut leprosi fierent, et quod plures ex eis fugientes de aliis regnis ad regna et terras nostras se transtulerunt, ubi sunt pro perpetrandis maleficiis supradictis. Nosque deceat licet iam inde vobis scripserimus tantis periculis providere cum sit difficile immo verius quodammodo impossibile tales cognoscere sive discernere et in dubiis sit via tutior eligenda. Idcirco volumus . . . incontinenti quilibet vestrum in jurisdictione sibi comissa cum diligentia perquiratis omnes alienigenas tam mares quam feminas, de quibus nulla notitia habeatur, quod suspicione careant predictorum, et eos cum inveneritis capiatis, et si quos ex eis leprosos inveneritis, contra eos de predictis cum summa diligentia inquiratis, et ipsos ac alios quos culpabiles inveneritis in predictis graviter puniatis, ceteros vero non leprosos captos a terra nostra eici faciatis sub fida custodia sit quod non possint [nocere], iniungentes eisdem in exitu quod extunc non redeant ad terras nostras aliter quod corporaliter punirentur. Insuper leprosos de partibus nostris in jurisdictione vestra constitutos qui iam sunt in certis domibus collocati faciatis sub arca clausura teneri plus solito sit quod exire inde nequeant ullo modo. Significantes eisdem quod si spreto mandato nostro inde exierint absque remedio morientur." The document is transcribed in full in Nirenberg, "Violence," pp. 328–330. There is also a partial transcription by Finke, *Acta Aragonensia*, vol. 2, no. 605.

[4] Patients with high resistance, for example, experience a very slow progression of the disease, called tuberculoid leprosy, and exhibit a wide variety of symptoms. Patients with low resistance suffer from the more severe lepromatous leprosy, whose symptoms form part of the popular image of the disease: skin lesions, progressive loss of nerve function in the extremities resulting in disfiguring injuries and deformations of the hands and feet, deformation of nasal passages, hoarsening of the voice, and so forth. A third, "indeterminate" form tends to evolve in its later stages toward one of the two basic forms. Without immunological techniques like the Mitsuda test, diagnosis is particularly difficult in the tubercular, intermediate, and early stages of the lepromatous forms of the disease.

anecdote that brought all these frustrations to the fore. He had just examined a man with severe lesions in the extremities but with no facial deformations:

> I wanted to absolve him, and I repeatedly asked him whether any sign had appeared in his face. He had remained quite like this for about twenty years, and he still lives with that ugliness of the extremities but without anything showing in his face. Hence I guess, with the conjecture closest to the truth, that it was not leprosy; nor does it seem possible that he would have lasted for so long without his face being disfigured. And therefore, even though I once thought differently, now that I have labored diligently in this work, I am of another opinion and I would no longer judge him leprous. However, God knows the truth, I do not know.[5]

Medieval medical theories of the spread of the disease doubtless contributed to King James's worries. It was thought, for example, that certain types of infectious lepers could hide their disease, at least in its early stages. According to some, children of lepers always inherited their parents' disease and could spread it by contact as casual as a glance of the eyes, though they might remain asymptomatic until much later in life. Women could also be hidden sources of leprosy, first because they were believed more resistant than men to the disease, and second because they could transmit it sexually. Though women who had sex with lepers would not themselves be infected (the walls of their wombs were dense and could not be permeated by the leper's sperm), the sperm would remain within the woman, infecting the next male to have sex with her, since the tissues of the penis were thought to be porous and easily penetrated by infectious agents.[6]

So the leprosy King James confronted in 1321 was both more common and a good deal more frightening than that with which modern readers are acquainted. It was deadly, difficult to diagnose, and insidious, and bound up as well with worries about sexuality, sin, and pollution.[7] King James was not ec-

---

[5]The translation is from L. Demaitre, "The Description and Diagnosis of Leprosy by Fourteenth-Century Physicians," *Bulletin of the History of Medicine* 59 (1985): 327–344, here p. 341. On Bernard of Gordon, see also Demaitre's *Doctor Bernard de Gordon: Professor and Practitioner* (Toronto, 1980). The literature on medieval leprosy diagnosis is vast. See, inter alia, E. Jeanselme, "Comment l'Europe au Moyen Age se protégea contre la lèpre," *Bulletin de la Société Française d'Histoire de la Médecine* 25 (1931): 1–155; F.-O. Touati, "Facies leprosorum: réflexions sur le diagnostic facial de la lèpre au Moyen Age," *Histoire des Sciences Médicales* 20 (1986): 57–66; and for an overview, Bériac, *Histoire des lépreux*, pp. 13–56. Increasingly the consensus among medical historians seems to be that by the fourteenth century physicians were diagnosing leprosy with a fair degree of accuracy.

[6]For belief in the heredity of leprosy see the texts quoted in Demaitre, "Description and Diagnosis," p. 332. It is not clear at what point such children were thought to be infectious. On the possibility of infection through mere eye contact (though in this case the example is of an adult infecting a child), see *The Prose Salernitan Questions*, ed. B. Lawn (London, 1979), p. 98. On the alleged immunity of women to leprosy, and their role in its sexual transmission, see D. Jacquart and C. Thomasset, *Sexuality and Medicine in the Middle Ages* (Princeton, 1988), pp. 188–193.

[7]Some of these worries were discussed in chap. 2. A few Iberian examples are given below. For more on the relationship among leprosy, sin, and pollution, see Pichon, "La lèpre et le péché"; N.

centric in his belief that it was "difficult, even impossible," to identify lepers, or that they might pose a danger to his kingdom. Nevertheless, his edict, while understandable in the context of medieval medical culture, is politically astounding. It creates a category of malefactor that is avowedly impossible to identify with certainty, thereby encouraging all the excesses of accusation that the king had apparently been at pains to avoid in his first edict. Even more surprising, it authorizes the imprisonment of virtually any foreigner—to my knowledge an unprecedented act in the Crown of Aragon. Because the edict so clearly lent itself to manipulation and (mal?)appropriation, the history of its reception provides an opportunity to describe the ways in which people argued over the terms and meanings of a concrete language of persecution. In the pages that follow, the edict's targets will be studied separately: first foreigners, foreign lepers, and others accused of well poisoning, then native lepers. Jews and Muslims, conspicuously unmentioned by the king, will be treated last.

. . . . .

In France the accusations against the lepers had been instigated by municipal interests, in defiance of the king. In Aragon such accusations were initially under royal control, and the king took a personal and aggressive interest in the capture of poisoners. On the 4th of July he wrote to officials of the town of Martorell, insisting that they hand over to his men one "master John," a leader of the poisoners. James admitted that Martorell was not under royal jurisdiction, but claimed that because this horrible crime touched upon the entirety of the public good and the king's person, jurisdiction in the case belonged to the Crown. Town officials seem to have been unpredisposed to agree, because James concluded by threatening that if they refused to hand master John over, the vicar of Barcelona had been commanded to force them to do so with his army.[8] The vicar had already captured several men on charges of well poisoning. At least some of the accused had powerful patrons. In the case of one man, captured carrying poisonous "powders," the king's daughter-in-law, the countess of Urgell, herself intervened. Such intervention by nobles and courtiers on behalf of defendants with some connection to them was quite common in the Crown of Aragon, but in this case the king was prepared to ignore patronage. All the vicar's prisoners were to be tortured and punished, and the king was to be informed of the results.[9] The countess's intercession did eventually earn her client the benefit of royal review: after two weeks James ordered the vicar to

---

Bériou and F.-O. Touati, *Voluntate Dei Leprosus: les lépreux entre conversion et exclusion aux XIIème et XIIIème siècles* (Spoleto, 1991).

[8] ACA:C 246:233 r–v (1321/7/4). The letter to the vicar is ACA:C 246:233r (same date). Both are transcribed in full in Nirenberg, "Violence," pp. 330–333.

[9] ACA:C 246:233r (1321/7/4).

send him the prisoner, now given a name (Jacobo Rotlandis), together with any confession and testimony in the case.[10]

Like the vicar of Barcelona, royal officials throughout the Crown were busy apprehending suspect foreigners. The *sobrejuntero* of Huesca and Jaca, whose bailiwick ran along the Pyrenean frontiers, sent the king confessions extorted from people accused of poisoning the waters of Toulouse (France). In Barbastro, also near the borders, two Basque men ("vascones") and one woman were arrested. They were to be sent to the vicar of Barcelona. The bailiff of Manresa was ordered to torture the eight foreigners he had captured, and to burn them if they confessed. In Montblanc the vicar captured ten men, some of them lepers, on the accusation of poisoning waters. Some of them were tortured, and all who confessed were to be burned. Again, eagerness to capitalize on the accusations seems to have generated jurisdictional conflict, but this time between royal officials. The castellan and bailiff of Montblanc complained that jurisdiction in the case was theirs, since the poisoners had been captured within the limits of the city.[11]

These cases seem to have been the most serious: so serious that the king insisted that all court records be kept secret, lest others learn to imitate such a horrible crime.[12] There was also a murkier world of accusation. King, officials, and private individuals alike could use the suspicion of poisoning to harass and extort. Here charges were less specific, and actions against foreigners much more widespread. It was fear of such action that prompted wealthier travelers to purchase letters of safe-conduct from the Crown: protection money of a sort. Thus Ponç de Rayes, a Basque, secured a letter from the king stating that he was not suspected of well poisoning and should therefore not be harassed.[13]

Basque travelers had special reason to be concerned. Because of the existence of "leper" lineages in the various regions described as "Vasconia," Basques were favored targets of accusations and extortions. In their home regions these lineages, known as "cagots" or "chrestiennes," as well as by other names, enjoyed a peculiar legal status predicated on the belief that their leprosy was transmitted through inheritance from generation to generation. In 1321, however, such

[10]ACA:C 173:197r–v (1321/7/18).

[11]For the suspects from Toulouse, ACA:C 246:234r (1321/7/5). For Barbastro, ACA:C 246:253v (1321/8/10). For Manresa, ACA:C 246:234r (1321/7/6). For the arrests at Montblanc, ACA:C 246:232v (1321/7/7), and on the jurisdictional quarrel, ACA:C 173:173r (1321/7/9).

[12]ACA:C 246:239v (1321/7/13): ". . . ne tam nephandi et horribilis criminis actus gentibus patefiant vel transeant in exemplum vobis dicimus et mandamus quatenus processus inquisitionum seu confessionum factos vel faciendos coram vobis contra dictos leprosos et alios de predictis inculpatos non publicetis neque pandatis alicui seu aliquibus nisi in quantum de necessitate fuerit et pro exequtione justitie fuerit opportunum." The document is transcribed in full in Nirenberg, "Violence," pp. 334 f.

[13]Safe-conduct for Ponç de Rayes, ACA:C 173:206v (1321/7/15). For other safe-conducts to foreigners from Bruges and elsewhere, see ACA:C 173:194r (1321/7/17), ACA:C 369:80r (1321/7/23).

ancestry became dangerous. Thus when the physician Amonaut, "de partibus vasconie," decided to move to Aragon, he wrote to the king that he feared harassment, because "it is said that he is from a lineage of lepers." King James ordered that if Amonaut was not a leper himself, he should be permitted to enter the kingdom despite being of such a lineage. Amonaut did indeed move to Aragon and seems to have assimilated fairly well, but Basques in upland Aragon would remain vulnerable to this type of accusation for many years to come.[14]

Whatever the concerns of the Basques, the Genoese were the group most ferociously attacked, and their plight makes clear to what extent the ways in which fear of poisoning were manifested depended on the political vulnerabilities and strategic needs of the moment. Genoa and Barcelona were commercial rivals of long standing, a rivalry exacerbated by being subsumed within the broader struggle between Angevins and Catalans for political hegemony in the western Mediterranean, and between Guelfs and Ghibellines for power in Italy. In 1321 tensions ran particularly high as James II concluded military and diplomatic preparations for yet another (not the last) confrontation with the Genoese, the invasion of Sardinia. In Sicily, these tensions were manifest in a riot between Catalans and Genoese that left three hundred dead. In the Crown of Aragon, they merged with the rhetoric of poisoning and resulted instead in judicial violence.[15]

---

[14]Amonaut was granted permission to enter Aragon by Infant Alfonso in ACA:C 371:5v (1322/7/19). A decade later, in ACA:C 445:33v–34r (1331/3/17), it was stated by "Monautus, cirurgici de partibus vasconie," that "in the time when it was said that the lepers were poisoning the waters, the said Monaut moved from Vasconia to the kingdom of Aragon with six horses." See also M. McVaugh, *Medicine before the Plague: Practitioners and Their Patients in the Crown of Aragon, 1285–1345* (Cambridge, 1993), p. 220. The bibliography on "cagots" is growing. See most recently F. Bériac, *Des lépreux aux cagots: recherches sur les sociétés marginales en Aquitaine médiévale* (Bordeaux, 1990); A. Guerreau and Y. Guy, *Les cagots du Béarn: recherches sur le développement inégal au sein du système féodal européen* (Montrouge, 1988); F. Idoate, *Documentos sobre agotes y grupos afines en Navarra* (Pamplona, 1973). On pp. 15 ff. Idoate describes the imprisonment of many lepers in Navarre during the persecution of 1321 and suggests that many lepers fled the country. Monaut may have been one of these. For much later examples of such accusations against Basques in upland Aragon, see ACA:C 1898:160r–161v (1391/2/1), published by J. Riera i Sans, "Supuestos agotes vascos en Monzón," *Príncipe de Viana* 36 (1975): 465–470, where seventeen individuals from ten families of Basque provenance were accused by their enemies of being lepers and "segregated Christians" (*Cristians apartats*). Not even a medical examination could quell the rumors against them. On the use of the term *Crestian* see F. Bériac, "Le vocabulaire de la lèpre dans l'ouest des pays de Langue d'Oc," *Annales du Midi* 96 (1984): 331–355, here pp. 338–343.

[15]For the riot in Palermo, see ACA Perg. Jaume II, extra inventario, nos. 48, 100. The state of relations between Genoa (and other Italian states) and the Crown of Aragon is exceedingly complicated. For a summary of the diplomatic maneuvers over Sardinia in the period between 1317 and 1324, see A. Arribas Palau, *La Conquista de Cerdeña por Jaime II de Aragón* (Barcelona, 1952), pp. 98–119. On Catalan-Genoese relations, see G. Fiaschini, "Genovesi e Catalani nel basso Medioevo: un problema storiografico aperto," in *Atti del Iº congresso storico Liguria-Catalogna (ottobre 1969)* (Bordighera, 1974), pp. 572–601; and G. Pistarino, "Genova e Barcellona: incontro e scontro di due civiltà," in ibid., pp. 81–122. The contemporary chronicle of Ramon Muntaner conveys a sense of

It seems that the king ordered the arrest of all Genoese in his kingdoms and the forfeiture of their property to the Crown. The arrests left hardly a ripple in the documentation. Were it not for a case of ambiguous identity, we would not even know they had occurred. More than a year after the arrests, the town council of Elx wrote to the king. Following the king's orders, the bailiff of Elx had arrested a Genoese man called Andriol de Vandrechi. But, the council pleaded, this man was married to a Catalan woman and had lived for more than twenty years in Elx. In all those years he had been an honest merchant and paid taxes to the Crown. Could not the king be merciful and treat this man as a citizen?[16]

Genoese were not the only Italians captured. Shortly before Christmas 1321 the king ordered that proceedings be concluded in the case of two Florentines arrested in Valencia. Despite the fact that the Florentines had paid a surety of five hundred maravedis (a huge sum), officials were slow in reaching a verdict. But only the Genoese were singled out by special edict from foreigners in general. Like the king's original edict ordering the capture of foreigners, the anti-Genoese activity in 1321 suggests that in Aragon enmity, or at least enmity powerful enough to motivate a plot like poisoning the wells, was conceived as running along political and mercantile boundaries. And this was not just a royal construction. In the town of Teruel it was asserted by the populace that royal officials were lax in enforcing the ban on foreigners, and the king believed that charges to this effect contributed to riots there. What is clear is that during the poison scare of 1321 in the Crown of Aragon, what mattered most was political, not religious, identity.[17]

. . . . .

Catalan attitudes toward the Genoese, a description of whose perfidy, he writes, would demand more paper than that produced by the mills of Xàtiva. Muntaner presents Aragon's enemies in the Sardinian war in terms of sins that assimilate them to lepers and Jews: lewdness, avarice, the practice of usury, helping the Muslims against Christendom, gambling, and enmity to God. See chaps. 282–287; for an English translation see *The Chronicle of Muntaner*, vols. 1–2, trans. Lady Goodenough, The Hakluyt Society, 2d ser., vols. 47, 50 (London, 1920–1921; Liechtenstein, 1967).

[16]ACA:C 176:276r–v (1322/10/19). The king agreed and ordered Andriol freed. The document states that Andriol was arrested as per "mandati nostri universaliter vobis et aliis officiales nostris [sic] dictae partis facti super capiendis quibuscumque januensem et eius bonis qui in dicta parte invenirent seu degerent." In ACA:C 222:105v (1322/10/20), the king orders "Odonem de Gaui, januensem," freed because he is now a subject of the king of Mallorca, who has interceded on his behalf. For a detailed treatment of the dangerous career of one Genoese merchant operating within this geopolitical nexus see M. Sánchez Martínez, "Mallorquines y Genoveses en Almería durante el primer tercio del siglo XIV: El proceso contra Jaume Manfré," in *Miscel.lània de Textos Medievals* 4 (1988), *La frontera terrestre i marítima amb l'islam*, pp. 103–162.

[17]For the case of the Florentines, see ACA:C 172:202r–v (1321/12/19), addressed to Pere de Queralt, vice-regent for the procurator in Valencia. For the riots in Teruel, in which a Jew and a Christian were killed and royal officials attacked, see below, and ACA:C 246:240r (1321/7/14), transcribed partially, below, n. 40, and in full in Nirenberg, "Violence," pp. 335 f. James's actions against the Genoese may have owed something to similar actions taken earlier by the king of France.

More problematic than foreigners, because less easily definable, were the lepers. We have already seen how, in his second edict "on the affair of the lepers," the king had stressed that the lepers were dangerous because they could not be identified. The king distinguished between two types of lepers, those who lived in leprosaria and those who did not. The latter were to be imprisoned, presumably because their lack of segregation made them doubly dangerous. Edicts like this one, as well as an (apparently lost) edict that ordered the confiscation of leper property to the Crown, created the possibility of violence on two fronts. Known lepers, whether in leper houses or not, could be attacked and their property seized. Second, anyone could be accused of being a leper, an accusation that, in the contemporary climate, was bound to attract the harsh attention of royal justice.[18]

Despite the king's concern with nonsegregated lepers, leper houses seem to have suffered most in 1321, perhaps because their property made them an attractive target. The leprosarium of St. Mary Magdalene in Cervera provides the best-documented example. The leprosarium was an old one, dating at least to the twelfth century. Together with a house for the lepers, it also possessed a spacious church dedicated to their use. The church of St. Mary Magdalene, which still stands, was rebuilt in 1192, and King Peter I is said to have heard mass there in 1202. Over the portal stood a statue of St. Mary, now decapitated, and carvings within the sanctuary represented the biblical scene "noli me tangere," touch me not.[19]

No record of an accusation against the lepers of Cervera appears to survive, but one must have been made, because a later document recalls the time "when the lepers . . . were sent away and expelled from the house in which they lived, and many of them were condemned to death."[20] If the burning and expulsion of the lepers was not chronicled, the seizure of their property was. The king immediately appointed Pere de Cardona, of the royal household, as administrator of the lepers' goods and by December 1, 1321, had decided, at the request of the municipal council of Cervera, to grant the property for the foundation of a new convent of Minorite sisters. Two thousand sous' worth of the property was to be retained for the sustenance of future lepers. The balance was delivered to the procurator of the Minorite friars.[21]

[18]The king's order to seize property belonging to lepers is hypothesized from documents concerning the execution of such an order, e.g., ACA:C 246:264v (1321/9/1); ACA:C 221:132v–133r (1321/12/5); ACA:C 172:254v (1322/1/17); ACA:C 221:170v–171r (1322/2/16); and esp. ACA:C 174:46v–47r (1322/2/16). These cases will be discussed more extensively below.

[19]For the early history of the leprosarium given here, see P. Sanahuja, "El monestir de Santa Clara de Cervera," Estudis Franciscans 47 (1935): 301–333, 457–482, here p. 301. During an invasion in the year 1200 it was used as a fort by the inhabitants of the town. On the church of St. Mary Magdalene, see A. Duran y Sanpere, Llibre de Cervera (Tarrega, 1972), pp. 213–217.

[20]Sanahuja, "El monestir," pp. 302, 460. Sanahuja reproduces an earlier transcription of AM Cervera no. 278 (1328/8/23): "Noverint universi quod, cum tempore quo leprosi cum infirmitatibus exigentibus et alias ex rationabili causa fuissent remoti seu expulsi ad domibus in quibus morabantur ac etiam plures eorum ad {ultimum} suplitium compdemnati fuissent."

[21]ACA:C 221, pt. 2, fol. 133r, transcribed by Sanahuja, "El monestir," p. 457. See also fols. 132v–133r.

The struggle over the property of the quondam lepers of Cervera did not end here. By 1323, the procurator of the Friars Minor feared expropriation of the lands formerly owned by the lepers. Despite subsequent royal reconfirmation of the monastery's rights, important factions on the town council were insisting that the land be returned to the lepers. The property was redivided between convent and leprosarium, but this arrangement proved equally temporary. In 1331, delegates from Cervera attended the parliament ("Cort") held at Tortosa and told King Alfonso "the Benign" that the lepers would starve if they did not recover all of their property. The king agreed. Why the townspeople of Cervera were so eager to reclaim property for the lepers is unclear. Perhaps the new convent proved more independent than the lepers had been, or perhaps the municipality feared that if it did not regain the property, it would be forced to come up with other revenues to sustain its afflicted. Whatever the reasons, within a decade the confiscations of 1321 had been reversed, the lepers repossessed.[22]

The arrests and confiscations that occurred at Cervera in 1321 were duplicated in other towns, though they have not left so clear a trail. The goods of the leprosarium in Morelle (in northern Valencia) were granted by the king to the Minorite sisters as well, with the "domus" to be converted into a convent. The three lepers who remained in the town, and others who might appear, were to be supported by income from the houses and lands they possessed in the town.[23] In Tàrrega leper properties were donated to the Friars Minor, who were permitted to sell the lands, with the condition that whoever bought them would agree to take care of any lepers who might appear in the future.[24] A slightly different grant was made in favor of the abbess of the Minorite sisters of Vilafranca del Penedès. Upon certification that there were no longer any lepers in Vilafranca, she was granted the "house" of the lepers and its properties, with the proviso that, should lepers appear, they would be sustained by the convent. In just over a week's time the abbess was complaining "that the sworn men of

[22]For the complaint in 1323, see ACA:C 181:211r (1323/3/10). Rights were reconfirmed in ACA:C 475:112v–113r (1328/6/19). In the 1328 document from the AM Cervera cited above, the pro-leper faction is mentioned: ". . . quidem dicta universitas ipsius villae, tam jurati quam alii plures de dicta universitate dictae villae insurgentes contra dictas donationes et concessiones . . . eo etiam quia leprosi aliqui veniebant ad villam Cervariae et non habebant locum aliquod in quo possent sustentari, et instarent quod ipsi leprosi redirent ad ipsam domum et estarent in eadem prout antea." The property, described as insufficient to support the construction of a new convent, is listed and divided. The donation is again reconfirmed in ACA:C 481:208v (1330/6/16). The reversal of the donation is contained in ACA:C 483:279r–v (1331/9/7). The documents have been published by Sanahuja, "El monestir," pp. 457–465.

[23]ACA:C 221:170v–171r (1322/2/16).

[24]ACA:C 222:43v–44r (1322/7/5): ". . . sub hac cum conditione quod quicumque hospicium hereditamenta et alia bona sedentia supradicta emerit obliget se et obligare se habeat quod futuris leprosis oriundis de dicta villa Tarrage provideat in suis vite necessitatibus competenter."

Vilafranca and others, maliciously and against Our grant, are impeding the said abbess and convent" from gaining title to the lands.[25]

Not all confiscated leper property went to religious orders. The goods of leprosaria in the environs of Tarazona and Borja were retained by the Crown. Nor was all leper property confiscated. When Artaldo de Luna took the goods of the leper house of St. Lazar, in the village of Sadava (which I have not been able to locate), he was ordered by the king to return them, as the king did not want them seized.[26] Surprisingly, these confiscations did not create vigorous resistance from local nobles or other individuals, as they had in France.[27] What significant opposition there was to the confiscations came from the municipalities. We have already seen how, in Cervera and Vilafranca, some municipal officials resisted the granting of leper property to religious orders. The most interesting case, however, comes from Tarazona. When King James issued an order to confiscate the property of leper houses in the cities of Borja and Tarazona, royal officials interpreted it to include the "Hospital of St. Lazar," in Tarazona. The hospital with its house and fields had belonged to Dominic de Sant Lazar, a leper, and on his death had passed to his daughters, Jordana and Agneta, also lepers. The Hospital of St. Lazar was, in short, a private hospital, created by a "leprous" individual from his own properties, transmitted through inheritance, and eventually giving its name (Lazarus was a patron saint of lepers) to the family that owned it. Presumably the hospital enjoyed certain privileges as a "charitable institution": exemption from tithes, perhaps, or a right to ask for alms in church. Akin to the early medieval *Eigenkirchen*, the Hospital of St. Lazar straddled the line between private property and a privileged, semiecclesiastical institution.[28]

---

[25] For the original grant to the abbess, ACA:C 222:64v (1322/8/6). For the complaint, ACA:C 222:71r (1322/8/15).

[26] For mention of the order concerning Tarazona and Borja, see ACA:C 174:46v–47r (1322/2/16), transcribed in full in Nirenberg, "Violence," pp. 324–326. The letter to Artaldo de Luna is in ACA:C 246:264v (1321/9/1).

[27] I have found but two complaints from individuals. One claimant insisted that land the king had confiscated from the lepers of Tarrega and then granted to the Friars Minor of the town should revert to her, because of improvements she had made on the land. The other, perhaps more typical, concerned pious bequests. Johanna, a woman from the area of Jaca, stated that her nephew had willed two vineyards to the lepers called "of the crown," on the condition that they burn candles for him in the lepers' church of St. Stephen. Because the lepers, now killed or imprisoned, could not meet the conditions stipulated in the will, Johanna argued that the vineyards should revert to her. See ACA:C 172:254v (1322/1/17); ACA:C 371:7v–8r (1322/7/18).

[28] The hospital is briefly described in ACA:C 174:46v–47r (1322/2/16), transcribed in Nirenberg, "Violence," pp. 324–326. In some leper hospitals the administratorship was transmitted through inheritance. See ACA:C 145:40v (1310/7/4): ". . . quod dictus Simon Martini tenuit dum vixit jure successionis aministrationem domus infirmorum Sancti Lazari Turolii," and said right "transtulit in quendam filium commune dicti Simonis et ipsius Macdalene." As charitable organizations hospitals were considered religious institutions for juridical purposes even when they were not administered by the Church, a fact with significant tax implications. See A. Rubio Vela, *Pobreza, enfermedad y asistencia hospitalaria en la Valencia del siglo XIV* (Valencia, 1984), pp. 64–65. In

The events of 1321 gave the municipality of Tarazona a chance to challenge these privileges. In a settlement arbitrated by Gondiçalvo Çapata, canon of Tarazona, and Pedro Juan de Mallet, the town council agreed to restore to Jordana and Agneta de Sant Lazar the house and certain surrounding fields that had belonged to their father. Other lands, however, the council was allowed to keep for itself. These were to be put out for sharecropping, with the tenant keeping half the harvest and the municipal council the rest. Given this settlement, the council asked the king to order his officials to release the property, to which the king agreed. The council went further, sending a separate delegation to plead for the release of the two women, who had been arrested along with the other lepers of Tarazona. They may also have been responsible for the information that reached Infant Alfonso in Zaragoza. The lepers who had been arrested by the *sobrejuntero* of Tarazona were starving to death owing to negligence, he was told. The prince responded that those foreign lepers being held at Tarazona should be promptly expelled, while native lepers should be restored to the status they enjoyed at the time the king issued his original edict, and should be provided for from their goods.[29]

The accusations of well poisoning in 1321 did have widespread and devastating effects upon lepers in the Crown of Aragon. In one case, that of Cervera, we know that some lepers were burned, others expelled from the town, and all their property confiscated. In a few other cases we hear only of confiscations and imprisonments, and in the vast majority of cases we hear nothing. We are not told what happened to the leper houses in the most important cities of the realm, Barcelona, Valencia, Zaragoza.[30] Perhaps their privileges and patrons

parts of the Pyrenees outside Aragon the juridical status of "leper lineages" carried with it a variety of special privileges and responsibilities. These included the duties of begging from door to door every Saturday and holiday, "in honor of God," and making coffins for the dead; the privileges of tax exemptions and perhaps the right to lend at interest. See F. Bériac, "Comment les Bearnais consideraient les Crestians vers 1450–1500," in *Minorités et marginaux en France méridionale et dans la peninsule Ibérique (VIIe–XVIIIe siècles) (Actes du colloque de Pau, 27–29 mai, 1984)* (Paris, 1986), pp. 55–70; and her monumental *Des lépreux aux cagots*.

[29]The plea on behalf of Jordana and Agneta is in ACA:C 221:242v (1322/5/24): "Cum pretextu mandati per nos facti super capiendis leprosis ceperitis Agnetem et Jurdanam, mulieres comorantes in domo leprosorum Sancti Lazari civitate predicte, et adhuc teneatis inclusas, et nuntii civitatis predicte nunc ad nostram praesentiam destinati supplicaverint nobis ut eas mandaremus absolvi." The infant's order is in ACA:C 370:47v (1322/4/5): "Cum vos ex mandato domini regis custoditos detineatis aliquos leprosos, et intellexerimus quod leprosi ipsi fame moriuntur, nec est a[l]liquis qui eisdem provideat. Idcirco vobis dicimus et mandamus quatenus illos ex dictis leprosis qui naturales domini regis non sint a terra regia eiciatis. Naturales vero domini regis reducatis in statu in quo erant cum ipsos dominus rex mandavit custodiri, et de bonis eorum illis satisfaciatis qui in provisionibus eorumdem aliquid expenderunt." Both documents are transcribed in full in Nirenberg, "Violence," pp. 326 f., 342 f.

[30]For these important leper houses see: for Valencia, Rubio Vela, *Pobreza, enfermedad y asistencia hospitalaria*, pp. 40, 45, and passim; for Barcelona, J. Mutgé Vives, *La ciudad de Barcelona durante el*

were powerful enough to protect them. It seems likely, however, that there were many more people in positions like that of Jordana and Agneta: incarcerated almost a year, forced to compromise with municipal authorities in exchange for protection, restored eventually to diminished holdings. Yet it is worth remarking that over time the lepers also found a good deal of support. Partial restitution took a year in some places, full restitution (as at Cervera) a little longer. It seems that the interests of towns, Crown, and lepers came quickly back to equilibrium.

. . . . .

Known lepers were not the only ones to suffer in 1321. Because lepers were so hard to identify, and because the king's edicts made the consequences of identification as a leper so serious, a new form of strategic accusation was created almost immediately. Neighbors, business rivals, enemies of all sorts could bring accusations of leprosy before local courts with the certainty that the charges would at least be investigated by royal officials. In this society where people were always willing to try new ways of mobilizing powerful but relatively inert (because lightly staffed) structures of royal power on their own behalf, the charge of leprosy was quickly adopted not just against foreigners but against more intimate enemies as well.

Such accusations were not entirely new, since a diagnosis of leprosy seems to have had some significance in both Christian and Muslim law before 1321.[31] In fact the word "leper," like "sodomite," "whore," "traitor," or "Saracen" (to a non-Muslim), represented an insult actionable as slander when used against "respectable" people.[32] Accusations of leprosy, like those of infamy, seem to have been used by communities to expel people perceived as troublemakers. In 1311, for example, the neighbors of Guillermo Porta of Cervera complained that he

---

reinado de Alfonso el Benigno (1327–1336) (Barcelona, 1987), pp. 35–36, and A. Pérez Santamaría, "El hospital de San Lazaro o Casa dels Malalts o Masells," in La pobreza y la asistencia a los pobres en la Cataluña medieval, ed. M. Riu, 1:77–115, Anuario de Estudios Medievales, anejo 9 (Barcelona, 1980); for Zaragoza, ACA:C 683:160v–161v (1356/3/29), transcribed in Nirenberg, "Violence," pp. 358–361. There were also leper houses in Teruel (see ACA:C 145:40v [1310/7/4]), Huesca (see ACA:C 521:7v [1329/3/27]), Manresa (see McVaugh, Medicine before the Plague, p. 224), and presumably in many other places.

[31] For example, in Muslim customary law in at least some parts of Catalonia, leprosy (of the wife) could constitute grounds for divorce. See Un tratado Catalán medieval de derecho islámico: el llibre de la çuna e xara dels moros, ed. C. Barceló (Córdoba, 1989), pp. 18, 52.

[32] R. Serra Ruiz, Honor, honra e injuria en el Derecho medieval Español (Murcia, 1969), pp. 32, 47, 66, 83, 95, 139, 150. For Castile, see also M. Madero, Manos violentas, palabras vedadas: la injuria en Castilla y León (siglos XIII–XV) (Madrid, 1992), p. 62. For an example of a couple's being fined for calling a woman "sarraynaça! de natura de sarrayns!" see P. Bertran y Roigé, "Conflictes socials a Cervera, segons el llibre del batlle Antoni de Cabrera (1356–1357)," Miscel.lània Cerverina 6 (1988): 53–70, here p. 59.

was infected with leprosy, and asked that he be removed from the town lest he infect them. The best way to protect oneself from such an accusation was to be declared nonleprous by a panel of doctors. A widow in the village of Gorga (Valencia) was maliciously accused of being a leper, so she obtained such a certificate from two physicians. When people continued to call her a leper, she obtained a letter from the king, addressed to all officials of the realm, instructing them to ignore such accusations against her.[33]

Local officials had local loyalties and might be tempted to ignore such a letter. Barcelona, a "poor and miserable woman," complained to the king that Francesc Constant, justice of the village of Ontinyent (Valencia), had expelled her husband from the town insisting that he was a leper. The husband, Bernat Cubelles, was received at the Hospital of St. Lazar in Valencia, but a panel of physicians there deemed him not leprous, so he returned to the village. The justice refused to accept this verdict and sent the poor man back to Valencia, where the doctors again refused to admit him to the leprosarium and sent him back with a letter, which they sealed, explaining their diagnosis. Barcelona felt that the justice's actions had caused her family harm and demanded an inquiry, to which the king agreed.[34]

Before 1321, such accusations do appear in royal documentation, but much less frequently than other accusations of infamy, such as adultery, usury, or concealing treasure trove, perhaps because examination by a panel of doctors provided a relatively effective safeguard against abuse.[35] With the royal edicts of 1321, however, the accusation of leprosy found renewed popularity and was aimed at rich and poor alike.

Monuaut, a "pauper" living in Jaca, was arrested "because, in the time of the rumors about the poisoning of the waters, he was accused of being a leper." He was examined by physicians in Huesca and found to be healthy, so he appealed to have his property returned to him, then claimed that the bailiff of Jaca was refusing to return his property. The bailiff countered that he had never seized any property from Monuaut, so there was nothing to recover.[36] Again, in the foothills of the Pyrenees near Huesca, Bertrand Guillermo, his wife Dulce, and

<hr>

[33] For Guillermo Porta, ACA:C 148:59v (1311/8/13). For Gorga, ACA:C 144:197r (1310/4/9). Both documents transcribed in Nirenberg, "Violence," pp. 313–315.

[34] ACA:C 164:200v (1318/1/26).

[35] Although Moore (*Persecuting Society*, pp. 78, 134) suggests that this was a much later development, assessment of leprosy by a medical jury, rather than by a local jury or by lepers, seems to have become routine in the Crown of Aragon by 1300, as the cases above suggest. (In France, medical juries remained uncommon until the second half of the century.) This does not mean, however, that medical diagnoses were uncontested by "the public," accusers, royal officials, or even other doctors. Much like expert testimony today, a medical evaluation, regardless of its accuracy, was but one strategy to be used in a conflictual situation. (For an opposing viewpoint, see McVaugh, *Medicine before the Plague*, pp. 222, 224–225.)

[36] On Monuaut's troubles, see ACA:C 370:214v–215r (1322/6/22); ACA:C 370:228v (1322/6/28); ACA:C 370:242v (1322/7/5).

their children were all accused of being lepers and their property seized. They too were found healthy by the physicians, and the king ordered that their property be returned.

The most interesting case occurred at the opposite end of the Crown, at Guardamar in the kingdom of Valencia, and at the opposite end of the economic spectrum. Events were clearly described by the king in his letter to Simon de Belloc, vice-regent for the procurator in Valencia:

> The news has recently reached us that, with the pretext of an order recently sent by us to all our officials about proceedings against any lepers because of the temerity that they attempted, officials of the village of Guardamar, at the instigation of some enemies as it is said, moved or intend to move against some inhabitants of the said town of Guardamar who are called "the Masquefas," collectively and singly, because they claim that some of the aforenamed lineage of the Masquefas are lepers.

The king stated flatly that it was not reasonable to proceed against an entire lineage ("genera," "parentela") because one member was afflicted with leprosy. He did not, however, suspend the proceedings. The Masquefas were to be examined for leprosy. Anyone who was not "touched" by the disease was to be freed, and the town crier was to forbid anyone to insult healthy Masquefas by calling them lepers, under penalty of fine. Masquefas who were diagnosed as leprous, on the other hand, were to be incarcerated, as per the king's edict.[37]

It is quite clear from this document that accusations of leprosy were perceived by contemporaries as "strategic," weapons to be used against one's enemies. Equally suggestive is the stress on lineage. Either leprosy in Valencia was thought to be transmitted through the generations (as with the *cagots* in the Pyrenees), or the Masquefas had creative enemies and these enemies had the ear of local officials.[38] The Masquefas were a prominent family in Guardamar and Oriola who surface regularly in royal documentation as landowners, town

---

[37] ACA:C 172:9v (1321/9/8): ". . . pretextu mandati . . . per nos facti super procedendo contra leprosos . . . , officiales loci de Guardamar, ad instigationem quorumdam emulorum, ut asseritur, aliquorum vicinorum dicti loci de Guardamar qui nominatur los Masquefes, processerunt sive procedere intendunt contra eosdem et singulos eorumdem, cum asserant aliquos ex genere prenominatorum dels Masquefes esse leprosos. Cum autem non sit rationi consonum neque decens quod licet aliqui de dicto genere dels Masquefes casu fortuite leprosi efecti fuerint ut asseritur contra alios qui de ipso genere ex morbo predicto tacti non sunt neque fuerunt ut fertur totaliter procedatur. Idcirco . . . contra predictos nominatos de Masquefa quos sciveritis seu inveneritis tactos non fore morbo leprosie predicte [sic] quamvis in genere sive parentela eorum aliqui leprosi fuerint minime procedatis. Immo voce praeconia inhiberi faciatis . . . quod nequis audeat . . . proclamare predictis . . . qui de dicto morbo tacti non sint leprosos, seu aliam motam eis imponere ex causa premissa. Si vero inveneritis aliquem seu aliquos ex dicto genere esse leprosos contra illos mimime procedere obmittatis." For a full transcription, see Nirenberg, "Violence," pp. 317 f.

[38] A host of ancient and medieval medical authorities believed leprosy to be hereditary, though Hansen's disease is not. On this belief and its consequences in France see the splendid study by Bériac, *Des lépreux aux cagots*, esp. pp. 209–297.

councillors, and royal officials.[39] Perhaps in the leprosy accusation against the Masquefa "parentela" we should see a local faction's attack upon a rival clan. If so, it was ultimately unsuccessful: the Masquefas continued to rise through royal service and local office. That it was attempted at all demonstrates the rapidity with which strategies of accusation were adapted to "national" political events by local populations seeking to meet local needs.

.   .   .   .   .

Lepers, foreigners, locals with creative enemies: in the Crown of Aragon these suffered more from the accusations of poisoning in 1321 than Muslims and Jews, despite the fact that historians have focused only on the latter. But even the few incidents involving minorities—one involving native Jews and a handful of native Muslims—demonstrate the processes of negotiation and contextualization that shaped the general charges to local needs.

In mid-July, complaints reached the king from the town of Teruel that royal officials were negligent in arresting strangers and barring entry to foreigners. Their negligence had already led to a "scandal," probably a riot, in the town, and the king ordered an investigation into the conduct of his officials.[40] Unfortunately, no details of this first unrest are preserved. Two weeks later, however, on the 29th or 30th of July, events took an ugly and well-documented turn. The events are described in a letter from the lieutenant of the bailiff in Teruel to the king, though it should be kept in mind that the writer was himself under investigation for lax enforcement of the king's edicts against foreigners, and this

[39]Masquefas figure as royal bailiffs in Catalonia already in the twelfth century. They received lands in Oriola and its environs in the first distributions after the reconquest, and the family remained prominent in the region throughout the fourteenth century. G. de Masquefa was bailiff of Piera in 1193: T. Bisson, *Fiscal Accounts of Catalonia under the Early Count-Kings (1151–1213)*, 2 vols.(Berkeley, 1984), 1:208, 265, 284; vol. 2, no. 96. In 1339 the Masquefa family purchased the lordship of Albatera: M. T. Ferrer i Mallol, *Les aljames sarraïnes de la governació d'Oriola en el segle XIV* (Barcelona, 1988), p. 8. In 1324, Bernat Masquefa formed part of a consortium to lease the *almoixerifat* of Oriola for 5,560 sous, ibid., p. 152. In 1319 the wife of Guillem de Masquefa of Oriola received permission to sell some land she owned to Muslims, ACA:C 217:205r (1319/11/10). Jaume Masquefa was bailiff of Oriola in the 1320s, and lieutenant of the procurator's vice-regent in the 1330s. See ibid., pp. 56, 162. See also idem, *La frontera*, pp. 125, 164, and *Organització i defensa*, pp. 106, 115, 119, and index, sub Masquefa. A Pere Masqueffa purchased licenses from the king to export grain from Valencia to Barcelona and elsewhere in the Crown: ACA:C 245:169v (1318/1/11). In 1321, Guillem Masquefa of Guardamar and a partner from Oriola were involved in a legal dispute over a mill and fishery. See ACA:C 175:198r–v (1322/6/30), which is an appeal by Masquefa and Tomas Pont of an earlier sentence against them.

[40]ACA:C 246:240r (1321/7/14): ". . . pro parte aliquorum asseritur quod in scandalo nuper suscitato apud Turolum super quo per vos procedi providimus officiales nostros culpam comisisse dicatur, immitendo inibi gentes extraneas seu eas prohibere nolendo ac non capiendo quosdam encarcatos." For a full transcription, see Nirenberg, "Violence," pp. 335 f.

may have colored his presentation. As the writer frankly states, "I notify you of these things, lord, so that I might not be reproached by you for negligence."[41]

On a Thursday with two days remaining in July, our informer writes, a man named Diego Perez of Daroca was arrested in the village of Rivuhuelos, in the hinterlands of the town of Teruel, on charges of throwing powders in the waters. He was brought to Teruel, where the municipal judges and members of the town council had him tortured "in order to know the truth." He admitted under torture to poisoning fountains in Rivuhuelos, Mora, and Valbona, and when asked for accomplices, mentioned "a Breton." Then he changed his mind and implicated "two Jews, the richest in Serrion." In fact, there were only two Jews living in Serrion: Samuel Famos and Yaco Alfayto. A judge went to the village and arrested these Jews, as well as some other Jews who did not live there, and brought them captive to Teruel.

Since the Jews of Teruel had a privilege that they could be judged only by the king or his bailiff, not by the municipal courts of Teruel, they asked the bailiff to intervene and assert his jurisdiction, as they feared a miscarriage of justice. The justices and alcaldes refused to surrender the Jews. Worse, members of the town council attacked the bailiff's house, smashed down the doors, and seized two other Jews whom the bailiff was also holding on suspicion of poisoning. The councillors, judges, and alcaldes then proceeded to torture Samuel Famos, who refused to confess to the crime. When the judges saw that Diego Perez stuck to his story (because he had been promised liberty if he implicated the Jew, according to the bailiff), and that the Jew refused to confess, they sent a man disguised as a priest to interrogate Diego under the guise of spiritual confession. Diego admitted to the "priest" that he had implicated the Jews only because he would rather die than be tortured, and because he had been promised freedom if he did so.

Faced with this retraction, the judges and alcaldes could scarcely convict Samuel, though a faction of the council was agitating strongly for his death. Instead, Diego Perez was condemned to death as a confessed poisoner. Then the town council contrived to deliver Samuel for lynching to "some people" they assembled hurriedly. Samuel's body was smashed, dismembered, and burned. "No sentence was given against him, nor did the alcaldes wish to render one, because they did not find him guilty." "As I and many others see it," wrote the bailiff, "the said Jew was killed unjustly."

The incident as interpreted by Carlo Ginzburg is a typical example of scapegoating:

> The authorities and judges who exert pressure so that the accusation will fall upon those who are already candidates for the role of scapegoat; the accused who yields,

[41] ACA:C cr. Jaume II, box 85, no. 5 (1321/8/18), published by Baer, *Die Juden* vol. 1, no. 177, pp. 224–228.

terrorized by torture; the mob unleashed against those presumed guilty; all this seems predictable, even obvious. . . . The authorities' version could spread and take root because at all levels of the population there was a willingness to accept, indeed to anticipate, the guilt of the lepers and Jews.[42]

The bailiff, however, presented the entire event as a jurisdictional quarrel. There is no mob, only a group organized by the councillors. The rest of the bailiff's letter goes on to detail further jurisdictional strife: the judges of Teruel tried to confiscate Samuel's goods notwithstanding the bailiff's assertion that they belong to the king.[43] Despite the previous turmoil over the leniency of royal officials against suspected poisoners, the town council was unable to convict a single Jew, even in its own courts. Nor was it able to unleash any violence except the lynching of the unfortunate Samuel, which the council itself organized directly. Far from spreading, what Ginzburg calls the official version (though in fact it was but one official version) got nowhere.[44]

. . . . .

Muslims suffered more than Jews from accusations of well poisoning in 1321, though here, too, the scope of the accusations was very limited.[45] In some respects, the greater vulnerability of Muslims to such charges is not surprising. Though studies of 1321 in France have assigned to the Muslims a "purely symbolic" role of distant enemy in the accusations, in Spain they represented an immediate and more convincing political threat than the Jews did, since Muslim, not Jewish, armies threatened Christendom.[46] Given the real and constant fear of Muslim incursions along the Valencian frontiers (Oriola, Alacant, Guard-

---

[42] Ecstasies, p. 51.

[43] Samuel's goods included pawns received from Christians and IOUs. Samuel was a debtor, too, and had given a variety of items in pawn to Christians. The IOUs had been given for safekeeping to two Christian women of Sarrion by Samuel's wife and son-in-law (yerno). Samuel's wife and some other Jews reclaim some of the confiscated goods in ACA:C 172:6r (1321/9/7).

[44] Quite some time after receiving the bailiff's letter, the king wrote to the judges and alcaldes of Teruel commanding them to desist from proceeding against Jews and to return the property of Jews they had seized when they broke into the bailiff's house. "If this was perpetrated by you, [it is] most horrible and we deem it done with maximum temerity and audacity." ACA:C 172:5v–6r (1321/9/7).

[45] Pace Lourie, "Anatomy of Ambivalence," who writes that "members of both minorities might be dragged out of jail and lynched, but significantly, only a Jew was strung up by a mob for 'poisoning the waters.'"

[46] On the perception of Muslims as "political," rather than "religious," enemies, see D. Carpenter, "Minorities in Medieval Spain: The Legal Status of Jews and Muslims in the Siete Partidas," Romance Quarterly 33 (1986): 275–287, here p. 276: "In essence, Jewish-Christian relations were defined and ofttimes determined by historico-theological considerations, while Muslim-Christian contacts in the Iberian Peninsula were governed by pragmatic concerns resulting from religio-bellicose confrontations."

amar . . .), it is curious that most accusations against Muslims came not from these borderlands but from the long-reconquered northeast.[47]

In Catalonia especially royal officials seem to have been very active. The magnates Oto de Montcada and Berenguer de Entencia complained to King James that his vicar in Lleida, together with an assessor, notaries, and an armed troop, had visited Oto's castles at Aytona and Gilsuto, and Berenguer's castle of Seros, and demanded that the bailiffs there surrender Muslims "accused of infecting the waters." The bailiffs had refused, so the vicar was proceeding against them. All of this, the nobles complained, was against custom and ancient usage. Perhaps because these were important people, the king ordered his vicar not to infringe their rights.[48] It is hard to know what lay behind this excursion into seigneurial territory: a conflict between royal and seigneurial officials? Between municipality and landed magnates? Were the nobles protecting suspected poisoners, or asserting their rights to judge them themselves?

Another episode is equally cryptic. In early August, King James wrote to the justiciar of Aragon and to the *merino* and town council of Zaragoza. He acknowledged receipt of a transcript they had just sent him from the trial of a group of Muslims who were charged with poisoning the waters at the request of the lepers. "Truly," he wrote, "it does not appear to us that the aforesaid accused Muslims are guilty in the aforesaid [affair], but because some of them have confessed [under torture, presumably] against themselves," the king would not mind if those who were found guilty were "atrociously punished." As for another Muslim held on a related charge, he could be tortured, "since he is a Saracen and the crime is very horrible." In short, the king did not believe the charges but was willing to let the executions take place "only taking great care lest other Saracens who are innocent of the aforesaid be drawn into the scandal."[49]

The limited extent of anti-Muslim activity in 1321 is best illustrated by the treatment of a Muslim leper, as likely a candidate for popular suspicion as one could hope to find. A Muslim named Micho, from San Esteban de Litera, was

[47]Only one accusation is recorded from the entire kingdom of Valencia: Raro, a Muslim of Murla, was accused of being a poisoner, though the characteristic formula "accused of infecting the waters" was not used in his case. ACA:C 246:243r (1321/7/21).

[48]ACA:C 173:233v (1321/8/1) is the more detailed document, although it was canceled and replaced by the briefer ACA:C 173:235v (1321/8/1), which does not mention the bailiffs' refusal. The former is transcribed in Nirenberg, "Violence," pp. 321 f.

[49]ACA:C 246:250r–v (1321/8/4): "Et vere non videbatur nobis quod inculpati sarraceni predicti in premissis obnoxii existant, quamquam contra se aliqua confessi fuerint, tamen bene placet nobis quod si culpa in eis reperta fuerit propter severitatem criminis atrociter puniantur. Quantum vero ad sarracenum illum quem captum detinetis pro receptatione predictorum, placet nobis quod si aliqua contra eum reperiuntur indicia adversus eum ad tormenta, cum sit sarracenus et casus valde orribilis, procedatur. Cavendo tamen sollicite ne aliis sarracenis in predictis inoxiis possint hac de causa scandala provenire." For a full transcription see Nirenberg, "Violence," pp. 336 f.

adjudged leprous by a panel of physicians. He was remanded to the custody of his wife and friends, who were to maintain him in an isolated place and guarantee his seclusion or be fined 1,000 maravedis of gold (an astronomical sum). Sometime during or before May 1322, Micho was found dead in an irrigation cistern, proof positive that he had not been adequately secluded, so the king instructed his officials to collect the fine.[50]

This "Micho" was probably the same person as a better-documented Muslim leper of San Esteban called Jucef de Celles. In February of 1322 Jucef had complained that some time ago he had been falsely accused of being a leper, and that a medical examination in Lleida had exonerated him. Nevertheless, Jucef claimed, the *sobrejuntero* of Ribagorza still ordered that he be secluded. If Jucef was not a leper, the king commanded, he should be exempt from seclusion. If he was "besmattered by said disease," the seclusion should continue. In a separate document issued the same day, Jucef and "some other Saracens" complained that the bailiff of Ribagorza had expelled them unjustly from some fields they and their ancestors had owned since time immemorial. Was this encroachment related to the accusation of leprosy?

What Jucef did not mention in his letter to the king is that he had been accused and arrested "on the occasion of the rumors of the infection of the waters." In the event, he had been remanded to the custody of his family and friends, who pledged a bond of 1,000 maravedis if they failed in their guardianship. But on the day they were required to bring Jucef before the *sobrejuntero*, they could not produce him and so incurred the fine. The king was gracious. Taking into account the "poverty" of the Muslim guarantors, he reduced the fine from 1,000 maravedis, a sum so huge as to be symbolic, to 1,700 sous, which was still a small fortune. On top of this, they owed the Crown 153 sous for the sealed letter of absolution. The entire sum was paid by Mahomat de Conillo, a Muslim of San Esteban who was not one of the guarantors, and who gained thereby the right to seize the goods of the guarantors until his expenses were satisfied.[51]

[50]On Micho, see ACA:C 385:199r (1322/5/22): "Cum vos ut audivimus intruseritis quendam sarracenum Sancti Stephani de Littera [vocatum Micho] in quendam separatum locum pro eo quia erat leprosus per fisicos judicatus, et ipse sarrace[. . .] ac eius uxor necnon et quidam alii saraceni dicti loci obligaverint se et bona sua sub pena mille morabetinorum auri quod sarracenus predictus non exiret modo aliquo dictum locum, et nunc ut precepimus sit inventus extinctus in quodam aljubio, et propterea prefati saraceni incure[rent] penam predictam quam per vos exigi volumus et levari." For a full transcription, see Nirenberg, "Violence," pp. 343 f.

[51]On Jucef de Cellas, see the two documents in ACA:C 174:45r (1322/2/13), the first concerning unjust expulsion from fields, the second (transcribed in Nirenberg, "Violence," pp. 323 f.) claiming possession of a doctor's certificate stating that Jucef is not a leper and should therefore not be secluded. The documents concerning the fine are ACA:C 386:78r (1322/7/16) (transcribed in Nirenberg, "Violence," pp. 344 f.) and ACA:C 386:79v (1322/8/11). The guarantors were Alboen Davinear, Mahomat de Lop, Mahomat de Cellas, Abdella son of Alema de Abdella, and Ferva, wife

The events involving Micho/Jucef(?) are confused. Did the doctors condemn or absolve him? Both were claimed, and both could be true, since patients might visit several doctors hoping to get a satisfactory verdict. The accusations themselves remain a complete mystery. Only two things are reasonably clear. The accused and his guarantors, largely his relatives, were not poor people: else such a large fine could not have been paid. Nor was a Muslim leper accused during the poison scare perceived as a particularly serious threat. The accusation was treated much like any other, with the defendant "released on bail" into the guardianship of his family. In San Esteban the poison scare of 1321 fomented a new type of accusation, but not mob violence against Jews and Muslims. In this respect events there conformed to a pattern that seems to have prevailed throughout the Crown of Aragon.

.   .   .   .   .

This is not to say that no one in the Crown of Aragon attempted to draw the kind of linkages among lepers, Muslims, and Jews that had been elaborated in France. Just as accounts of lepers as poisoners led individuals and groups to make new types of claims and accusations in their competitive relations with other individuals and groups, French stories of Jews and Muslims as accomplices might have a similar effect. The important point here is that such linkages were simply claims. Like a price uttered in a bazaar, their truth value was determined by the outcome of the bargaining they engendered.[52] Municipal councils, for example, could attempt to renegotiate particularly competitive or conflictual relationships by asserting that, in light of the information from France, certain activities of the Jews represented a public danger. Such claims were made in the Crown of Aragon, though rarely, and they invariably failed.

Consider the case of Montblanc. A good number of poisoners had been captured there, leading to a conflict of jurisdiction between the bailiff and castellan of the town. Some of those arrested were lepers; none was Jewish. At roughly the same time a series of riots broke out against the Christian elites of the town. One Berenguer de Cagestan and his friends attacked the bailiff and his retinue. Worse, "some people of the said place rose up against the rich men and broke into some homes with axes, and committed violence in the city and its regions against many men."[53]

---

of Jucef de Cellas. "Micho" may well have been a nickname for Jucef, in which case the reason his guarantors could not produce him is that he was lying dead in a cistern.

[52]Simile adapted from Rosen, *Bargaining for Reality*, p. 4.

[53]ACA:C 173:223v–224r (1321/7/29): ". . . alcuns gens del dit loch se levaren contra los richs hommes e ab destrals trencaren alscuns alberchs et feren violencia dins la vila e el terme a molts hommes."

In this context of unrest the town council passed two ordinances aimed in part at the Jews. First, the council mandated a moment of prayer in the city streets. Each day a bell would be struck, and everyone about the town, Christian or Jew, was to kneel and pray. The Jews complained that some people would insult and stone them during the prayer, claiming that their knees were not bent. Two Jews had been injured on such an occasion, and the bailiff had refused to defend them. Infant Alfonso took the part of the Jews, ruling that it made no sense that Jews, "who are utterly segregated from Christian communion, could be forced in any way to pray with them." This is a curious ordinance, and the council's motivation in passing it is unclear. According to the Jews, however, its effect was to harass them by extending the scope of sacred violence from strictly delimited festivals into the everyday.[54]

The council's second ordinance is perhaps more clearly related to issues of contagion and disease. According to the Jews, the council had decreed or intended to decree that Jews were forbidden to touch bread, meat, fish, fruit, or other victuals in the market but had to accept foodstuffs from the seller without touch, "sine tactu." This was a tremendous disadvantage for Jewish buyers—they were forced to rely on the goodwill of merchants who reserved their best wares for favored clients—but the Jews did not approach the court with this argument alone. The problem with the edict, they told Prince Alfonso, was that it could instigate the populace, "who already hold them in contempt," to riot and murder.[55]

Whether the populace of Montblanc was ready to riot against the Jews is impossible to tell. The fact is that they did not do so, even as they rioted against the rich and royal officials. Further, Jewish communities often argued their interests in the language of violence: Jews and their allies pressed for legislation they thought beneficial by asserting that it would protect the Jews, and fought against prejudicial legislation by arguing that it would increase violence against them (see chapter 1). Nevertheless, the document is curious, and it is this type

[54] ACA:C 369:86r (1321/7/29): ". . . quia proceres dictae villae ordinamentum fecerunt de oratione facienda ad signum cimbali diebus singulis in dicto loco, gentes eiusdem loci et potissime plebeii, quia judei dicta oratione durante euntes per villam acas[. . .] non erant flexis genibus cum eisdem, verberant, vilipendiunt, lapidant et molestant eosdem judeos, contra eos populum etiam concitando. Et quod vos . . . non vultis inde inquirere nec ipsos judeos defendere a molestationibus supradictis. . . . Quocirca nos, attendentes fore absonum rationi ut judei, qui a comunione xristianorum sunt penitus segregati, ad orandum cum eis modo aliquo compellantur, vobis dicimus." For a full transcription, see Nirenberg, "Violence," pp. 341 f. On sacred violence, see chap. 7.

[55] ACA:C 369:85v (1321/7/29): ". . . nobis extitit cum querimonia intimatum quod proceres dictae villae ordinant . . . quod judei in emendo panes, carnes, pices, fructus et alia victualia in dicto loco ea non tangant set sine tactu ea emant et a vendentibus accipiant, ex quo ordinamento ipsi judei timent nec inmerite ne dum dampnificari in emptione predicta, verum etiam ex populi comotione quae iam eos ingratos [habent] periculum mortis et [a]valotamenti ac scandalum maximum incurrere." See Nirenberg, "Violence," pp. 340 f., for a full transcription.

of market legislation that has led Maurice Kriegel to posit a widespread popular view of the Jew as "untouchable," a source of impurity and disease.[56] If this was indeed the case, it is doubly curious that in the charged atmosphere of 1321 the councillors did not make any explicit connection between Jews and lepers or between Jews and infectious disease in order to strengthen their case.[57] And while it is striking that in 1321 a group of Christians, in this case an "elite" group in the town council, asserted that Jews should not be allowed to touch foodstuffs in the market, it is even more striking that the assertion was not accepted as "true": the council's decree was struck down.

There is one case of segregatory measures against the Jews linked directly to the poison scare, but it was proposed by a royal official, not a municipal council. The vicar of Barcelona and Valles, who appears to have been most active in the persecution of the plot, proposed to ban Jews from entering any Christian homes that were equipped with wells, unless they had previously posted a bond to guarantee that they were not poisoners. Why the vicar proposed such a rule is unknown, but his actions provide us with our first indication of royal attitudes toward the accusations emanating from France: "We see [no reason] to fear on this [issue] from our native Jews," wrote the king, and he ordered the vicar to take no action that might restrict free conversation of native Jews with Christians, or Jewish access to Christian homes.[58]

The king's distinction between native and foreign Jews quickly took on a great deal of significance. Three days after his letter to the vicar of Barcelona, he wrote to all the officials of his realms:

> Concerning the Affair of the Lepers: . . . Since from approximately the time when rumor arose against those who were attempting to poison the waters many foreign Jews have entered our lands and have not ceased to do so, in order to remove all suspicion we wish to eject them from our land. Therefore we tell and command you

[56] Kriegel's argument that Jews were considered "untouchable" is based on market regulations like this one, though he is unaware of this particular document and relies primarily on postplague documentation. It should be noted that some market regulations forbade *anyone* to touch certain foodstuffs, e.g., *Llibre de les ordinacions de Torroja*, ed. J. Torné i Cubells and E. M. Vallejo i Fidalgo (Tarragona, 1989), pp. 47–48. Kriegel's arguments are made in "Un trait de psychologie sociale," pp. 326–330. But compare N. Coulet, "Les juifs en Provence au bas moyen-age: les limites d'une marginalité," in *Minorités et marginaux en France méridionale et dans la peninsule Ibérique (VIIe–XVIIIe siècles) (Actes du colloque de Pau, 27–29 mai, 1984)* (Paris, 1986), pp. 203–219.

[57] Such connections are explicitly drawn in some Spanish Muslim market regulations. See for example É. Lévi-Provençal, *Séville musulmane au début du XIIe siècle: le traité d'Ibn ʿAbdun sur la vie urbaine et les corps de métiers* (Paris, 1947), pp. 112–113.

[58] ACA:C 173:179v (1321/7/10): "Cum intellexerimus quod vos ordinastis seu ordinare intenditis praeconitzationem fieri ut judei non intrent domos aliquas xristianorum ubi aliqui sint putei nisi certa cautela adhibita, et quod ad hoc procesistis seu procedere intenditis ut aquas non possent inficere. Nosque super hiis ex judeis naturalibus nostris timendum fore non videamus. Immo intendamus absque suspicione aliqua posse conversari cum eisdem et hospiciorum liber aditus hac de causa negari non debere eisdem." Transcribed in full in Nirenberg, "Violence," p. 319.

to expel immediately any of the aforesaid Jews who entered our land at about that time, ordering them on pain of corporal punishment to leave our land immediately and not presume to return. And take special care lest henceforth any foreign Jews manage to enter our land in any way, expelling them in a similar way if they should enter.[59]

More than a month after the border had been closed to lepers, and three weeks after it was closed to foreigners in general, the entry of Jews was barred. The edict may have directed official hostility against foreign Jews: in Lleida, a Castilian Jew was accused of poisoning the waters.[60] Its implementation was not, however, clear. Jews had been immigrating into Aragon from France in large numbers over the past several decades. Most recently, the Shepherds' Crusade had driven hundreds of Jews across the borders.[61] How long need a Jew have lived in Aragon in order to be considered native? Fortunately, the bailiff of Calatayud asked these questions, and the king's answer survives. Jews who had entered the Crown within the past year were to be expelled; all others could remain. The king's letter is dated August 18: presumably refugees from the shepherds could remain.

In the case of Calatayud, which is the only documented one, recent Jewish immigrants were to be identified by the Jewish community itself. Jewish officials were to gather the information by solemnly proclaiming excommunication (alatma), though who was to be threatened by excommunication is not specified. The order had unforeseen implications. Just as the king's earlier edict about the identification of lepers had opened a new category of accusation for Christians, the identification of immigrants did so for Jews. An Inquisition trial held some two decades later, in 1342, attests to the tensions French immigration

---

[59]ACA:C 246:239r (1321/7/13): "Cum a tempore citra quo contra illos qui aquas nituntur inficere rumor invaluit non nulli judei extranei terram nostram ingressi fuerint et adhuc ingredi non cessent. Nosque ad tollendam omnem suspicionem eosdem a terra nostra eici velimus. Idcirco vobis dicimus et mandamus quatenus judeos prefatos a dicto tempore citra terram nostram ingressos quos in jurisdictione vestra inveneritis abinde protinus expellatis, iniungendo eisdem sub pena corporum ut exeant incontinenti de terra nostra nec ad eam redire presumant, ac caveatis sollicite ne deinde alii judei extranei terram nostram intrare valeant ullo modo, eos si ingressi fuerint assimili expellendo. In exequendo autem huiusmodi mandato nostro solliciti intendatis." For full transcription, see Nirenberg, "Violence," pp. 333 f.

[60]ACA:C 246:242r (1321/7/22). The bailiff of Lleida was contesting jurisdiction over "quendam judeum castellanum suspectum de negotio potionum leprosorum" with the vicar and paers of the town. The king ruled that "quia dictus judeus extraneus est et potiones leprosorum ordinate erant fieri contra xristianos et in eorum dispendium, intendimus quod dicti vicarius et paciari et non vos debeant cognoscere de predictis" (emphasis added).

[61]Although it is clear from the king's order translated above, and from the documentation concerning the pastoureaux in the previous chapter (recall the seventy immigrant Jews who were murdered), that hundreds of Jews were immigrating into Aragon from France in 1320–1321, these immigrations are not mentioned by Y. T. Assis, "Juifs de France réfugiés en Aragon (XIIIe–XIVe siècles)," RdÉJ 142 (1983): 285–322.

had caused in the Aragonese Jewish community, and demonstrates how these tensions could find an outlet in accusations made under the new edict.

Jucef de Quatorze, a Jew from the area around Calatayud, was charged in 1342 with encouraging the relapse of a Jewish convert to Christianity. In keeping with inquisitorial procedure he was asked for a list of his mortal enemies. Many of his enemies were Christians, including the bailiff of Calatayud and his retinue, but among the Jews was one Cuxo, "gallicus." When asked why Cuxo was an enemy, Jucef stated

> that Cuxo is a Frenchman, and exercises the trade of a merchant; and he thinks he is an
> enemy because during the time of the inquests conducted against the French, the said
> Cuxo sheltered them [French Jews] in his home, and he still does so; the said Jucef was
> very angered by this, because many men of his lineage had lost all their goods for this
> reason; for all these reasons, the said Jucef accused the said Cuxo, along with all the
> Jews of Calatayud, saying that it would be a good thing if, and doing everything in his
> power so that, the said Cuxo might leave the land, since such a man should not remain
> in it.[62]

Jucef's kinsmen presumably lost their goods in the inquisitional activity that followed the expulsion from France, activity aimed at French Jews who might have converted to Christianity in France and relapsed once they reached the safety of Aragon. Such accounts as this cast doubt on Yom Tov Assis's claim that French refugees were always warmly received by Aragonese Jews. They also demonstrate how quickly Jews, like Christians, seized on new types of accusation created by royal policy in order to pursue old enmities.[63]

This edict against the immigration of Jews from France seems to have remained in effect for at least a year. In July of 1322 a group of Catalan Jews about to travel in France (in itself surprising) on business took the precaution of obtaining a letter from the king ordering royal officials not to arrest them at the borders on their return, since they were Catalan, not French.[64] The edict must

---

[62]Cathedral of Barcelona, Codex no. 126, fol. 53r. The document is partly transcribed in J. Perarnau i Espelt, "El procés inquisitorial barceloní contra els jueus Janto Almuli, la seva muller Jamila i Jucef de Quatorze (1341–1342)," *Revista Catalana de Teologia* 4 (1979): 309–353, here p. 323.

[63]On inquisitorial activity against French immigrants, see Assis, "Juifs de France," p. 300. The Inquisition returned to Calatayud to pursue similar charges in 1324–1326. Collection of the fines continued into Alfonso's reign. See Baer, *Die Juden*, vol. 1, no. 184, pp. 244–245, and add to the sources cited there ACA:C cr. Jaume II, box 135, no. 395; ACA:C cr. Alfons III, no. 306 (but two among many other documents on the case). For Assis's claim that refugees were warmly received, see "Juifs de France," p. 302. The extreme suspicion with which Aquinet, a young French Jew, was received in Vilafranca del Penedès (he was denounced to the bailiff of the town by the secretaries of the aljama) may be more typical. Vilafranca del Penedès, Museu del Vi, Arxiu de la Comunitat, Registre de la Cort del Batlle Ferrer Oller, 1325, fol. 116r, transcribed in Perarnau, "El procés inquisitorial barceloní," pp. 323–324n.23.

[64]ACA:C 175:248v–249r (1322/7/14): ". . . cum aliqui judei cathalani naturales terrae nostrae cathalonie extra dominationem nostram diu est se contulerint in Franciam tam causa negotiationis

therefore have had some effect on the immigration of those Jews forced to leave France in 1322, despite Assis's belief that James II "remained faithful to his traditional politics" in favor of Jewish immigration.[65] But whatever its implications for Jewish immigration, the edict clearly cast suspicion outward, across the borders. Catalan Jews, "our Jews," were not to be feared.

.   .   .   .   .

The preceding pages have documented the effects an extraordinary set of accusations had on social relations in the Crown of Aragon in 1321. These effects were not limited to majority relations with minority communities. Within both majority and minority communities, ways of perceiving enmity and reacting to it were momentarily transformed along axes of religion, disease, and political allegiance. What were the long-term effects of this transformation? Were the events of 1321 in Aragon part of, or did they contribute to, the formation of a religious, medical, and political discourse increasingly intolerant of Jews, lepers, Muslims, and other minorities within Christian society?

The answer to the first question seems to be "none." Most of the actions taken in 1321 against target groups were reversed within a year. Almost as soon as leper property was confiscated, pressure began to mount to have it returned. The use of leprosy accusations that had been sparked by the king's edicts concerning lepers ceased almost immediately.[66] Fear of contagion decreased almost as quickly. By February 1322, for example, a patient petitioned the king to free a leper and let him remain in the kingdom, since the leper was a surgeon and the patient needed him to complete a cure.[67] Unlike France, in the Crown of Aragon there were few attempts to carry out the full institutionalization of lepers, but, as in France, what attempts there were failed. Thus in 1349 Juan "the Gascon," administrator of the leper hospital in Zaragoza, complained that, although a previous king (James II in 1321?) had ordered that all those found to

---

quam aliter, et a vobis et aliis in reditu eorum ad partes dominationi nostri timeant forsitan capi et impediri et molestari in personis et rebus ac bonis eorum pretextu praeconizationis de mandato nostro publice facto quod aliquis extraneus judeus qui de partibus Francie veniret non posset terra nostram intrare, et qui intraverant expellerentur a terra." Catalan Jews faced considerable danger traveling in France. On July 15 and August 11, 1321, King James wrote to the *sénéchal* of Carcassonne requesting that he free two Catalan Jews who had been arrested by that official when the king of France ordered all the Jews of his kingdom captured. The *sénéchal* refused. See ACA:C 173:195r (1321/7/15), transcribed in Nirenberg, "Violence," pp. 319 f.; ACA:C cr. Jaume II, box 133, no. 3 (1321/8/11). The *sénéchal*'s response is in ACA:C cr. Jaume II, box 135, no. 173, dated Wednesday after the Assumption of the Virgin, 1321.

[65] Assis, "Juifs de France," p. 312.

[66] Though just as such accusations predated 1321, they postdated it too. For the case of Pere Teixidor, tried at Vic in 1333, see McVaugh, *Medicine before the Plague*, p. 221. See also ACA:C 1058:28v–29r (1341/10/5) for an outbreak of concern over nonsegregated lepers in the Vall d'Aran, and n. 14, above, for a flurry of accusation in 1390.

[67] Two documents, ACA:C 247:14r–v (1322/2/21).

be leprous in the kingdom of Aragon should be forced to bring their property and enter the leprosarium at Zaragoza, the order was unenforced.[68]

This is not to say that the rhetoric of magic, poisoning, or other "horrible crimes" lost all of its force. Just as such rhetoric existed long before 1321, it continued after. But the accusations were ecumenical and did not target particular groups. Already by November of 1321 the king was being told of "Christians, Jews, and Saracens" who were experimenting with magic, necromancy, and poisons, crimes so horrible as to offend the name of God. Even in the atmosphere of accusation still lingering at that date, the king's informers gave no religious specificity to their charge.[69]

Nor, in the years following 1321, were famines and pestilence seen as part of a plot against Christians. The famines of 1333, remembered later as "the first bad year," caused riots in Barcelona against municipal councilmen, not against the Jews. When the Carmelite friar Bernat Puig preached on Christmas Day 1333, instead of "sowing peace" and "inducing the populace, as he ought, to endure the high wheat prices patiently," he said only that the city councillors had caused the famine by hoarding grain, and that "it was fitting that God should give the city tribulations and anguishes, because of its evil government [regimen]."[70] Famines in Valencia were perhaps more severe, and events there took a different turn. In 1326 the Valencian municipal council attempted to restrict contacts among Christians, Muslims, and Jews in order to control sinful activity that was raising the wrath of God against the city. In 1335 the council again wrote to the king, informing him of their certainty that hideous sins had been committed in the city and its hinterlands, namely, sexual liaisons between Christians and Muslims, as well as sodomy between Muslims. These sins, it was said, were the cause of the present troubles, since they corrupted the air, and

---

[68] ACA:C 657:87r–v (1349/7/2); ACA:C 683:160v–161v (1356/3/39), the latter transcribed in Nirenberg, "Violence," pp. 358–361. The document is of special interest because it describes the collection of alms for the lepers. When the procurator of the leper house arrived at a given town on a feast day, town officials were to gather together all the citizens to hear the procurators plead for alms to relieve the misery of the lepers. On the failure of institutionalization in France see Bériac, Histoire des lépreux, pp. 197–198.

[69] ACA:C 246:305r (1321/11/20).

[70] The riot against the councillors (for selling grain at high prices) is described in AHCB, Llibre del Consell, 13, fols. 75v–76r (1334/4/16). The homes of several councillors were pillaged, their wine barrels smashed, and the like. See also ACA:C 529:26v (1334/4/23). The friar's sermon, as well as another sermon in which he encouraged the audience to pray for King Alfonso's victory in his war with the Muslims, but not in his war with Christians (i.e., the Genoese), is described in a petition from the town council asking that the friar be punished, AHCB, Llibre del Consell, 13, fol. 49r (1334/1/4): "Quoniam, idem frater, die natalis Domini in ecclesia sedis civitatis predicte, predicans verbum Dei, quia in ipsa civitate erat et est maxima caristia, et debuisset populum induxisse ad tollerandum pacienter ipsam caristiam . . . idem frater . . . totam plebem contra consiliarios et presidentes civitates predicte excitavit dicendo . . . quod, ob hec, dignum erat quod Deus daret dicte civitati tribulationes et angustias propter malum regimen predictorum." J. Mutgé kindly provided me with transcriptions of these documents. See also her La ciudad de Barcelona, pp. 44–45.

since God punished them by beating his people with pestilence, drought, sudden deaths, and famine.[71] These were complex claims, with complex motivations. They did not, however, attribute any malevolence to groups. What was at issue was the propensity of individuals (especially Muslims and Christians) to certain types of sin. If society was at risk, it was not from corporate enmities (Jews, lepers, Muslims, Templars, or any other group plotting against society) but from the disruptive behavior of sinful individuals.[72]

It is especially striking that the municipality of Valencia did not further pursue the equation made in 1321 of Jews or Muslims with poisoners, because it did so in the case of another group: women. The belief that women (especially midwives and herbal healers) could use their medicines both to cure and to kill was an old one, already formulated, for example, by Plato.[73] A similar theme appears in the Visigothic code, which itself became a source for later law in the Crown of Aragon. The thirteenth-century *fuero* of Albarracín, for example, dedicated a number of articles to women who prepared abortifacients, potions, and poisons.[74]

In 1329 the physicians of Valencia, working through the municipal council of the city, built upon this tradition in order to reinforce their monopoly on medical licensing by banning women from practice: "No woman may practice

[71] AMV, MC, A-1, fols. 280v–281r (1326/9/16): "Com, per pecats públichs e notoris perpetrats e feyts, lo nostre senyor Déus enjendrà en l'àer diverses tempestats a cominació o menaces que.s departescha hom de pecats." AMV, Ll.M., g³-1, fol. 51v (1335/11): ". . . per los quals peccats, axí enormes e molt greus, l'àer se corromp e nostre senyor Déus, al qual és desplaent, dona de grans verdugades, que s'acosten a bastonades, per pestalències de pedra e de enula e de sequedat, per minva d'aygües pluvials, morts soptanes e greus malalties e caresties de viandes." These documents are partially transcribed in A. Rubio Vela, *Peste negra, crisis y comportamientos sociales en la España del siglo XIV: La ciudad de Valencia (1348–1401)* (Granada, 1979), pp. 20–21. The latter is more fully transcribed in idem, *Epistolari de la València medieval* (Valencia, 1985), pp. 353–354. For more on interfaith sexuality, see chap. 5. On Christian stereotypes of Muslims as sodomites, see J. Boswell, *Christianity, Social Tolerance and Homosexuality: Gay People in Western Europe from the Beginning of the Christian Era to the Fourteenth Century* (Chicago, 1980), pp. 198–199, 278–283.

[72] Relations between the city of Valencia and seigneurial Muslims living in the villages that surrounded it probably structured the council's claims, especially those about miscegenation. Complaints from Valencia about the mixing of Christian prostitutes with Muslims in outlying areas like Paterna and Quart, for example, were fairly common. See, e.g., ACA:C 452:120r (1332/10/1), and chap. 5.

[73] Plato, *Theaetetus* 149–150. Anxiety about the double nature of medicines, killing and curative, was to some extent a general phenomenon in various European societies. See J. Derrida, "Plato's Pharmacy," in *Dissemination*, trans. B. Johnson (Chicago, 1981), pp. 70, 97–98, 129–132; M. Mauss, *The Gift: The Form and Reason for Exchange in Archaic Societies*, trans. W. D. Halls (New York, 1990), pp. 63, 152–153; idem, "Gift, gift," in *Mélanges Charles Andler* (Strasbourg, 1924). It was, however, heightened in the case of administration by women.

[74] *Leges Visigothorum* 3, 4, 13; on which see A. Niederhellmann, *Arzt und Heilkunde in den Frühmittelalterlichen Leges* (Berlin, 1983), p. 96. For the *fuero*: *Carta de población de la ciudad de Santa María de Albarracín*, ed. C. Riba y Garcia (Zaragoza, 1915), pp. 163–164. Similar laws were included in other *fueros*. The *Laws of the Alamans and Bavarians*, trans. T. J. Rivers (Philadelphia, 1977), pp. 50–51, made special provision for women who called each other "poisoner," and for the judgment of women accused of poisoning. No similar provision is made for men.

medicine or give potions, under penalty of being whipped through the town; but they may care for little children, and women—to whom, however, they may give no potion."[75] Monica Green has pointed out that later medieval medical licensing regulations were intended to restrict women's activities in the medical profession, while others have suggested that this particular regulation was aimed at Muslim *metgesses* (female doctors), since Muslims constituted the majority of women seeking medical licenses in fourteenth-century Valencia. Both of these arguments may be true, but even so the prohibition was implicitly based on claims that women, as a group, were especially likely to use poison. Hence the particular danger in their potions (in Catalan, *bouratges*).[76] Despite the events of 1321, such claims would not successfully be made about Jews or Muslims in the Crown of Aragon until many years after the coming of the Black Death.[77]

. . . . .

What, then, are we to make of cataclysmic events, like those of 1321, which are so discretely bound in time that they seem both to be unprecedented and to have no immediate afterlife? The answer does not lie in the *longue durée*. For centuries before 1321, stereotypes of leper malevolence and infection coexisted

[75] *Furs* of Valencia of 1329, provisions for control of medical practice. Transcribed by G. Colón from AMV, Furs de València, MS B of Boronat Péra, fols. 119v–120r, published and translated in L. García-Ballester, M. McVaugh, and A. Rubio Vela, *Medical Licensing and Learning in Fourteenth-Century Valencia* (Philadelphia, 1989), pp. 60–61.

[76] M. Green, "Women's Medical Practice and Health Care in Medieval Europe," *Signs: Journal of Women in Culture and Society* 14 (1989): 434–473, here pp. 446–452; García-Ballester, McVaugh, and Rubio Vela, *Medical Licensing*, pp. 29–32. For a discussion of women's roles in the transmission of pharmaceutical knowledge, of gynecological potions in particular, see M. Cabré i Pairet, "Formes de cultura femenina a la Catalunya medieval," in *Més enllà del silenci: les dones a la història de Catalunya*, ed. M. Nash (Barcelona, 1988), pp. 31–52, here pp. 34 f., discussing the pharmacological treatise *Flor del tesoro de la belleza: Tratado de muchas medicinas o curiosidades de las mujeres*, ed. J. de Olañeta (Barcelona, 1981).

[77] Individual Jewish doctors were accused of poisoning (e.g., Jucef de Berlanga, a physician of Calatayud accused of poisoning a cleric of Daroca under his treatment [ACA cr. Jaume II, box 134, no. 140]), but such accusations were not tied to stereotypes about Jews as poisoners. In 1356 the physicians of Valencia did complain, with some success, that Peter IV was granting licenses to "Jews, Muslims, and apostates." See A. López de Meneses, "Documentos culturales de Pedro el Ceremonioso," *Estudios de Edad Media de la Corona de Aragón* 5 (1952): 669–771, here doc. no. 37, p. 701. The argument for exclusion, however, was based on a concern that non-Christians would interfere with the administration of last rites to dying patients, not on propensity to poison. For what evidence there is for the stereotype, see McVaugh, *Medicine before the Plague*, pp. 59–60. The link between Jews and poison was stronger in Italy, but even there it was seldom invoked to bar Jews from municipal medical offices. On Italy see A. Toaff, *Il vino e la carne: Una comunità ebraica nel Medioeva* (Bologna, 1989), pp. 276–281. In Castille (and France) the link was invoked to some effect as part of Trastamara propaganda during the civil war against Peter the Cruel, but once the war was over the stereotype seems to have been once again contained. See in general J. Valdeón Baruque, *Los judios de Castilla y la revolucion Trastamara* (Valladolid, 1968), pp. 37–43; and more specifically idem, *Los conflictos sociales en el reino de Castilla en los siglos XIV y XV* (Madrid, 1975), p. 132, both of which overlook a good deal of material.

with ideals of the leper as object of charity, without engendering massive violence, and the same is true of the centuries after 1321. The lepers were not crushed by the slow accretion of stereotypes,[78] but by revolutionary accusations. Certainly these accusations made reference to a host of age-old ideas about their targets, but they did so within unique contexts and they were crafted with specific aims.

The process itself is most apparent in France. Earlier (chapter 2) I discussed how a series of rebellions against the monarchy were cloaked by violence and accusations first against Jews, then against lepers, and finally against Jews again. The accusations that "justified" this violence were not new. They drew upon ancient discourses about sacred monarchy, poison, the relationship of Jews to Christians, the relationship between disease and sin, and the like. It is in these discourses that the accusations sought their legitimation. But the accusations were novel in the work they were being asked to perform: providing the ideological legitimation for action that could be perceived as rebellious.

Behind the accusations in France we should see not the panic of irrational masses, nor a closely planned conspiracy coordinated by some unidentifiable elites, but the formulation and widespread adoption of a rhetoric that momentarily "worked." Nor should we underestimate the resistance encountered by this rhetoric or overestimate its causal importance. The "truth" of the accusations was established (to the extent that it ever was) only through sharp struggle with the monarchy, and this struggle took place along many fronts: taxation, coinage, inquisitorial justice, usury charges, jurisdictional complaints. In other years and contexts, the accusations of 1321 might have met the same fate as the Toulouse petition of 1320, gathering dust in some archive, unanswered and unread.

If in France the meanings of the accusations against the Jews, lepers, and Muslims were created out of conflict with the Crown, in Aragon they were determined, at least initially, by the king himself. As in the case of the Templars over a decade before, King James was provided with claims ready-made and already accepted by other monarchs.[79] James directed these claims in particular directions: away from the Jews, for example, and toward lepers. Such direction represented the Crown's interests, protecting its most precious assets (Muslims and Jews) while allowing it to claim the property of the lepers, a group whose complex status and privileges had placed them outside royal control. But the king's construal of the accusations was sharply contested by groups with different interests. Municipalities and individuals were eager to expand the implications of this new accusational tool, the Crown eager to constrain them. Both positions evolved in dialogue with each other. Foreigners and recent Jewish immigrants came to be included in target groups, and accusations of leprosy

---

[78] The model proposed generally by Cohn, *Europe's Inner Demons*; Beriac, "La persécution," p. 203; and Ginzburg, *Ecstasies*.

[79] For the reception of charges against the Templars in Aragon, see most recently J. M. Sans i Travé, *El procés dels Templers catalans*, 2d ed. (Lleida, 1991), and the bibliography contained therein.

against neighbors and enemies temporarily widened, but native Jews and most Muslims remained largely outside the scope of accusational activity. This was an evolutionary process driven by conflict and negotiation, not by a tendency to accept all such accusations as true.

There is a comparative note worth making. The same accusations, drawing upon the same sets of medical and religious stereotypes, had very different effects in France and the Crown of Aragon. An adequate explanation of this difference would require a comparative cultural, social, and political history too complex to undertake here. Consider the specific example of the lepers: why was the violence against them in Aragon so different from that against lepers in France?

Both regions shared common cultural and medical attitudes toward leprosy. The status of the leper as a source of corruption and sin does not differ significantly between the Catalan sermons of St. Vincent Ferrer and the *Gesta Romanorum*.[80] Nor were ideas about the disordering potential of bad kings lacking in the Crown of Aragon. In an argument reminiscent of the French material presented in chapter 2, the Catalan writer and physician Arnau de Vilanova stressed that unjust rulers, those who oppress the poor with taxes, debase the coinage, or allow the punishment of crimes to be remitted with monetary fines, would suffer rebellion and hardship in their realms along with illness and sterility in their bodies, whereas just rulers would enjoy victory and prosperity, as well as bodily health and fertility.[81] But there were also important differences between France and the Crown of Aragon. It may be, for example, that lepers (and other minorities) were better assimilated into majority social and economic structures in the Crown of Aragon than they were in the south of France, though we should not exaggerate the limits assimilation places on violence. Other differences, though less obviously connected to the status of minorities, nevertheless affected it greatly. Aragon, for example, had no "sacred monarchy." Catalan writers did draw links between just rule and the health of a monarch's body and kingdom. But Aragonese sovereigns, unlike those of France, did not construct an ideology of sacral kingship to justify their rule. Nor

---

[80]For a sense of the similarities between French and Iberian stereotypes about leprosy, compare the French material on the relationship between leprosy and sin in chapter 2 with St. Vincent Ferrer, sermon 145 (in *Sant Vicent Ferrer: Sermons*, vol. 5, ed. G. Schib [Barcelona, 1984], pp. 15–20), where leprosy is presented as the physical representation of pride, avarice, excessive sexual desire, envy, gluttony, anger, a propensity to resort to divination, and laziness. See too the *Cantigas de Santa Maria de Don Alfonso el Sabio*, ed. Real Academia, 2 vols. (Madrid, 1889), cant. 189, where a Valencian pilgrim encounters a dragon (sin) in the dark, defeats it, but is rendered leprous by its poison; or cant. 93, where a burgher excessively indulgent in sins of the flesh is punished by God with leprosy but is cured at the intercession of the Virgin Mary. The Iberian material, like the French, situates itself within a nexus of ideas about sin, disease, poison, contagion, and the like.

[81]Arnau de Vilanova, "Allocutio christiani," fols. 222v–223v, 224v–225r. Arnau bases his argument on a mixture of natural law, medical similes, and biblical proof texts, particularly Ecclus. 10:8: "Regnum a gente in gentem transfertur propter iniustitias." For an edition see now J. Perarnau i Espelt, "L'*Allocutio Christini* d'Arnau de Vilanova," *Arxiu de Textos Catalans Antics* 11 (1992): 7–135, here pp. 102–115. Compare Arnau's material with the texts discussed in n. 77 to chap. 2.

were they thaumaturgic. They invoked no healing touch as evidence of their special relationship with God.[82] Again unlike the kings of France, the count-kings of Catalonia-Aragon separated their treatment of minorities sharply from their self-presentation as Christian monarchs. Then too, after more than half a century of constitutional conflict between unions and monarchy in the Crown, resistance to royal power could follow a variety of clearly marked routes without being deflected against minorities. These differences, along with others such as differing structures of taxation and fiscality, may have restricted the spread of accusations against lepers, Jews, and Muslims in the Crown of Aragon by limiting their usefulness in broader social conflicts. In France, these accusations became affairs of state. In the Crown of Aragon they furthered more local enmities, pursued face to face.

The translation of events from France into Aragon in 1320–1321 suggests an obvious conclusion: although the form and vocabulary of stereotypes about and accusations against minorities (poison, magic, sexuality, and so forth) may seem very similar across time and geographic space, their function and effect are closely dependent on social context and conflict, and therefore differ greatly from time to time and place to place. There are more specific implications to such a conclusion. One is that explanations of violence against minorities that dwell exclusively in the history of stereotypes, that overemphasize similarities in vocabularies of hatred, or that depend upon the rise of a pan-European persecuting mentality fail to account for this diversity both in the reception of accusations against minorities and in the ability of such accusations to provoke violence. To account for this diversity a comparative approach, even the limited one presented here, is necessary.[83] Another is that cataclysmic violence cannot be understood separately from more common forms of violence and accusation through which conflict and competition are regularly pursued in a society. In this chapter, for example, we have seen how the charge of poisoning shaped strategies of accusation in the Crown of Aragon and was in turn transformed and redirected by these strategies. To represent adequately the complexity of this dialectical process, we need to study how persecuting discourses were put into action, not only in the rare moments of collective violence with which medieval history is punctuated, but also in the vast stretches of calmer relations in between. The charting of these calm but dangerous waters, what we might call the shoals of everyday violence, is the goal of Part Two, to which we now turn.

---

[82] Unfortunately, very little work has been done on the ideology of the Catalano-Aragonese monarchy. See, however, B. Palacios Martín, *La coronación de los reyes de Aragón, 1204–1410* (Valencia, 1975). For Castile, see T. Ruiz, "Une royauté sans sacre: la monarchie castillane du bas moyen age," *Annales: ESC* 39 (1984): 429–453. Compare epilogue, n. 60.

[83] One such study is that undertaken for leprosy in the Latin kingdom of Jerusalem and France by Pegg, "Le corps et l'autorité." Pegg's approach is taken up and championed by M. Douglas, "Witchcraft and Leprosy: Two Strategies of Exclusion," *Man*, n.s., 26 (1991): 723–736, here pp. 734–735.

PART TWO

❖ ❖ ❖ ❖ ❖ ❖ ❖ ❖ ❖ ❖ ❖ ❖ ❖ ❖ ❖ ❖ ❖

Systemic Violence: Power,

Sex, and Religion

Chapter 5

SEX AND VIOLENCE BETWEEN MAJORITY AND MINORITY

> Be consecrated unto me, for I, Yahweh, am holy, and I shall set
> you apart from all these peoples, for you to be mine.
> (Lev. 20:26)

T HE PREVIOUS CHAPTERS emphasize the relationship between the collective and the local, between stereotype and strategy, within episodes of large-scale violence. Such episodes have come to memorialize for historians the fragility of minority existence, but they tell us only part of the story of how religious difference generated violence. To address this latter question, we must lower our gaze from the thunderbolts of mass violence to the sparks generated by friction between groups, and specifically to the threat of violence arising from the everyday transgression of "religious boundaries" by individuals (through conversion, blasphemy, interfaith sexuality, commensality, dress, topography). This background static of violence never receded from practical consciousness. It influenced the daily actions and strategies of minority and majority alike: what clothes to wear, what route to take to work, how to accuse an enemy of a crime—the list is endless.

The list is so long because religious boundaries were themselves multiple. Depending on the needs of the moment, people might attempt to invoke or efface a great variety of implications from religious difference. In chapter 1, for example, a Christian ridiculed the barrier between Christian and non-Christian cooperation in feuds. At the opposite end of the spectrum, a Barcelonan scribe whose house was uncomfortably close to a "Jewish" sewer argued that non-Christian feces should be barred from flowing through his (Christian) neighborhood, since their odor offended the nostrils of the Virgin of the Pine, patroness of the parish church.[1] Transgression of such "situational" boundaries needed a great deal of amplification by circumstances before it could provoke violence. There were, however, some religious boundaries that were more highly charged and whose crossing was accomplished only at considerable risk.

Conversion is the most famously conflictual crossing of these boundaries. Not surprisingly, conversion in medieval Europe was meant to take place in only one direction: toward Christianity. Conversion from Christianity to Juda-

[1] For the sewer, see ACA:C 437:101v (1330/6/22). See also Mutgé, *La ciudad de Barcelona*, p. 277.

ism or Islam, on the other hand, rendered the convert infamous, occasioned the forfeiture of the convert's property, and was punishable by death.[2] The institutionalized violence represented by the Inquisition was a product of the anxiety that this boundary of conversion might be transgressed in the wrong direction. Yet in the Crown of Aragon this anxiety did not become generalized before the forced conversions of 1391. Certainly there were exceptions. Inquests into the "relapse" of Jewish converts to Christianity were not uncommon in the mid–fourteenth century.[3] Further, there were worries about the conversion of Christians to Islam, not surprising in a society bordering so closely with an Islamic state, borrowing extensively from Islamic culture, and containing a large population of Muslims. Such conversions did occur, but reactions to them seem to have been relatively moderate.[4]

The greatest amount of anxiety and violence surrounded a different type of crossover: that of sexual intercourse between members of different religious groups. Of all borders between communities, this was perhaps the "hottest" both because of its ability to provoke blinding flashes of violence and because its charge was most frequently tapped and put to work by individuals through accusations at law.[5] This, then, is a chapter about accusational or judicial vio-

[2]Documented conversions of "old" Christians (as opposed to the apostasy of recent converts to Christianity) to Judaism in medieval Europe are few. There are some famous exceptions, however. See, for example, F. Maitland, "The Deacon and the Jewess: or, Apostasy at Common Law," in his *Collected Papers*, ed. H. Fisher, 3 vols. (Cambridge, 1911), 1:385–406; A. Cabaniss, "Bodo-Eleazar: A Famous Jewish Convert," *Jewish Quarterly Review* 43 (1953): 313–318. In Spain, conversion from Christianity to Islam seems to have been more common than to Judaism (see below). On conversions between Islam and Judaism see chap. 6.

[3]We saw in the previous chapter how Jucef de Quatorze denounced some French Jews because he was afraid that they might be suspected of being relapsed converts. On the early history of the Inquisition in the Crown of Aragon see J. Vincke, *Zur Vorgeschichte der Spanischen Inquisition: Die Inquisition in Aragon, Katalonien, Mallorca und Valencia während des 13. und 14. Jahrhunderts, Beiträge zur Kirchen- und Rechtsgeschichte* 2 (Bonn, 1941). Cf. also Baer, *Die Juden*, 1:204–205; *The Jews*, 2:10–11.

[4]The most famous example of such a conversion is that of Anselm Turmeda, on whom see most recently M. de Epalza, *Fray Anselm Turmeda (Abdallah Al-Taryuman) y su polemica islamo-cristiana* (Madrid, 1994). See also R. I. Burns, "Renegades, Adventurers, and Sharp Businessmen: The Thirteenth-Century Spaniard in the Cause of Islam," *Catholic Historical Review* 58 (1972): 341–366. D. Carpenter, "Alfonso el Sabio y los moros: algunas precisiones legales, históricas y textuales con respecto a Siete Partidas 7.25," *Al-Qanṭara* 7 (1986): 229–252, here pp. 231 f., briefly notes the concern of the *Siete Partidas* with Christian conversion to Islam. Such conversions are well documented in the ACA; witness this nonexhaustive list from the reign of James II: ACA:C cr. Jaume II, box 57, no. 7,022; ACA:C 195:119v; 220:97r; 221:176r–v; 385:96v. ACA:C 220:12v–13r (1321/5/18) provides more detail than most. Here, Sibil complains that her husband, Bernat Nadal, converted to Islam while on a trip to North Africa. Bernat's father went to Africa, brought back his son, and reconciled him before the bishop of Tortosa. But when the father died some time later, the vicar of Tortosa first imposed a large fine upon Bernat and then claimed that because of apostasy the whole estate was forfeit. Bernat promptly relapsed and fled to North Africa with the inheritance. Sibil asks that the fine (already paid) be returned as charity for her children, and the king agrees.

[5]I am borrowing this typology somewhat metaphorically from P. Sahlins, *Boundaries: The Making of France and Spain in the Pyrenees* (Berkeley, 1989), pp. 1, 8–9. See also R. Gross, "Registering and

lence, not the violence of crowds or individuals. Accusational violence differs
from the more direct sort in that the violence is conditional (it depends upon
the charge's being believed and acted upon by officialdom), and the actual
violence is carried out (by judge, torturer, or executioner) in the name of the
collective. In the Crown of Aragon, as in medieval Europe generally, direct and
accusational violence were to a certain extent interchangeable, as when a Christian of Daroca first hit a Muslim on the head and then, when the Muslim tried
to bring suit for assault, charged the Muslim with interfaith sex to scare him into
dropping his case.[6]

Above all, this chapter is about the barriers to sexual intercourse between
people of different faiths erected within the fourteenth-century Crown of Aragon and the function of those barriers in both creating and containing violence. These two topics are not quite the same, and the chapter is divided
between them. The first half is panoramic. Its goal is to map sexual boundaries
more complex than we usually allow because created by three communities and
two sexes interacting in myriad asymmetries of power. Only with such a map in
hand can we identify those active borders where stress and violence were most
likely to accrue. These are the subject of the second half, which focuses on the
bodies of Christian prostitutes and asks how their disproportionate role in the
specific construction of miscegenation anxiety in the Crown affected the tenor
and force of violence against minorities.[7] This is a different set of questions from
those normally asked by historians of minorities, and it requires that we adopt
the point of view of the dominant majority, Christian and male. To do so is not
to trivialize the violence suffered by minorities, or to legitimate the inequalities
of power that such violence was meant to perpetuate. It is, however, to experience from another vantage point the vertigo induced by the precipices of privilege that separated the dominant from the weak.

.   .   .   .   .

Christian anxiety about marriage and sexual intercourse with non-Christians
was an ancient phenomenon, a feature of the earliest churches (e.g., 1 Cor.,
7:12–16) and the subject of canonical restrictions well before it drew the atten-

---

Ranking of Tension Areas," in *Confini e regioni: il potenziale di sviluppo e di pace delle periferie* (Trieste,
1973), pp. 317–328, cited in Sahlins, introduction, n. 1.

[6] ACA:C 175:264v (1322/7/21). See also the examples in chap. 1, and n. 43 there.

[7] The word "miscegenation" is a nineteenth-century neologism whose first extensive use seems
to have been in the United States immediately following the Civil War. Though it generally means
"a mixture of races; esp.: marriage or cohabitation between a white person and a member of another
race," I am using it here in an etymologically stricter sense, to indicate a mixing of categories (Latin
miscere and *genus*), in this case defined primarily along religious lines. Some of the ways in which
medieval notions of miscegenation differ from modern ones will be discussed more explicitly
below. The definition cited above is from *Webster's Third New International Dictionary* (1961). The
Oxford English Dictionary further specifies the races as "white" and "negro," though it gives instances
of other usages (e.g., "Christian" and "pagan").

tion of newly converted Christian Roman emperors as a fitting subject for secular law.[8] This it did soon enough. The "union" of Jews with Christian women (or at least with those who worked in imperial weaving factories) was forbidden by the emperor Constantius as early as 339.[9] By 388 the prohibition was generalized:

> No Jew shall receive a Christian woman in marriage, nor shall a Christian man contract a marriage with a Jewish woman. For if any person should commit an act of this kind, the crime of this misdeed shall be considered as the equivalent of adultery, and freedom to bring accusation shall be granted also to the voices of the public.[10]

This edict would have momentous consequences. Not only did it make intermarriage a crime susceptible to public accusation, but its preservation in the amber of the Theodosian Code encouraged its reincorporation into later medieval adaptations of Roman law.[11]

The prohibition on intermarriage was often reiterated in the early Middle Ages, though most frequently in conciliar, not secular, legislation.[12] These pronouncements suggest that intermarriage was a continuing problem, and one not always addressed by secular authorities.[13] By the turn of the millennium, how-

[8]The earliest council whose acts survive, the pre-Constantinian Spanish council of Elvira (ca. A.D. 300–309), included a canon forbidding intermarriage between Jewish men and Christian women unless the Jew was willing to convert. Sexual relations with pagans and heretics were also discouraged. See canons 16 and 78 in La colección canonica hispana, vol. 4, Monumenta Hispaniae Sacra, ed. G. Martínez Díez and F. Rodríguez (Madrid, 1984), pp. 247, 267. See also S. Laeuchli, Power and Sexuality: The Emergence of Canon Law at the Synod of Elvira (Philadelphia, 1972).

[9]Codex Theodosianus 16.8.6. It is not entirely clear whether this edict is concerned with intermarriage, conversion, or both, an ambiguity elided in the translation by J. Marcus, The Jew in the Medieval World: A Source Book (315–1791) (New York, 1969), pp. 4f.

[10]Codex Theodosianus 3.7.2; 9.7.5. Cf. A. Linder, The Jews in Roman Imperial Legislation (Detroit, 1987), pp. 178–182. Compare this strategy of fomenting accusations against Jews with the complaint in Lactantius, De mortibus persecutorum 13.1 (PL 7.214), that Diocletian encouraged all accusations against Christians but would not allow Christians to bring charges of adultery and theft on their own behalf.

[11]In the East the Codex Justinianus 1.9.6; and in the West the Lex Romana Burgundionum 19.4; the Breviarium of Alaric, 3.7.2, 9.4.4; and the Lex Visigothorum, 12.2.14, among others, all took up the prohibition on intermarriage in the Codex Theodosianus. The latter two had a considerable influence on the later development of Aragonese law.

[12]For papal condemnations of intermarriage see G. D. Mansi, Sacrorum conciliorum nova et amplissima collectio (Paris, 1901–1927), 12.294, canon 27 (A.D. 731), and MGH, Legum sectio III, Concilia, vol. 2.1, ed. A. Werminghoff (Hanover, 1906), p. 16, canon 10 (A.D. 743). A host of church councils addressed the issue of intermarriage. For Visigothic examples, see III Toledo (A.D. 589), canon 14; IV Toledo (633), canon 63; X Toledo, canon 7 (in La colección canonica hispana, vol. 5, Concilios Hispanos: segunda parte, ed. G. Martínez Díez and F. Rodríguez [Madrid, 1992], pp. 120–121; 239–240; 551). For the early medieval prohibitions on intermarriage see, inter alia, J. Parkes, The Conflict of the Church and the Synagogue (London, 1934); B. Bachrach, Early Medieval Jewish Policy in Western Europe (Minneapolis, 1977).

[13]IV Toledo, for example, ordered that "those Jews who have Christian women to wife be advised by the bishop of their city that if they wish to remain with her, they must become Christian,

ever, such flexibility seems a thing of the distant past, and with all intermarriage effectively suppressed, attention shifted from marriage to fornication and adultery (the two terms were used nearly interchangeably in the Middle Ages).[14] Between the eleventh and the fourteenth centuries, canon lawyers elaborated an extensive literature on the impermissibility, not just of marriage, but of any sexual contact between Christian and non-Christian, despite the fact that such contact outside of marriage was nowhere specifically forbidden in any of the major decretal collections. Their reasoning was straightforward. If Christians and non-Christians were explicitly banned from bathing or dining together, and from other forms of social intimacy, then surely the church fathers had also intended to ban the most intimate of social relations: sexual intercourse.[15] Not all lawyers agreed with this reasoning. Oldradus de Ponte, defending a Jew accused of intercourse with a Christian woman in early-fourteenth-century Avignon, argued that no ecclesiastical law demanded that the Jew be punished. But the fate of Oldradus's client demonstrates how unconvincing the argument was: Pandonus was castrated, his amputated flesh displayed publicly before the royal palace as a stark symbol of transgression.[16]

Not surprisingly, given this practical reality, Iberian secular law in the High Middle Ages ignored the issue of intermarriage and focused its concerns on the

---

and if, being warned, they refuse, they shall be separated." In Visigothic Spain the prohibition was both ecclesiastical and secular law, and enforcement was a real possibility. (IV Toledo, however, may have been concerned with originally Jewish couples in which the wife had converted to Christianity.) In Merovingian France, on the other hand, ecclesiastical sanction may have been the only practical action. At the Second Council of Orleans, in 533, the assembled bishops ordered the excommunication of any Christian who married a Jew but contemplated no further action (canon 19). For II Orleans, see *MGH, Legum sectio III, Concilia*, vol. 1, ed. F. Maassen (Hanover, 1893), p. 64. See also p. 67 for a similar pronouncement from Auvergne (535).

[14]Technically fornication included all intercourse other than that between husband and wife, while adultery was more narrowly sex by a married person with someone other than his or her spouse. In many of the documents discussed here, however, adultery was used more broadly to mean any intercourse other than that sanctioned within the bonds of marriage. For the technical distinction as used by Gratian and others, see J. Brundage, *Law, Sex, and Christian Society in Medieval Europe* (Chicago, 1987), p. 246.

[15]There are now a great many studies on the status of non-Christians in canon law pertaining to marriage. See most recently J. Brundage, "Intermarriage between Christians and Jews in Medieval Canon Law," *Jewish History* 3 (1988): 25–40; and W. Pakter, *Medieval Canon Law and the Jews* (Ebelsbach am Main, 1988), pp. 263–291. See also E. Bussi, "La condizione giuridica dei musulmani nel diritto canonico," *Rivista di storia del diritto italiano* 8 (1935): 459–494; F. Cantelar Rodríguez, *El matrimonio de herejes: Bifurcación del impedimentum disparis cultus y divorcio por herejía* (Salamanca, 1972); P. Herde, "Christians and Saracens at the Time of the Crusades: Some Comments of Contemporary Canonists," *Studia Gratiana* 12 (1967): 359–376; J. Muldoon, *Popes, Lawyers, and Infidels: The Church and the Non-Christian World, 1250–1550* (Philadelphia, 1979).

[16]For the text of Oldradus's argument, see N. Zacour, *Jews and Saracens in the Consilia of Oldradus de Ponte* (Toronto, 1990), pp. 30–32, 68–70, 90. See also Brundage, "Intermarriage," n. 47; "De his qui foris sunt," in Pakter, *Medieval Canon Law*, 275–276, 534–535. Compare n. 22 below, where the emphasis on spectacle and the public is even more apparent.

act of sexual intercourse itself. The prohibition enunciated in the *Costums* of Tortosa is representative:

> If Jewish or Muslim males are found lying with a Christian woman, the Jew or Muslim should be drawn and quartered and the Christian woman should be burned, in such a manner that they should die. And this accusation can be brought by any inhabitant of the town, without the penalty of "talio" or any other [penalty].[17]

The law in cases where Christian men had intercourse with non-Christian women was only slightly different. In the *Furs* of Valencia, for example, Christian males and Jewish women caught together were to be burned. Those caught with Muslim women were to be whipped naked through the streets together with their partner in crime.[18]

That these laws provoked judicial violence is evident from the archival record, a record that predates even the redaction of any of the law codes cited above.[19] In 1022 the lands of a Jew of Barcelona named Isaac were confiscated because he "committed adultery with a Christian woman." Isaac's life seems to have been spared in exchange for his acceptance of baptism.[20] By the thirteenth and fourteenth centuries, references to the punishment of Muslim and Jewish males on such charges are a bureaucratic commonplace. The passion of a Muslim convicted of intercourse with a Christian woman in 1388, for example, is recorded only in a note made by an official of the justice of Valencia that he paid a carter some thirty-four sous for the wood used to burn the prisoner.[21] This

---

[17] *Costums de Tortosa* (*Código de las costumbres escritas de Tortosa*, ed. R. Foguet and J. Foguet Marsal [Tortosa, 1912]), 9.2.7; Cf. *Furs*, 9.2.8–9, both parties condemned to be burned; and *El Fuero de Teruel*, ed. J. Casteñé Llinás (Teruel, 1991), no. 386, p. 533: "Similarly if a [Christian] woman is surprised with a Muslim or a Jew, and they can be captured, let both be burned together." Many more texts could be added. These are chosen as examples of the law in three principal polities of the Crown. The crime of miscegenation was considered so horrible as to be excluded from standard royal pardons and safe-conducts. For one among countless such safe-conducts, see ACA:C 880:132r (1345/2/20). For a remission, see ACA:C 520:260v (1329/2/6). Other crimes usually excluded from standard pardons included sodomy, abetting heretics, poisoning, false moneying, and lèse-majesté.

[18] *Furs*, 9.2.8–9. Cf. F. Roca Traver, "Un siglo de vida mudéjar en la Valencia medieval (1238–1338)," *Estudios de Edad Media de la Corona de Aragón* 5 (1952): 115–208, here p. 162; Boswell, *Royal Treasure*, p. 346. For more on the complex issue of the differential treatment of intercourse between Christian males and, on the one hand, Muslim females, on the other, Jewish, see below.

[19] Both the *Furs* and the *Costums* were redacted in the latter half of the thirteenth century (though the *Furs* continued to expand over time). The *Costums* (1272) codified older custom. On the sources of the *Costums*, see J. Massip, *La gestació de les costums de Tortosa* (Tortosa, 1984).

[20] Mention of Isaac's case is preserved in the *Liber Antiquitatum*, ACB, no. 448. fol. 170, published by F. de Bofarull, "Jaime I y los judíos," *Congrés d'Historia de la Corona d'Aragó, dedicat al rey en Jaume I i la seva época* (Barcelona, 1913), pp. 818–943, here pp. 821 f. See also Baer, *Die Juden*, vol. 1, no. 4, p. 2.

[21] Another official of the same court was paid five and one half sous for the work involved in publicly whipping a Jew for the same crime at roughly the same date. R. Narbona Vizcaíno, *Pueblo, poder y sexo. Valencia medieval (1306–1420)* (Valencia, 1992), p. 140

dry bureaucratization should not obscure the nature of the Muslim's fate. His consumption by the flames was meant as a vividly horrifying public example to others, even if its annotation was lost in a pile of routine receipts.[22]

The desire to prevent sexual contact between Christian and infidel led to the creation of other complementary boundaries as well, though these carried a lesser charge of violence. By the thirteenth century, fear of such intercourse came to justify the most extensive attempts at segregation undertaken by the medieval church. At the Fourth Lateran Council in 1215, it was decided that since the physical similarities among Christian, Jew, and Muslim led to sexual intercourse between Christians and non-Christians, Jews and Muslims would henceforth be required to dress differently from Christians.[23] This attempt to differentiate clearly between Christian and non-Christian, to draw visible boundaries between the two groups, would create an explosion of new rules and legislation stipulating how Muslims and Jews (and sometimes Christians) could attire themselves: the Jewish cape and wheel of colored cloth and the Muslim haircut and dress. We should not forget, however, that these emblems of difference were enacted and justified as visual representations of a sexual boundary not to be transgressed.[24]

.   .   .   .   .

Though this chapter focuses on Christian concerns about intercourse with non-Christians, and for its purposes Christian evidence is the most important, similar concerns and restrictions existed in both minority traditions. These minority concerns had their own histories and motivations, but they were also bound up

[22]Horrifying to the victim, though perhaps ludic for Christians in the audience. Compare the order of the judges of Mantua in 1569 that the testicles of a Jew be cut off as punishment for having had sex with a Christian, because this punishment would provide "a most beautiful carnivalesque spectacle." Cited in S. Simonsohn, *History of the Jews in the Duchy of Mantua* (Jerusalem, 1977), p. 115; Toaff, *Il vino e la carne*, p. 18. Toaff believes that Christian-Jewish intercourse in medieval central Italy was common, but cf. Bonfil, *Jewish Life in Renaissance Italy*, pp. 111–114.

[23]See canon 68 of the Fourth Lateran Council (1215), in *Constitutiones concilii quarti lateranensis una cum commentariis glossatorum*, ed. A. García y García, *Monumenta Iuris Canonici, Corpus glossatorum*, vol. 2 (Vatican City, 1981), p. 107. Similar requirements had been instituted a century before in the Crusader Kingdoms, where Frank and Muslim lived in close proximity. See, for example, the Council of Nablus (1120), c. 12, 15, 17, in Mansi, *Sacrorum conciliorum*, 21:264, and the discussion in J. Brundage, "Prostitution, Miscegenation and Sexual Purity in the First Crusade," in *Crusade and Settlement*, ed. P. Edbury (Cardiff, 1985), pp. 57–65, here 60–61.

[24]A. Cutler, "Innocent III and the Distinctive Clothing of Jews and Muslims," *Studies in Medieval Culture* 3 (1970): 92–116, argued that the distinction was imposed not to prevent sexual intercourse but to humiliate minorities. In Aragon, however, the documentation repeatedly stresses sexual boundaries as the motivation behind distinctive clothing. See, for example, ACA:C 384:48v–49r, concerning the Jews of Apiera; ACA:C 1090:10 r–v (1373/11/8), concerning the Muslims of Valencia. See also Brundage, "Intermarriage," p. 30; Lourie, "Anatomy of Ambivalence," p. 54. That distinctive clothing is meant to reinforce sexual boundaries is also evident in the Castilian *Siete Partidas* 7.24.11. See Carpenter, *Alfonso X and the Jews*, pp. 100–101.

with their Christian context, so that in this matter as in so many others the three communities shaped and were shaped by each other.[25]

For Jews, problems of miscegenation had been (and still are) a constant concern in a long history of living among other peoples. Mixed marriages were forbidden in Deut. 7:3 ("you must not intermarry with them"), and in Neh. 10:31 ("We will not give our daughters in marriage. . . nor allow their daughters"), while in Num. 25 Phinehas averted God's anger from the Israelites and ended a "plague" of miscegenation when he transfixed with a spear an Israelite man and a Midianite woman who were together in a tent.[26] Medieval Iberian rabbis, though less dramatic than Phinehas, nevertheless agreed with him. Maimonides, with characteristic clarity, outlined what was at stake: "for it is in these matters that the Omnipresent one has sanctified us and separated us from the heathens, namely in matters of forbidden unions and forbidden foods."[27] He went on to reiterate the Torah's prohibitions on intermarriage and to approve later prohibitions against adulterous intercourse as well, "as a precaution, lest such intercourse should lead to intermarriage."[28] Perhaps out of similar prophylactic concerns, miscegenation came to violate a number of taboos, including that of blood, since "the Sages have decreed that all heathens, whether male or female, are to be regarded as in a permanent state of flux

[25] For a discussion of miscegenation between Muslims and Jews, see chap. 6. The issue of the relationship between Jewish and Christian concerns about miscegenation is too complex to address here. For a polemical juxtaposition of the two, see H. Arendt, *Eichman in Jerusalem* (New York, 1963), p. 5. Compare J. Katz, *Exclusiveness and Tolerance: Studies in Jewish-Gentile Relations in Medieval and Modern Times* (Oxford, 1961), p. 3: "Every attitude of the Jew towards the non-Jew has its counterpart in a similar attitude of the Gentile towards the Jew."

[26] But there are also examples of sanctioned intermarriage or intercourse in Jewish scripture. Cf., inter alia, Genesis 34, where Simeon and Levi earn Jacob's reproof for murdering their sister Dinah's Gentile rapist/bridegroom; Genesis 40, which reports without negative comment Joseph's marriage to Asenath, daughter of Potiphera, priest of On (though later traditions present her as adopted, the biological daughter of Dinah and Shechem); and the Book of Ruth. For biblical and Talmudic laws on the subject of intermarriage, see L. Epstein, *Marriage Laws in the Bible and the Talmud* (Cambridge, MA, 1942); idem, *Sex Laws and Customs in Judaism* (New York, 1948). On Phinehas, see S. Reif, "What Enraged Phineas?: A Study of Numbers 25:8," *Journal of Biblical Literature* 90 (1971): 200–206.

[27] Maimonides, *Mishneh Torah*, introduction, summary of Sefer Kedushah (SK). Though for some purposes (and after much debate) the rabbis chose to define Muslims and Christians as nonheathens (e.g., for business purposes such as the lending of money or the selling of cattle), within the context of miscegenation there was no such relaxation, as the following quotations make clear. See also Katz, *Exclusiveness and Tolerance*, pp. 32–36, and chap. 4.

[28] *Mishneh Torah*, SK 12.1–10 (trans. L. Rabinowitz and P. Grossman, *The Code of Maimonides, Book Five: The Book of Holiness, Yale Judaica Series,* vol. 16 [New Haven, 1965], pp. 80–83). The quotation is from 12.2. Maimonides approves of the actions of zealots who, like Phinehas, kill Jews engaged in public miscegenation, but his equation of public with ten or more Israelite witnesses renders the approval more theoretical than practical. See SK 12.4–6, 14. For early rabbinic discomfort with Phinehas's actions, see TJ Sanh. 27b. R. Isaac ben Yedaiah, writing in Provence in the thirteenth century, emphasized that miscegenation could lead to apostasy. See M. Saperstein, *Decoding the Rabbis: A Thirteenth-Century Commentary on the Aggadah* (Cambridge, MA, 1980), p. 96.

insofar as cleanness and uncleanness are concerned, whether they actually have a flux or not."[29]

Maimonides was writing a legal commentary, and his concerns are hard to connect with specific events. More easily contextualized are the writings of the late-thirteenth-century Toledan rabbi Yehuda ben Asher ben Yeḥiel, who insisted that any Jewish man who practiced "harlotry with the daughter of a foreign God" should be placed under *ḥerem* (ban), and that it was everyone's responsibility to denounce before the Jewish courts any Jewish males who had committed harlotry with "Ishmaelite" or Christian women.[30] It is true that Yehuda was writing in a specific polemical context, reacting to a setting (Toledo ca. 1280) that produced poems like this one by Ṭodros Abulafia:

Yea, one should love an Arab girl
Even if she's not beautiful and pure.
But stay far away from a Spanish girl
Even if she's radiant as the sun! . . .
Her clothes are filled with crap and crud,
Her hems are blotted with her uncleanness.
Her harlotry is not taken to heart; she is
So ignorant of intercourse she knows nothing.
But every Arab girl has charm and beauty. . . .
She knows all about fornication and is adept at lechery.[31]

Yet Rabbi Yehuda's remarks are not unrepresentative of rabbinic attitudes in the thirteenth- and fourteenth-century Crown of Aragon. Thus Naḥmanides wrote to his son that "whoever goes astray with Gentile women desecrates the covenant of Abraham."[32] So strong was this sense of boundary that it could even be used to legitimate Jewish prostitution. In one Castilian community it

[29]SK 4.4 (*Code*, p. 26). Cf. Sk 12.2: "He is guilty through her of intercourse with a menstruant, a bondswoman, a heathen woman, and a harlot" (*Code*, p. 81). The legal issues that underlie this statement are complex and beyond my competence. See, by way of comparison, the treatment of Samaritans in Niddah 31b–39b, and of flux in Niddah 72.

[30]R. Yehuda ben Asher, *Zikhron Yehuda* (Berlin, 1846), no. 91. In no. 63 he invokes the zealots against such men.

[31]Note that this is a polemic in which Yehuda had the upper hand: Ṭodros was lucky to escape excommunication. For more on Ṭodros's precarious position, see R. Brann, *The Compunctious Poet: Cultural Ambiguity and Hebrew Poetry in Muslim Spain* (Baltimore, 1991), chap. 5. The translation of Ṭodros's poem is from Brann, p. 145.

[32]H. D. Chavel, *Kitvei Rabenu Moshe ben Naḥman*, vol. 1 (Jerusalem, 1964), p. 370; *The Zohar* 2, 3a–b (cited in Baer, *The Jews*, 1:262), and 2, 87b. For additional citations see B. Dinur, *Yisrael ba-Golah*, vol. 2 (Tel Aviv, 1969), pp. 291–292; Epstein, *Sex Laws and Customs in Judaism*, pp. 172–173. A rich and detailed treatment is that of Y. T. Assis, "Sexual Behaviour in Mediaeval Hispano-Jewish Society," in *Jewish History: Essays in Honour of Chimen Abramsky*, ed. A. Rapaport-Albert and S. Zipperstein (London, 1988), pp. 25–59, here pp. 38–41. See also Saperstein, *Decoding the Rabbis*, p. 246; and I. Epstein, *Studies in the Communal Life of the Jews of Spain*, 2d ed. (New York, 1968), p. 88, citing Rabbi Solomon ben Adret of Barcelona.

was explicitly argued that Jewish prostitutes, though a source of sin, should not be expelled, lest Jewish men seek out Christian harlots and "mix the holy seed with Gentile women."[33]

Muslims, or rather Muslim males, encountered within their own tradition somewhat less stringent prohibitions on miscegenation than Christians and Jews did, at least in theory. According to classical Islamic jurisprudence, Muslim men could marry Christian or Jewish women (the children would be Muslim), but Muslim women could not marry non-Muslim men.[34] This law was predicated, of course, on Muslim political superiority. In areas where Muslims were subject to Christians, however, as in the Crown of Aragon, such laws could not be observed in practice, since Christian law denied Muslim males the same right Muslim jurisprudence allowed them. Though it is difficult to find evidence of these practical limitations in the surviving Mudejar law codes, which repeat the precepts of classical jurisprudence even when these are inapplicable to the reality of Muslim life as a minority,[35] they are clearly apparent in handbooks of religious instruction like the so-called *Breviario Sunni*, written by Yçe de Gebir, a Segovian Muslim, in 1462. Here the prohibition on interfaith sexuality is absolute: "Whether men or women, they shall not sleep with nor marry infidels."[36]

Despite Yçe's evenhandedness, there was something of a double standard in the enforcement of antimiscegenation laws in minority (as in majority) communities. Jewish men often slept with non-Jews (generally Muslims: see the following chapter) with little formal sanction from their communities. Jewish women suffered corporal punishment, exile, or death for the same crime. Because Oro de Par, a Jewish woman of Zaragoza, consorted with Muslim (and

[33]*Zikhron Yehuda* 17, cited by Assis, "Sexual Behaviour," p. 45, along with further evidence for Jewish prostitution in the Crown of Aragon.

[34]For a summary of these rules see J. Schacht, *An Introduction to Islamic Law* (Oxford, 1964), pp. 131–132. For specifically Maliki law on the subject (the school of law most influential in Muslim Iberia and North Africa), see D. Santillana, *Istituzioni di diritto musulmano malichita con riguardo anche al sistema sciafiita* (Rome, 1925–1938), 1:207 f. The Maliki school, perhaps more than others, tended to frown on mixed marriages, especially if they occurred in lands not ruled by Muslims.

[35]See, for example, the fourteenth-century Castilian Mudejar law code transcribed as *Leyes de moros del siglo XIV*, ed. P. de Gayangos, *Memorial Histórico Español*, vol. 5 (Madrid, 1853), pp. 1–246, esp. title 14, p. 20. Title 83, p. 63, is concerned with the complications created when one member of a Christian couple converts to Islam; elsewhere Christians who convert to Islam and then relapse are to be beheaded (title 179, p. 143). The late-fourteenth-century Valencian *Llibre de la çuna e xara* (ed. C. Barceló under the title *Un tratado Catalán medieval de derecho islámico* [Córdoba, 1989], here p. 90) assigns the death penalty to married Muslim males who commit adultery, no matter what the religion of their accomplices. Similarly, unmarried males who sleep with unmarried females receive the same number of lashes regardless of the religion of the women.

[36]*Suma de los principales mandamientos y devedamientos de la ley y çunna por don Içe de Gebir . . .* (= *Breviario Sunni*): "Ni duerman, ni casen con ynfieles, asi hombres como mugeres." Ed. P. de Gayangos, *Memorial Histórico Español*, vol. 5 (Madrid, 1853), pp. 247–421, here p. 341. The most recent study of the *Breviario* is that of G. Wiegers, *Islamic Literature in Spanish and Aljamiado: Yça of Segovia (fl. 1450), His Antecedents and Successors* (Leiden, 1994), pp. 115–133 and passim.

Christian) men, the Jewish aljama asked the king to have her disfigured and exiled. Jewish officials were afraid to act on their own, the petitioners claimed, because they feared violence from Oro's Christian lovers. Family, too, could move to protect these boundaries: it was the brothers of a Jewish woman from Zaragoza who were accused of murdering her because she was pregnant by a Christian. Of course not every Jew shared this vigilant attitude, certainly not the Jewish butcher of Zaragoza who, together with some associates, kidnapped the daughter of another Jew and delivered her to a Christian "so that he might deflower her."[37] But it was normative.

Even more markedly, Muslim communities focused most of their attention on patrolling the interfaith sexuality of Muslim women, not men. The Muslim aljama of Valencia, for example, purchased King Peter's confirmation of its privilege that whenever a Muslim woman was found guilty of adultery (that is, any sexual intercourse) with a non-Muslim, the death penalty would be imposed upon her without possibility of monetary remission.[38] In individual cases, action was often taken by the families of the women involved, or by the local community. The Crown's registers are clogged with notices of Muslim women sentenced to death, flogging, or enslavement by their communities for adultery, whether with Muslim, Christian, or Jew.[39]

This emphasis on the transgressivity of female exogamous sexuality in minority communities is not surprising, both because it replicates concerns in the classical traditions of both communities and because minority male sexuality was the focus of so much majority attention. That said, there is a clear interrela-

---

[37] For the case of Oro de Par, which occurred in 1356, see ACA:C 691:127r–v. For the murder of the pregnant sister, see ACA:C cr. Jaume II, 30, no. 3804 (1311/1/15). A similar document concerning the case is published in Baer, Die Juden, vol. 1, no. 164, pp. 201–203, from ACA:C 239:18v–19r. For the kidnapping of Genton Ovay's daughter by Ebrahim Araria, "carnifex judeus cesarauguste," and her delivery to an unnamed Christian "ut eam defloraret," see ACA:C 1065:33v (1351/1/25). Cf. chap. 6 on the importance of this issue in Muslim-Jewish relations.

[38] For the edict of 1347 confirming the execution of Muslim adulteresses, see ACA:C 884:167r–v, published in Ferrer, Els sarraïns, p. 271. The edict was included in the compendium of Valencia's privileges entitled Aureum opus regalium privilegiorum civitatis et regni valentie (Valencia, 1515), "In extravaganti," 8, fol. 236 (p. 531 of the 1972 facsimile edition), with the incorrect date of 1348. For an earlier example, see ACA:C 61:101v (1283/4/23) (= Régné no. 1045), in which the Muslims of Xàtiva ask that the prohibition on adultery between Christians and Jews on the one hand, and Muslim women on the other, be enforced.

[39] Women condemned to death would be turned over to the Christian authorities for punishment, which generally consisted of enslavement. Alternatively, they might be redeemed for a sum of money by their families, by protectors, or through charity. For example, a poor married Muslim woman from the village of María was caught in adultery in 1342 and condemned to receive one hundred lashes. As she stood naked in the plaza about to be whipped, some Muslims from Zaragoza took pity on her and "for the love of God" paid her fine of seventy sous. See the account book edited in Orcástegui and Sarasa, "Miguel Palacín," p. 104. The frequency of these convictions stands in jarring contrast to the seeming difficulty of proving adultery accusations in the Qur'ān (e.g., Sūrah 4:15) and in classical sharīʿa (cf. N. J. Coulson, A History of Islamic Law [Edinburgh, 1964], pp. 126 f.), both of which require four eyewitnesses.

tionship between the treatment of women within a given minority community and the place of that community's women in the majority sexual economy, a point to which we will return below. Here the essential point is a more obvious one: that Jewish and Muslim communities each constructed sexual boundaries congruent with, and reinforcing, the Christian prohibition of miscegenation, though for very different reasons.

. . . . .

While it is true that all three communities, minority as well as majority, officially disapproved of miscegenation and were willing to use violence to discourage it, there were important differences in the forms miscegenation and violence took among the various groups. For the sake of simplicity, both interfaith sexuality and the violence it generated can be divided into two types, that involving majority males and minority females, and that of majority females with minority males.

By far the more common of these was the former, specifically between Christian males and Muslim females, and its violent result was generally the enslavement or (much less frequently) the execution of Muslim women.[40] These women committed two crimes when they had sex with Christians: they violated Christian laws against miscegenation, and they violated Muslim legal prohibitions on sexual intercourse outside of marriage. Both these crimes carried severe penalties of death or its equivalent (e.g., whippings of more than one hundred lashes), penalties that were routinely commuted to the "social death" of enslavement to the Crown.[41] Since this proved extremely profitable both for the Crown and for accusers, who received as reward a portion of the enslaved woman's sale price, Muslim women who slept with Christians ran a high risk of "losing their persons." Accusations against such women were often brought by their own families, or by officials of the Muslim aljama, but they could also come from Christians eager for profit, or even from the woman's sexual partner. This last possibility was vividly illustrated by John Boswell in the context of a royal grant to the monastery of Roda. In 1356 King Peter granted to the monastery rights over all Muslim women under its jurisdiction convicted of sleeping with Christians but had to alter his grant in 1357 to exclude those women

[40]Because the legal consequences of intercourse between Christian men and Muslim women have been extensively studied, they will be treated only briefly here. See Boswell, *Royal Treasure*, pp. 346–350; Ferrer, *Els sarraïns*, pp. 18–28; Lourie, "Anatomy of Ambivalence," pp. 69–70; M. Meyerson, "Prostitution of Muslim Women in the Kingdom of Valencia: Religious and Sexual Discrimination in a Medieval Plural Society," in *The Medieval Mediterranean: Cross-Cultural Contacts*, Medieval Studies at Minnesota 3, ed. M. J. Chiat and K. L. Reyerson (St. Cloud, 1988), pp. 87–95; and C. Verlinden, *L'esclavage dans l'Europe Médiévale*, vol. 1, *Péninsule Ibérique-France* (Bruges, 1955), p. 420.

[41]Boswell, *Royal Treasure*, p. 346. On slavery as social death, see O. Patterson, *Slavery and Social Death: A Comparative Study* (Cambridge, MA, 1982).

convicted of sleeping with the monks themselves. Evidently the monks of Roda (and there are other examples) sought both financial gain and sexual recreation by "seducing" Muslim women, then denouncing the objects of their desire and having them enslaved.[42]

It is not enough to attribute this vulnerability of Muslim women to "colonial" exploitation by Christians. It was this, but it was also the product of a Muslim society in which the competition for family honor was carried out (in part) through emphasis of restrictions on female sexuality. The colonial context did not create this emphasis, though it sharpened it by adding a level of competitive signification: interfaith adultery impugned the honor of the Muslim community as well as of the woman's family. Thus it was the Muslim community itself that policed the bodies of its women and condemned their sexual transgressions, at times even asking the Crown to ban its officials from commuting execution or otherwise exercising leniency.[43] There were various ways Muslim women could hope to escape punishment for miscegenation. They could convert to Christianity, as did two shepherdesses who abandoned their flocks and ran off with a Christian prostitute, adopting her trade.[44] They could even touch the king's compassion by telling him of the wrongs they had endured. When Fatima was accused, she explained to King Peter IV that she had been raped by a Christian when she was nine years old, had a child by him, and was then given by him to a Muslim in marriage. She had left that marriage because the husband was wasting her possessions, and then had sex with a number of Christians. The king forgave her the consequences of this past.[45] Such stories suggest that, vulnerable as Muslim women were to the violence generated by miscegenation boundaries, those same boundaries could sometimes give them unusual opportunities to escape the control of their families and communities. From the point of view of the male Muslim community, however, each such act of royal leniency not only lessened the community's honor vis-à-vis the dominant faith

[42] For Boswell's example, see *Royal Treasure*, p. 348, citing ACA:C 1149:23 and ACA:C 1070:23. In 1337 Peter pardoned a Muslim woman named Fatima for sexual relations with Sancho de Martes, a member of the royal household, on the condition that she never again have intercourse with a Christian, but later revoked the pardon and granted her as slave to Sancho himself. See ACA:C 860:130r (1337/1/20) and 861:207v (1337/3/22), cited in Ferrer, *Els sarraïns*, p. 21.

[43] This Muslim concern has been well noted by Meyerson, "Prostitution," pp. 90–91. For an example of Muslim requests to forbid leniency, see n. 38, above. A fear of assimilation may have contributed to this restrictive emphasis. For an example of a society shifting from "permissive" female sexuality to "restrictive" as (in part) a reaction to colonial sexual exploitation, see R. Gutiérrez, *When Jesus Came the Corn Mothers Went Away: Marriage, Sexuality, and Power in New Mexico, 1500–1846* (Stanford, 1991), p. 156.

[44] On the two shepherdesses (who belonged to the noble Guillem d'Entencia), see ACA:C 172:21r–v (1321/9/8). Conversion often protected Muslim women from punishment for miscegenation (e.g., ACA:C 896:21r, 1353/5/21), but not always (e.g., Verlinden, *L'esclavage*, vol. 1, doc. 9 [with wrong date], ACA:C 211:269r). Cf. Boswell, *Royal Treasure*, p. 347.

[45] See ACA:C 869:204r–v (1340/8/22) and 871:165r (1341/2/20), discussed in Ferrer, *Els sarraïns*, p. 22.

but also weakened its ability to regulate the sexuality of its women, and was therefore doubly resented.

The frequency of Christian male sex with Muslim women is interesting, among other reasons, because it muddies the illusion of a neat congruence in Christian attitudes toward sex with Muslims on the one hand and with Jews on the other. There are already hints of disparity in the law codes, as for example in the *Furs* of Valencia, where Christian males caught with Jewish women are to be burned, whereas those caught with Muslim women are to be whipped naked through the streets.[46] Intercourse between Christian men and Jewish women did occur. In the mid-1260s, for example, a Jewish woman named Goig de Palafols petitioned King James I for an extension on his previously granted permission for her to live with her Christian lover Guillemó. Goig writes that she has brought Guillemó "into her house, her living quarters, and her bed-chamber." The couple is "burning in their love for each other," and now that the term on their permission to cohabit is about to expire, they feel like "a thief whom the lord has ordered to be hanged."[47] Such things happened, but they were much rarer, and less likely to be tolerated, than relations between Christian men and Muslim women.[48]

The question of why this might be so deserves a chapter in itself, one focusing upon the theological as well as the social.[49] Here, however, in a vast oversimplification, I will limit myself to one issue: the relative power of the two communities. The Muslim community was comparatively poor, predominantly agricultural, its political influence fragmented among a multiplicity of lords. Perhaps more important, Muslims were a conquered people, defeated in past battles of a war whose end was not yet in sight. All foreign Muslims were *de bona guerra*, enslavable upon capture, and native Mudejars, though protected by law, could sometimes be enslaved illegally, or (more frequently) legally as punish-

[46] *Furs* 9.2.8–9, cited above, n. 17.

[47] The king's answer to Goig's plea is not recorded. For her letter, see ACA cr. Jaume I, box 1, no. 19 (undated). The letter is transcribed and discussed in L. Berner, "On Western Shores: The Jews of Barcelona during the Reign of Jaume I, 'el Conqueridor,' 1213–1276" (Ph.D. diss., University of California, Los Angeles, 1986), pp. 267–274, 543–544. Goig was a prominent woman, perhaps even a creditor of the king's. The permission may have been necessary as much to protect her from legal action by the Jewish community as to protect the couple from Christian law.

[48] See, for example, ACA:C 221:145r (1321/12/17), a remission for Pere de Villanova, Christian of Valencia, accused of having had sex with Balida, wife of Astrug Mossetes, Jew of said town. Pere paid eight hundred sous reials for the remission. I know of no such fines involving Christian-Muslim relations. The rape of Jewish women by Christian men also seems to have triggered more violent conflict than that of Muslim women. Cf. ACA:C cr. Jaume II, box 133, no. 65 (1324/7/24), where an attempt by a group of Christians in Lleida to rape some Jewish women led to a battle in which both Jews and Christians were injured.

[49] For example, did the foundational relationship of Judaism vis-à-vis Christianity lead Christians to insist on greater sexual separation from Jews than from Muslims, whose religion was less threatening because its validity did not have to be accepted on any level?

ment for a great variety of crimes.[50] By definition, in fact, any Muslim woman involved in miscegenation lost her freedom and her person. The enslavement of Muslim women involved in such relations diffused much of the tension inherent in them (from a Christian point of view). Sex with slaves was a common practice throughout the Mediterranean, among adherents of all three faiths, and the Crown of Aragon was no exception. Such sex expressed and reproduced relationships of domination and dependence within the household.[51] Further, when a Christian penetrated a Muslim woman/slave, he reiterated those very acts of conquest and degradation that formed much of the basis for Iberian Christian ideas of masculinity and honor. From the point of view of Christian males, then, sex with Muslim women reaffirmed religious, gendered, and economic hierarchies and created no problematic kinship ties.[52]

The Jews, on the other hand, were closely tied to the Crown and had a good deal of financial and political power that they could use to reinforce the sexual boundary around their community.[53] And Jews were not a conquered people subject to enslavement (except in a quasi-mythical and theoretical sense: see chapters 1 and 7). A Jewish woman accused of miscegenation might be fined, tortured, mutilated, or even executed, but she could not become chattel. Goig's case provides a clear example of the confusions this could create: a Jewish

---

[50]Cf. Boswell, *Royal Treasure*, pp. 50–51; Burns, *Islam under the Crusaders*, p. 252; Lourie, "Anatomy of Ambivalence," pp. 62–68; with similar examples in Verlinden and Ferrer. Foreign Muslims could be exempted from enslavement through treaties made between their rulers and Christian monarchs.

[51]In the Crown of Aragon sex with slaves became problematic only when it involved people from outside the household. Hence James II's edict, issued at the request of the city of Valencia and other towns of that kingdom, forbidding anyone to have sex with an owner's slave unless they were of the owner's "parentela." Violators were to be whipped naked through the streets. See ACA:C 219:321r (1321/5/1). On sex with slaves more generally see Brundage, *Law, Sex, and Christian Society*, p. 518. Of course the relationships expressed and established through such sex varied greatly between, for example, Islam (where the concubine's *um walid* status produced free and legitimate offspring) and Christianity. For sex with slaves in Islam, see S. Marmon's summary article "Concubinage, Islamic," in *Dictionary of the Middle Ages* (New York, 1983), 3:527–529. The explicit Islamic literature on the purchase of slaves for sex is generally lacking in Christian Europe. For a sample of such literature see Abu'l-Ḥasan al-Mukhtār ibn al-Ḥasan Ibn Buṭlān, *Risāla fī Shirā al-Raqīq*, ed. ʿAbd al-Salām Ḥārūn (Cairo, 1373/1954), pp. 354–358, 371–378; English translation in B. Lewis, *Islam*, vol. 2, *Religion and Society* (Oxford, 1987), pp. 243–251. See also F. Malti-Douglas, *Woman's Body, Woman's Word: Gender and Discourse in Arabo-Islamic Writing* (Princeton, 1991), pp. 33–38.

[52]In Christian Spain sexual exploitation was primarily a problem for slave women, though one finds hints that the power of female slave owners could be used to similar effect. Cf. *Cantigas* 186, where a Christian woman forces her male Muslim slave to participate in the entrapment of her daughter-in-law on charges of miscegenation. I do not have enough information about homosexual miscegenation involving Muslim slaves to hazard an opinion on the subject.

[53]Thus in 1277 the Jews of Calatayud obtained from King Peter III a charter fining any Christian male caught by witnesses in bed with a Jewish woman three hundred maravedis, and giving the Jewish community the right to arrest him. See ACA:C 39:155r-v (= Régné no. 674, and doc.10).

woman, moneylender to the king, using her political connections to allow her access to a Christian lover. Far from domination, this bordered on dangerous inversion.[54] Such relations posed a threat to Christian hierarchies and needed to be ringed with a thick hedge of taboo.[55]

Though the violence generated by intercourse between Christian men and minority women had differential affinities, it remains true that even the most tolerated form of miscegenation from the Christian point of view (i.e., Christian males with Muslim females) was capable of provoking collective anxiety and a potential for violence. Like a variety of other widely tolerated but disapproved-of activities (e.g., gambling, or the frequenting of prostitutes by married men), engaging in such intercourse was considered a sign of bad character, and bad character, if it was formalized in a charge of "mala fama," entailed serious judicial disabilities such as susceptibility to torture or banishment.[56] Even more revealing is the elevation of these issues of individual character to subjects of community concern and censure in times of crisis, such as the advent of famine, drought, or plague. These crises were thought to be a punishment for the moral failings of a community and its individuals. A graph of the dates of such crises coincides precisely with that of the dates of municipal decrees against miscegenation and other "crimes against nature," which suggests that though the transgressive character of Christian male miscegenation could be overlooked, it was never forgotten.[57] It is in this vein that we should read the complaint of St. Vincent Ferrer: "Today the law is not obeyed. [Christian men] want to taste everything: Muslims and Jews, animals, men with men; there is no limit."[58] Religious identity was viewed as a "natural" limit to sexual contact, as "natural"

---

[54] A concern made clearer in Castilian literature than in Catalan. See, e.g., E. Aizenberg, "Una judía muy fermosa: The Jewess as Sex Object in Medieval Spanish Literature and Lore," La Corónica 12 (1984): 187–194.

[55] Compare J. Kovel, White Racism: A Psychohistory, 2d ed. (New York, 1984). Kovel makes a distinction between "dominative racism" and "aversive racism." In the former, which he terms phallic, the subjugation of the minority woman through slavery makes intercourse with her un-problematic for the majority male. When such categorical domination is impossible, however, "phallic" domination is replaced by aversion, by repression and fears of pollution, a state Kovel terms "anal." Cf. S. Freud, "On the Universal Tendency to Debasement in the Sphere of Love," in vol. 11 of The Standard Edition of the Complete Psychological Works of Sigmund Freud, trans. and ed. J. Strachey (London, 1957), pp. 177–190, esp. 182–183, 189. Such a model makes some sense if we accept the argument of T. Glick's "The Ethnic Systems of Premodern Spain" (Comparative Studies in Sociology 1 [1978]: 157–171), with its distinction between "paternalistic" and "competitive" systems in which Muslims are viewed paternalistically, Jews competitively.

[56] See Villanueva's transcription from the canons of the Synod of Tortosa (1359), in Viaje literario, 5:362; and Boswell, Royal Treasure, p. 346n.71.

[57] For the linkage between crisis and moral failing, see below, as well as chap. 4., n. 71, and the epilogue. For Narbona's graphing of the dates of famine and plague against moral legislation in Valencia, see his Pueblo, poder y sexo, p. 75.

[58] St. Vincent Ferrer, Sermons, vol. 1, ed. J. Sanchis Sivera (Barcelona, 1932), "Sabbato [post pentecostes]," p. 224.

as boundaries between the sexes, or between humans and animals. Such boundaries could be crossed, but not effaced.

. . . . .

Christian female intercourse with minorities was far more explosive an issue, albeit probably less frequent, than that of Christian males. We have already seen examples of the violence such acts could bring upon the minority males involved: burning, castration, torture. Christian women, too, confronted the stake. The risks involved are evident in the behavior of those accused. In 1311 Prima Garsón fled her hometown of Daroca in fear when rumors implicated her in an affair with a local Muslim named Ali, who was burned at the stake in her absence. When she was captured, a medical exam proved her virginity and therefore her innocence (as well as the unfortunate Ali's), none of which had served to assuage her terror when the rumor was first bruited about.[59] Elvira, a Christian widow of Oriola who had two daughters by a Muslim of Crevillent, skipped town as soon as her affair became gossip, escaped to Granada, and converted to Islam.[60]

Absent the possibility of legal marriage between Christian and non-Christian, three permutations of this type of miscegenation existed: within a minority marriage in which one spouse converted to Christianity, within an adulterous relationship, or between prostitutes and their clients. The first of these was relatively rare (at least until the mass conversions of 1391), and authorities seemed willing to extend a large degree of latitude in such cases. Gonsalvo García, a carpenter of Teruel converted from Islam to Christianity, lived for over a decade with his Muslim wife Nuça "so that he could convince her and [their] children to convert" before some of his enemies convinced the bailiff to prohibit their cohabitation. Even then, the king granted Gonsalvo's wife an additional year in which to come to the faith.[61] A more relevant case, because it involved a Christian woman, is that of a Jewish couple, Samuel Baruch and his wife Aldonça. When Aldonça converted to Christianity in 1391, her father (also a convert) publicly interrogated his son-in-law before the notary of Santa Coloma de Queralt, the rector of les Piles, and several other witnesses. He presented Samuel with two possibilities: convert to Christianity and continue the marriage, or, alternatively, remain a Jew but still keep her as his wife, without prejudicing her Christian faith. Samuel opted for a third way, probably much

---

[59]Ferrer, *Els sarraïns*, p. 32, citing ACA:C 239:32v, 95r, 125r, 205v; ACA:C 241:117r.

[60]Ferrer, *Els sarraïns*, citing ACA:C 207:184r (1311); ACA:C 150:65v–66r (1312).

[61]ACA:C 455:181r (1332/7/11). Similarly, a Muslim named Zorba was arrested in 1334 because she was living with her husband, who had converted, but the king ordered her freed and allowed her to continue cohabiting with her husband in the hopes that he might convert her. See ACA:C 502:211v (1334/4/11), in Ferrer, *Els sarraïns*, p. 243.

more common: divorce—which should not overshadow the fact that as late as 1391 such a choice was not a foregone conclusion.[62]

Nor, in general, do contemporaries seem to have been as concerned about the possibility that married women might engage in interfaith adultery as one might expect in a culture where familial and community honor were so inextricably interwoven with female sexuality. Each group did have a good deal of competitive interest in the morality of the other groups' women. Muslims and Christians, for example, were well represented in the crowd of spectators packing the synagogue of Zaragoza for the adultery trial of the Jewess Doña Lumbre. The crime itself, however, was an intrafaith affair.[63] Even the exceptions seem relatively unconflictual. When Çalema Abinhumen was accused of sexual relations with Arnaldona, the wife of Ramon d'Aguilar, of Lleida, Ramon denied any knowledge or suspicion of the deed, and Çalema was acquitted.[64] True, husbands might have a number of reasons to deny such suspicions.[65] Nevertheless, the rarity of miscegenation accusations against married women and women "of good repute" in the archives suggests that these were not the primary locus of miscegenation anxiety.[66] Women of bad repute were.

Prostitutes are by far the most frequently mentioned class of Christian women in miscegenation cases. It is in some ways easy to see why this might be so. Sexually active, relatively unsupervised, mobile, and dependent on clientele, prostitutes had greater motive and opportunity, so to speak, than other

[62] AHPT, Man. 4017 (Santa Coloma), 1391–1392, fols. 79v–80v, transcribed by Secall, La comunitat hebrea, pp. 118–119: ". . . e si xipia nous volets fer si volets fer habitacio ab la dita filla mia en la vila d Tarrega tinent aquella com a muller com ella es presta e aparellada de star ab vos e de servir vos be axi com muller deu fer a marit sens contumelia dela fe xipiana." Secall does not notice that the passage allows cohabitation should Samuel fail to convert. For an example of a more straightforward divorce, see pp. 116–117. For the canon law treatment of marriages in which one spouse converts to Christianity, see Brundage, "Intermarriage," p. 29.

[63] On this fascinating trial, which occurred in 1368, see A. Blasco Martínez, "El adulterio de Doña Lumbre, judia de Zaragoza," Michael 11 (1989): 99–120, here p. 114: ". . . en la sinoga, en la qual se suelen diversas gentes de christianos et de moros plegar quando tales actos se fazen en grant multitud." See also her "Avance de estudio de un caso de adulterio en la aljama de Zaragoza (siglo XIV)," Proceedings of the Ninth World Congress of Jewish Studies, Division B, vol. 1, The History of the Jewish People (Jerusalem, 1986), pp. 105–112.

[64] ACA:C 876:60v–62r (1344/4/2), cited by Ferrer, Els sarrains, p. 31, published by Mutgé, L'aljama, pp. 298–302.

[65] The Jew who struggled with a naked Gentile he found hiding under his wife's bed chose to believe his wife's story that the man had given her his pants and shirt to repair, since if he doubted her she would be forbidden him by Jewish law. Adret 1:1187. Cited by Assis, "Sexual Behaviour," p. 47.

[66] The few examples in literary sources seem to support this conclusion. See, e.g., Cantigas 186, where a mother-in-law seeks to entrap her son's wife by forcing a Muslim slave to get in bed with her while she sleeps. The wife is condemned to the flames, but her innocence is established when the Virgin Mary has the fire devour the Muslim but leave her untouched. None of this is to suggest that this type of miscegenation did not occur, only that it did not form a focus of public discourse.

women.[67] In part as a result of this, prostitutes became the focus of discussion about miscegenation in all three communities. Christians wanting to craft believable accusations against a Jew, for example, knew the importance of putting a prostitute at the center of the story. When two converts to Christianity wanted to embroil the Jew Boniach Deuslosal, a former associate of theirs, with the Christian authorities, they spun a narrative of a business trip in which the three met a Christian woman on a country road and each had sex with her. The prostitute, whom the accusers described as "young and energetic," had conveniently left for the Balearics, but the two converts were willing and able to provide details: who paid how much, in what order they lay with her.[68] If the judge was not convinced, it was not because the story was implausible. Here as in so many cases the topos gained its force from reality.[69]

Boniach was fortunate to escape unscathed. In other cases, prostitutes could prove a lightning rod for judicial violence on a massive scale. Eighteen Muslims from the Vall d'Uxó were condemned to death for sexual relations in a field with a Christian prostitute. The remission cost them 4,120 sous of Barcelona: a fortune.[70] Minority communities were alert to this danger of "prostitutes as boundary" and took steps to limit it by attempting to keep "public women" at a remove. The strategy of the Jews of Daroca is typical. They complained that Christian prostitutes resided on the route the Jews had to take in order to draw water from the river, a proximity that was dangerous insofar as it could provide

---

[67] On the many forms of prostitution, formal and informal, legal and clandestine, in fourteenth-century Valencia, see the thoughtful article of M. Carmen Peris, "La prostitución valenciana en la segunda mitad del siglo XIV," in *Violència i marginació en la societat medieval* (= *Revista d'història medieval* 1 [1990]), 179–199, here pp. 180, 187, 189. Most of the examples of miscegenation that follow occurred with informal or clandestine prostitutes, i.e., with those not enclosed in a supervised brothel. From the licensed brothel of Valencia city, for example, only three occurrences of miscegenation reached the courts in the period between 1367 and 1399. (The figure is somewhat deceiving, since the charges against the convert Gil García were that he had arranged for a great many Muslims to lie with Christian prostitutes by telling the women that the men were Christian. Gil was condemned to burn.) See ibid., pp. 183, 185. This is due to the fact that licensed brothels were subject to a great deal of official supervision. The gallows erected just outside the entrance to the Valencian brothel was meant as a reminder of this, doubtless an inhibiting one for non-Christians. (The description of the gallows is from the much later (1501) account of Antonio de Lalaing, in *Viajes de extranjeros por España y Portugal*, vol. 1, ed. J. García Mercadal [Madrid, 1952], pp. 478 f.)

[68] Perhaps the accusers, like Naḥmanides, had heard the proverb preserved in the latter's *Vikuaḥ*: "They say in our land: 'he who wishes to tell lies should send his witnesses far away.' "

[69] There are many such accusations preserved. This one is mentioned because the sixty-two-page trial transcript for the case (against Boniach Deuslosal, Jew of Puigcerda) survives and is a valuable example of accusation techniques, particularly *converso* ones. A good deal of the case is concerned with an incidental accusation of receiving stolen consecrated Hosts. Boniach was acquitted on all counts, and the case did not proceed to torture. See ACA:C Procesos 23/3 (1377/10/31 forward).

[70] ACA:C 221:231v–232r (1322/5/8). Cf. Ferrer, *Els sarraïns*, p. 35n.85.

occasion for accusations.[71] The Muslims of Valencia city, using similar arguments, expended a great deal of time and effort in an ongoing battle to expel Christian prostitutes from the Muslim quarter, efforts that were sometimes stymied by that enigmatic figure, the *rex arlotum* (king of prostitutes) of Valencia.[72] Both communities demonstrated a refined awareness of the prostitute as site of miscegenation, and of the politics and dangers of such transgression. Prostitutes were an important boundary, albeit a movable and corporeal one, between Christian and non-Christian. It was in fact this motility and corporeality that rendered them so dangerous.

No one was more aware of the prostitutes' role in the economy of miscegenation than the women themselves, since they were not spared by the violence channeled through their bodies. Unless they could prove that their clients had passed as Christians, they faced the flames. (Though how often they were actually executed is hard to determine, since the death of a prostitute was of little official consequence and therefore rarely recorded. We know, for example, that Thoda met her death by fire, but we know it only because she exonerated a few of the Muslims accused just before her execution, which generated a record of their absolution.)[73] For prostitutes accused of interfaith sex, markers of identity became a matter of life and death. Hence the frequent emphasis on dress in miscegenation cases: were the Jews dressed as Jews? did they carry weapons? were the Muslims wearing their proper haircut?[74] Because prostitutes were the Christian women most likely to come into sexual contact with non-Christians, the task of identification fell disproportionately upon

[71] ACA:C 447:182r–v (1331/8/31). The king decreed that if this was true, the prostitutes should be moved.

[72] For the "rei dels arlots" in Valencia see ACA:C 863:189v, collected in *Aureum opus*, privilege 8 of Peter II, p. 265, where his office is revoked. Cf. Narbona, *Pueblo, poder y sexo*, p. 150; V. Graullera, "Los hostaleros del burdel de Valencia," *Revista d'història medieval* 1 (1990): 201–213, here p. 201; M. Carboneres, *Picarones y alcahuetas, ó la mancebía de Valencia* (Valencia, 1876; reprint, 1978), pp. 19–20. On the office of "king of prostitutes" in France, see J. Rossiaud, *Medieval Prostitution*, trans. L. Cochrane (Oxford, 1988), pp. 58–59, 65. For conflict between the Muslims of Valencia and the "rei," see ACA:C 235:120v (1304/7/28) and the discussion in Ferrer, *Els sarraïns*, p. 4. Even Christians could adopt this strategy to rid their lands of unwanted prostitutes, as when Rodrigo Diez argued that they should be expelled from his village because Muslims often walked through it and slept with the prostitutes, pretending they were Christians. See ACA:C 452:120r (1332/10/1).

[73] See ACA:C 385 bis:118r–v (1322/2/23). Similarly the judicial "suffocation" of a Christian prostitute is mentioned only because an official is being investigated in connection with it. See ACA:C 384:27r–v (1321/2/17).

[74] For an example of these questions being asked in the case of Jews, see Proceso 23/3, cited above (n. 69), fols. 4r–v, 10v. For a Muslim, see, inter alia, the case of Ybrahim del Crespo in ACA:C 652:135r (1348/8/13); and ACA:C Proceso 12/14, discussed below. Many of these indicators were not particularly decisive. Plenty of Muslims neglected to wear the prescribed haircut, and Jews frequently carried weapons (especially while traveling), despite prohibitions. In ACA cr. Pere III, box 23, no. 3148 (1336/8/14), for example, the fact that Vidal Avençora is carrying a sword, lance, and javelin is mentioned without negative comment.

them.[75] It was through the fulfillment of this task that the prostitute came to play, in a literal sense, the role of recognizer of difference.

The prostitute's role in identification and the recognition of difference suggests her importance as a boundary marker, an importance I would allegorize in the story of Alicsend de Tolba and Aytola the Saracen. Alicsend was a Christian prostitute who, together with one colleague, made her way to a shepherds' camp near Xivert on the ninth day before the calends of December of 1304. After a time, the two prostitutes asked the shepherds if there were any other likely customers among them, but were told that only "un moro" (a Moor) remained. It was then, according to witnesses, that "Lorenç Pastor" (Lorenç the Shepherd) went to the Muslim called "Aytola Sarray" (Aytola the Saracen) and asked him if he would not like to sleep with Alicsend. Aytola objected, quite naturally, that he was a Muslim, and besides, he had no money. Lorenç not only offered to loan Aytola the money but gave useful advice as well: "He told the said Moor to say that his name was Johan, to speak in . . . , and to say that he was from the port."[76]

To this point the story seems an idyllic example of *convivencia*: an interfaith community of shepherds willing to obscure the religious differences that divided them. In any event the illusion was shattered by a woman's voice: Alicsend's scream of *Viafors* (roughly translated: "Help!") when she "recognized that he was a Moor in his member."[77] Aytola fled, and Alicsend denounced both him and Lorenç to the lieutenant of the commander of the Temple in Xivert for falsity and deviousness "in dishonor of God and of the Catholic faith."[78] In this case it is Aytola's expulsion from Alicsend that identifies him as alien, an "other-

---

[75] This is implicit in the laws stipulating the specific dress of minorities in order to avoid sexual intermixing. These laws are concerned, not with respectable Christian women, but with the large number of (mostly poor) women who at some point in their lives engaged in prostitution, whether part-time as a supplement to their incomes or even as a way of saving money for a dowry, or full-time as a way of making a living. For women prostituting themselves to save money for a dowry, see T.-M. Vinyoles, "L'esdevenir quotidià: treball i lleure de les dones medievals," in *Més enllà del silenci: les dones a la història de Catalunya*, ed. M. Nash (Barcelona, 1988), pp. 73–89, here p. 80.

[76] ACA:C Procesos, new numeration 12/14 (1304), fol. 2v, testimony of Pedro, fil d'en Enegot Saragoça. Unfortunately the advice as to how Aytola should speak is illegible. "John" seems to be the name of preference among Muslims seeking to pass as Christians. For another case, see ACA 528:285r–v, 1334/2/28.

[77] ACA:C Procesos, new numeration 12/14 (1304), fol. 2v: "[ha]via conegut que ere moro en son menbre."

[78] This is a notarial formula used often in cases of blasphemy or miscegenation (in this case see, e.g., fol. 9r). Aytola fled town before the accusation was made. Lorenç was tried and defended himself on three counts: first, he was a good Christian and would never do such a thing. Second, he could not be tried for complicity in a crime in which the perpetrator was not available for trial. Third, Alicsend's testimony should not be believed, since as a prostitute she was of "mala fama." The document is in very poor condition, but it seems Lorenç was acquitted, despite the fact that the testimony of several shepherds supported Alicsend. Why this transcript from a seigneurial court is preserved in the royal archive is not clear.

ness" that not coincidentally is physicalized and recognized in his sexual member. I will return to contextualize this theme. Here it is enough to insist that because the prostitute is a site at which difference is policed, she becomes quite literally a marker of difference, as well as an active agent in its surveillance.

.   .   .   .   .

The previous pages represent an attempt to display the workings of a complex system of sexual interaction and violence along a bewildering number of axes of gender and religious identity. The description is tentative, since we know almost nothing about gender in any of the communities of the Crown of Aragon and have few models for treating Christian attitudes toward both minority religions simultaneously. Indeed, so complex were the effects of sexual and religious identities upon one another in the fourteenth-century Crown that we should perhaps think of it as a society of six dynamically related genders, rather than of two genders and three religions. In each religious community masculinity and femininity emerged from a matrix of relations with the other communities and genders.

Given this complexity, we need as detailed a picture as possible of our historical subjects' attitudes toward sexual mixing if we are to avoid treating these attitudes as congruent with those of other times and places, such as our own. This is a particular problem in the case of miscegenation, since the near universality of such concerns in plural (i.e., multiethnic, multireligious) societies has deadened our sense of difference and contingency by naturalizing the object of inquiry. Thus one of the most sensitive historians of the Mudejars likens fourteenth-century collective anxiety over Muslim-Christian sexuality to that over black-white intercourse in the postbellum United States.[79]

One danger of such universalizing gambits is that they make certain basic questions seem naive. We tend not to ask why fourteenth-century Catalan anxiety about religious intermixing should focus on sex and not on other types of interaction such as (for example) eating together, because we have so many other examples from European history before us. This tendency is based on the false and ethnocentric proposition that all ethnic or religious groups fear exogamy.[80] But even accepting this proposition, we should still admit that such fear can take many different forms, and that these differences have consequences for interaction between groups. It matters, to take an abstract example, where the

[79]Boswell, *Royal Treasure*, p. 344n.60.

[80]J. Pitt-Rivers points out the greater Judeo-Christian-Islamic emphasis on group endogamy relative to other cultures in *The Fate of Shechem, or the Politics of Sex: Six Essays in the Anthropology of the Mediterranean* (Cambridge, 1977), pp. 119–124. One need not accept his argument to recognize that Hindu, Amerindian, or sub-Saharan African (to name three cultures studied extensively by anthropologists of marriage) attitudes toward exogamy and miscegenation are not our own.

SEX AND VIOLENCE 149

boundary line is drawn. The effect of Muslim prohibitions on the marriage of Muslim women to non-Muslim men is very different from that of the Jewish ban on intermarriage for both sexes, especially because the latter was elaborated through a great many other prohibitions on social intercourse whereas the former was not.[81] We need, therefore, to ask specific questions. In this case, stories like that of Alicsend urge us to ask, "Why sex?" and, in particular, "Why sex with prostitutes?"[82] The lack of popular lynchings on charges of miscegenation in the Crown of Aragon and the existence of long-term affairs between religiously mixed couples raise the question of the function of this anxiety and the violence it provoked.[83] Did it foment intolerance, as we tend to assume, or contain it? Finally, the accusational nature of many of our records forces the issue of agency. How and to what effect did individuals invoke this type of anxiety, and the judicial violence it made possible, in their face-to-face interactions?

The question "Why sex?" may serve as a broad introduction to these issues. In favor of universalism is the fact that many multiethnic societies erect barriers to sexual activity across group boundaries, proclaiming as their intent the prevention of mixing, generally of self-styled "superior" with "inferior" races. In the case of Jews, one need only think of the Nuremberg laws of 1935 and their prohibition of Jewish-German intermarriage under the rubric *Rassenschande* ("race pollution"); or of the early modern Spanish obsession with *limpieza de sangre* ("purity of blood") and restrictions on the descendants of Jewish converts

---

[81] With apologies to the classical idea of rabbinic law as a "hedge around the Torah," one might say that many of the prohibitions on social interaction in Jewish law were hedges around the procreative body. The prohibition on sharing wine with non-Jews, for example, was interpreted by the Talmudists as a barrier to miscegenation: "Their wine was forbidden on account of their daughters." BT 'A.Z. 36b.

[82] By comparison, sexual intercourse between black men and white *prostitutes* (as opposed to "respectable" white women) provoked little anxiety in the southern United States before the early twentieth century. In this regard, the Scottsboro trial of the early 1930s represents something of a turning point. On Scottsboro, see D. Carter, *Scottsboro: A Tragedy of the American South*, rev. ed. (Baton Rouge, 1979); J. Goodman, *Stories of Scottsboro* (New York, 1994). For Scottsboro's role in making whites aware of sex between black men and white female prostitutes, see J. D. Hall, *Revolt against Chivalry: Jessie Daniel Ames and the Women's Campaign against Lynching* (New York, 1979), pp. 201–206. On changing attitudes toward black-white miscegenation in the southern United States more generally, see J. Johnston, *Race Relations in Virginia and Miscegenation in the South, 1776–1860* (Amherst, MA, 1970); M. Hodes, "Sex across the Color Line: White Women and Black Men in the Nineteenth Century American South" (Ph.D. diss., Princeton University, 1991).

[83] The few riots that are documented are complicated by jurisdictional quarrels. Thus the justice of Daroca and his men attacked the house of the lieutenant of the bailiff general when the latter proposed to free a Muslim accused of sex with a Christian woman, doubtless alleging that the Muslim should be punished. I know of no such cases that do not involve competing officials. On this case, cf. ACA:C 239:59r–v (1311/4/16) and ACA:C 239:62v–63r (1311/4/19); Ferrer, *Els sarraïns*, pp. 28–29, 225–226.

to Christianity.[84] These anxieties focus on sex because they are concerned with the reproduction of racial categories, categories whose very existence seems threatened by miscegenation.

Such concerns are, however, very different from those of the fourteenth-century Crown of Aragon, though they share with them a certain sexual vocabulary. Prior to the mass conversions of Jews to Christianity in 1391, anxiety about the reproduction of racial categories, or even evidence for such categories, is difficult to find. There is, for example, little evidence that descendants of converts were in any way stigmatized as "racially impure" or of dubious orthodoxy before the fifteenth century. A convert's descendants seem to shed completely the appellation *baptizat* or *converso* after the first generation. Further, Christian (and Jewish) men were willing to marry converted Muslim women, and there are even cases of Christian men petitioning the Crown to have their illegitimate sons by Muslim slave women declared their legitimate heirs.[85] This was, of course, a calm predicated on a certain confidence in the efficacy of conversion. (That such confidence existed is attested by the numerous cases in which charges of miscegenation against Jewish or Muslim males were dropped once the defendant converted to Christianity.)[86] It was predicated, too, on the arrogant conviction that any child with a Christian biological parent was by definition Christian if the parent cared to claim it.[87] When Christian officials seized the Muslim Adambacaix's son Mahomet because the Christian Antoni Safàbrega had declared on his deathbed that the child was the product of his adulterous relationship with Adambacaix's deceased wife Axa, they were not

---

[84] See Y. Yerushalmi, *Assimilation and Racial Anti-Semitism: The Iberian and the German Models*, Leo Baeck Memorial Lecture 26 (New York, 1982).

[85] For example, Domingo Carbonell of Xàtiva married a converted Muslim woman ca. 1310. Such cases are rarely recorded because they were unremarkable. Domingo's is preserved in the archives only because his wife's brother tried to break into the Muslim quarter to retrieve some of her goods. The brother later converted as well. See Ferrer, *Els sarraïns*, pp. 19, 76, and ACA:C 207:176v, transcribed on p. 222. A similar but much later case is that of ACA:C 3653:157r–v (1498), discussed by Meyerson, "Prostitution," p. 88. There are also cases of Christians marrying *baptizats* and then converting to their spouse's original Islam (e.g., ACA:C 12:28v [1263], in Burns, "Renegades," p. 346). In cases where illegitimate sons of a Muslim woman and a Christian man converted but were not legitimized, they were nonetheless referred to in legal documents as "illegitimate son of such and such a man," as in ACA:C 172:187r (1321). For the sake of comparison, consider how different the treatment was of offspring from unions between white males and black slave women in the antebellum southern United States.

[86] Though we know distressingly little about Christian attitudes toward converts in the thirteenth- and fourteenth-century Crown, the problem is too large to approach here. For an example of remissions granted converts, see ACA:C 1152:159r–v (1357/4/16), where a Muslim who has been condemned to execution by burning for having had sex with a Christian woman is absolved on the condition that he is baptized and abandons Islam. The price: fifty sous of Jaca. See Mutgé, *L'aljama*, p. 321.

[87] In the case of offspring produced by intercourse between a Christian and a Muslim slave, for example, the status of the child was carefully legislated. In all cases, however, the child was Christian. See, e.g., *Costums de Tortosa* 6.1, paragraphs 12, 14, 17, 18.

acting out of fear that boundaries of exclusion were necessary to the maintenance of racial integrity.[88]

In the face of such difference, it seems worthwhile to return to the question "Why sex?" in the context of fourteenth-century Iberia. A passage from a law code of the thirteenth-century King Alfonso the Wise of Castile purports to provide something of an answer and can serve as a starting point:

> Since Christians who commit adultery with married women deserve death, how much more so do Jews who lie with Christian women, for these are spiritually espoused to Our Lord Jesus Christ by virtue of the faith and baptism they received in His name. . . . And the Christian woman who commits such a transgression . . . shall receive the same punishment as the Christian woman who lies with a Muslim.[89]

The logic of the passage is clear. Each Christian woman, wed or unwed, is the bride of Christ, just as the collective Christian Church, the *ecclesia*, is traditionally represented as his bride. Through such synecdoche, miscegenation becomes the cuckolding of Christ.[90]

By invoking a link between the bodies of women and the honor of God, Alfonso has transported us to the province of anthropology. His focus on women as the site of dishonor gestures toward the concept of "honor and shame" so beloved among students of Mediterranean societies.[91] Here, God's

[88]For a description of the case, see Ferrer, *Els sarraïns*, pp. 27–28, citing ACA:C 2132:114v–115r; 121r–v; 139v–140r. The events occurred in 1401.

[89]*Siete Partidas* 7.24.9. The translation is Carpenter's, *Alfonso X and the Jews*, p. 35. For the punishment of Muslims, see *Siete Partidas* 7.25.10, briefly discussed in Carpenter's "Minorities in Medieval Spain," p. 283.

[90]Alfonso's synechdocal move, though deployed quite specifically here, is within a well-established and ancient tradition. Compare Eph. 5:25–30. Corporeal similes and metaphors, even sexual ones, are of course common ways of representing entire religious communities. For the Christian and Jewish traditions, the Song of Songs is a proof text. See, e.g., G. Cohen, "The Song of Songs and the Jewish Religious Mentality," in *The Samuel Friedland Lectures, 1960–1966* (New York, 1966), pp. 1–21. Compare the early rabbinic commentary on Deut. 33:4 in *Sifre Deuteronomy* §345 [C], where "the Torah is betrothed to Israel and has therefore the status of a married woman in relation to the nations of the world," so that any Gentile who touches the Torah is sexually violating Israel's wife. These allegories, however, are quite different from the synecdoche described above. On *Sifre Deuteronomy* see S. Fraade, *From Tradition to Commentary: Torah and Its Interpretation in the Midrash Sifre to Deuteronomy* (Albany, 1991), here pp. 57–58. For the translation cited here, see *Sifre: A Tannaitic Commentary on the Book of Deuteronomy*, trans. R. Hammer (New Haven, 1986), pp. 357 f.

[91]Because this model has already been applied to the medieval Mediterranean, I limit myself here to a few citations. For the Crown of Aragon, see Meyerson, "Prostitution," p. 90; idem, *Muslims of Valencia*, chap. 6. For the anthropological literature, see, inter alia, the following essays collected in *Honour and Shame: The Values of a Mediterranean Society*, ed. J. Peristiany (London, 1965): A. Abou-Zeid, "Honour and Shame among the Bedouins of Egypt," pp. 245–259; P. Bourdieu, "The Sentiment of Honour in Kabyle Society," pp. 191–243; J. Caro Baroja, "Honour and Shame, a Historical Account of Several Conflicts," pp. 79–139. See also J. Schneider, "Of Vigilance and Virgins: Honor, Shame and Access to Resources in Mediterranean Societies," *Ethnology* 10 (1971): 1–24; Pitt-Rivers, *The Fate of Shechem*.

patriarchy is spiritual, though expressed in carnal terms, and all Christian women are his kin group. Likewise, Alfonso's raising of the individual woman's body to the level of the collective seems inspired by a careful reading of Mary Douglas. Consider her view of the ways in which group identity is expressed: "The image of the human body [is used] to express both the exclusive nature of the allegiance and the confused social experience. The group is likened to the human body; the orifices are to be carefully guarded to prevent unlawful intrusions."[92] The fears of pollution that arise when the boundaries of such groups come under pressure are expressed through metaphors of the body: the female body becomes the site of fears of penetration and corruption, the male of diffusion and enfeeblement.[93]

This "Alfonsine" model accounts for the rhetoric of castigation (significantly not the same as Douglas's "corruption") that pervades contemporary discussions about the repercussions of miscegenation. When the municipal council of Valencia agonized over the consequences of the many enormous sins, notably miscegenation, committed in their city, they wrote of the horrific divine punishment such sins would bring upon the community: "for which sins, so enormous and grave . . . our Lord God . . . gives great whippings, even canings" in the form of plagues and bad weather.[94] It seems that in fourteenth-century Catalonia-Aragon the transgression of boundaries was feared, not so much because it brought about corruption or enfeeblement, but because it was inevitably followed by harsh discipline. God and his lash hovered over those places where religions met and mingled.

Some elements of this model, such as the use of body metaphors, seem quite common, even universal; others are more historically specific. Of the latter, the most surprising as well as the most ironic is the identification of the prostitute's body as the most dangerous of these places of mingling to the fourteenth-century Catalano-Aragonese mind. Why would a community invest its honor with women whom the community itself defined as without honor?[95] Why assign to an internal "other" such an important role in identifying and rejecting the external "other"? Why should the socially peripheral prove so symbolically central?[96]

[92]M. Douglas, *Natural Symbols: Explorations in Cosmology* (New York, 1982), p. viii.

[93]M. Douglas, *Purity and Danger: An Analysis of the Concepts of Pollution and Taboo* (Boston, 1966), pp. 122–128.

[94]This example is from AMV, Ll.M., g³-1, fol. 51v (1335/11). For its text, see chap. 4, n. 71. Punishment could, however, take the form of corruption—for example, corruption of the air, i.e., plague. This is, admittedly, a fine distinction.

[95]Recall that prostitutes were by definition of "bad repute" and could not even give valid testimony (at least in theory). It was for this reason, in fact, that Alicsend's miscegenation complaint had been dismissed.

[96]See B. Babcock, *The Reversible World: Symbolic Inversion in Art and Society* (Ithaca, NY, 1978), p. 32: "What is socially peripheral is often symbolically central." See more recently the delightful introduction to P. Stallybrass and A. White, *The Politics and Poetics of Transgression* (Ithaca, NY, 1986), pp. 1–26.

These questions, and particularly the last, cannot be approached without a sense of the prostitute's symbolic role, as opposed to her literal function, in the interfaith sexual economy. Prostitutes were, above all, public women. Our documents speak, not of whores, sluts, prostitutes, but of "public women," sometimes of "women who sin publicly."[97] It is the public nature of their sexuality—as opposed to that of respectable women, which is constrained by the bounds of private property and the household—that makes prostitutes infamous in the Middle Ages. Thus, in the Catalan version of the *Golden Legend*, when St. Mary of Egypt wished to make clear the sinfulness of her previous life, she stated, "And I lived there twelve years, sinning publicly with my body, denying it to no man."[98]

In denying her body to no man, St. Mary was also acting in the stereotypical fashion of a prostitute. An early-fifteenth-century French version of her life is more explicit:

To all I am abandoned,
To each one; have no fear,
Here is my body, which I present
To all who want to have it.

Ruth Karras (like Simone de Beauvoir before her) has pointed out this sense of "prostitutes as common to all, the property of all men . . . because they were the property of none," a sense "reflected in regulations of brothels across medieval Europe that forbade prostitutes to refuse any customer or even to have particular lovers." It was reflected, too, in the occasional legal conclusion that prostitutes could not by definition be raped, since they could not withhold consent from any man.[99]

[97] For the vocabulary in Valencia, see Carmen, "La prostitución," p. 189. "Putana publica" is the term used in *Costums de Tortosa* 9.2.3. Other words, such as *meretrix*, appear in the documentation as well. The public nature of prostitution was also stressed in canon law, e.g., in the insistence of Cardinal Hostiensis (d. 1271) that only public promiscuity rendered women prostitutes. See J. Brundage, "Prostitution in the Medieval Canon Law," *Signs: Journal of Women in Culture and Society* 1 (1976): 825–845, here p. 827n.6. Of course there were plenty of popular terms for prostitute that had nothing to do with the public nature of their activities (e.g., *bagassa*), but these were insults, not legal terms.

[98] *Vides de sants rosselloneses*, vol. 2, ed. C. Maneikis Kniazzeh and E. Neugaard (Barcelona, 1977), p. 393.

[99] From the Passion play of Eustache Marcadé, cited in Rossiaud, *Medieval Prostitution*, p. 141; and in R. Karras, "Holy Harlots: Prostitute Saints in Medieval Legend," *Journal of the History of Sexuality* 1 (1990): 3–32, here p. 22. The quotation is from "Holy Harlots," p. 10. Cf. *The Second Sex*, trans. H. Parshley (New York, 1974), p. 619: "The [wife] is protected by one male against all the others; the [prostitute] is defended by all against the exclusive tyranny of each." For brothel regulation emphasizing the common ownership of prostitutes, see Karras, "The Regulation of Brothels in Later Medieval England," *Signs: Journal of Women in Culture and Society* 14 (1989): pp. 399–433, here pp. 405, 425; L. Otis, *Prostitution in Medieval Society: The History of an Urban Institution in Languedoc* (Chicago, 1985), pp. 68–69, 84–85; L. Roper, "Discipline and Respectability: Prostitu-

It was this very commonality that undergirded the conceptual edifice justifying and legitimating the existence of prostitution, the brothel, and even the individual prostitute herself. Medieval social theorists (and also lawyers for prostitutes and brothel managers) referred frequently to an annotator's interlinear gloss to Augustine's *De ordine* 2.4.12: "The public woman is in society what bilge is in [a ship at] sea and the sewer pit in a palace. Remove this sewer and the entire palace will be contaminated." For many medieval commentators, the prostitute was the terminus of a complex plumbing system, emptying (male) society of the fetid waters of fornication that always threatened to overwhelm it. Hence the view that the prostitute exercised a *ministerium*, an office "ordained for the service of the commonality."[100] As such, the individual prostitute could stand for the collective lust of a community, an allegorization enacted, for example, in the repentance scene from the Catalan version of the life of St. Taysis (Thaïs). Here Taysis carries her property to the center of the town, calls the entire populace before her, and cries out, "Come, all you who sin with me, and you shall see how I burn all that you have given me": a public and communal renunciation of her public and communal role.[101]

Already we can suggest, albeit abstractly, that the prostitute represented manhood because she represented male sex rights in women, because with her all men could enact their masculinity.[102] That this was a manhood limited to Christians is clear, especially when Christian prostitutes were involved.[103] But I would like to claim that the prostitute embodied the Christian community of men in an even more powerful way: that the overlap between her role as receptacle of communal Christian male lust, on the one hand, and medieval theories about the physical and spiritual bonds created by intercourse, on the other,

---

tion and the Reformation in Augsburg," *History Workshop* 19 (1985): 3–28, here p. 6. For regulations concerning rape, see the above as well as M. Pilosu, *La donna, la lussuria e la chiesa nel medioevo* (Genoa, 1989), p. 73; and J. Brundage, "Rape and Marriage in the Medieval Canon Law," *Revue de Droit Canonique* 28 (1978) (*Etudes offertes à J. Gaudemet*), pp. 70 f. For a Catalan example, see the *Costums de Tortosa* 9.2.3, where the rape of a "putana publica" is not compensated.

[100]Rossiaud, *Medieval Prostitution*, p. 81, citing similar views from Thomas Aquinas, Ptolemy of Lucca, and Boccaccio, and providing instances of the invocation of this concept in legal briefs. The second quotation is from ibid., p. 103, citing a fifteenth-century source. The same arguments are commonplace in the Crown of Aragon. See, for example, Francesc Eiximenis, *Lo Crestià*, ed. A. Hauf (Barcelona, 1983), chap. 574, pp. 155 f. Cf. Narbona, *Pueblo, poder y sexo*, p. 151.

[101] *Vides de sants*, 3:343: ". . . ela pres tot so que avia guasayat per peccat e portà-ho enmig de la ciutat e fe aquí venir lo pòbol dient:—Venits, vosautres qui pecquets ab mi, e veyats con cremaré eu tot so que m'avets donat—." For other representations of the prostitute's role as communal, see Rossiaud, *Medieval Prostitution*, pp. 81–83, 103, 123–124, and passim.

[102]See the formulation of C. Pateman, *The Sexual Contract* (Stanford, 1988), chap. 7, "What's Wrong with Prostitution," esp. p. 199.

[103]And perhaps also when they were not. The very act of visiting prostitutes could be presented as a custom of Christian men alone, as in the charge against the Jew Lop Abnexeyl of "going at night to prostitutes, in the manner of Christian men." See ACA:C 382:137r–138r (1318), published in Baer, *Die Juden* vol. 1, no. 171, p. 211.

transformed the prostitute into a concrete representation of a community of men united to each other by a common sexual bond.[104] In the case of the fourteenth-century Crown, this was a community delimited in terms of religious identity. All Christian males could, in the words of St. Paul, "become one body" with a Christian prostitute, but through her (and this St. Paul did not say) they also became one with each other.[105]

To see how this might be so we need only glance at the complex networks of affinity medieval people, or at least medieval theologians, believed were created by sexual intercourse. When a man ejaculated inside a woman's vagina, there was established between the two a bond of consanguinity similar to that with a blood relation or a godparent. The two were enmeshed not only with each other, but within each other's kinship networks as well, establishing incest taboos between themselves and their partner's relations as powerful as those created by biological affinity. Pope Celestine III could even rule that if a couple fornicated before marriage, the exchange created an incest barrier between them, a canonical impediment to their subsequent marriage. The mechanisms of this bonding were often expressed in terms of the exchange of blood. In the words of a canonist, "unity of flesh" was achieved whenever there was "mixing of blood."[106] The mechanism behind such mixing was clearly spelled out in medieval medical theories of spermatogenesis. Sperm was "man's purest blood," distilled throughout the veins and arteries of the body, whipped up to a steaming white froth by male heat, then ejaculated into the womb, where it mixed with the cooler blood of the female.[107]

[104]Roper makes a related point in "Discipline and Respectability," pp. 4, 6, 20, e.g., p. 4: "here . . . masculinity, virility and membership of the polity were intimately connected." See also her " 'The Common Man', 'the Common Good', 'Common Women': Gender and Meaning in the German Reformation Commune," *Social History* 12 (1987): 1–21, here pp. 2f. See, too, E. Sedgwick's model of "male homosocial desire" in *Between Men: English Literature and Male Homosocial Desire* (New York, 1985), pp. 21–27.

[105]1 Cor. 6:16–17: "You surely know that anyone who links himself with a harlot becomes physically one with her (for Scripture says, 'the pair shall become one flesh'); but he who links himself with Christ is one with him, spiritually."

[106]On the affinities created by intercourse see the legal and canonistic material collected by Brundage, *Law, Sex, and Christian Society*, p. 356nn. 155–156, where "sanguinis commixtionem" is equated with "carnis unitatem." See also idem, "Marriage and Sexuality in the Decretals of Pope Alexander III," in *Miscellanea Rolando Bandinelli Papa Alessandro III*, ed. F. Liotta (Siena, 1986), pp. 59–83, here p. 71. It should be noted that these theoretical barriers were often overlooked by the Church in the interests of regularizing informal unions and legitimizing illegitimate births. Compare the modern Greek explanation cited in J. du Boulay, "The Blood: Symbolic Relationships between Descent, Marriage, Incest Prohibitions and Spiritual Kinship in Greece," *Man*, n.s., 19 (1984): 533–556, here p. 546: "If you drink water it becomes part of you. So it is with blood." That medieval theorists fit prostitutes within this framework is evidenced by Gratian's ambiguous resolution in the *Decretum* to the question of whether a prostitute could marry a former client. See Brundage, "Prostitution in the Medieval Canon Law," p. 844.

[107]On spermatogenesis and blood see especially Jacquart and Thomasset, *Sexuality and Medicine in the Middle Ages*, p. 60 and passim.

Within this system of sexual and blood relations, the prostitute, available to all and denying none, can be thought of as the center of a circle, bound by radiating blood relations to all males with sexual rights in her. Christian men, through their relation to the prostitute, are likewise related to each other, incorporated in her person as a blood brotherhood of Christian males.[108] In the synecdochic language of the body so beloved of our sources, the prostitute's skin bounded the Christian community, her orifices, when penetrated by Christians, reinforced it. Hence the danger of a miscegenation that could achieve, at least symbolically, the clandestine admittance of the non-Christian into the Christian community through the body of the prostitute. From this point of view we can see how the prostitute's body might become the site of abjection, the place at which the "self" (i.e., the collective group, the Christian community) recognized and (ideally) rejected the "other," as it did in the case of Alicsend.[109]

. . . . .

In identifying a symbolic context for the prostitute's role in the interfaith sexual economy of fourteenth-century Aragon, I do not mean to imply that such a role was universal or inevitable. In fact, this emphasis on the prostitute is historically

---

[108]Taken to its extreme, of course, such a model would create infinite and impossible incest taboos. But the world of prostitution was one in which such taboos were attenuated. Still, some theologians, focusing on theoretical extremes, did criticize prostitution for precisely this reason. See, for example, the thirteenth-century Dominican friar Laurent of Orleans's *Somme le roi*, which complains that prostitutes "aucunes fois sunt mariées, ou de religion, et ne refusent nelui, ne frere, ne cousin, ne fil, ne pere" (cited in C.-V. Langlois, *La vie en France au Moyen-âge*, rev. ed., vol. 4 [Paris, 1928], p. 163). Compare Thomas of Chobham's concern that prostitutes do not know if their client is "married, or excommunicated, or priest, or monk, or Jew, or if he is the father, or brother, or consanguineous relative of one with whom they have already lain previously," in his *Summa confessorum*, ed. F. Broomfield, *Analecta Mediaevalia Namurcensia* 25 (Louvain, 1968), p. 349. For similar anxieties in antiquity and the early Middle Ages, see J. Boswell, *The Kindness of Strangers: The Abandonment of Children in Western Europe from Late Antiquity to the Renaissance* (New York, 1988), pp. 3, 96, 112–113, 157–167. Concern with the possibility of unknowingly committing incest with a prostitute is an ancient phenomenon. See, e.g., the story of Judah and Tamar in Genesis 38.

[109]In arriving at this formulation of the prostitute's body as a representation of the body social, and in locating sites of abjection on this body that function as a "boundary-constituting taboo for the purposes of constructing a discrete subject through exclusion," I have learned much from J. Kristeva, *Powers of Horror: An Essay in Abjection*, trans. L. Roudiez (New York, 1982), esp. pp. 64–72, as well as from the comments of I. Young, *Justice and the Politics of Difference* (Princeton, 1990), pp. 143–145; and J. Butler, *Gender Trouble: Feminism and the Subversion of Identity* (New York, 1990), pp. 133 f. (whence the above quote). My borrowing, however, is very loose, and none of these authors would recognize their arguments in mine.

quite specific and unusual, even the obverse of miscegenation fears in other times and places.[110] Nor should it be viewed as incidental, a logical consequence of the effective repression of miscegenation involving respectable women. We do not know how effectively such miscegenation was repressed, only that women of good repute seldom appear in the criminal records. Further, we can perfectly well imagine miscegenation *anxiety* focusing on a wider field of relations, or focusing on respectable women, even absent the *reality* of such miscegenation. Anxieties and accusations need not and often do not correspond to social fact. Attitudes toward miscegenation in the fourteenth-century Crown of Aragon were a historically specific and structured way of expressing anxiety about the risks interaction posed to group integrity.[111]

From this position, we can ask how this particular set of anxieties affected the possibilities for other types of interaction among Christian, Muslim, and Jew. The question is important because there were many such possibilities. Despite repeated ecclesiastical condemnation, Christians, Muslims, and Jews drank together, gambled together, went to war together, lived in the same neighborhoods (sometimes in the same house), established business partnerships, engaged in all forms of commercial exchange, even watched each other's religious ceremonies and processions. Were these opportunities for interaction expanded or contracted by the specific form miscegenation anxiety took in the fourteenth-century Crown of Aragon?

We can approach this question at an abstract level by imagining a more homogeneous world where barriers to miscegenation do not exist, as in the famous, though problematic, formulation of yet another anthropologist:

A continuous transition exists from war to exchange, and from exchange to intermarriage, and the exchange of brides is merely the conclusion to an uninterrupted process

---

[110]E.g., in the United States, on which see n. 82 above, or in Mexico, on which see P. Seed, *To Love Honor and Obey in Colonial Mexico: Conflicts over Marriage Choice, 1574–1821* (Stanford, 1988), pp. 146 f.

[111]We need not look far afield to see how specific these anxieties were. Consider how different the situation was in France, where in 1321 towns from the regions of Toulouse, Albi, and Carcassonne petitioned the king to expel the Jews, alleging (among other things) their attempts to seduce Christian women (see chap. 2, n. 39). French Jews also seem more concerned than their Aragonese counterparts about the possibility that Jewish women will be attracted to Christians: "She too will court the man who is uncircumcised in the flesh and lie against his breast with great passion, for he thrusts inside her a long time because of the foreskin. . . . When an uncircumcised man sleeps with her and then resolves to return to his home, she brazenly grasps him, holding on to his genitals, and says to him, 'Come back, make love to me.' This is because of the pleasure that she finds in intercourse with him, from the sinews of his testicles—sinew of iron—and from his ejaculation—that of a horse—which he shoots like an arrow into her womb." Circumcised Jews, on the other hand, not only give their wives little pleasure, but are often too tired to have sex at all, since they work so hard in Gentile lands. See Saperstein, *Decoding the Rabbis*, pp. 94–99 (here p. 98), translating from R. Isaac b. Yedaiah's commentary on Midrash Rabbah.

of reciprocal gifts, which effects the transition from hostility to alliance, from anxiety to confidence, and from fear to friendship.[112]

Here the exchange of women appears as the culmination of processes of interaction, processes ranging from war to alliance and kinship, as the most precious and basic form of gift giving. But it has its own particularities, although in the above passage they are elided. Like all forms of exchange, it "provides the means of binding men together." However, to "the artificial links . . . of alliance governed by rule" that other forms of exchange create, the exchange of women adds "the natural links of kinship."[113] More than other forms of exchange, it has the potential to "naturalize" more "artificial" forms of exchange such as commercial relations. If this naturalizing exchange of women is the culmination of other forms of exchange, then it renders these other forms more dangerous (from a fourteenth-century Catalan point of view), since they become one in an uninterrupted series of steps across boundaries.

The Crown of Aragon, however, was not such a thoroughly Lévi-Straussian world.[114] In it, deep fissures obstructed the naturalizing exchange of women, fissures that defused the tensions in other types of interaction and exchange, since these were by themselves incapable of achieving a "transition from hostility to alliance," from "other" to "self." We almost lose sight of the deeper of these fissures, the prohibition upon intermarriage, ignored in our sources because taken for granted. The other, the prohibition on interfaith fornication and adultery, constituted the bodies of prostitutes as the limits of legitimate and nonthreatening exchange, and devolved upon "public women" the task of maintaining the boundary between "natural" and "artificial." In terms of art, the circle within which the prostitute could legitimately be exchanged inscribed boundaries as sharp as those created by limitations on the exchange of brides. By fulfilling this task of boundary maintenance, the bodies of women of ill repute drained other types of interaction of the violence with which they might otherwise have been imbued and accumulated this violence within themselves.

We can see this process at work in the tavern life of villages such as Paterna on the outskirts of Valencia. One witness, Tomas Marques, stopped at such a tavern in Benimahabet (not located) sometime in early 1307 and found there Christians, "baptized [Muslims] from Paterna" (i.e., converts to Christianity),

[112] C. Lévi-Strauss, *The Elementary Structures of Kinship*, ed. R. Needham, trans. J. H. Bell, J. R. von Sturmer, and R. Needham (Boston, 1969), pp. 67–68.

[113] Ibid., p. 480. Though here my use of Lévi-Strauss's model is mechanistic, I have profited from G. Rubin, "The Traffic in Women: Notes on the 'Political Economy' of Sex," in *Toward an Anthropology of Women*, ed. R. Reiter (New York, 1975), pp. 157–210; and M. Strathern, *The Gender of the Gift: Problems with Women and Problems with Society in Melanesia* (Berkeley, 1988), pp. 330–332 and elsewhere, especially in my conceptualization of prostitutes above.

[114] Compare Pitt-Rivers, *The Fate of Shechem*, p. 120: "There is however one area of the world which, though it is noted for being traditionally organised in corporate and even in kin groups, refuses to exchange women: the Mediterranean."

and Muslims from Quart, all playing dice together and getting drunk. Tomas of course joined in, but he and a Muslim from Quart named Morsuch had a losing day and had to pawn their clothes to a Christian named Bernat Bosser. Present amid all this interfaith gambling, drinking, and moneylending, Tomas tells us, was the prostitute Marieta de Murcia. When Jacme Camarido visited the same tavern, there were three prostitutes present who would be taken by winning Christian gamblers to the neighboring vineyard. A similar picture of interfaith conviviality was reported in the tavern of Paterna, where a prostitute joined in the dice game. But the limits to this sociability were always made clear by the women. Thus Tomas tells us that Marieta made a trade "of her body in the said place to any man who wanted [it] who was a Christian."[115] The existence of this boundary rendered all the rest less threatening, almost (but never quite) unremarkable, despite the fact that this interfaith conviviality in the presence of prostitutes was expressly condemned by law.[116]

.   .   .   .   .

Thus far my analysis has focused on the specific forms taken by a collective anxiety about sexual interaction: first, on showing how these anxieties create between groups boundary-maintaining taboos so highly charged that they generate institutional violence; and second, how, though we generally treat them as symptomatic of intolerance, such taboos and the violence they generate might serve to render other types of interaction less conflictual, lessening their potential for violence. But this is only part of the story, read at the level of the collective. We still need to descend to the level of strategic action in order to see how individuals put the collective to work in the transactions of their daily lives, transactions that both shaped, and were shaped by, collective discourses about interfaith sexuality.

[115]The information presented here is a pastiche of testimony from ACA:C Proceso 515/10 (old numeration) (1307), a partial transcript of a lawsuit between Romea Lopis, the wife of the knight Martin d'Oblites, and Sancho Garçes over who owns the rights to a "sotsalcaydia" (a judicial office). Sancho wins the case. The information on tavern life is mentioned only in an attempt to argue that the testimony of several of the witnesses is invalid bacause they are of "mala fama," since they lend at interest, frequent taverns, and sleep with prostitutes. See in particular fols. 7v–8r (Tomas); 9v (Jacme); 10v–11r (Bernat d'Oriola, ferrer); 11v (Pere de Teragona, esparter). All of these witnesses mention the presence of numerous prostitutes, e.g., Marieta de Murcia and Marieta d'en Bayard (a.k.a. Marieta puta xica, "the small whore": see fol. 14r for the nickname). The document is full of information on the organization of village prostitution. See, for example, fols. 39v–50r, where (inter alia) various taverners and others are accused of recruiting men and women for prostitution and transporting them from village to village.

[116]Or soon would be. Decrees forbidding conversation between Christian prostitutes and Muslims in taverns throughout the kingdom of Valencia were issued in 1311 and 1312 by James II, though there may have been earlier ones as well. These are published in *Aureum opus* 50, p. 162, and 56, p. 166.

At first glance, the kinds of individual action preserved in archives seem to support the first of the conclusions I just mentioned and to rebut the second. It is clear that contemporaries were aware of the immense potential for violence that accrued in charges of miscegenation—so aware, in fact, that they resorted to such accusations constantly in attempts to tap into that violence.

We might start by returning to those very prostitutes whose bodies were constituted as boundaries, as sites for the recognition and rejection of the non-Christian. I say "were constituted" because individual women did not necessarily view themselves as boundary markers, though they were aware of the normativity of such roles and of the risks and possibilities inherent in them. Alicsend's scream in the shepherds' camp was motivated not only by the shock of difference, but also by a situational calculus. Had Lorenç conspired to entrap her as an opportunity for extortion? If so, her scream argued for her ignorance and innocence. Conversely, she was herself now in a position to extort: to this her scream staked public claim. As it was, she pressed charges only when Lorenç's promise to blackmail Aytola and share the proceeds with her became unfulfillable after the Muslim's flight.[117] Even here, then, in the cases of prostitutes who formed the front lines, so to speak, in the struggle of identity and difference, there was room for the strategic actions and choices of the individual.

The strategic nature of miscegenation anxiety is most evident at a slight remove from the prostitutes themselves, in those many moments when individuals used accusations of interfaith sexuality in an effort to channel the violence accruing about this issue into conflicts arising from less heightened interactions. The accusation of miscegenation was commonly used against Jews and Muslims precisely because it was highly charged and therefore particularly effective at prompting judicial action.[118] Individuals used such accusations to raise other-

[117]Authorities often suspected that prostitutes only denounced their non-Christian clients when they feared that they themselves might otherwise face charges. For a detailed example in which Infant Martin himself instructs officials on how to carry out an interrogation in hopes of catching a prostitute in contradiction, see ACA:C 2077:9v–10r (1389/1/20), discussed and transcribed in Ferrer, *Els sarraïns*, pp. 37, 329–330.

[118]Recall how as early as the fourth century Roman law invited such accusations by exempting accusers from the penalties for informing, and how in the fourteenth the blanket pardons and safe-conducts issued by the Crown expressly excluded miscegenation from their "coverage." Both of these conditions made miscegenation a useful accusation. For a somewhat ironic example, see the documents in ACA:C 468:200v–201v (1335/7/27), where Bonmacip Abrae and Jucef Lupelli are accused of violence against Jews and Christians and of raping Christian women. Unmentioned in the charge is the fact that the two had obtained on behalf of the aljama a general pardon for all crimes (with the usual exception of miscegenation, etc.) at a cost to themselves of 1,500 sous, which the aljama now refused to pay. In the ensuing conflict, the aljama resorted to charges of miscegenation. (The conflict over payment, though not the charge of miscegenation, is presented with a great deal of ignorance and anti-Semitic vitriol in R. Corbella i Llobet, *L'aljama de jueus de Vic* [Vic, 1909; reprint, 1984], pp. 84–92.) To point out that such accusations were useful and powerful is not, of course, to suggest that they may not also have sometimes been true.

wise relatively mundane legal disputes to the level of defense of the faith, as when a Christian debtor complained first that a loan was usurious, then that his goods had been unfairly seized by his Jewish creditor, and finally that the creditor had tried to rape the debtor's daughter.[119]

Some of these charges were quite vague, made in the hopes that torture or character witnesses might uncover particulars. Others went to great lengths to provide a suitable lightning rod in the form of a woman, most often a prostitute. Often, the accusers' motives were quite clear, at least to the plaintiff. Such was the case with Jahuda Avenbruch, a Jew of Lleida, who complained in 1286 that while he had been visiting Albesa, some men of the place together with a Christian woman broke into the house where he was staying and claimed to have found him lying with their accomplice. According to Jahuda they used this as a pretext to rob him, and the count of Urgell used their accusation to extort from him thousands of sous in fines. He was now worried that a coreligionist might seek to make hay out of the same accusation.[120]

Among other things, Jahuda's story makes clear that Christians were not the only ones to bring accusations of miscegenation against minorities. Members of minority communities themselves frequently tried to use the judicial apparatus against their enemies. Jewish aljamas complained constantly of lower-class Jews' bringing such accusations against wealthy ones, and attempted to forestall this by prohibiting accusations by Jews against other Jews in Christian courts. Hence (in part) the extensive and largely ineffectual Jewish legislation against *malshins* (informers, i.e., accusers in Christian courts), a type of legislation that was explicitly imitated by Muslim communities by the end of the fourteenth century.[121]

In both Muslim and Jewish communities, accusations of miscegenation became a preferred tool of factions fighting for power, prestige, or community office. The host of accusations made against members of a leading Muslim clan of Teruel, the Olleros, is typical. The accusations took as broad an aim as possible. The patriarch of the clan, Mahomat Ollero, and his sons Jucef and Galip (Galip was holding the office of *amīn* [a financial and judicial officer] at the time the charges were made) were all accused of a variety of excesses, including murder and assault. But sex crimes peppered the list. Thus one of Mahomat's

---

[119]Cf. chap. 1, n. 64, for a discussion of ACA:C 365:188v–189r (1320/12/13), in which Pedro Domingo of Ayneto complains that Jaco, the son of his creditor Jucef Abutarda of Daroca, has tried to seduce his daughter and wrongfully seized some chickens. For more on Jaco's career, see below.

[120]ACA:C 70:23r (= Régné no. 1693), published in Régné, pp. 439–440. Compare ACA:C 172:263r–v (1322/1/20), where a Christian of Zaragoza and his concubine conspire to frame Samuel Alaçar.

[121]See, for example, ACA:C 519:111r–v (1328/5/31), where Abraam, a.k.a. Recandell, is accused of theft and of extorting money from other Jews by threatening to denounce them "coram inquisitor heretice pravitatis" for sleeping with Christian women. On the issue of *malshins*, see chap. 1, n. 65.

daughters was accused of sleeping with a Christian man, one of his sons of sleeping with a servant to whom he was related, and one of Jucef's sons of sleeping with a Christian woman.[122] Even Christian officials were at risk, since they could be fined or dismissed on charges of tolerating miscegenation or punishing it too leniently.[123] Officials, on the other hand, could use sex accusations to persecute their enemies, or just to raise some revenue. This practice was so common that the guidelines for inquisitional proceedings against royal officials stipulated as a point of regular investigation whether alcaydes had used prostitutes in order to frame individuals on charges of adultery and force them to redeem themselves.[124]

These accusations are obviously attempts to generalize the violence normally reserved for very specific transgressions and apply it to a great variety of everyday conflicts. As such, they seem to challenge the argument that heightening sexual boundaries reduces tension in other forms of interaction, or at the very least to suggest a constant tension between delimiting and generalizing conflict. Such a tension does exist, but it is more complex than may at first appear. We tend to forget that accusations of miscegenation, like all accusations, were merely claims. Their truth value was established through negotiation and contextualization, never taken as apparent. These processes of negotiation tended to constrain the violent potential of any accusation. Hence, although the registers of the Crown are crammed with records of accusation, convictions (except in the case of Muslim women) are a very rare event. Some cases, like that of the Muslim Hilel Mallul, ended in acquittal, with the accusing official ordered to publicize the accused's innocence and good name; others in an acquittal obtained for a fee; still others in the purchase of a remission from guilt or a pardon. A majority probably never made their way into the courts or the documentary record.[125] The violence generated by sexual boundaries was not easy to tap.

---

[122]ACA:C 246:190r (1321/4/6). Such accusations were common. Cf. ACA:C 121:66v (1301/6/30), where a Muslim *faqīh* (jurist) of Zaragoza is accused by municipal officials of magic and miscegenation (cited in Ferrer, *Els sarraïns*, p. 33).

[123]Cf. ACA:C 219:266v (1321/3/27), cited by Ferrer, *Els sarraïns*, p. 38, in which a Christian royal official is prosecuted for having absolved too leniently a Christian woman accused of sleeping with Muslims. Compare ACA:C 528:239v, where Valerius, alcalde of the Muslims of Zaragoza, is accused by the Muslims of tolerating sex between Muslims and Christians (the accusation is later quashed by the king as malicious).

[124]ACA:C 519:20v–26r (no date, ca. 1327/12) contains a list of standard charges to be used in inquisitional proceedings against a variety of types of officials. Various sexual issues are mentioned on fols. 25r–v, including the issue of trumped-up charges and also the possibility of alcaydes selling married people "licenses" to commit adultery without fear of punishment. For testimony against one Muslim on such charges, see the depositions against Jaale Abunacia of Miravet contained in ACA:C Procesos 502/11 (1309). In the furtherance of his extortions, Jaale is even said to have accused one man's daughter of being pregnant, despite the fact that she was "only a little girl." The document is in Catalan, with subscriptions in Arabic. Cf. Lourie, "Anatomy of Ambivalence," p. 45.

[125]For Hilel, see A. Conte Cazcarro, *La aljama de Moros de Huesca* (Huesca, 1992), p. 40, citing

This was due in part to the fact that the strategic nature of such charges was no mystery to contemporaries. Consider the case of Jaco Abutarda, Jew of Daroca. Jaco regularly flouted the authorities. When the community's tax collector came knocking on his door, Jaco punched him in the face. Such behavior made him enemies who had to be dealt with. Jaco seems to have been exquisitely aware that enmity against minorities often took the form of accusations, and he took suitable precautions. Hence he always carried with him an amulet of "names, characters, and precious stones," which he boasted protected him from the king's justice. The amulet must have worked, because Jaco was absolved of the charges of miscegenation against him, albeit at the cost of a considerable sum of money.[126]

The workings of this economy of accusation were relatively clear to everyone. Muslims and Jews could be tried only in the courts of their lords, who both passed judgment and executed it. Accusations thus became a form of extraordinary taxation in which lords convicted their own subjects in order to extract money from them. This system limited violence in two ways. First, by monetizing it, the system converted physical violence into, at least in the most extreme cases, something that resembled a licensing fee. This process was transparent to everyone, though it was in bad taste to say so. Hence the accusation against Salomon Churchulu, a Jew of Daroca, stated not only that he slept with women of all three faiths, including Christian prostitutes, the wives and daughters of other Jews, and Muslims of unspecified status, but also that he bragged of his ability to avoid punishment simply by paying a fine. Likewise space was found among the numerous accusations against Johan Sibili, Jew of Valencia, to add one of untruthful boasting. Though Johan trumpeted that he had purchased a royal remission for all his crimes at a price of 10,000 sous, his denouncers charged, he had in fact gotten only a partial remission, and for the much more modest sum of 500 sous, at that.[127]

ACA:C 163:155r (1317). Lourie points out that defendants could often buy pardons for such offenses, but even innocence could prove expensive. See Lourie, "Anatomy of Ambivalence," pp. 54–55. For a sampling of accusations, fines, and the like against Jews see Assis, "Sexual Behaviour," pp. 42–44. Assis knows of only one case that ends with the death penalty imposed on both the Jewish male and the Christian female accused, and that case, in 1381, involved a nun (p. 44, citing Villanueva, *Viaje literario*, 21:219); and A. Morel-Fatio, "Notes et documents pour servir à l'histoire des Juifs des Baléares sous la domination aragonaise du XIIIe au XVe siècle," *RdÉJ* 4 (1882): 37.

[126] ACA:C 488:52v–53v (1334/8/16): ". . . deferendo tecum nominas, caractaras ac lapides preciossas asserendo quod propter hoc nos vel aliquis nostro nomine contra te cum justitia procedere non possemus." The document, which constitutes Jaco's remission for these crimes, detailed other charges as well. See also ACA:C 529:21r–v (1334/3/30). On Mediterranean Jewish amulets see the introduction to L. Schiffman and M. Swartz, *Hebrew and Aramaic Incantation Texts from the Cairo Genizah* (Sheffield, 1992). On their decoration and use as jewelry see S. Goitein, *A Mediterranean Society: The Jewish Communities of the Arab World as Portrayed in the Documents of the Cairo Geniza*, vol. 4, *Daily Life* (Berkeley, 1983), pp. 218 f.

[127] For Salomon's case, see ACA:C 650:79r–v (1347/12/15). For Johan Sibili, ACA:C Procesos 115/19 (1346/3/24), transcribed in Lourie, "Mafiosi and Malsines," appendix A. Among the

Second, this system of accusation limited violence by contextualizing it within interest groups. Lords, for example, might be eager for the bits of extraordinary revenue such accusations brought in, but they were also extremely sensitive to the fact that excessive arbitrariness would depopulate their minority communities through emigration and kill the goose that laid the golden egg.[128] And just as lords might be willing to despoil or even execute someone else's Muslim or Jew, they wanted to protect their own.[129] The result of what one might call these checks and balances was that the violent charge inherent in accusations of miscegenation was diffused to the point where it was rarely lethal, though often a costly nuisance.[130] This is something of a circular equilibrium. The potential for conflict in everyday social relations between groups was concentrated onto charges of miscegenation centered on the bodies of prostitutes, while at the same time these very charges were drained of virulence by their constant invocation and contextualization within everyday relations.

Of course there were moments when the power of this boundary flashed out in full and horrific force. I think of Pandonus; of Ali "Killer of Lions," the Muslim burned to death on charges of sex with a Christian girl who proved on later examination to be a virgin; of Thoda the prostitute; or of the Muslim grain trader, a vassal of the Templars, who was traveling through lands belonging to his lords' enemies when they seized his ship and cargo, injured and killed some of the friends who tried to save him, and burned him on charges of miscegenation when his distant lords proved helpless to protect him.[131] In some ways such

---

many accusations against Johan was predictably included that of sex with Christian women (no. 11, p. 90). The false boast was the last accusation (no. 23, p. 92).

[128] Complaints that accusations are depopulating a given Muslim or Jewish aljama were frequent. For one example, a letter from the Infant Alfonso to King James II concerning Teruel's aljamas, see ACA:C 385 bis:145v (1321/2/17).

[129] A few of many examples: in ACA:C 534:35v–36r (1331/11/22), the countess of Terranova halts an accusation of theft against her Muslims by complaining to the king that it is depopulating her *alqueria*. The viscountess of Cardona's complaint that one of Infant Peter's officials had arrested one of her Muslim women vassals on charges of adultery with a Christian prompted the king to ask the archbishop of Zaragoza to investigate the case: see ACA:C 534:126r (1333/4/18). In ACA:C 886:182r–v Lope de Luna, seigneur of Sogorb, complains that people accuse his Muslims of, among other things, miscegenation, solely for purposes of extortion. For a case involving Jews, see ACA:C 533:111v, where the master of Calatrava intervenes on behalf of his vassal Jucef Abinfalvo. Representative of the other point of view is the complaint of the city of Barbastro, which argued that the noble Guillem d'Entencia had interfered with its right to execute a Muslim condemned to burn because he had sex with two Christians. Guillem was insisting that since the Muslim was his vassal, he could be tried only in his courts.

[130] These checks and balances were to some extent enshrined in the *furs nous*, the new "constitutions" issued to Valencia by Alfonso the Benign. These provided for a division of the revenue of justice between the Crown as judge and the lord of the person tried. For the *fur*, see *Furs* 3.5.78, 3.5.81, 3.5.85 (3:127–130, 133, 136–138 in the ed. of G. Colon and A. Garcia). Cf. Romeu, "Los fueros de Valencia y los fueros de Aragón," pp. 100 f. For a case insisting on the principle, see ACA:C 456:99v.

[131] Ferrer, *Els sarraïns*, pp. 29–30, ACA:C 118:31v–32r (1301/3/14) (transcribed in Ferrer, pp. 214–215); ACA:C 121:27v (1301/6/19).

moments were exceptional, which is precisely what makes them good foci for the study of the network of relations that intermeshed minorities with majority. The victims were individuals stripped of the customary protections and social relations that tended to be mobilized by such accusations and to attenuate their force. Equally important, however, these moments were also systemic. They were the product of a society whose stability depended in part on the display, only occasional but with terrifying clarity, of the violent consequences of difference.

Chapter 6

MINORITIES CONFRONT EACH OTHER: VIOLENCE

BETWEEN MUSLIMS AND JEWS

T HE PREVIOUS CHAPTER moved from a set of anxieties arising at a particular religious boundary to the strategic deployment of these anxieties in a competitive world: a move from structure to context, so to speak. But we can also take the opposite tack and ask how particular and contingent historical situations encourage the emergence of intolerant religious discourses and give them strength. Such a vast question is best answered by example, in this case that of Muslim-Jewish relations in the Christian Crown of Aragon. Though some have found in the "horizontal" relationship between minority communities materialist conflict and violence undistorted by the screen of Christian religious discourse,[1] in fact Muslims and Jews not only acted and argued out their conflicts in their own religious languages but also sought access to explicitly Christian discourses. Even when they did not seek to have their conflicts transcend the realm of the material, we should not forget that their interactions were structured by Christian institutions (economic, political, judicial, and so forth) and the ideologies supporting these. The need to function within such institutions forced non-Christians to participate in their logic and to adopt those modes of argument that were most effective within them. One remarkable consequence of this is the adoption by Muslims of Christian anti-Jewish discourse and violence in the Crown of Aragon, a filiation that will, I hope, become clear as we tread the path from context to discourse, from situations of Muslim-Jewish conflict (moneylending, meat markets, sex) to invocations of the Crucifixion.[2]

There are some unfortunate practical difficulties specific to the study of Muslim-Jewish relations in the Crown of Aragon that deserve mention as caveats. The first is a problem of sources. Both groups are most accessible in the documentation of their Christian kings, a documentation concerned with taxes, privileges, and criminal and jurisdictional complaints. Not surprisingly, Christian-Muslim and Christian-Jewish relations, not Muslim-Jewish ones, feature most prominently in the evidence. As for Muslim records, the emigration of elites from much of the Crown (Valencia excepted), later attempts to suppress the use of Arabic, and finally the expulsion of the Moriscos all ensured that

---

[1] Thus J. Hinojosa Montalvo can write that "there were tensions between Jews and Muslims, although the religious factor was absent and the disputes arose out of economic reasons." *The Jews of the Kingdom of Valencia: From Persecution to Expulsion, 1391–1492* (Jerusalem, 1993), p. 170.

[2] This is in some sense a rejoinder to N. Cohn, cited in the introduction.

what Arabic material survives from the period is sparse and scattered. Jewish sources, too, suffered in the expulsions of 1492 and in any case were never rich in material concerning their Muslim neighbors. When Jews did write of "Ishmaelites," they often meant those sovereign Muslims across the sea, not the impoverished Mudejars with whom they shared a subject status within a Christian land. This lack of sources is mentioned, not by way of excuse for what follows, but as a partial explanation for the near total lack of interest historians have shown for the topic of Muslim-Jewish relations in Spain.

Herein lies a second problem. The study of minority interaction is undertaken in a historiographic vacuum. Virtually no work has been done on Muslim-Jewish relations under Christian rule in the Iberian Peninsula, so we know little of the material infrastructure of these relations.[3] The one area of minority interaction that has received attention, that of high culture, has led to idiosyncratic conclusions. Thus one historian has recently argued that fifteenth-century Spanish Jews felt a cultural affinity for Muslims and Islam. Some Jews, he points out, spoke Arabic and admired its qualities as a language. They respected the great Muslim thinkers and partook of a culture permeated by Muslim cuisine, music, and poetry. "All this," he claims, "is hardly compatible with a view of Spanish Jewry as antipathetic and distant to Arabic culture."[4]

It is certainly true that Arabic high culture enjoyed prestige among learned Jews, but this model leaves much unsaid. First, this often-eulogized respect for Arabic culture was scarcely a universal or uncontested position, even among the learned. There were doubtless plenty of Jews who, like the erudite fourteenth-century Catalan Joseph ben Shalom Ashkenazi, attacked the Muslims as idolaters and ridiculed their religious practices in the most scatological terms.[5] True, Joseph ben Shalom was a Kabbalist, writing against a rationalist philosophical tradition saturated with Arabic influence. But his attack against an "Islamicizing" philosophical elite is part of a long tradition of antirationalist polemic that one should not minimize when assessing the extent of Jewish affinities for Muslim culture.[6]

---

[3]Boswell (*Royal Treasure*) and Lourie ("Anatomy of Ambivalence") have both dedicated valuable pages to the subject as part of broader projects, as has (in his many works) R. I. Burns. M. Meyerson is in the midst of a broadly comparative study, first fruits of which are cited in n. 23 of the introduction.

[4]E. Gutwirth, "Hispano-Jewish Attitudes to the Moors in the Fifteenth Century," *Sefarad* 49 (1989): 237–261, quotation from p. 242. For Jewish comparisons of life under Islamic and Christian polities see the work of B. Septimus: " 'Better under Edom Than under Ishmael,' the History of a Saying," *Zion* 47 (1982): 103–111 (in Hebrew); idem, "Hispano-Jewish Views of Christendom and Islam" (unpublished paper). See also, but with care, Roth, *Jews, Visigoths and Muslims*, esp. pp. 163–203.

[5]See G. Vajda, "Un chapitre de l'histoire du conflit entre la kabbale et la philosophie: la polémique anti-intellectualiste de Joseph ben Shalom Ashkenazi de Catalogne," *Archives d'histoire doctrinale et littéraire du Moyen Age*, 1957, p. 135 (text provided below).

[6]For more on this controversy, see S. M. Stern, "Rationalists and Kabbalists in Medieval

Second, we really know very little about the attitudes of Muslim and Jewish cultural elites toward each other, as distinguished from their attitudes toward each other's ideas. Here we should heed the words of Elena Lourie. As she points out in a different context, the notables whose writings have received so much attention are scholars and philosophers praising famous, but long-dead, Muslim intellectuals. They formed part of an interfaith "Republic of Letters" whose adherents (in all three religious groups) borrowed ideas from one another in a great variety of fields, including medicine and philosophy. But cultural borrowing does not equal tolerance: Aquinas could praise Maimonides while at the same time advocating discrimination against the Jews.[7]

For this reason the pages that follow address only tangentially the existing work of intellectual historians on Muslim-Jewish relations. I focus instead on material and social interactions that cluster around familiar settings: moneylending, meat buying and selling, civic processions, sexuality, conversion, polemics. These are sites already well known to historians of Christian relations with Jews or Christian relations with Muslims, but the documents of minority-minority affairs cluster around them as well. Indeed, it is difficult to think of a type of interaction, or a barrier to interaction, that did not concern members of minority groups as much in their relations with other minorities as in those with the majority. We think of the segregation of neighborhoods, of markets and economic life, of communal baths and social centers, as techniques of avoidance used by the majority, but they are those of minorities as well.[8] Much the same issues polarizing majority-minority relations polarized those between minorities, with the difference that minorities had less obvious tools with which to move against their competitors. The chapter explores some of these spheres of

---

Allegory," *Journal of Jewish Studies* 6 (1955): 73–86; Kriegel, *Les Juifs à la fin du Moyen Age*, pp. 145–179.

[7] See Lourie, "Anatomy of Ambivalence," p. 72. On the "rencontre" between intellectuals of different faiths at the level of philosophy, see G. Dahan, *Les intellectueis chrétiens et les juifs au moyen âge* (Paris, 1990), p. 322.

[8] Thus in 1365 during the war with Castile, when the Crown's needs increased Muslim bargaining power, the Muslims of Castro and Alfandequiella forced King Peter to promise them that no Jews (or Christians) would be allowed to live among them. See ACA:C 1204:63 (1365/4/8): ". . . que nengu crestia ne juheu no puxa poblar ab ells"; published in Boswell, *Royal Treasure*, pp. 367, 494 ff. In ibid., p. 69, in discussion of ACA:C 721:135 (1365/1/2), a Jew of Tortosa asked the king to induce an exchange of property with a Muslim in order to avoid proximity. For the objections of minority groups to the sharing of wax ovens in Castellón, see ACA:C 478:237v–238r (1329); on shared bread ovens in Tarazona, ACA:C 486:16r (1333). There are many other examples; these are chosen as representative. For what may be a contrary example of Muslims and Jews in Tortosa struggling to maintain their rights to share their own bathing facilities against municipal attempts to force them to use municipal baths, see ACA:C 48:190r (1280/11/30), and the discussion of related documents in D. Romano, "Los judíos en los baños de Tortosa," *Sefarad* 40 (1980): 57–64. Other areas will be discussed in more detail below. (Of course Muslims and Jews also attempted to segregate themselves from Christians, but that is not the subject of this chapter. For Muslims, see, e.g., ACA:C 215:205r [1317], in Ferrer, *Els sarrains*, p. 232. For Jews, see, e.g., ACA:C 219:344v [1321] and 413:42r–v [1328].)

conflict and competition between minorities: for economic power (meat markets and moneylending), for civic prestige, for sexual access to women, and for converts. In each of these cases, analysis lingers over the violence (accusational and physical) such conflicts caused and the religious rhetorics that emerged to justify such violence.

.   .   .   .   .

It is difficult for modern consumers to imagine the barriers to free exchange that existed in the corporatist and therefore deeply riven markets of the Middle Ages. In the medieval Crown, rights to sell, purchase, or produce a given commodity might depend upon one's town of residence, guild affiliation, tax status, liege lord, religion, the time of year, week, or day, or any combination of these factors—and this is by no means an exhaustive list. These were barriers that invited manipulation, conflict, and violence. Some of this complexity is clearly evident in the market for meat, which can serve as an introductory example.

It is not surprising, given the place of dietary restrictions in all three religious traditions, that the sale of food should provide a point of conflict between groups.[9] In the case of Muslims and Jews, dietary laws separated their communities from others. Christians, though not in principle barred from partaking "of everything that God created," achieved in practice a similar separation by reiterating in countless ecclesiastical councils prohibitions on dining with Muslims and Jews, or eating food prepared by them. As St. Vincent Ferrer put it in his emphatic way, "Don't buy their victuals . . . because we have no greater enemies . . . if they send you bread, throw it to the dogs; if they send live meat, accept it, but not dead; because Holy Scripture says against these sins: 'Do you not know that a little leaven corrupts the whole dough?' "[10]

The most intense conflicts related to food arose over the exchange of meat between Jew and Christian. It is not entirely clear why this is so. Some scholars have blamed such tensions on the belief that the Jews were "untouchable," a source of pollution; others on the association of meat markets with blood, a liquid of rich signification in the Middle Ages.[11] Two other, perhaps more

[9]Compare the prohibitions in the Pentateuch (e.g., Leviticus 11) and the Qurʾān (E.g., Sūrah 5:3, "The Table") with the criticism of such prohibitions in the writings of St. Paul (esp. Romans and Galatians).

[10]The criticism that Muslims err in not permitting themselves everything of God's creation is from Bernardo Pérez de Chinchón's 1532 *El libro llamado Antialcorán*, cited by L. Cardaillac, *Moriscos y cristianos: un enfrentamiento polemico (1492–1640)* (Madrid, 1977), p. 328. St. Vincent's quotation is from his *Sermons*, vol. 3, no. 56, p. 14. His scriptural citation is from 1 Cor. 5:6. Synodal prohibitions on the Christian purchase of Jewish or Muslim meat were common, but not universal. Cf. the Synod of Tortosa of 1359, which revoked earlier conciliar decrees mandating excommunication as the punishment for eating Jewish or Muslim meat. See Boswell, *Royal Treasure*, p. 102, and Villanueva, *Viaje literario*, 5:358.

[11]On Jews as "untouchables," Kriegel, "Un trait de psychologie sociale," pp. 326–330. On the association of ritual murder accusations against Jews with meat markets, Jordan, "Problems of the

convincing, explanations arise. The first is an economic consequence of ritual practice. Without some commercial outlet for meat that proved unkosher after slaughter (usually because of tubercular lesions in the lungs), Jewish meat consumption would become prohibitively expensive. The sale of such meat to Christians and Muslims at a reduced price provided a solution to this dilemma, but it also irritated Christian butchers who saw their municipally regulated prices being undercut. Furthermore, some Christians saw such sales as demeaning to their faith. It was not fitting, according to the divines, that a Christian should eat meat rejected by a Jew, an argument that reached its apogee in the bull issued by Benedict XIII in 1415 threatening with excommunication anyone who accepted foodstuffs from a Jew, "vel carnes per eos refutatas quas tryffa vocant" (or the meats rejected by them which they call *ṭrefah*). [12]

Municipal councils were only too willing to borrow this religious argument for a different reason. Meat markets may well have been the most regulated aspect of medieval life. The seigneur had rights over the butcher table itself, but the price of the meat, as well as its importation, the pasturage of the flocks as they awaited slaughter, even the salaries of the guards who watched those flocks—all were regulated by municipal ordinance. [13] Taxes on meat, whether on herds in transit, on the pasturage that fed them, or collected at the point of sale by the butcher, might be imposed by the Crown, local lords, the Jewish or Muslim aljama, or the town council. [14] In this complex process of moving meat across geographic and jurisdictional space from the countryside to urban markets, Jewish butchers depended on and cooperated with Christians. [15] But with

Meat-Market of Beziers," 37–39. Lourie writes that "no place could have aroused uglier associations or be better designed to instil fears . . . of ritual murder." See her "A Plot Which Failed? The Case of a Corpse Found in the Jewish *Call* of Barcelona (1301)," *Mediterranean Historical Review* 1 (1986): 187–220, here p. 189.

[12] Here I am following J. Riera i Sans, "La conflictivitat de l'alimentació dels jueus medievals (segles XII–XV)," in *Alimentació i societat a la Catalunya medieval* (Barcelona, 1988), esp. pp. 305–310. For Benedict's bull, see Amador de los Ríos, *Historia social, política y religiosa*, 2:551. For the bull's confirmation in Aragon, see ACA:C 2395:122r–126v (1415/7/23), here fol. 124r, published by F. Vendrell de Millás, "En torno a la confirmación real, en Aragón, de la pragmatica de Benedicto XIII," *Sefarad* 20 (1960): 1–33, here p. 27.

[13] On meat market regulations in Catalonia see F. Carreras y Candi, "Ordinacions urbanes de bon govern a Catalunya (segles xiii a xviii)," *Boletín de la Real Academia de Buenas Letras de Barcelona* 11 (1923–1926): 293–335, 365–431; and 12 (1926–1928): 37–63, 121–153, 189–208, 286–295, 368–380, 419–423, 520–533. For an example of conflict between municipality and minority butchers over pricing in Borja, see ACA:C 620:177v–178r (1342/11/12). For conflicts over pasturage and guards in Luna, see ACA:C 2076:82r–v (1388/4/10), ACA:C 2077:76v (1389/5/17), both cited in Riera, "La conflictivitat," p. 300.

[14] The most detailed work on the complex problem of monopolies and taxes on foodstuffs in Aragon has focused on wine. See A. Blasco Martínez, "La producción y comercialización del vino entre los judíos de Zaragoza (siglo XIV)," *Anuario de estudios medievales* 19 (1989): 405–449.

[15] Mossetes, a Jewish butcher of Girona, was probably typical in forming part of a "societas" with Christian butchers for the purpose of purchasing livestock. See ADG Ll. Ep. 25, fols. 121r–v (1354/11/6), where his widow Regina sues his former associates for the return of some money and animals, "tam grossa quam minuta."

their autonomous butcher tables, tax structures, and royal privileges, the Jews often found themselves at odds with Christian butchers and municipal officials, and it was at these jurisdictional fault lines that anti-Jewish rhetoric and violence often arose.[16]

It is not obvious that these issues should strain Muslim-Jewish relations as much as Christian-Jewish ones. After all, Christian polemicists against Muslims often faulted them for "judaizing" in dietary matters because they observed similar rules in the slaughtering of animals.[17] But again fiscal issues pulled the minority communities apart. Because both Muslims and Jews formed part of the "royal treasure," the Crown sometimes treated its rights over them jointly.[18] Monopolies could be assigned on ovens, meat markets, and even jails to be used by members of both religions. Joint meat markets were almost always under Jewish control, probably because Jewish aljamas had more wealth with which to purchase the privilege, and perhaps because Jewish rules for ritual slaughter satisfied most Muslim requirements, while the reverse was not true.[19] In such a situation, Muslims became something of a captive market for ritually slaughtered Jewish meat that proved unkosher, subsidizing Jewish meat prices and paying taxes via Jewish collectors. The case of Tortosa provides a good example of the conflicts that could arise from this.[20]

In 1321, after a lengthy lawsuit between the two minority communities, King James II granted the Muslims of Tortosa the right to build their own meat market, despite the Jews' claim that the Muslims were legally obliged to purchase the unkosher meat slaughtered by the Jews. The Muslims were to pay six

---

[16]Some of this violence was institutional, as in the 1415 edict confirming the bull of Benedict XIII, which stipulated that Jews who sold meat to Christians were to be whipped through the town (see n. 12 above). At other times the violence was only implicit, as when the butchers of Apiaria attached a pole with an effigy dressed in Jewish clothes to the stall reserved for the Jews, a move that the Jews feared was meant to incite a riot. See ACA:C 438:225r–v (1330/5/11).

[17]E.g., in El libro llamado Antialcorán, cited above, n. 10: "Vosotros [Moriscos] soys peores que los judíos, que no osays comer de todo lo que Dios crió. . . . dezís mal de los judíos y guardays lo más principal de su ley." For earlier examples see R. Southern, The Making of the Middle Ages (New Haven, 1953), p. 41, citing Giraldus Cambrensis, and J. Kritzeck, Peter the Venerable and Islam (Princeton, 1964), p. 95, citing Herman of Dalmatia's Doctrina Mahumet. See also Cutler and Cutler, The Jew as Ally of the Muslim, p. 411n.52.

[18]For a general survey of minority, particularly Muslim, meat markets, see Boswell, Royal Treasure, pp. 95–103.

[19]For a general statement of the permissibility for Muslims of meat slaughtered by Jews, see F. Denny, An Introduction to Islam, 2d ed. (New York, 1994), p. 284. The Prophet Muhammad was reported to have eaten Jewish food: see Ibn Qayyim al-Jawziyya, Aḥkām ahl al-dhimma, ed. Ṣubḥī Ṣāliḥ, pt. 1 (Beirut, 1983), pp. 244–245, 270. Cf. Cohen, Under Crescent and Cross, p. 132. For a polemical Jewish attack on the laxity of Muslim dietary laws, see Cutler and Cutler, The Jew as Ally of the Muslim, p. 439n.61. But in Iberia Jews may have been more moderate on the issue. Cf. a responsum of Ibn Adret on a related issue, Adret, vol. 1, no. 345.

[20]The case of Tortosa is partly described in R. Mayordomo Font, "Notas históricas sobre la carnicería de la aljama sarracena de Tortosa (siglo XIV)," in Homenatge a la memòria del prof. Dr. Emilio Sáez (Barcelona, 1989), pp. 223–231.

hundred sous of Barcelona per year for their privilege.[21] In order to appease the Jews, however, the king later restricted the placement of the Muslim meat market so that it would not compete with that of the Jews, and allowed all Muslims not actually from the town of Tortosa to continue purchasing meat from the Jews, or anywhere else. Later that year, when the Jews complained again, he ordered the Muslim meat market destroyed and relocated within the Muslim quarter in order to further limit its clientele.[22] Of course, once the Muslims had their own meat market, they encountered the same types of conflict with Christian municipal institutions as Jews did. By 1328, the Muslims of Tortosa were tussling with the Christians over taxes on meat, not with the Jews over monopolies.[23]

Even in towns where each denomination had its own butcher, conflict arose. Because Jews often sold unkosher meat at prices below those charged by other butchers, any non-Jew might be tempted to purchase it. Christian authorities reacted to this with municipal and ecclesiastical prohibitions, and so did the Muslims. In Tarazona, the Muslims explicitly allied with the Christians when the two groups issued a joint ordinance barring the Jewish meat market to patrons of either faith.[24] The Muslim aljama of Zaragoza emancipated its butcher table from that of the Jews sometime in the 1320s but then found itself competing with both sides. In 1333 it complained to the king that Muslims were shopping at the Jewish table, while at nearly the same time the Christians were complaining that the Muslims' low prices were attracting Christians to their butcher shop. A decade later the Muslims passed an ordinance punishing any Muslim who bought meat from Jewish butchers with a fine of five sous or five lashes. They also argued along religious lines. Echoing Christian complaints about Jewish rejects, they told the king that Jews sold Muslims suffocated meat and other unclean things which the Jews would not eat and which were ritually forbidden to the Muslims.[25]

---

[21] ACA:C 219:306v–307r (1321/5/1), transcribed in Mayordomo, "La carnicería," p. 229. Most curious is the Jews' claim that the Muslims were obliged to buy their rejected meat: ". . . videlicet quod asserebatur per dictos judeos vos dictos sarracenos debere recipere et emere de carnibus *trufatis* per eosdem judeos decolatis in macello vocato de Remolins et non alibi, vobis dictis sarracenis contrarium asserentibus" (emphasis added). Ironically, King James II had granted the Muslims the right to purchase meat at the Jewish meat market at the Muslims' request as a special concession, and one that had been bitterly contested by the Christian municipal officials, who claimed that Muslims were obliged to buy their meat at municipal stalls. On the issue of impurity, see ACA:C 196:232v (1298/5/21).

[22] The first restriction is in ACA:C 220:15r (1321/5/25), the Jews complaining that ". . . dictum macellum, si infra limitationem predictam fieret, fore in eorum non modicum detrimentum." The destruction and reconstruction is ordered in ACA:C 220:40r–v (1321/6/28).

[23] ACA:C 430:28v (1328/10/18).

[24] ACA:C 101:260r–v (1295/7/27), cited by Lourie, "Anatomy of Ambivalence," p. 43n.138. King James overturned the ordinance as an innovation.

[25] In 1320 the Jews of Zaragoza complained that the Muslims had violated their obligation to buy from the Jews and had opened their own table, a move that the king condemned as an innovation.

Meat markets are only one example of how fiscal structures could pull apart the two minority communities, though a distinctive one in that they involve a similarity of ritual interests. In general, fiscal issues could be expected to stress relations between the two groups, since Muslims and Jews had different relationships to their common protector, the king. A majority of Muslims were rural vassals of lords other than the king, even if the king claimed theoretical jurisdiction over them, whereas the great majority of Jews were urban and depended directly on the sovereign.[26] Most of those Muslims who were urban lived in royal aljamas, but these were generally poorer than their Jewish counterparts, if tax records are any indication.[27] The sums paid by Jews in taxes to the Crown vastly overshadowed those contributed by Muslims, a fact that may have had some weight in the king's arbitration of disputes between them. These differences are best summed up in the stereotypical statuses of Muslims and Jews: Muslims were thought of as manual laborers (see chapter 1), Jews as royal dependents and sources of revenue. Hence the words with which the city of Valencia resisted royal attempts to impose a new tax upon it: "It is nothing other than to turn each of his cities into a Jewry . . . we will not give in to such a request, for we would rather die than be like Jews."[28]

This differential status revealed itself in a number of ways. The Crown, for example, sometimes used Jews as its agents in fiscal affairs involving Muslims, either by farming out royal monopolies to Jews (as in the case of meat markets,

---

See ACA:C 170:267v (for a similar complaint in Calatayud, see ACA:C 171:5r [1320/12/13]). By 1333 the Muslim table was a fait accompli. For the Muslim complaint that Muslims were going to the Jewish butcher, see ACA:C 458:27v–28r (1333/7/15); for the Christian complaint of Christians buying from Muslims at lower prices see ACA:C 458:39v–40r. ACA:C 625:29r (1343/10/15): ". . . aliqui sarraceni et sarracene ipsius aljame . . . ibant ad carniceriam judeorum dicte civitate et in ea emebant carnes contra ordinationem dudum factam per dictam aljamam sarracenorum eo quia in dicta carniceria judeorum vendebantur eis carnes suffocaate [sic] et alie inmunde quibus judei nullatenus vestebantur." Similar complaints had even been made by Muslims in Islamic Spain. Cf. Abū Isḥaq al-Ilbīrī's poem attacking the Jewish prime minister of Granada, Yūsuf ibn Naghrīllah, in which he complains that Jews sell Muslims their nonkosher leftovers. Cf. B. Lewis, "An Anti-Jewish Ode: The Qasida of Abu Ishaq against Joseph ibn Nagrella," in *Salo W. Baron Jubilee Volume*, ed. S. Liebermann (Jerusalem, 1974), 2:657–668. For the Arabic text, see J. Monroe, *Hispano-Arabic Poetry: A Student Anthology* (Berkeley, 1974), pp. 206–213, here line 34.

[26] For more on these differences, see chaps. 1 and 5.

[27] The fact that taxes on Muslims yielded the king much less than taxes on Jews has often been noted, most recently by C. Guilleré, "Les finances de la Couronne d'Aragon au debut du XIVe siècle (1300–1310)," in *Estudios sobre renta, fiscalidad y finanzas en la Cataluña bajomedieval*, ed. M. Sánchez Martínez (Barcelona, 1993), pp. 487–507, here p. 495. The urban Jewish community, like the urban Muslim one, consisted mostly of small tradesmen, but the Muslim community lacked the tiny layer of the very rich who were so prominent in Jewish administration. Cf. Lourie's comparison of the wealth of the Muslim Bellido clan with that of the Alatzars, "Anatomy of Ambivalence," pp. 36–37.

[28] For Muslims as the prototype of exploitable agricultural labor, see chap. 1. The quotation about Jews and taxes is from AMV, Ll.M., g³ 4, 108v (1378/10/26), cited in Bramon, *Contra moros y judíos*, p. 67.

ovens, and notaries), or more directly by appointing them as tax collectors in Muslim communities. Like Christians, Muslims resented such appointments. Unlike them, they sometimes lacked the power to do much about it. Individual Jews in positions of authority could be beaten up, but their existence as a class could not be challenged by Muslims on religious grounds as easily as it had been by Christians. Consequently, Muslim-Jewish economic relations were not as closely regulated as those involving Christians, a lack of structure that could itself lead to conflict.[29]

Moneylending is typical of these economic activities, both because it was frequent and because it formed the basis for much of the differential treatment of Muslims, Christians, and Jews by the Crown. In some ways the market for money was indifferent to faith, with bankruptcy the only heresy.[30] By the fourteenth century, Jews, Muslims, and Christians lent and borrowed from each other in all conceivable combinations. Contra stereotype, we find the Jewish aljama of Zaragoza pleading for grace in its repayment of a loan to a Muslim official, and the aljama of Sogorb borrowing money from Muslims to redeem its Torah scrolls from impoundment.[31] Nevertheless, religious identity mattered. There is no doubt, for example, that the lending of money at interest by Jews and the subsequent taxation of their profits by the Crown was one of the primary paths of monetary flow toward the royal fisc.[32] And though Muslims did lend at interest, and Christian rentiers dominated high finance, it was the Jews and the consumption loans in which they specialized that were associated with usury.

[29] On Jews as intermediaries in Muslim fiscal affairs see, for the early period, R. I. Burns, *Medieval Colonialism: Postcrusade Exploitation of Islamic Valencia* (Princeton, 1975), p. 272 and passim. On a Jew as notary of a Muslim aljama, see Boswell, *Royal Treasure*, pp. 502–503. For a case of violence, see, e.g., ACA:C 367:76r–v (1322), where the *alamin* of Cocentayna and four other Muslims were accused of beating up Mosse, a Jew of Elx collecting taxes on behalf of the noble Roger de Lauria.

[30] Cf. F.-M. Voltaire, *Lettres philosophiques* (Paris, 1964), letter 6 "On the Presbytereans," p. 47.

[31] Muslims figure frequently as creditors of Jews. See, for example, ACA:C 462:122r–v (1333/5/25), where Samuel Albala, Jew of Alagon, complains that he is being defrauded by his Muslim creditor Abdalla Abinamir, son of the *alamin* (Arabic *amīn*, a local administrator) of Pedrola. In 1334, the Jewish aljama of Zaragoza pleaded that it could not afford to pay Abdalla's father, the *alamin*, what it owed him (ACA:C 465:271v). The case of Sogorbe is recorded in a *responsum* of Rabbi Isaac ben Sheshet Perfet, no. 282, on which see J. R. Magdalena Nom de Déu, "La aljama judía de Segorbe en un 'responsum' de Rabí Ishaq bar Séset Perfet," *Boletín de la Sociedad Cast-ellonense de Cultura* 59 (1983): 385–393; and F. Baer, *Studien zur Geschichte der Juden im Königreich Aragonien während des 13. und 14. Jahrhunderts* (Berlin, 1913), p. 202, who gives the creditor as a Christian. For the transcript of a judgment against several Jews of Barbastro for nonpayment of debts to two Muslims, see ACA:C Procesos 563/10, dated 1325/1/30.

[32] Little makes the general point in his *Religious Poverty*, pp. 45–46: "The Jews could thus drain off a layer of money from the population at large and pass it on to the royal treasury without the king's having to get approval to levy a tax or his having to pay the costs of collecting a tax. Therefore the Jews, prior to the development of a general and regular system of taxation, had in effect, if unofficially, become royal tax collectors." For the importance of Jewish taxes to the count-kings, see Sánchez, "Fiscalidad real," esp. p. 118.

Such an association was not unfounded. Secular laws about moneylending were explicitly designed to achieve three goals: to discourage Christians from the infamous sin of usury by assigning the task to the Jews, to protect Christians from usurious rates of interest, and to fill the royal treasury.[33] The pursuit of these goals came to shape contemporaries' perceptions not only of Jews but also of the monarchy, since the registration of loans, requests for loan moratoria (delays in repayment issued by royal authority in exchange for a fee), and the litigation of disputes were among the most common contacts ordinary people had with the Crown and its courts.[34]

In a Christian context, the implications of this association of Jews with moneylending and royal fiscality in shaping anti-Jewish attitudes and violence have received a great deal of attention, but they are important in Muslim relations as well. If anything, Muslims experienced the link more powerfully, since compared to Christians they were at significant disadvantage in their credit relations with Jews. Much of the usury legislation that fixed the maximum legal interest rate on Jewish loans to Christians at 20 percent per month did not protect Muslims.[35] Privileges to Jewish communities, both seigneurial and royal, often explicitly excluded Muslims from coverage by usury legislation, authorizing instead any interest rate agreed upon mutually by the borrower and lender.[36]

[33] Not everyone thought that the solution favored by Aragonese (and other) monarchs for the attainment of these goals was a good one. Indeed some went so far as to suggest that the Aragonese kings were, by some sort of commutative principle, usurers. Cf. Guillaume de Montlauzon's commentary on the *Clémentines*: "Numquid ergo rex Arragonie vel eius officiales, qui levant magnum tributum a Iudeis seu Sarracenis regni sui, propter usuras quas permittunt eos exercere ibidem, si repetitores ab istis iudeis impediantur per istos, incidentne ipse rex vel eius officiales in sententiam infra scriptam?" Cited in Dahan, *Les intellectuels*, p. 214n.72.

[34] The importance of Jewish moneylending to royal bureaucratic activity is perhaps best illustrated by the dramatic drop in the volume of notarial activity produced after the massacres of Jews in 1391. Public perception of the link between royal enforcement of usury laws and the royal bureaucracy's desire to generate fine income is evident in ACA:C cr. Jaume II, box 135 nos. 383–384, where judge Rodrigo Gil Tarín complains that municipal authorities in Monzón, San Esteban de Litera, and other towns refuse to cooperate in his inquest and denounce usurers, maintaining that the fines generated by royal justice will only drive up the cost of credit.

[35] Though earlier examples existed, it was the legislation of James I that formed the basis for most later usury regulation in the Crown of Aragon. These regulations were explicitly based on religious premises: (1) that Christians sinned in permitting usury, whereas Jews were allowed it by their law (at least as creditors of non-Jews); (2) that Christians should be protected from Jewish rapaciousness. It is not clear where the Christian authorities thought Muslims fit within this system.

[36] See Alfonso's confirmation in 1328 of the (much older) privileges of the Jews of Fraga, in ACA:C 476:136r–140v. Muslims are explicitly excluded from the coverage of usury legislation, since "Dominus Jacobus . . . et praedecessores sui sub dicto coto sive constitutione sarracenos sive sarracenas minime intellexerint comprehendi." (Published in J. Salarrullana de Dios, "Estudios históricos acerca de la ciudad de Fraga: la aljama de judíos de Fraga," *Revista de Archivos, Bibliotecas y Museos*, 3ª epoca, año 23, 40 (1919): 69–90, 183–206, 431–446, here p. 75.) Its language on mutual agreement is similar to that used in Peter IV's reconfirmation of privileges granted by Peter III, James II, and Alfonso to the Jewish aljama of Zaragoza: ". . . in mutuis quae sarraceni receperant a judeis faciant et solvant prout componere vel convenire possunt interse" (ACA:C 863:207r–208v).

The implications were obvious: lords were not willing to extend the protection of the Christian rhetoric of usury to Muslims, since this might reduce the income they could extort from the Jews.[37]

Of course Muslims did attempt to invoke Christian rhetoric by bringing usury accusations against Jews. Perhaps equally often, they found themselves forced to argue in terms of the religious differences between themselves and the Jews. A Muslim *qāḍī* (judicial official), for example, might attempt to protect his coreligionists by arguing that Muslim religious law (*sunna*) allowed debts to accumulate interest for only six (or seven or ten) years, an argument that echoed both privileges accorded Christians and the Pentateuch's concept of sabbatical years. In 1296 the Jews of Borja, Zaragoza, and Tarazona countered this claim of religious privilege by arguing that Muslim jurists were invoking "their Muslim *sunna* invented and newly made by the said Muslims" in order to avoid paying debts.[38]

Religious solidarity was another way of invoking difference, one frequently apparent in the behavior of Muslim local officials. The registers of the Crown of Aragon are full of Jewish complaints about the refusal of Muslim (and Christian) officials to administer justice to them in their litigation with Muslims. Indeed, Muslims seem to have expected this type of solidarity from their officials. One witness against Jucef Alhudali, *faqīh* (jurist) of Tarazona, admitted that he hated Jucef and considered him his enemy because the *faqīh* had enforced the court judgments that a Jewish creditor had obtained against him.[39] In extreme cases, the king could threaten disciplinary action, as when he threatened to depose the Muslim *faqīh* of Borja because of that official's bias against Jewish plaintiffs.[40]

Even when religious solidarity was not explicitly invoked, disputes over loans could easily degenerate into violence between Muslims and Jews. Moneylenders sometimes planned on the possibility of such violence, as did the Jew of Zaragoza who took the precaution of having Prince Peter write to the Muslims of Alfamen warning them against harming him when he passed through the area collecting his debts.[41] This type of violence was often preceded by the

[37] Lourie makes a related point in "Anatomy of Ambivalence," p. 31.

[38] ACA:C 103:218v–219r, 299v–300r (1296), cited in ibid., p. 32, and further references in her n. 107. See also Boswell, *Royal Treasure*, p. 219, citing ACA:C 901:205r (1357/11/15), in which the king states that Muslims are not protected by the six-year statute that applied to Christians. The details of legislation on debt duration were complicated (hence frequently litigated) and cannot be dealt with adequately here. Suffice it to say that the Muslim claim that their law limited the length of time interest could accrue to six years was disingenuous, not only because classical Muslim law prohibited the charging of interest altogether, but also because it discouraged claims that time could extinguish legal obligations (*suqūṭ bi-murūr az-zamān*). See Santillana, *Istituzioni di diritto musulmano malichita*, 2:110 f.

[39] ACA:C Procesos 523/11 (old numeration), fols. 44r–v (dated 1323?).

[40] ACA:C 109:359v–360r, cited in Lourie, "Anatomy of Ambivalence," p. 48n.149. In 1333 some Jews of Borja claimed to be so impoverished by litigation with their Muslim debtors that they could not pay the scribes assigned to the case (ACA:C 460:99v).

[41] ACA:C 85:206v (= Régné no. 2371) (1291/7/11).

exchange of insults. Such was the experience of the Borjan Jew Issac Franco, who found that some Muslims of Malexant, presumably his debtors, cut down and uprooted his vineyard after "aliqua dissensiona verba."[42] From violence against property it was but a short step to violence against persons. The murder of moneylenders as they traveled the countryside collecting their debts was not uncommon, and Muslims participated in such violence, sometimes alongside Christians. Three Jews of Lleida, for example, were murdered in 1364 by two Christians (including the bailiff) and eight Muslims of Ajabut.[43] Such violence could be classified as "situational" in that it sprang from specific relationships between individual Muslims and Jews, and not from ascriptive "religious identity," but it was nevertheless connected to the same issues of legal and religious status that structured Christian-Jewish relations.

The beating and imprisonment of a Jewish creditor by the Muslim vassals of the abbot of Valdigna in 1377 provides a case in point.[44] Abraham Atarela, a Jew of Algezira, had gone to the village of Umbria to collect a debt from a Muslim called Azmet Aeça. When he was in the Muslim's house, "the said Muslim, moved by an evil spirit, ignoring God all-powerful and royal authority, and ignoring the fact that this Jew and all other Jews are under the guard and protection of the lord king," picked up a lance and tried to kill Abraham.[45] The Jew fled to the house of a neighboring Muslim, but Azmet raised the hue and cry, rousing the Muslims to riot against Abraham, and claiming falsely that the Jew had injured him.[46] After beating Abraham, the Muslims handed him over to their lord the abbot, who threw him in jail on the pretext that he had injured Azmet, and starved him until he agreed to pay a fine of one hundred florins of gold in exchange for his release. The abbot also seized, it was alleged, a sack full of silk worth more than one hundred Valencian pounds that Abraham was carrying when he was attacked.[47]

Thus far the incident appears merely local, but the legal arguments made in the case revealed the incident's connection to issues of Jewish legal status funda-

---

[42] ACA:C 247:283r (1323/6/12).

[43] ACA:C 721:88 (1364/12/3), published in Boswell, *Royal Treasure*, p. 431.

[44] For transcripts of the proceedings against the abbot by the royal fiscal procurator, see ACA:C Procesos, 126/2 (1377/1/3). The final sentence is preserved in ACA:C 2101:38v–40r.

[45] Fol. 6r–v: "E com lo dit juheu fon en la dita alqueria ana a casa del dit moro e demana a aquell los dits diners, e lo dit moro induhit d'esperit maligne, no guardan deus tot poderos ne la senyoria real, ne guardant com lo dit juheu e tots los altres juheus son sots proteccio e guarda del dit senyor rey . . . pres .i. basto e ab aquell irrui contra lo dit juheu per matar e consumar aquell," and then grabbed a lance.

[46] This is, of course, the argument of the royal procurator, not of the abbot's lawyer: fol. 6v, "comença de cridar grans crits de viafora e avalota los moros de la dita alqueria e per ço quels dits moros matassen e consumassen lo dit juheu, dix a aquells quel dit juheu lo havia nafrat jassia no fos ver, e de aço es fama."

[47] Fol. 7r: ". . . qui non volien donar a menyar al dit juheu pres ans aquell maltractaven per ço que per força sagues a rescatar, feu composicio forçada ab lo dit abat de Valldigna e ab sos officials per preu de Cent florins d'or."

mental to the position of Jews vis-à-vis Muslims and Christians. The king insisted that jurisdiction over the case belonged to the bailiff general of Valencia, a royal official. All Jews were "of the king's chamber," "the king's treasure," and any case involving them, whether it occurred on seigneurial or royal lands, or involved Muslims or Christians, came under royal jurisdiction.[48] Not so, argued the abbot. It is true that Jews belong to the king no matter where they travel, but jurisdiction over crimes Jews commit belongs to the lord of the place in which they are committed.[49] This summarized neatly the conflict between nobles and their vassals on the one hand, the Crown and its Jews on the other. Since the majority of Muslims were seigneurial, not royal, vassals, jurisdictional conflicts such as this one tended to polarize the two communities.[50]

We need not assume that this type of violence was the norm. The vast majority of Muslim-Jewish credit relations were unremarkable, like those between Jews and Christians. Nevertheless, Muslims were just as capable as Christians of generalizing from particular situational violence to broader anti-Jewish activities. In 1358, for instance, King Peter was forced to intercede on behalf of the Jews at Borja because he "learned that numerous inhabitants of the city of Borja, Christians and also Muslims, hate the Jews of the aljama [of the city] and try to harm them, jointly and individually, confiscating their property and committing other injustices against them without justification for their actions."[51]

This does not mean that Muslims and Christians were united by a common hatred of the Jews. Relations between Muslim and Christian were as difficult, albeit in their own way, as relations between Christian and Jew, or Muslim and Jew, and alliances were constantly shifting. Earlier in the same town of Borja, the Muslims had complained that Jews and Christians together had insulted and violently attacked some Muslims, severely injuring them.[52] Nor do such acts of violence always reflect broader social attitudes. Famet el Crespo and Famet el Muntesio were Muslims of Daroca who, under the protection of a local knight, attacked Jews and Muslims alike. Their actions should not be overburdened

---

[48]Fols. 5v–6r for the initial argument.

[49]Fol. 16r.

[50]A conflict more subtly evident in texts like ACA:C 880:133v (1345/2/28), where Peter IV grants to the Muslims of Grisén, at the request of their lord Hugh, viscount of Cardona, "quod quotiescumque contigerit eos habere aliquos quaestiones cum aliama judeorum civitatis Tirasone vel aliquibus ipsius aliama . . . liceat ipsis sarracenis habere aliquem vel aliquos sarracenos vel xristianos que ipsos defendere valeant in judicio sive extra, non obstante littera quacumque per nos concessa in contrarium aliame judeorum civitatis predictae."

[51]". . . perpendimus [ut] aliqui habitatores ville Burgie tam Christiani quam Sarraceni odio habentes judeos aljama ipsius ipsos et eorum singulares vilipendere conantur, pignorando et alias injusticias nulla de cause pereuntes, ut fertur, eis faciendo. . . . Idcirco nos in tuitione, praesidio ac defensione vestra commendamus aljamam jamdictam et singulares de eadem." ACA:C 691:166 (1358/1/31), published in Boswell, *Royal Treasure*, p. 375.

[52]ACA:C cr. Pere IV, box 2, no. 148 (1337/1/21).

with meaning.[53] Further, many instances of cooperation between Muslim and Jew exist, particularly at the individual level. Commercial contacts, for example, were frequent.[54] More intimate partnerships also existed. When the king impounded the Zaragozan Jew Samuel Golluf's "palace" and the goods contained therein, it was the Muslim Ali Alvalencia whom Samuel asked to help him steal back the goods.[55] No model that does not allow room for such cooperation will do justice to Muslim-Jewish relations in Aragon.

Nevertheless, fiscal and economic structures often pitted the interests of Muslims and Jews against each other, whether at the corporate level of the aljama, when privileges and monopolies dependent on the "state" were involved, or at the levels of individuals acting in oppositional relationships closely structured by "state" institutions, as, for example, when borrowing money. In such a competition, royal fiscal considerations (though not necessarily seigneurial ones) often favored the Jews. No medieval Muslim or Jew would have been surprised by the advice of Queen Elionor to her son Prince Martin in 1374, when she told him to ignore the complaints of the Muslim aljamas of Sogorb, la Serra d'Eslida, Almonesir, Paterna, and Benaguasil about the weight of their debts to the Valencian Jew Jafuda Alatzar. After all, Jafuda alone paid more taxes to the Crown than virtually all the Muslim aljamas of the kingdom of Valencia combined.[56]

. . . . .

To this point the focus has been on competition between minorities within fiscal or economic hierarchies, but there were other (not unrelated) arenas for conflict as well. Like financial competition, relations within these other spheres tended to be less systematically regulated, and therefore in some ways more conflictual, than those between minority and majority. Consider the world of urban ritual. Neither minority group harbored illusions that its place in a given ritual hierarchy lay anywhere but below that of the Christians. In the following

---

[53] ACA:C 525:58v–59r (1331/9/7): "Famet el Crespo et Famet el Muntesio . . . se sub protectione et comanda quorundam militum vel potentium dictae villae posuerunt, ob quorum favorem vulnerarunt quendam judeum in carraria maiori dictae villae necnon .iii. sarracenos dictae villae letaliter vulnerarunt." The two carried out several other attacks as well. When they were arrested by the Muslim amīn they, together with some Christians, attacked that official and beat him.

[54] One example must suffice: see A. Blasco Martínez, La Judería de Zaragoza en el siglo XIV (Zaragoza, 1988), doc. nos. 8–11, 13–15, 17, 20, 21, 33, for a multitude of occasions on which the Jews of Zaragoza hired Muslim builders to carry out construction on their homes.

[55] ACA:C 444:162r (1332/1/25): ". . . dictus judeus petiit in moraria Cesarauguste Ali Alvalencia qui Ali, simul cum dicto judeo, abstraxerunt de dicto palacio pannos, peccuniam et alia jocalia seu majorem partem ipsorum non obstante empara praedicta."

[56] The queen's advice is from ACA:C 1582:107r–108r (1374/11/1). The tax contributions are from a war subsidy request of 1363, ACA:C 1185:219v–221r and 1187:212v–214r. See J. Riera i Sans, "Jafudà Alatzar, jueu de València (segle XIV)," Revista d'Història Medieval 4 (1993): 65–100, here pp. 76, 79.

chapter we will see how the annual rearticulation of such a hierarchy during Holy Week could contribute to the stability of Christian-Jewish relations. This one argues the converse case: that the lack of a powerful discourse capable of establishing a clear hierarchy between Muslims and Jews, and of rituals capable of rearticulating that hierarchy, manifested itself in unique forms of inter-minority physical and rhetorical violence.

Civic processions provide a good example. Processions are a well-known scene of conflict between Christians and Jews, and the peaceful participation of Jews in them has been held up by at least one historian as a barometer of Christian tolerance. In fact, I have found no case of violence between the Christian majority and either minority in civic (as opposed to religious) processions during the fourteenth century.[57] If such a barometer is valid, then relations between Muslims and Jews were stormy. In 1291, the Jews of Daroca complained to the king that, when they heard of the death of King Alfonso, they prepared a "representation" of his corpse and bore it on a bier ("scannum") through the town of Daroca. When they passed through the Muslim aljama, the Muslims attacked the bier with swords, damaging it and injuring the Jews.[58] Later in King James's reign, in 1324, the Muslims of Huesca were fined 50,000 sous of Jaca, a staggering sum, for attacking the Jews as they processed through the Muslim aljama in a celebration of Prince Alfonso's victory in Sardinia. Twenty Jews were seriously injured. The Muslims maintained that the altercation, which occurred in the "Carraria de Salis," had been started by the Jews.[59]

This type of conflict recurred throughout the century. Again in Daroca, Muslims and Jews attacked each other as they processed "leaping, dancing, and making many other expressions of joy" in celebration of the birth of the Infant Ferdinand. The attack was described as "in the fashion of public war" and in this

[57]N. Coulet, "De L'intégration à l'exclusion: la place des juifs dans les cérémonies d'entrée solennelle au moyen age," *Annales: ESC* 34 (1979): 672–683. The participation of Muslims and Jews in festivities in honor of princes was an ancient phenomenon in Iberia. See, e.g., the *Chronica Adefonsi Imperatoris*, ed. L. Sanchez Belda (Madrid, 1950), §157, pp. 121–122, relating how all three faiths took to the streets with music and chant to celebrate the entry of Alfonso VII into Toledo in 1139. For some fifteenth-century examples see R. Menendez Pidál, *Poesia juglaresca y origenes de las literaturas romanicas* (Madrid, 1957), p. 98. Violence during religious processions was more common, as in the attack upon Muslim and Jewish bystanders launched in 1328 by clerics and confraternity members during a Corpus Christi procession in Calatayud. See ACA:C 519:122v–123r and related documents.

[58]ACA:C 85:196r (1291/7/8) (= Régné no. 2367). For a brief discussion of Jewish participation in this type of ceremony, and for an analysis of this particular document, see E. Lourie, "Jewish Participation in Royal Funerary Rites: An Early Use of the *Representatio* in Aragon," *Journal of the Warburg and Courtauld Institutes* 45 (1982): 192–194. A. Duran y Sanpere, *Referències documentals del call de juheus de Cervera. Discursos llegits en la "Real Academia de Buenas Letras" de Barcelona* (Barcelona, 1924), pp. 28–29, discusses a Jewish funeral procession for King Alfonso in 1450.

[59]Discussed in Basáñez, *La aljama sarracena de Huesca*, p. 77, citing ACA:C 248 (pt. 2), fols. 133v–134r, 135r–v, 154r and 160r. The fine is reduced to 20,000 sous at the request of Queen Elisenda, as is detailed in ACA:C 226:26v, published by Basáñez as doc. no. 20, pp. 151–152.

case seems to have been reciprocal.[60] Two years earlier, King John granted a remission to the Muslim aljama of Fraga for the price of one thousand florins of gold. The Muslims had assaulted the Jews of Fraga during a solemn procession mourning the death of Peter the Ceremonious, John's father. Apparently, the two groups had argued over who should have precedence in the procession, and the Muslims attacked the Jews when the Jews marched first.[61]

The conflict over precedence was carried out in the chancery as well as on the streets. In a very informative document issued in 1392, apparently at the request of the Muslim aljama of Huesca, King John stated that he desired to put an end to the conflicts and scandals which occurred at all occasions of official celebration or mourning in the city of Huesca: the deaths and births of princes, the advents of kings. To this end, the king decreed that on all such occasions the Muslims should march first, since Muslims risked their lives in military service for the king while the Jews did no such service, and the honor should be commensurate with the risks. The king may have reversed himself some years later, however, agreeing with the Jews that they should have precedence because of the greater antiquity of their religion.[62]

In all of these examples, the competition for prestige at a civic level is apparent between the two minority groups. The fact that this competition took place in processions designed to show allegiance to the royal family reinforces an obvious conclusion: the acts by which Muslims and Jews defined themselves against each other were often performed for a Christian audience. It could not

[60]ACA:C 1819:141r (1389/5/7): "Pridem dum judei et sarraceni aliamarum nostrarum civitate Daroce post felicem incliti infantis Ferdinando domini regis atque nostri carissimi primogeniti nativitatem solempne festum celebrantes accederent per diversas partes ipsius civitatis tripudiando, ludendo et plura alia gaudia faciendo, et quidam ex dictis judeis spiritu diabolico inducti . . . cum pluribus lapidibus, coltellis et aliis diversorum armorum generibus acriter insurgerent . . . contra dictos sarracenos, et aliqui ex sarracenis contra dictos judeos, quorum praetextu plura sunt vulnera et percussiones inter eos." See also ACA:C 1818:136r–137v, which ordered the Muslims and Jews to appear and give testimony on the case, and uses the phrase "irruendo . . . ad modum belli publici expugnarunt."

[61]ACA:C 1890:52r–53r (1387/1/23): ". . . contra vos, alaminum, juratos et alios sarracenos aljame sarracenorum villae predictae, delatos seu inculpatos quod dudum quando fiebant sive celebrebantur ut moris [sic] est in villa ipsa per xristianos, judeos et sarracenos exequie seu funerarie domini regis Petri . . . fuit contentio inter judeos predictos et vos super modo et ordine incedendi, videlicet si dicti judei in processione quae tunc celebrabatur in exequiis sive funerariis predictis deberent vos praecedere et vos subsequi vel econtra. Super quaquidem [sic] contentione cum judei predicti vos in ipsa solempnitate precederent, vos seu aliqui vestrum nullatenus metuentes tante solempnitati [sic] scandalum et turbacionem inferre, judeos ipsos per modum seditionis et avaloti cum lapidibus, fustibus, et aliter inhumaniter invastis[sic], ipsos seu majorem partem ipsorum letaliter vulnerando."

[62]For the decision on behalf of the Muslims, see ACA:C 1903:52v–53r (1392/8/12). The document is published by Basañez, *La aljama sarracena de Huesca*, doc. no. 92, p. 231. J. Riera i Sans informed me of the later revocation on behalf of the Jews, but I have not been able to find the document.

be otherwise in a Christian polity, though with both groups unable to tap convincingly into the religious discourse that structured power in the Crown of Aragon, any victory could only be temporary, contingent on pragmatic political or economic allegiances of the moment.

.   .   .   .   .

The same is true of another sphere of competition, that over women. The previous chapter discussed the constraints on such competition between minority groups and the majority, some of the ideological grounds for such constraints, and their role in fomenting or limiting violence. Miscegenation was an equally important issue between minority groups; perhaps more so, since these groups had greater reason than the majority to fear assimilation and the erosion of boundaries. In this field as in others, however, minorities struggled to find modes of violent action and argument that could legitimate the creation of barriers between non-Christians within a Christian polity.

One way to establish sexual boundaries along religious lines was through legislation—that is, the purchase of privileges from the Crown. The Muslim aljama of Valencia, for example, purchased King Peter's confirmation of its privilege that whenever a Muslim woman was found guilty of adultery (here defined as any sexual intercourse outside of marriage) with a non-Muslim, the death penalty would be imposed without possibility of monetary remission.[63] In individual cases, action was often taken by the families of the women involved, or by the local community. Amiri, a Muslim woman of Zaragoza, was twice caught in miscegenation, with both Christians and Jews. On both occasions her community intervened to prevent her sale into slavery (the standard penalty), on the condition that she never commit adultery with Christian or Jew again. When she was again found by night in the Jewish quarter committing adultery with Jews, the two communities apparently came to blows, "wishing to kill each other over her." She was sold to a Christian for 120 sous, of which the person who informed against her (Christian? Muslim? Jew?) received 30 and the Crown the rest.[64]

The issue in Amiri's case was not adultery, as the promise required of her makes clear, but adultery with non-Muslims, particularly Jews. Though Muslim society in the Crown of Aragon (and elsewhere in the Mediterranean) was organized around the concepts of ʿaṣabīya and family honor, and was intolerant of women's sexual activities outside of marriage, nevertheless adultery with co-

[63] For the edict of 1347 confirming the execution of Muslim adulteresses, see ACA:C 884:167r–v, published in Ferrer, *Els sarraïns*, p. 271. The edict was included in the compendium of Valencia's privileges, *Aureum opus*, "In extravaganti," 8, fol. 236 (p. 531 of the facsimile edition), with the incorrect date of 1348.

[64] For the case of Amiri, which occurred in 1301, see Orcástegui and Sarasa, "El libro-registro de Miguel Royo," pp. 111–112. See also Lourie, "Anatomy of Ambivalence," p. 71.

religionists could be forgiven.[65] In 1342 a married Muslim woman from the village of María was caught in adultery. She was condemned by the qāḍī to receive one hundred lashes (roughly equivalent to a sentence of death). Because she was poor she could not redeem herself in cash, yet as she stood naked in the plaza about to be whipped, some Muslims from Zaragoza took pity on her and "for the love of God" paid her fine of seventy sous.[66] Adultery with Jews was more serious.

Jewish aljamas shared this dim view of sexual intercourse across religious boundaries. Recall from the previous chapter the case of Oro de Par, a Jewish woman of Zaragoza, whose intercourse with Muslim (and Christian) men prompted the Jewish aljama to ask the king to have her disfigured and exiled. This is not to say that individuals could not have different attitudes. The Muslim of Zaragoza who participated in the gang rape of a Muslim woman in the company of two Jews does not seem to have had the same feelings of "community honor" as his coreligionists involved in the incident with Amiri.[67] But such exceptional cases may be treated as proving the rule.

In the struggle to maintain sexual boundaries vis-à-vis the Jews, Muslims had several disadvantages. One was the prevalence of Mudejar prostitutes, itself partly a by-product of the Christian exploitation of Muslim women discussed in chapter 5.[68] There was little Muslims could do to prevent intercourse between such prostitutes and Jewish men. Hence cases like the one reported in Huesca in 1444, where a group of Muslims seized a Jew they found visiting a brothel in the Muslim quarter, stripped him, and left him naked in the street: an act of aggression for which they paid a heavy fine.[69] Such violence was relatively rare, perhaps because the activities of Muslim prostitutes did not raise serious reproductive challenges for the community: presumably the offspring of a prostitute followed the mother's religion.[70]

[65] Meyerson, "Prostitution," pp. 87–95, esp. p. 90. For an example from the anthropological literature, see Abou-Zeid, "Honour and Shame."

[66] For the record of her redemption, see the account book edited in Orcástegui and Sarasa, "Miguel Palacín," p. 104.

[67] Cf. chap. 5. For the case of the gang rape in 1301, see Orcástegui and Sarasa, "El libro-registro de Miguel Royo," p. 113. The Muslim involved in the gang rape was poor. For the case of Oro de Par, which occurred in 1356, see ACA:C 691:127r–v. For a rabbinic opinion about a case involving a Jewish woman and a Muslim male, see She'elot u-Teshuvot le-Harav Rabenu Asher ben Yeḥiel (New York, 1954), 18.13.

[68] The role of Muslims in the world of prostitution is well documented, though relatively unstudied. For the fifteenth century, see Meyerson, "Prostitution." On the fourteenth, see Boswell, Royal Treasure, pp. 348–351. On the numerical prominence of Muslim prostitutes in Valencia, see Roca Traver, "Un siglo," p. 161.

[69] The case, recorded in AHPH Pr. 83, fols. 264v–265v (1444), is cited by A. Conte, La aljama de moros de Huesca, p. 41. The religion of the prostitute is not mentioned, but she is unlikely to have been a Christian, since if she were, the Jew would not have dared go to the authorities with his complaint.

[70] The point is hypothetical, since I know of no evidence.

The prevalence of Muslim slavery and one of its by-products, concubinage, was a more serious disadvantage because it did threaten to produce offspring whose Muslim religious affiliation was likely to be contested. Christian law forbade Christians to work in Jewish households, but Muslim slaves, male and female, were commonly owned by Jews. The preservation of sexual boundaries was difficult in such a situation, particularly for women, since slave owners (Jewish, Muslim, and Christian) often engaged in intercourse with their Muslim slaves.[71] In one convoluted case from Zaragoza, a Jew was even accused of poisoning his son because they were both in love with one of their Muslim slaves. The son, it was said, had threatened to convert to Christianity if the father did not stop sleeping with the slave.[72]

Slavery also challenged religious categories because it encouraged conversion. Muslim slaves owned by Jews had a clear incentive: conversion to Christianity could provide them with a route to freedom, and many slaves exercised this option.[73] Some others converted to Judaism, a move that at least theoretically improved their status within the Jewish community, though it brought other complications, a point to which I will return. Even when conversion of the slave was not at issue, the children born of these mixed unions created problems for both communities (a complication missing when Christians were involved). Thus, for example, in 1321 Chresches de Turri and some of his kinsmen, Jews of Girona, had to purchase a license from King James II permitting them to circumcise a Muslim boy who was the child of Chresches by a Muslim slave, and to convert him to the Jewish religion. Some forty years earlier, Chresches's ancestor Abraham de Turri, also of Girona, had taken an alternative course, suffocating his two children by one of his Muslim slaves.[74] At about the same time, in Huesca, the conversion of a female Muslim slave to Judaism created a curious legal problem. The slave had borne a child by her (former?) owner, the Jew Cecrim Abraham. Cecrim was trying to establish

---

[71]See chap. 5 and Lourie, "Anatomy of Ambivalence," p. 71. On Jewish attitudes toward Muslim concubines in Aragon, see especially Assis, "Sexual Behaviour," pp. 36–40.

[72]ACA:C cr. Jaume II, box 30, no. 3804 (1311/2/15), a similar version of which is published in Baer, *Die Juden*, vol. 1, no. 164, pp. 201–203, from ACA:C 239:18v–19r.

[73]For some of the rules governing such conversions (including required cash payments to the Jewish owner), see ACA:C 40:16v–17r (1277/8/17) published in Régné, pp. 424–425. For a typical example of the types of problems that arose over such conversions, ACA:C 91:25r (1292/2/5). Muslims slaves of Christians also converted in significant numbers. Cf. Burns, "Muslims in the Thirteenth Century Realms of Aragon," p. 79.

[74]For the circumcision, see ACA:C 385:19r: ". . . concedimus de gracia sp[ecialiter] vobis . . . possitis in civitate predicta, videlicet in calle judayco ipsius civitatis, quendam filium cuiusdam sarracene serve et captive vestre facere judeum et ad ritum pervertere judeorum et ipsum facere circumscidi, iuxta legem et consuetudinem ebreorum" (1321/12/17). For the suffocation, see ACA:C 62:136v–137r (1285/3/15), published in Régné, pp. 428–430: "Item quod tu, dictus Abraham, suffocasti duos infantes natos de quadam sarracena, que a te ipsos suscepit. Item quod tenebas publice in domo tua quandam sarracenam de Palia nomine Axian in tuo contubernio, cum qua habebas rem, quotiens volebas et quae a te suscepit plures partus."

ownership over the child, arguing that "according to the custom of the city" the children born from the union of a Jewish master and a Muslim slave belonged to the master. Apparently the convert was alleging that her conversion enfranchised her offspring.[75]

Outside of the institutional framework of slavery, free Muslim women might opt to cohabit with Jewish men. Abulfacem, a Jew of Mula (Murcia) lived in concubinage with Axona, a Muslim, for which reason they were arrested by the king's brother and procurator in Murcia. The couple jointly appealed to the king, who ruled that they should be allowed to cohabit unmolested, since neither was a Christian, a ruling that makes explicit the relatively unregulated nature of Muslim-Jewish sexual relations.[76] Such arrangements need not have been rare. We know, for example, that some Jewish communities pronounced bans upon Jews who had Muslim concubines but did not marry them "with betrothal and *ketubah* [marriage contract]." In one *responsum*, a Jew argued that he should be allowed to continue living with a concubine he had converted from Islam to Judaism and married, even though he had not given her a *ketubah*. Rashba disagreed.[77] Common or not, it was precisely this type of interaction that Muslim edicts against adultery with Jews sought to prevent.

These examples make clear something not very surprising: that competition for women and competition for converts are related. Given my invocation of Lévi-Strauss in the previous chapter, we should expect such a correlation, and indeed of the conversions from Islam to Judaism that I have found, a disproportionate number were by women apparently in positions similar to that of Axona, the concubine of Abulfacem. Among these, the case of Maria is the best documented.[78] She surfaces anonymously on the 12th of August, 1356, when, at the request of the Jews of Lleida, King Peter ordered his bailiff there to release a Muslim woman arrested for converting to Judaism. The conversion, according to the king, was not a crime punishable by imprisonment.[79] Two weeks later, the king issued the following privilege to Martin Eiximin:

[75] ACA:C 67:1r (1286/5/1) (= Régné no. 1543): ". . . Cecrim Abnabe (?), judeus Osce, genuit genuit [*sic*] ex quadam sarracena sua quandam prolem, et quod fecit ipsam sarracenam converti ad legem judaycam, et quod est consuetudo civitate Osce si aliquis judeus generat prolem ex sarracena captiva sua [. . .] proles quam ex ea habeat pertenuit ad[. . .]." The conversion may well have enfranchised the mother. Cf. Assis, "Sexual Behaviour," p. 39.

[76] ACA:C 110:34v (1298/3/26): "Unde cum supradictae personae alieni sint a lege nostra et non videamus causam propter quam vos de facto huiusmodi intromitere debeatis." My thanks to M. T. Ferrer for the reference.

[77] Adret, vol. 5, no. 245. The concubine involved in this incident was probably not a free Muslim, at least not before the marriage. For more general comments on Jewish attitudes toward concubinage, see Assis, "Sexual Behaviour," pp. 36–40.

[78] Maria's case was first noted, and partially documented, by Boswell, *Royal Treasure*, pp. 351 f. See also my "Maria's Conversion to Judaism," *Orim: A Jewish Journal at Yale* 2 (1984): 38–44.

[79] ACA:C 690:31v (1356/8/12): "Conquerendo expositum est nobis pro parte aljame judeorum Ilerde quod vos cepistis quandam sarracenam pro eo quia legem ebraycam assumpsit vel assumere

We hereby grant and concede to you, the said Martius, all rights which we do hold, or might or should hold over Maria, a Jewess who had been a Muslim, both for her having recently abandoned the religion of perfidious Muhammad and embraced the law of the Hebrews, and for the crime of adultery which she is alleged to have committed with Jews while still a Muslim. . . . And we accord and allot to you, the said Martius, full power and authority to settle with the said Muslim on that amount of money upon which you shall be best able to agree with her, . . . as well as [authority for] absolving and sentencing this Jewess for the aforesaid and whatever other crimes may have been committed by her.[80]

The Muslim aljama of Lleida was apparently infuriated by this action. For two years the aljama fought the lenient treatment accorded Maria, as attested by a document issued in May of 1358, in which the Muslims asked King Peter to intervene against any Christian who attempted to obstruct the punishment of a Muslim convert to Judaism. They argued that according to a "general constitution of Catalonia recently published and enacted at Tarragona, no Muslim man or woman should dare in any manner to convert to the law of the Jews, and that if any Muslim violates this he shall incur both corporal and financial punishment." According to the Muslims, the license accorded by the king to a recent conversion (presumably Maria's) set a bad example to others who might be thinking of conversion, and harmed the aljama.[81]

Minority communities fought against such conversions indirectly, by patrolling sexual boundaries, and directly, by seeking to outlaw conversions between minority religions. Throughout the Crown of Aragon, for example, Muslim aljamas attempted to put Muslim conversion to Judaism on an equal footing with Christian conversion to Judaism: the penalty they demanded was death. The earliest evidence is contained in a statute passed by the *corts* (parliamentary assembly) in Tarragona in 1235, as part of a regulation concerning moneylending: "We declare that Saracen men and women may not become Jews, nor may

---

intendebat, quam captam ad huc penes vos detinetis pretendendo quod dicta sarracena debet condempnari pro eo quia de[. . .] quid in dimitendo sectam suam et assumendo legem ebraycam, qua de causa supplicatum nobis fuit ut dignaremur super predictis de justitia providere. Nos itaque dicta supplicatione admissa vobis dicimus et mandamus quatenus si dictam sarracenam praedictam de causa et non alia captam tenetis ipsam a dicta captione absolvatis et contra ipsam vel judeos dicte aljame vel aliquos singulares ipsius praetacta occasione minime procedatis."

[80]ACA:C 899:60r (1356/8/22), published and translated in Boswell, *Royal Treasure*, pp. 351–352, 442. Adultery here may refer to the practice of prostitution without royal license.

[81]ACA:C 691:232r-v (1358/5/18): "Q[uaprop]ter iuxta quamdam constitutionem generalem Catalonie dudum in civitatem Tarracone editam sive factam nullus sarracenus nec nulla sarracena valeat seu presumat quovismodo ad legem judaycam se transferre, et si contrarium per aliquem sarracenum vel sarracenam fit, quod incurrat illic talis pena corporalis et bonorum. . . . quapropter per eosdem adelantatos nomine dicte aljame fuit nobis humiliter suplicatum ut ad tolendum omnem perjudicium quod ipsi aljame et eius singularibus possit propterea in futurum de facili eveniret digna remedia predictam constitutionem omnino facere observari." The king ordered that in the future the constitution should be enforced. Cf. the partial transcription in Boswell, *Royal Treasure*, p. 380.

Jewish men and women become Saracens. Those who do so shall lose their persons."[82] In 1337 King Peter the Ceremonious, at the request of the Muslim aljama of Valencia, confirmed the right of that aljama to condemn to death those of its members who converted to Judaism:

> It has been humbly brought to our attention on behalf of the Muslim aljamas of the kingdom of Valencia that Muslims are permitted by their law to put to death any Muslim or Muslims converted to the Jewish faith, but when it occurs that some male or female Muslim is converted to the said Jewish faith, numerous Christians nevertheless endeavor to defend the said converted Jews and to prevent justice from being done to them according to their [the Muslim] law, to the detriment of the Muslims, and in flagrant violation of their law. We, therefore, in response to the humble request made to us on their behalf, direct and command you that whenever it should happen that a male or female Muslim is converted to the Jewish faith, you permit them to be judged and punished entirely by Muslim judges in accordance with their law, and without mercy, financial compromise, or any kind of remission or interference whatsoever.[83]

In practice, it seems that these rights were unevenly enforced. Maria's case is a good example, and there are others. In 1292 James II granted permission to Perfet Gravei and his brother, Jews of Barcelona, that they might convert a Muslim slave of theirs called Hauha. Moreover, any Jew who wished was permitted to cathecize Hauha in the "more judayco."[84] In 1315 James II wrote to his bailiff in Lleida, commanding him to punish a Muslim woman who had converted to Judaism. The wording of the edict makes clear that James had forgotten the law requiring "loss of person" passed in 1235 in the reign of "his grandfather of happy memory." He had been reminded of it by the previous bailiff of Lleida, who brought it up as justification for having arrested the woman in the first place. James suggested that the law be enforced, unless the

---

[82] "Item statuimus quod sarracenus vel sarracena non possit fieri judeus vel judea, nec judeus vel judea non possit fieri sarracenus vel sarracena. Et qui hoc fecerint, amittant personas suas." *Cortes* 1.126 (French summary in Régné, no. 9). The motivations and legal justifications for this law are unknown, and the punishment it prescribes unclear. It may refer either to enslavement or to capital punishment (probably the former: enslavement of Muslims to the Crown often substituted for capital punishment). For an example of similar legislation in Castilian territories, see the *cortes* of Seville of 1252, art. 44, cited in J. F. O'Callaghan, "The Mudejars of Castile and Portugal in the Twelfth and Thirteenth Centuries," in *Muslims under Latin Rule: 1100–1300*, ed. J. M. Powell (Princeton, 1990), pp. 11–56, here p. 50.

[83] ACA:C 862:121r (1337/1/12), published and translated by Boswell, *Royal Treasure*, pp. 378–379, 436–437. I have slightly altered his translation.

[84] ACA:C 260:97r (1292/6/25): ". . . Damus et concedimus vobis, Perfeto Gravei (?), iudeo . . . quod possunt vos aut . . . frater vester facere iudeam quandam sarracenam vestram nomine Hauha, concedentes vobis quod omnes illi tam iudeae quam iudei qui interesse voluerint ad factionem ipsam iudea possunt interesse ac facere ea quae in talibus more judayco sunt fieri assueta." My thanks to M. Echaniz Sans for the reference. What is meant by the latter part of the concession is not completely clear.

present bailiff determined that it had been repealed.[85] Lleida was again the scene of a Muslim's conversion in 1335, this time of a male. The Jewish aljama of the town complained to the king that the bailiff had imprisoned an unnamed Muslim because he had adopted or was planning to adopt "legem ebraycam," i.e., Jewish religion. The king instructed the bailiff to release the Muslim if he was being held on no other charge, and not to prosecute the Jewish aljama or any of its individuals on this matter.[86]

In 1361, King Peter blocked the prosecution of the Jewish aljama of Barcelona for its conversion of the Muslim Lopello de Serrah Mahomet, who changed his name to Abraham. The king had previously licensed the conversion, but opposition was so strong that the Jewish aljama had to obtain a remission (presumably at some expense) to avoid litigation.[87] Twenty years later, the bailiff of Valencia beyond the Xixona wrote in his account book that he had received a fine of 165 sous from two Muslim women of Alacant, Fotoix and Axena, who had converted to Judaism and changed their names to Jamila and Simfa. The fine was levied for "conversion without license," and no other punishment is mentioned.[88] Both these documents suggest that in the latter half of the century conversion from Islam to Judaism was a matter of licensing fees, not of criminal courts. If so, they may have been more numerous than would appear from the chancery documentation, which mentions only those episodes where things went wrong. In any event, such cases make clear the reasons why Muslim communities had difficulties imposing the death penalty: the strapped royal treasury welcomed the income that licenses and remissions brought in.

Jewish conversions to Islam also occurred. They too were met with demands for the death penalty from Jewish communities, who apparently had more success than the Muslims, perhaps because they had more resources. In 1280 a flurry of documents were issued concerning the conversion to Islam of three Jews from the hinterlands of Zaragoza. The Jews were arrested, transferred to

---

[85] ACA:C 242:163r–v (1315/6/13), published by Ferrer, *Els sarrains*, p. 230.

[86] ACA:C 471:138v (1335/3/31): "Conquerendo exponitum est nobis pro parte aliame judeorum Ilerde quod vos cepistis quendam sarracenum pro eo quia legem ebraycam asumpsit [sic] vel assummere intendebat, quem captum ad huc penes vos deti[neritis] asserendo quod dictus sarracenus debet condempnari pro eo quia deliquit [sic] in dimitend[i] sectam suam et assumendo legem ebraycam, qua de causa suplicatum nobis fuit ut dignaremur super praedictis de justitia providere. Nos vero dicta suplicatione admissa vobis dicimus et mandamus quatenus si dictum sarracenum praedicta de causa et [n]on alia captum tenetis, ipsum a dicta captione absolvatis, et contra ipsum vel judeos dictae aliame vel aliquos singulares ipsius praetacta occasione minime procedatis."

[87] ACA:C 905:68 (1361/1/4). As a Muslim Abraham was already circumcised; his circumcision upon conversion would have consisted in the giving of a drop of blood. See Maimonides, *Mishneh Torah, Sefer Kedushah* 1.14.5. See also B. Z. Wacholder, "Attitudes towards Proselytizing in the Classical Halakah," *Historia Judaica* 20, no. 2 (1958): 87–88, and compare Baer, *The Jews*, 2:48, referring, however, to slaves. None of the individuals whose cases are examined here were described as slaves. On Jewish circumcision of slaves and Church attitudes toward it, see S. Grayzel, *The Church and the Jews in the Thirteenth Century* (Philadelphia, 1933), pp. 23–26.

[88] ACA:RP, MR 1722:49r, cited in Ferrer, *Els sarrains*, pp. 82–83.

Zaragoza, prosecuted, and punished, all apparently at the insistence of an important Jewish courtier and royal official, Jucef Ravaya, the king's treasurer.[89] What the punishment was we can only guess, but a document dated 1284 concerning a different case leads one to presume the worst: "To the justiciar of Xàtiva, that he deliver to death a certain Jewess named Maulet who turned Saracen, since the king in a similar case pronounced the same sentence."[90] Presumably the trials at Zaragoza provided the precedent.

Apart from these four early cases, I have found no further traces of Jewish conversion to Islam in archival records.[91] This does not mean that the threat was not real. Joseph ben Shalom Ashkenazi's polemic was obviously concerned with the possibility that ignorance and poverty or, worse, wealth and familiarity with Arabic learning might lead to such conversions:

> Consider attentively the stupidity of those of our coreligionists who praise and exalt the religion of the Muslims, thus transgressing the precept of the law: "you must not accord them any grace" [Deut. 7:2]. Not content with this, when the Muslims profess their faith at the hour of their assembly, those poor Jews who have no part of religion associate themselves with them, reciting beside them the "Hear O Israel." Then they make the most vivid praise of the nation of that contemptible individual [Muhammad]. This attitude has the result that they attach themselves, they and their children, to the Muslims, that they vilify the blessed religion of Israel, renege the law of the Lord of hosts, and follow the nothingness and vanity of a despicable people. I am not astonished that the simple folk of our people allow themselves to go praise [Muhammad], [but by] those who pretend to be of the religion of Israel, I mean certain notables of our communities, proclaiming the praise of the Muslims and testifying to their unitary faith.[92]

This text is deliciously unclear and rich in possibilities: one can only imagine the setting in which Muslims and poor Jews prayed their respective prayers side by side. It is not, however, sufficient evidence for formal conversions from Judaism

---

[89] ACA:C 48:139v, ACA:C 48:159r, ACA:C 48:159r (dated 1280/9/1 and 9/26), published by D. Romano, "Conversión de judíos al Islam," *Sefarad* 36 (1976): 336, doc. nos. 1, 2, and 3.

[90] ACA:C 46:221v (1284/7/6), in Romano, "Conversión de judíos al Islam," p. 337, doc. no. 4. The document has also been (less accurately) transcribed by F. Roca Traver, *El justicia de Valencia, 1238–1321* (Valencia, 1970), doc. no. 154, p. 476, and by Burns, "Renegades," p. 348n.16.

[91] Hence I think M. García-Arenal overstates the case when she says that "la conversion spontanée de juifs à l'Islam finit pas [*sic*] poser un vrai problème dans les territoires de la couronne d'Aragon aux XIIIe et XIVe siècles." "Rapports entre groupes dans la péninsule ibérique: la conversion de juifs à l'islam (XIIe–XIIIe siècles)," in *Minorités Religieuses dans l'Espagne Médiévale, Revue du Monde Musulman et de la Méditerranée* 63–64 (1992): 91–101, here p. 98.

[92] I translate here from the text given by Vajda, "Un chapitre de l'histoire du conflit," p. 135. I do not follow some of his interpretive insertions, such as "in spirit" after "poor," since the text could easily be implying some distinctions between rich and poor, vulgar and educated. The context of the polemic may mitigate its value as evidence for conversion. See the beginning of this chapter. Kriegel, *Les Juifs à la fin du Moyen Age*, pp. 82–83, and Lourie, "Anatomy of Ambivalence," p. 72, refer to this passage as well, though to different ends.

to Islam in the fourteenth-century Crown.[93] Conversions between minority groups were far too conflictual, violated too many secular and religious laws, and offered too many opportunities for accusation and extortion to have been passed over in silence, yet it is of silence that the judicial record of conversions from Judaism to Islam consists.

If judicial records provide a sense of the comparative frequency of conversions between minority groups, they reveal almost nothing of the religious competition that such conversions both symptomized and caused. Judicial records suggest fiscality as arbiter, and little else. Yet beneath the smooth fiscal surface of these cases we can sometimes detect a turbulence of competitive religious discourses, all articulating different views of divine history and different religious hierarchies within which conversion should be understood.

A vestige of such an argument is perhaps preserved in a *consilium* of Oldradus de Ponte, a fourteenth-century lawyer (d. 1337?) who may have spent some time teaching in Lleida: "A Jew went over to the sect of the Saracens. The Question is put, should he be punished?"[94] Oldradus has few doubts: "Evidently not, since we tolerate both sects. If each is in a state of damnation it does not matter to which sect he belongs because there is no distinction between equivalents." His second argument, however, is much less evenhanded. If apostasy is a turning back, a movement from the better to the worse, then Jewish conversion to Islam was not apostasy, since "the Saracen sect is not as bad as that of the Jews, according to the word of the Lord." "The Church makes sufficiently clear that they are worse, for when it prays on Good Friday for all people there is no genuflection for Jews, though there is for pagans [i.e., Muslims]." In the case of Jewish conversions to Islam, Oldradus's reasoning is clear: they are not to be punished. For conversions in the other direction, his arguments conflict, an ambiguity not without consequences. Oldradus also makes explicit an important aspect of the competition over conversion between minority groups. The fight over such conversions was, among other things, a fight about prestige before a Christian audience, conducted of necessity in the language of that audience.[95]

---

[93] Mechanisms for the formal conversion of Jews to Islam did exist in the legal traditions of al-Andalus, but there is not much evidence for their use after the tenth century. Whether they were known among Mudejar jurists is an open question. See M. Abumalham, "La conversón según formularios notariales andalusíes: valoracíon de la legalidad de la conversíon de Maimónides," *Miscelánea de Estudios Arabes y Hebráicos* 34 (1985): 71–84; P. Chalmeta, "Le passage à l'Islam dans al-Andalus au Xe siècle," in *Actas del XII Congreso de la U.E.A.I. (Málaga, 1984)* (Madrid, 1986), pp. 161–183; and García-Arenal, "Rapports," p. 94, citing the previous works.

[94] *Consilia* are legal opinions, often requested of jurists by courts trying a particular case, but also issued about hypothetical questions not being litigated at the moment. In this case Zacour believes that the question is hypothetical. Cf. Oldradus's opinion cited in chap. 5, clearly issued in an actual case.

[95] On Oldradus, see W. C. Stalls, "Jewish Conversion to Islam: The Perspective of a *Quaestio*," *Revista Española de Teología* 43 (1983): 235–251; Zacour, *Jews and Saracens in the Consilia of Oldradus*

Oldradus's evidence is indirect in that his arguments cannot be tied to a specific case, but what may have been for him a theoretical exercise was for others a practical matter of life and death. The vicious pitch such struggles could achieve is nowhere clearer than in a record of another conversion from Islam to Judaism, that of a young woman in Talavera sometime in the first half of the fifteenth century, an event that apparently provoked a "great and scandalous discord."[96] The document contains few details of the conversion itself. The Muslim woman is not named, and we are told only that Yuda, a Jew from Talavera, "took a young Moorish woman from her father's house and converted her to Judaism." Whether this occurred with or without her consent is considered irrelevant: the writers infuriatingly state their confidence that the archbishop is aware of the facts and needs no further information. Whatever else we learn about the specifics of the case, such as the rumor that Yuda had been "mixing" sexually with the young woman for some time before the conversion, emerges only incidentally.[97] Instead, the two sides (Christian clerics on behalf of the Muslims on the one hand, the Jews and their Christian lawyer on the other) focus most of their arguments about the permissibility of the conversion upon one issue: are the Jews or the Muslims closer to Christ?[98]

The Jews begin broadly, citing Oldradus. Had he not written that since both Muslims and Jews were outside the Church, it should not concern itself with

---

de Ponte, pp. 21–22, 42–43, 77. The translation here is by Zacour, pp. 42–43. The biblical reference is to Matt. 11:24.

[96] See BNM Res. 35, fols. 101r(b)–112v(b), which preserves the arguments against the conversion by the dean of Talavera, the prior of Santa Catalina, and Fernando Alonso, a canon of the town; and those in favor of it by the Jews of Talavera and their lawyer. My thanks to Kathryn Miller for telling me of the manuscript and providing me with a microfilm. The manuscript is undated and was apparently copied at the request of Alfonso de Cartagena from the original records of the proceso held in the archbishop of Toledo's court (fol. 101r[b]: "Recibi una letra . . . en que me enbiava pedir aquel proceso . . . sobre el judio que avia tornado la mora judia . . . sobre la qual fue nacido aquella grande discordia"). Alfonso, himself a convert from Judaism and author of a defense of the conversos (Defensorium unitatis christianae), was born in 1385, became bishop of Burgos in 1435, and died in 1456, dates that may serve as termini post and ante quem. Though late and from Castile, many of the document's arguments have parallels in the fourteenth-century Crown. For a brief description of BNM Res. 35, see H. Santiago-Otero and K. Reinhardt, "Escritos de polémica antijudía en lengua vernácula," Medievalia 2 (1993): 185–195, here pp. 193 f.; and, with less detail, H. Santiago-Otero, "The Libro declarante: An Anonymous Work in the Anti-Jewish Polemic in Spain," Proceedings of the Tenth World Congress of Jewish Studies, Division B, vol. 2, ed. D. Assaf (Jerusalem, 1990), pp. 77–81, here p. 77. On the scandal, see fol. 101r(b), 101v(a).

[97] Fol. 101v(b): ". . . saco una moça mora de casa de su padre e la torno judia, lo qual ser de consentimiento de ella o non no curamos." If rape or abduction was involved, it is not explicitly stated. That the Jew, "contra Dios e contra su ley, aya seydo mesclado, segund se dize ser notorio, mucho tiempo ante de esta muger" is mentioned only as a further abomination.

[98] That Christian clerics are pleading on behalf of the Muslims is explicit throughout the document. For Christian participation on behalf of the Jews, see, inter alia, the signature of the letrado for the Jews on fol. 105r(b) and the reference in the rebuttal on 105v(a) to ". . . un escripto que por parte de los judios, non sabemos si por algun xristiano."

conversions between them (104r[a–b])? In any event, once the woman has chosen the Jewish faith, she should not be compelled to change that choice, just as no one is compelled to choose the Catholic faith.[99] In all this, write the Jews, Oldradus is correct. The only doubt is whether "the Jew, who has laws and prophets which we believe and honor as holy, can receive the law of the Moors, and not whether the Muslim, who has a lying prophet and an inane and ridiculous law, can receive the law of the Jews" (104r[b]).[100] In brief, Oldradus is wrong to suggest that Christianity considers Muslims better than Jews: "el contrario es la verdad" (104v[a]).

The Jewish law is better than the Muslim law: first, because it comes from God, whose authorship of Mosaic law is accepted by all; and second, as Augustine put it, because it contains the laws and prophecies that proclaim the coming of Christ.[101] Just as the law of the Jews is closer than that of the Muslims to Christianity, so are the Jews closer to Christ, for they are branches cut from the olive tree that is Christ. "It follows that the Jew is closer to the Church, who is a branch cut from the olive that is Christ and has a greater part in him, than the Moor, who has no connection with him."[102] The future, like the past, proves the superiority of Jew over Muslim: at the end of days 144,000 Jews will fall fighting against the Antichrist on behalf of the Christian faith, whereas the Muslims will fight for him.[103] As for Muslim law, it was authored by Satan.[104]

[99] Citing Gratian, D. 45 c. 5.

[100] ". . . [c]a mayor dubda es si el judio que tiene leyes e prophetas los quales nos creemos e onrramos asi como sanctos pueden recibir la ley de los moros, que non si el moro, que tiene propheta mentiroso e ley inane e ridiculosa puede recibir la ley de los judios."

[101] On the divine authorship of Mosaic law the advocate for the Jews cites all the standard patristic references. Like Oldradus, he also makes liturgical references, as when he points out that the liturgy asks for the intercessionary prayers of the patriarchs. Augustine's *Enarrationes in Psalmos* 40.14 is paraphrased to demonstrate the goodness of the prophetic contents of the law.

[102] 104v(b): "Siguese que mas cerca esta de la iglesia el judio ques ramo cortado del oliua que es xpo, e mas parte tiene en el, que no el moro que non ha [conexion?] alguno con el." The reference is to Rom. 11:17–24.

[103] 104v(b): Among other patristic sources, the text refers here to St. Jerome's *Commentary on Daniel*, which it claims follows Methodius in giving this toll of Jewish dead. I have not been able to identify any such passage in Jerome. The textual tradition of Pseudo-Methodian "revelations" is very complicated. All present the Ishmaelites (i.e., Muslims) as allies and forerunners of the Antichrist. But neither the early Latin versions published by E. Sackur (*Sybyllinische Texte und Forschungen* [Halle a.d.S., 1898; reprint, Torino, 1963]) nor the Greek and Syriac texts studied and published by P. Alexander (*The Byzantine Apocalyptic Tradition*, ed. D. deF. Abrahamse [Berkeley, 1985]) mention the figure of 144,000 Jews slain for Christ. Later Latin texts, however, do. See, for example, a Middle English translation roughly contemporary with BNM Res. 35: "Methodius: 'þe Bygynnyng of þe World and þe Ende of Worldes" (in *Trevisa's Dialogus inter Militem et Clericum, Sermon by FitzRalph and þe Bygynnyng of þe World*, ed. A. Perry, Early English Text Society, vol. 167 [London, 1925], pp. 94–112, here pp. 101, 105–107, 110–111) and the Latin texts upon which it is based (listed in Perry, pp. xxxvii–xliii, liv–lv).

[104] 104v(b), which adds that Muhammad wrote it at the instigation of a cardinal named Sergius who was angry at being passed over for pope. On Sergius, see N. Daniel, *Islam and the West: The*

The *alcoran* is a joke, not a law of God. Further, unlike Jewish law, it is full of blasphemy, for although it accepts that "our Savior was a holy prophet and Saint Mary was a virgin," it nevertheless states that Christ is not God and that he neither died nor was resurrected (105r[a]). Finally, when the Church prays for heretics and pagans, it says "remove iniquity from their hearts," but when it prays for the Jews, it says "remove the veil from their hearts." It is better to have the truth, even veiled, than to have only lies and falsehoods.[105]

Some of these arguments (and there are many more) are ingenious, such as the interpretation of Romans and the argument about the end of days; others predictable, like the invocation of the priority of Mosaic law. All of them, as well as other more technical points made by the Jews, emphasize the relative positions of the two minorities vis-à-vis Christ and Christianity. The same is true of the arguments made by the clerics of Talavera on behalf of the Muslims. After an initial nod to the issue of the Church's relations with non-Christians, and with the exception of a good deal of anti-Jewish invective there for its own sake, most of their energy is dedicated to a comparison of Muslim and Jewish affinities with Christianity.[106]

The Muslims' advocates do not mince words: "The Jews, in the rites of their religion as they currently practice it, are to a great degree of worse condition and more damnable and more abhorred by the Lord, and more corrupting . . . of us, than are the Moors who live among us."[107] The Moors, to be sure, are "bestial" and "filthy," but they have never received true law. The Jews have and have rejected it. Rejecting their prophets, they have become a synagogue of

---

Making of an Image (Edinburgh, 1962), pp. 84, 89. The legend of Sergius is well attested in Spain, e.g., in St. Pedro Pascual's *Sobre el seta mahometana*. The Jewish anti-Muslim presentation here collects a good number of stereotypes current in Christian anti-Muslim polemic, many of which are discussed by Daniel.

[105] 105r(a–b): ". . . se deve mas tener por burla que no por ley de dios"; ". . . quel nuestro salvador fue sancto propheta e que sancta maria fue virgen"; ". . . auferat iniquitatem . . . auferat velamen"; ". . . menos mal es tener la verdad, aun cobijada, que no tener no verdad alguna, ante mentira e falsedad."

[106] 106r(a) challenges Oldradus's emphasis on "de hiis [*sic*] qui foris sunt" and opposes to it St. Thomas Aquinas, *Summa Theologica* IIa, IIae, q. 10, a. 8, that though Jews and Muslims should not be compelled in matters of faith, "pero deven ser de los fieles conpelados en quanto podieren. . . . impiedad e turben la fe o la policia xristiana." 106r(a)–106v(b) focus on the issue of identifying the crime and the punishment. The crime is not apostasy because she was not a Christian, but the conversion insults the Church and is therefore punishable as blasphemy. Nor does punishing her imply that she is being forced to convert to Catholicism. She is simply being denied protection as a Muslim, since she abjured Islam, and as a Jew, since her conversion was not legal. She should therefore be enslaved and forbidden to practice either faith. As for the Jew, he should be punished more severely because he "did not fear to offend the Church so brazenly," and should be handed over to the secular authorities (i.e., he and all the Jews who participated should be burned: 18v[a]). The comparison between the two laws is taken up explicitly on 107r(a) forward.

[107] 107r(a): ". . . ca los judios en los ritos de la su observaçio que agora biven son de peor condiçion e mas damnables e al señor mas aborrecidos e a nos mas infestos e enpeçibles en mucho grado que non sean los moros que entre nos biven."

Satan, losing all title to Mosaic law and to the name of "Jews."[108] It follows that while the Jews are blasphemous, blind, and obstinate, the Muslims are only blind, because their "evil way of life is only a manner of bestial superstition and blind ignorance." Moreover, rather than blaspheme as the Jews do, the Muslims accept Christ: "They confess him and say he was a very holy envoy of God, conceived through the Holy Spirit in the womb of the glorious one Our Lady, she birthing without corruption, remaining virgin before and after the birth."[109] Over and over again the relative affinity of Muslims for Christianity is stressed. Mudejars, the archbishop was told, make more sincere converts to Christianity. And they do not seek to destroy Christianity as Jews do. Indeed, if the Church teaches that Muslims are to be avoided as much as Jews are, it is only because Muslims have been contaminated by Jewish ways, such as circumcision.[110] The same argument is applied to the apocalypse. The Antichrist will be born of the Jews. They will be his principal helpers, "and by them the Moors will be provoked to turn themselves to him."[111] Worse, it is conversions like the one at hand and those that have preceded it that will themselves bring about the coming of the Antichrist.[112] In the words of an ironic prophecy attributed to the Muslims of Talavera, and quoted with approval by the clerics in their argument, "the Antichrist is coming, and all should now convert to Judaism, since Christendom suffers and defends these improprieties of the Jews."[113]

The Talavera dispute is in essence an argument over which non-Christian

[108] 107r(a–b). The key reference is to St. Augustine, Sermons on St. John the Baptist: "By denying Christ they denied Moses and the Prophets. Destroying him they destroyed them and lost the law." 107v(a): ". . . avemos de dezir que estos malditos de dios e obstinados non son judios ni pueblo de dios mas sinoga de sathanas." (Cf. Apoc. 2:9: ". . . ab his, qui se dicunt Iudaeos esse, et non sunt, sed sunt synagoga Satanae."

[109] 108r(a): ". . . ca la su malvada bivienda solamente es por manera de una bestial spurçiçia e çiega ignorançia." 108r(b): ". . . los moros confiessem e dizen el aver seydo un muy sancto por dios embiado, concebido por obra de spiritu sancto en el vientre de la gloriosa nuestra señora, pariendo ella sin corrupcion, quedando virgen ante e despues del parto."

[110] The frequency of the Christian accusation that the Jews influenced Muhammad has often been noted, most recently by T. Burman, *Religious Polemic and the Intellectual History of the Mozarabs* (Leiden, 1994), pp. 42, 271–273.

[111] 108r(b): On Jews as serpents seeking to poison Christians. Muslims, on the other hand, do not seek to dispute Christianity (partly because they are rude, bestial, and without guile). 108v(b): "Ca si los sanctos doctores ya en nuestros tiempos quieren que sean los moros igualmente evitados, esto es por que segund ellos dizen ya que judayzan circumcidandosse." On Jews as bad converts compared to Muslims, see 108v(b), 110v(a). On the Antichrist, see 109v(a–b), here (b): ". . . e por ellos an de ser provocados los moros a se tornar a el e fasser esso mismo."

[112] A prior conversion is mentioned by the Jews as evidence that the toleration of such converts was not an innovation (105r(b)): ". . . parece que un alfaqui se ouo tornado judio en Soria, estando ende el rey nuestro señor, *e vino por la villa de Guadalajara predicando la ley de los judios, blasfemando e detestando la ley de los moros*, e la iglesia lo tolero e fue platicado en el consejo del rey por algunas de las razones desuso alegadas" (emphasis added).

[113] 110r(a): "Señor, bien lo dizen los moros que viene el antexristo, e que todos se devian (?) ya tornar judios, pues que la xristandad sufre e defiende estos improperios de los judios."

religion will have greater access to Christian discourse and the powerful subject positions it affords.[114] It is a peculiar case, tied to competition over women and converts, filtered through Christian spokesmen, late, and from outside the Crown of Aragon, but it is representative of the struggle between Muslims and Jews for Christian authorization in their relations with each other. That Christians were willing to grant such authorization is clear, and not only from texts as explicitly theological and adversarial as that of Talavera. In the thirteenth-century devotional songs called the *Cantigas de Santa Maria*, for example, the Virgin Mary works miracles for Muslims and makes clear her preference for Moors over Jews.[115] These comparisons by Christians focused on the question of which group was closer to Jesus and Mary, and the conclusion, as at Talavera, often revolved around the well-known fact that Islam accepted Mary's virginity after conception and considered Christ a prophet.[116]

In light of the Christian affinity for such arguments we should not be surprised to find a strategy of Mudejar and Morisco invocations of Christ and the Virgin in their competitions with the Jews. Such invocations are hard to disentangle from more traditional Muslim criticisms of Judaism. The *Qur'ān* itself stressed that the Jews had been damned because (among other reasons) they refused to believe Mary and defamed her, rejecting the prophecies of her son.[117] Given such an antecedent, the common and much-embroidered Mudejar and Morisco reiterations of this curse were to some extent internal to their tradi-

---

[114]In this context the qualification tacked on by the clerics of Talavera is at best rhetorical. 110v(b): ". . . non nos plaçe mucho en el negoçio presente disputar de las tales comparaciones, que son odiosas."

[115]The *Cantigas* emphasize Muslim respect for the Virgin. Cf. *cantigas* 165, 169, 329, 344 (e.g., 165: "O Soldan diss' ao mouro: / —En o alcoran achey / que Santa María vírgen / foi sempr', e pois esto sey, / guerra per nulla maneira / con ela non fillarey"). As a consequence of this respect, she works miracles on their behalf. As *cantiga* 181 puts it, "Pero que seia a gente / d' outra lëi descreuda, / os que a Uírgen máis aman / a esses ela aiuda." For her preference of Muslims to Jews, see *cantiga* 348 ". . . dos iudeus, seus enemigos, a que quer peor ca mouros." She sometimes prefers Muslims to Catalans as well, as in *cantiga* 379. See M. García-Arenal, "Los moros en las Cantigas de Alfonso X el Sabio," *Al-Qanṭara* 6 (1985): 133–151; and the articles of A. Bagby: "The Moslem in the *Cantigas* of Alfonso X el Sabio," *Kentucky Romance Quarterly* 20 (1973): 173–207; "The Jew in the *Cantigas* of Alfonso X el Sabio," *Speculum* 46 (1971): 670–688; and "Alfonso X el Sabio compara moros y judíos," *Romanische Forschungen* 82 (1970): 578–583.

[116]See, e.g., Qur'ān, Sūrah 21 ("The Prophets") 91: "And she who was chaste, therefor We breathed into her (something) of Our spirit and made her and her son a token for (all) peoples" (Pickthall translation); Sūrah 19 ("Mary") 27–34; Sūrah 4 ("Women") 155. Christian polemicists could, of course, exaggerate such affinities, as when the clerics of Talavera stated that Muslims believed that Mary remained a virgin after giving birth, a point not generally accepted among Mudejars. On Iberian Muslim beliefs concerning Mary's virginity, cf. M. de Epalza, *Jésus otage: Juifs, chrétiens et musulmans en Espagne (VIe–XVIIe s.)* (Paris, 1987), pp. 179, 182. Epalza provides an excellent survey of Muslim attitudes toward Jesus and Mary, though he does not ask how such material might be used by Muslims against Jews in a Christian context.

[117]Sūrah 4 ("Women"), 156: "And because of their disbelief and of their speaking against Mary a tremendous calumny. . . ."

tion.[118] Nevertheless, within a Christian context the repetition of these Muslim traditions could not avoid a strategic valence, one that could at times be adopted with brazen enthusiasm.[119]

It is from this perspective that we should view an anti-Jewish polemic written in Arabic by an Aragonese Muslim from the city of Huesca, in 1360. The competitive context of his work is made plain in his introduction:[120]

> When I saw that . . . the parties of the Jews grew strong in their homes and congregations, loosening their tongues in lies and calumnies and insulting our Prophet, Muhammad, upon him the blessing and peace of Allah, denying his revelation and

[118]Some examples are clearly not strategic. In BNM 9067, fol. 200v, for example, a Morisco (writing in Tunis) condemns the Jews' errors concerning Mary's virginity but does so within an anti-Christian polemic. See the edition by A. Rodríguez, *Leyendas aljamiadas y moriscas sobre personajes bíblicos* (Madrid, 1983), p. 335. In other cases a distinctly anti-Jewish polemical strand is visible, though its strategic use is not always evident. Cf., e.g., F. Pareja, "Un relato morisco sobre la vida de Jesús y María," *Estudios Eclesiásticos* 34 (1960): 859–871, translating Escorial MS no. M. 1668 (dated 1522), fols. 140v–144v. This is a detailed Arabic treatment of the life of Mary and Jesus, with emphasis on the Jews' attempts to harm them at the instigation of the Devil.

[119]One of the boldest examples is much later, from the Granada of Phillip II, where Moriscos forged Arabic texts purportedly written by Arab disciples of St. James the Apostle and hidden in Granada, that they might be revealed near the end of days as correctives to the corruption and sectionalism of pre-Parousia Christianity. The forgeries sought to create a foundational role for Arabs in Christianity, and to represent Muslims and Moriscos as the guardians of true Christian religion and uncorrupted gospel. Aiming perhaps at the conversos, the texts made explicit comparisons with the Jews, as when Mary told St. Peter that the Arabs and their tongue were the best of the offspring of Adam: "Los árabes y su lengua. . . . Como me dijo Jesús que ya habrá precidido sobre los hijos de Israel los que de ellos fueren infieles la palabra del tormento y destruición de su reino que no se les levantará cetro jamás. Mas los árabes y su lengua volverán por Dios y por su ley derecha, y por su Evangelio glorioso, y por su Iglesia santa en el tiempo venidero." See M. Hagerty, *Los libros plúmbeos del Sacromonte* (Madrid, 1980), pp. 123–124. This theme is repeated later, with the addition of St. Peter's prophecy that Jerusalem will be destroyed because the Jews deny Christ: "Y no quedará en ella piedra sobre piedra por su infidelidad y error y haber negado a Jésus Espíritu de Dios y su Evangelio Glorioso" (p. 208). For the charge that the Jews corrupted Scripture, see p. 255.

[120]*Ta'yīd al-milla*, Arabic MS, Colección Gayangos 31, Real Academia de Historia de Madrid. My thanks to John Boswell and Olivia Remie Constable for providing me with copies of the manuscript. For the sake of accessibility references will be to L. Kassin's edition and translation of the work in his "A Study of a Fourteenth-Century Polemical Treatise *Adversus Judaeos*" (Ph.D. diss., Columbia University, 1969), though my translations from the Gayangos manuscript occasionally differ from his. A Vienna manuscript, described by M. Steinschneider (*Polemische und apologetische Literatur in arabischer Sprache* [Leipzig, 1877], p. 34), is included in Kassin's edition. See also M. Asín Palacios, "Un tratado morisco de polémica contra los judíos," in *Mélanges Hartwig Derenbourg* (Paris, 1909), reprinted in *Obras escogidas* (Madrid, 1948), 2:247–273; M. Perlmann, "The Medieval Polemics between Islam and Judaism," in *Religion in a Religious Age*, ed. S. D. Goitein (Cambridge, MA, 1974), pp. 120 f.; A. Chejne, *Islam and the West: The Moriscos* (Albany, 1983), pp. 81–82 and passim. The date and place of composition are given by the author at the end of the document (Gayangos fol. 55v, Kassin p. 283). In "Muslim-Jewish Relations in the Fourteenth-Century Crown of Aragon," *Viator* 24 (1993): 251, I mistakenly attributed authorship to Muhammad ar-Raqilī, the scribe of the Vienna manuscript. For a discussion of authorship, see Kassin, though I find his hypothesis of the author's conversion from Judaism to Islam unconvincing.

prophetic role, and claiming that Allah, praised be He, did not reveal to any other people but them the religious law and scripture, and maintaining that Hagar, Ishmael's mother, peace be upon her, had not been Abraham's wife, peace be upon him, but his concubine. . . . I then studied the Torah and the Psalms and the Books of the Prophets, peace be upon them, and extracted from them proofs and testimonies to refute them [the Jews], and an account of how God rebuked and cursed them, and called them unbelievers.[121]

The proofs produced by our author are manifold. Here, I want to mention only the arguments of the fifth section of his polemic, dedicated to cataloging the infidelities of the Jews to God and demonstrating God's curse upon the Jews. The greatest of these infidelities was their rejection first of Jesus as prophet of God, then of Muhammad. For these (particularly for the first) they were expelled from their promised land and sentenced to perpetual enslavement. Our author does invite the Jews to repent, a repentance conditioned upon (1) their acceptance of Jesus as a messenger of God, and belief in Jesus' revelation, and (2) faith in Muhammad and his *Qurʾān*.[122] Nevertheless, he stresses that such repentance is impossible: the time when the Jews were allowed to repent is past. As evidence, he cites a curious eschatological *ḥadīth* of the Prophet: at the end of days, "when ʿIsa [Jesus], upon him be peace, descends from the heavens, he shall be a just judge upon the earth, shall break the cross and slay the pigs and the Jews, so that the Jew will hide near a rock. And the rock shall say to the believer: 'O believer, come, for there is a Jew near me: kill him!' "[123] Jesus is at the center of the Jews' crime and of their punishment, according to our Muslim author. His opinion had currency: the treatise was copied, translated into romance, summarized, and read.[124]

[121]Fol. 1v. Cf. Kassin, p. 105.

[122]Fol. 43v.

[123]Fol. 44r; Kassin, p. 244, mistranslated by me in "Muslim-Jewish Relations," p. 252. The *Tayʾīd*'s version seems to be a conflation of two traditions. Compare, for example, in al-Bukhārī, *Ṣaḥīḥ*, ed. and trans. M. Muhsin Khan (Beirut, n.d.), vol. 3, no. 425, and vol. 4, no. 657, where Jesus breaks the cross, kills the pigs, and abolishes the Jizya, with vol. 4, no. 791: "The Jews will fight with you, and you will be given victory over them, so that a stone will say: 'O Muslim, there is a Jew behind me: kill him!' " Independently, both traditions are common in eschatological *ḥadīth*. See, e.g., H. Lazarus-Yafeh, "Is There a Concept of Redemption in Islam?" in *Some Religious Aspects of Islam* (Leiden, 1981), pp. 48–57, here 51–53, on Jesus at the end of days, citing, inter alia, a version in which Jesus is sent to "kill the swine, break the cross . . . and kill the Christians." (She does not mention examples explicitly involving Jews.) For a sampling of traditions in which a rock (or a tree) calls aloud to reveal a hiding Jew, see G. Vajda, "Juifs et Musulmans selon le Ḥadīt," *Journal Asiatique* 229 (1937): 57–127, here p. 112, drawing primarily on the *Musnad Aḥmed* of Aḥmed b. Ḥanbal. But I know of no parallel to the *Taʾyīd*'s conflation.

[124]For examples of Aljamiado summaries, see, in the collection of the Miguel Asín Institute in Madrid, item 8, fols. 396v–418; item 9, fols. 205v ff., both presumably dating to the early seventeenth century. The items are described in the catalog of the collection, *Manuscritos Arabes y Aljamiados de la Biblioteca de la Junta*, ed. J. Ribera and M. Asín (Madrid, 1912), pp. 48 f., 52. The Gayangos manuscript contains interlineated aljamiado glosses by a later hand, e.g., fols. 4v, 5r.

The *Ta'yīd* is a manual for disputation, a briefing book for Muslims who wished to debate Jews face-to-face. As such, it contains information on a great many issues of contention between Muslims and Jews (e.g., the relative legitimacy of Ishmael and Isaac). Of these issues, the most inflammatory within a Christian context was the Jewish rejection of Jesus' mission, and it seems that Muslims focused upon it. Hence the famous Catalan rabbi Solomon b. Abraham ibn Adret (Rashba) included among his *responsa*, for the purposes of "teaching the sons of Judah to answer in honest words and rely on honest sources," a summary of a public debate he had engaged in with "an honored Ishmaelite scholar." The debate centered on the issue of whether or not the Messiah had come, a focus that has led one modern scholar to suggest that Rashba was really polemicizing against Christians. The very possibility of such an interpretation, it seems to me, is evidence for a Muslim strategy that turned Muslim polemical attacks on Judaism into a defense of Christianity, and Jewish attacks on Islam into attacks on the religion of the dominant.[125]

The violent potential of this polemical position will become clearer in the next chapter, whose focus is on how Holy Week riots against Jews articulated Christian views of the Jews' relationship to Jesus. A hint of the possibilities is already apparent in the prophetic curse given pride of place in book 5 of the *Ta'yīd*:

> And in return for not having served Allah your Lord . . . Allah shall empower over you your enemy, and you shall serve him in hunger and thirst, naked and lacking everything, so that he will put an iron yoke upon your neck until he has wiped you out. And Allah will send against you a nation from afar. . . . And your enemy shall shut you up in all your houses until he demolishes your lofty and impenetrable walls. . . . so that you shall eat the fruit of your womb, the flesh of your sons and daughters that Allah your Lord has given you, because of the siege and straitness to which your enemy shall confine you.[126]

Christian contemporaries would hear allusions here: to the Jews' crucifixion of Christ; to the siege and destruction of Jerusalem as punishment for this act; to the subsequent diaspora and "servitude" of the Jews; and, as the next chapter argues, to the annual evocation of these events through the Holy Week stoning

---

[125] Adret, 4:53–54, no. 187. See also a refutation of Ibn Ḥazm's anti-Jewish polemic ascribed to Adret, the "Ma'mar 'al Yishma'el," discussed in J. Perles, *R. Salomo b. Abraham b. Adereth. Sein Leben und seine Schriften* (Breslau, 1863), pp. 57, 77; and especially M. Schreiner, "Die apologetische Schrift des Salomo b. Adret gegen einen Muhammedaner," in *Zeitschrift der Deutschen Morgenländischen Gesellschaft* 48 (1894): 39–42. Lourie, "Anatomy of Ambivalence," p. 56n.175, believes that Rashba's *responsum* was actually a camouflaged attack on the Christians and not on the Muslims, since it discusses whether or not the Messiah had already come. But the Jewish refusal to recognize Jesus' (not to mention Muhammad's) revelation was part of Muslim polemical attacks against the Jews.

[126] Kassin, "A Study," pp. 249–252. This is an adaptation of the curse in Deut. 28:47–57. Cf. the similar usage in the *Libros plúmbeos*, above, n. 119.

of the Jews. That Muslims heard these allusions as well is evident in their adoption of a most Christian form of violence:

> We have learned, [King James writes,] that some Muslims living in Daroca, despite a proclamation that no one, during the eight days of Easter, dare stone or throw stones at our castle of Daroca where the Jews live, scaled the walls of that castle and then attacked the Jews living in that castle with rocks and swords, seriously injuring some of them and committing many other enormities against those Jews.[127]

In this violent act the Muslims of Daroca asserted their common bond with Christians. Both accepted the prophecy of Jesus, and both were willing to avenge his murder. Muslim-Jewish relations were brought momentarily into a Christian discourse, with the Muslims joining the majority. It seems fitting that, like so many other commentaries on religion and power in the Crown of Aragon, this one should be embedded in an act of violence.

[127] ACA:C 245:121r (1319/4/30): "Jacobus etc. fideli suo Egidio Garlon, vicino Daroce, salutem etc. Cum intellexerimus quod aliqui sarraceni comorantes in Darocha, dudum spreta preconitatione facta nequis auderet in octavio pasche illapidare sive jacere lapides adversus castrum nostrum Daroce in quo inhabitant judei, ascenderunt muros ipsius castri et postea cum lapidibus et gladiis irruerunt in judeos comorantes in dicto castro et quosdam ex eis fortiter vulneraverunt et plura alia enormia adversus eosdem judeos comiserunt. Idcirco cum predicta si vera existant debeant fortiter castigari volumus vobisque expresse dicimus et mandamus quatenus incontinenti visis presentibus de predictis inquiratis diligentissime veritatem." The incident was not unique. In 1285 the Muslims of Pina, together with Christians of the town, invaded the Jewish synagogue and broke into the cabinet where the Torah scrolls were kept. This probably occurred during Holy Week. See ACA:C 56:62v (1285/4/8), summarized in Régné no. 1335.

Chapter 7

THE TWO FACES OF SACRED VIOLENCE

> In the remainder of the cities of the Franks they have three days
> in the year that are well known, when the bishops say to the
> commonfolk: "The Jews have stolen your religion and yet the
> Jews live with you in your own land." Whereupon the
> commonfolk and the people of the town rush out together in
> search of Jews, and when they find one they kill him. Then they
> pillage any house that they can.

S O WROTE the Muslim polemicist Ahmad ibn Idris al-Qarāfī (d. 1285).[1]
For the Egyptian al-Qarāfī this annual event, the attacking of Jews
during Holy Week, was emblematic of the intolerant depravity of European Christians, and he used it (pace his Iberian coreligionists) to draw an unfavorable comparison of Christian violence against minorities with Muslim
tolerance.

Critics today might disagree about the overtly polemical comparative element of al-Qarāfī's claim,[2] but his reading of Holy Week attacks as emblematic
of intolerance is in line with that of the most up-to-date historians. In those few
moments when Easter riots surface from the footnotes of modern scholarship,
they mark a transition from tolerance to intolerance. The only existing extended commentary on such riots that I know of, on the attack of 1331 in
Girona, provides a good example:

[The riot was] symptomatic of the state of mind beginning to form among some
sectors of Christian society in Catalonia during the first half of the fourteenth century,
a state of mind increasingly unfavorable to the Jews. . . . the first symptoms of an anti-
Semitism that would gather momentum throughout the fourteenth century, and
would pour into the catastrophe of the Jewries, in the year 1391.[3]

---

[1] *Al-ajwiba al-fākhira ʿan al-asʾila al-fājira*, p. 4, cited by Cohen, *Under Crescent and Cross*, p. 191.

[2] Al-Qarāfī represents an early shot in the polemical debate over the relative tolerance of Muslim
and Christian societies, a debate in which Cohen's book itself is the most recent salvo. See
introduction.

[3] J. M. Millás Vallicrosa and L. Batlle Prats, "Un Alboroto contra el call de Gerona en el año
1331," *Sefarad* 12 (1952): 297–335, reprinted in *Per a una història de la Girona jueva*, ed. D. Romano
(Girona, 1988), 2:501–541, here p. 501.

The imagery in this passage makes its assumptions clear: Holy Week riots are the tremors that precede an earthquake, signs of escalating stress at the fault lines of society.[4] In this model, acts of violence are treated as symptoms of increasing intolerance and strung together to create a narrative culminating in tragedy. Such narratives generally focus on the changing power of persecuting discourses, with the violence itself treated as little more than a voltmeter. Hence readings like that of Delumeau's *Fear in the West*, where Holy Week violence (specifically the events of 1331) serves as evidence for the transformation of the "theological discourse" about Jews as Christ-killers from a specialized and local phenomenon into a generalized popular hatred of the Jews.[5]

While modern critics agree with al-Qarāf ī in treating Holy Week riots as uniformly negative signs of intolerance, their approach is at the same time more sophisticated and less well informed than his was. More sophisticated because they place the riots in a Christendom whose intolerance is evolving historically, whereas for al-Qarāf ī such intolerance was rather a defining and monolithic characteristic of (Western) Christianity. Less well informed in that they achieve this evolutionary explanation only by ignoring what al-Qarāf ī himself tells us: that Holy Week riots were annual, customary, and quasi-liturgical, not some aberrant symptom of a system gravely ill. Though both equate violence with intolerance, the tension between them is that between the diachronic and the cyclical, between the periodizing interpretations of historians and the rhythm and formal repetition of ritual life.[6]

Because Holy Week riots self-consciously represented a violent ritual paradigm for Christian toleration of Jews, one that persisted with little formal change over a period of centuries, their analysis can uncover some of the assumptions and tensions implicit in our (and al-Qarāf ī's) understanding of medieval violence and intolerance. First, however, we need to reconstruct Holy Week riots themselves: their frequency, their participants, their scripts. Only then can the search for contexts and meanings begin. The plural is deliberate, for the world of Holy Week violence was one in which the sacred was physically experienced, relations of power were criticized, the past became the present, and urban space was transformed. In and through these transformations and extravagances, Holy Week violence argued for the continued existence of

---

[4]Compare J. Riera i Sans, "Els avalots del 1391 a Girona," in *Jornades d'història dels jueus a Catalunya* (Girona, 1987), pp. 95–159, here p. 111.

[5]J. Delumeau, *La peur en occident (XIVe–XVIIIe siècles)* (Paris, 1978), p. 281: "Le discours théologique a donc puissamment et consciemment alimenté l'antijudaïsme. Il a généralisé la haine des Juifs, qui n'avait été longtemps que ponctuelle et locale." He cites the events of 1331 in Girona as a concrete example.

[6]For a classical statement of a tension between diachronic and cyclical in the analysis of ritual see Hubert and Mauss, "Étude sommaire," pp. 189–229. I am not arguing for continuity in meaning where there is continuity in form. See below, and the epilogue.

Clearly 1331 was no "anti-Semitic novelty" but one in a long series of annual Holy Week attacks on the Jewish *call* of Girona.[15]

Such attacks were even more widespread geographically than Berenguer Sariera thought. A cursory survey documents these events throughout the Crown, in Barcelona, Vilafranca del Penedès, Camarasa, Pina, Besalú, Daroca, Alcoletge, Valencia, Burriana, Apiera, and Teruel.[16] Obviously many more riots occurred than survive in the documentation: all the witnesses at the Girona inquest of circa 1302 swore the riots had been annual for decades, though only a very few surface in royal archives before that date. The Jews themselves seem to have been reluctant to appeal to the king unless matters got out of hand. A short time before the Gironese riot of 1331, a group of children dancing to the music of a *jongleur* named Bernard de Campdara had been incited by the *jongleur* to throw stones at a Jewish funeral procession. The bailiff arrested Bernard but later released him at the request of one of the secretaries of the aljama, who refused to press charges.[17] It was a Christian widow, not the Jews, who complained of the riots in Burriana. A house she rented to a Jew had been damaged by the rioters, and she wanted compensation.[18]

---

citra quae est .xx. annorum et ultra, vidit tam in civitate Gerunde et civitate Barchinone et Valencie quam etiam in aliis locis Cathalonie quod scolares et adolescentes prohiciebant lapides contra judeos, et etiam lapidabant eos die veneris sancto pasche et etiam diebus lamentationis, et ipse etiam testis [. . .] et observantiam qui est inde proiecit plures lapides contra iudeos et hospicia eorundem et credit quod usus praedictus et observantia duravit per .xxx. annos et ultra per maiorem partem Cathalonie." Other witnesses had even longer memories, reaching back almost half a century.

[15] For other examples of Holy Week riots in Girona, see ACA:C 242:141v, 145r (1315/5/5 and 1315/5/15) (published in J. Vincke, *Documenta selecta mutuas civitatis arago-cathalaunicae et ecclesiae relationes illustrantia* [Barcelona, 1936], pp. 163 f.); ACA:C 171:73v–74r (1321/1/13); ACA:C 428:123v–124r (1328/1/25). Local archives provide even more extensive evidence. See, inter alia, ADG, LL. Ep. 2 bis, 122r–v (1327/3/31), which explicitly states that the attacks are annual; AHCG, Llibre Verd, fol. 300r (1333/3/26); ADG, LL. Ep. 10, 185r (1347/3/19); ADG, LL. Ep. 21, 222v–223r (1353); ADG, LL. Ep. 60, 71r–v (1370). See now C. Guilleré, *Girona al segle XIV*, vol. 1 (Girona, 1993), pp. 128–130, which unfortunately came to my attention only as this book was going to press.

[16] Barcelona: ACA:C cr. Jaume II, box 27, no. 3477 (1308/4/22); ACA:C 434:49v–50r (1329/5/9); ACA:C 434:101r (1329/5/19); ACA:C 530:162v–163r (1335/5/8); ACA:C 654:128v–129r (1349/2/26). Vilafranca: ACA:C cr. Jaume II, box 57, no. 6974 (1322/3/21); ACA:C cr. Jaume II, box 134, no. 10 (1323/2/13). Camarasa: ACA:C 40:30r (1277/10/24) (= Régné no. 689). Pina: ACA:C 56:62v (1285/4/8) (= Régné no. 1335), not explicitly identified as Holy Week violence. Besalú: ACA:C 70:77v (1287/3/23) (= Régné no. 1710). Daroca: ACA:C 245:121r (1319/4/30). Alcoletge: ACA:C 383:40r–42r (1320/8/1) (= Baer, *Die Juden*, vol. 1, no. 175), not explicitly identified as Holy Week violence. Valencia kingdom: ACA:C 170:295v (1320/12/4). Valencia city: ACA:C 171:155r (1321/1/13). Apiera: ACA:C 457:224v (1333/3/21). Teruel: ACA:C 171:271v (1321/4/8). Burriana: ACA:C 173:77v (1321/5/7). For brief discussions of such events in Valencia, see J. M. Doñate Sebastia and J. R. Magdalena Nom de Déu, *Three Jewish Communities in Medieval Valencia* (Jerusalem, 1990), pp. 51–52; Hinojosa, *The Jews in the Kingdom of Valencia*, p. 162.

[17] ADG, box 24, A, no. 7, published in Millás and Batlle, "Un Alboroto," p. 317/521.

[18] ACA:C 173:77v (1321/5/7).

Even in years for we have no evidence of riots' occurrence, we know they were anticipated. Sometime in the decade of the 1370s, for example, a visitor to the *call* of Girona on Good Friday found it guarded by a number of lower-level royal officials ("curritores" and "sagiones"). The level of alert seems not to have been very high: the anonymous visitor was apparently so scandalized by the carousing of the officials and the Jews that he reported it to the Inquisition. According to the accusation, the officials ate, drank, and gambled with the Jews. When the bailiff came by on patrol and saw these activities, he fined the Christians for gambling outside of approved premises but took no further action. Bailiff and officials both were denounced.[19]

The hiring of guards, usually lower officials, to protect Jewish aljamas during Holy Week was customary. For Zaragoza, where I have found no record of riots, it may be significant that the salary of guards for Good Friday and a provision for alms to be distributed (to Christians?) on Easter were listed among those expenses most necessary for the aljama, along with payments of debts owed, taxes, maintenance of the royal lions, the salaries of rabbis, and Christmas presents for royal officials.[20] The earliest document I have found attesting to the use of Christian guards, from 1287, ordered officials of Besalú to ensure that the guards protecting the Jews were not molested on Good Friday.[21] Some two centuries later, in 1473, the Jews of Castellón refused to pay the lieutenant of the justice of that town the customary protection fee, arguing that instead of protecting them on Thursday, Friday, and Saturday of Holy Week, the lieutenant stoned them himself and incited others to do so as well.[22]

If hired police officials proved insufficient protection, a community would be obliged to defend itself. Vigorous self-defense had its dangers, however, since it could involve the Jews in feuds, retaliatory attacks, and royal fines for death or loss of limb. Perhaps this difficulty was behind the privilege issued by Infant Alfonso to Jewish settlers in Alcoletge:

[19] Unfortunately the accusation is undated. See J. Régné, "Rapports entre l'inquisition et les juifs d'après le mémorial de l'inquisiteur d'Aragon (fin du XIVe siècle)," *RdÉJ* 52 (1906): 224–233, here pp. 226–227. See also M. Omont, "Mémorial de l'inquisition d'Aragon à la fin du XIVe siècle," *Bibliothèque de l'Ecole des Chartes* 66 (1905): 261–268.

[20] ACA:C 939:99r–103v (1382/3/7), transcribed by Baer, *Die Juden*, vol. 1, no. 342, pp. 512–518, here 515. In a similar document limiting what expenses and bribes the secretaries of the aljama of Barcelona were authorized to pay, specific exception was made for the "salaries of the Good Friday guards, as is customary." ACA:C 948:114v–122v (1386/4/2), transcribed by Baer, *Die Juden*, vol. 1, no. 381, pp. 580–593, here p. 589.

[21] ACA:C 70:77v (1287/3/23) (= Régné no. 1710). Bonanasch Escapat, *elemosinarius* of the Jewish aljama of Vilafranca, testified in 1299 that he had been required to pay the royal judge of Vilafranca and the castle guards one maravedi each Easter, "as is the custom, for protection during Holy Week." ACA:C Procesos 506/1, discussed by E. Lourie in her important article "Jewish Moneylenders in the Local Catalan Community, c. 1300: Vilafranca del Penedés, Besalú and Montblanc," *Michael* 11 (1989): 60–61.

[22] ARV Bailía, 1155, fol. 58v, (1473/5/20), published by Doñate and Magdalena, *Three Jewish Communities*, pp. 148 f., and discussed on p. 52. The bailiff of Castellón had charged a Jewish official one hundred maravedis for nonpayment of the protection fee.

If perchance anyone, Christian or Muslim, impelled by audacity, wishes or attempts to invade or rob those Jews, their houses, or their goods . . . the Jews can defend themselves . . . against the aforesaid invaders and injurers, whosoever they be and of whatever status. And that if in said invasion or conflict the invaders are hit or injured, even if death is the result, no petition or demand can be made against the said Jews. . . . And if the friends of one thus injured or hit wish vindictively to inflict harm or damage upon those Jews, we and our officials are bound to defend and maintain the Jews and their goods.[23]

The phrase "Christian or Muslim" in this edict is not accidental, as we saw in the previous chapter. Muslim attacks against Jews during Holy Week are documented in Daroca (1319) and Pina (1285); others may have occurred. Muslim participation might suggest that the religious specificity of Holy Week riots against Jews had been worn down through custom and repetition. More likely it reflects the fact that, at least in their polemics, Muslims in Christian Spain attacked the Jews for rejecting Jesus' revelation. Through Holy Week violence Muslims aligned themselves with the Christian majority as avengers of Christ.[24] Aḥmad ibn Idrīs al-Qarāfī would have been most surprised.

. . . . .

Before we can talk of what these riots meant, how they functioned, or how they could be manipulated, we need to know what actually occurred in them. For the twentieth-century historian, haunted by memories of the pogroms of the Pale and Kristallnacht, it is easy to imagine a scene of uncontrolled and murderous fury, violence, and looting:

At twelve o'clock at noon [in April 1881], the air echoed with wild shouts, whistling, jeering, hooting, and laughing. An enormous crowd of young boys, artisans and laborers was marching. The entire street was jammed with the barefoot brigade. The destruction of Jewish houses began. Windowpanes and doors began to fly about, and shortly thereafter the mob, having gained access to the houses and stores, began to throw upon the streets absolutely everything that fell into their hands. Clouds of feathers began to whirl in the air. The sound of broken windowpanes and frames, the crying, shouting, and despair on the one hand, and the terrible yelling and jeering on the other, completed the picture. . . . Shortly afterwards the mob threw itself upon the Jewish synagogue, which, despite its strong bars, locks and shutters, was wrecked in a moment. One should have seen the fury with which the riff-raff fell upon the [Torah] scrolls, of which there were many in the synagogue. The scrolls were torn to shreds, trampled in the dirt, and destroyed with incredible passion. The streets were

---

[23] ACA:C 383:40r–42r (1320/8/1). For the Latin text, see Baer, *Die Juden*, vol. 1, no. 175, pp. 217–218.

[24] See chap. 6; Nirenberg, "Muslim-Jewish Relations," pp. 251–252, 265–268.

soon crammed with the trophies of destruction. Everywhere fragments of dishes, furniture, household utensils, and other articles lay scattered about.[25]

Consider how different from this image is the picture that emerges from eyewitness accounts of royal officials present during the Girona riot of 1331:

On Holy Thursday, the bailiff "heard that clerics were attacking and invading the walls and gates of the aforesaid *call*, and . . . immediately went to the said gate, and . . . saw many tonsured students or clerics ranging in age from ten to twelve years, who fled when they saw this witness . . . with them there were a few boys between fifteen and eighteen years of age. . . . [He] then inspected the said wall and gate and saw that . . . some few stones had been removed from it. . . ." Similarly the next morning, he "went with some other officials of the said court to the said *call*, and when he got there, he saw nobody over twelve years of age, and he saw there a large rock wedged against the door. . . . Later that day . . . he heard that the *call* was being invaded and attacked, and he went to the *call* immediately but saw no one there, and he inspected the said wall and gate and saw that the props of the gate were moved away from the gate toward the wall, and this witness immediately had it pushed back. . . ." He also heard that "the aforesaid gate was set afire by a tonsured son of Raymond Alberti, some fourteen years of age, and by a son of the said vicar, a tonsured cleric . . . some twelve years of age, and by a[nother] tonsured cleric some twelve years of age, which fire was extinguished by the Jews of the *call* . . . and no evil resulted from this." Another witness out for a stroll saw "many clerics . . . throwing rocks against the *call*."[26]

The "attack and invasion" of the *call* of Girona in 1331 was an attack upon its walls and gates. This is what is meant by the phrase "they stoned the Jewish *call*" that appears in this and other documents.[27] This type of attack was not limited to Jews: people often threw stones at the houses of their enemies, or at official buildings. King Alfonso, for example, angrily ordered the justice of Ejea to announce a sixty-sou fine for anyone who dared throw rocks against the walls or roof of the royal palace in that city.[28] What is emphasized in the 1331 ac-

---

[25] *Razsvet* (St. Petersburg), 19 (May 8, 1881), translated and published as an eyewitness account of the Kievan pogroms by S. Berk, *Year of Crisis, Year of Hope: Russian Jewry and the Pogroms of 1881–1882* (Westport, CT, 1985), pp. 35–36.

[26] ADG, box 24, A, no. 7, testimony of Bernat de Bas, bailiff of Girona, and of Bonanat Tornavellis, citizen of Girona, transcribed in Millás and Batlle, "Un Alboroto" pp. 316–317/520–521.

[27] For example, ACA:C cr. Jaume II, box 27, no. 3477 (1308/4/22): "dilapidaverunt seu expugnaverunt callem judaycum Barchinone."

[28] ACA:C 523:97v (1330/8/21). For attacks on official buildings as a form of resistance to authority, see Mérindol, "Mouvements sociaux et troubles politiques," pp. 291–292. The throwing of rocks at the doors and houses of one's enemies was specifically forbidden in several law codes, e.g., the *fuero* of Teruel. See *El Fuero latino de Teruel*, no. 284, p. 220.

counts from Girona is not the sense of invasion, but of perimeter and boundary.[29]

Even when attacks were limited to stoning the walls of the Jewish quarter, they were dangerous and frightening. Jews could never be sure that officials would defend them, or that customary restraints would prevail. Furthermore, thrown stones could prove deadly:

> It was reported to the bailiff that during the holiday of Easter, a group of youngsters was playing next to the castle of the Jews of Daroca, and that Pero Xomonez, son of don Xomen de Palaçio, who was with them, threw a rock over the wall of the castle that injured a Jewish woman, from which injury the woman died. The bailiff pressed charges and the case came before the lord King. . . . [Fine received:] five hundred sous of Jaca.[30]

Nevertheless, although Jews were injured and terrorized, these attacks (at least as reported by Christian witnesses) lacked the face-to-face brutality we tend to associate with pogroms.

To Bertrand de Lauro, vicar of Barcelona in 1308, it was not so much the actions of the attackers as the noise they made that was noteworthy:

> On the Sunday on which this last Feast of the Palm Branches was celebrated, at about dusk, it occurred in the city of Barcelona that some men with rocks stoned and attacked the *call* of the Jews of Barcelona, for which reason there was tumult and a very great noise emitted, at which tumult and noise I immediately went out in order to put down and proceed against those found to be guilty. . . . They intend to pretend that in that event a woman who was one of those who were emitting the sounds was hit by a blow of a stick by one of my retinue.[31]

---

[29]The throwing of stones could even acquire a ritualized role in the law as a means of contesting property boundaries. Thus the formal denunciation of construction that infringed upon one's rights in Salamanca involved the hurling of nine stones against the structure. See M. Echániz Sans, "Las Mujeres de la Orden Militar de Santiago: el monasterio de Sancti Spiritus de Salamanca (1268–1500)" (Ph.D. diss., University of Barcelona, 1990), vol. 4, doc. no. 143 (dated 1449/4/7).

[30]ACA:RP, MR 1688:39v (1311), published by J. R. Magdalena Nom de Déu, "Delitos de los judíos de Aragón a inicios del siglo XIV (1310 a 1312): Aportación documental," *Anuario de Filología* 5 (1979): 221.

[31]ACA:C cr. Jaume II, box 27, no. 3477 (1308/4/22): ". . . die dominica quam fuit celebratum festum ramis palmarum proxime praeteritum circa crepusculum contigit in civitate Barchinone quod aliqui homines cum lapidibus dilapidaverunt seu expugnaverunt callem judaycum Barchinone, propterquod fuit ibidem tumultus et sonus maximus emissus, ad quem sonum et tumultum ego incontinenti exiui ut ea cedarem et procederem contra quos culpabiles invenirem. Sitque cepi aliquos ex ipsis quos inveni ibidem et qui dicebantur noxii in premissis, cuius occasione aliqui vicini et circumstantes et qui erant affines seu de parentela illorum qui capti fuerant ut est dictum irrueru[nt] contra aliquos de familia mea qui mecum advenerant ad predicta et eos conviciis et iniuriis corporalibus affecerunt, super quibus ego inquisivi. . . . Verum cum intellexerim quod, pro eo quia super predictis interpellatus et rogatus nolo supersedere, aliqui intendunt negotium predictum exponere coram vestra regia magestate et dirigere ut fiat per vos remissio de excessibus supradictis, intendentes pretendere quod in ipso actu q[uedam] mulier quae erat de illis qui sonum

Verbs of noisemaking run through the account of the 1335 riot in Barcelona as well: "vociferando," "faciendo rumore," "Emitterent sonum de viafors."[32] In Vilafranca, the crowd was "clamoring."[33] The bells, too, could be pealed in a tocsin, as occurred during James I's visit to Girona. Throughout much of the surviving documentation, Holy Week violence against the Jews seems a matter of noise and the stoning of the walls that enclosed the Jewish quarter.[34]

More extensive Holy Week violence did occur. Much of it, however, was directed not at the Jews but at the Christian officials who protected them. Our most detailed source for this is the inquest carried out in 1331 after the attack on officials who intervened to protect the Jews of Girona.[35] What follows is a narrative composite of the most important testimony.

On the Thursday of Holy Week the bailiff of Girona, Bernat de Bas, had it cried throughout the city that anyone who harmed or insulted the Jews would be fined one hundred sous. At about ten o'clock on that Thursday, the bailiff together with seven or eight *sagiones* (police officials) walked around the *call* to make sure no one was harming the Jews. The officials confiscated weapons from clerics they encountered and ordered groups of clerics and children who were throwing stones at the *call* to disband. Near the cathedral, the bailiff saw some twenty armed clerics, servants of clerics, and students who were throwing rocks at the *call*. When they saw the bailiff, the clerics ran into the church; when questioned about their intentions, they complained that the Jews, who should have been shut up in the *call*, were still walking about the city and had fought with the clergy, a charge that the officials denied. When an official tried to take a knife from one of the clerics, the clerics attacked, throwing stones, making a great noise, and yelling. A knife-wielding cleric hit the head of an armed citizen who was trying to help the bailiff and it looked like a mortal stroke, but since he used the flat of the knife and not the edge, the citizen was not injured and went home. Another cleric threatened the bailiff with a dagger to his chest but did not stab him. Two *sagiones* fled into the house of a cleric of the cathedral chapter, where they were found and surrounded by their attackers. Two canons of the cathedral, apparently leaders of the clerical group, pushed up to them and said: "You dog, son of a dog, what are you doing here, you people, you come to disturb our offices. You will have an evil day, you and the others, and we will

---

emitebant fuit percussa quodam ictu baculi per quendam de familia mea." For a full transcription see Nirenberg, "Violence," pp. 362–364.

[32] ACA:C 530:162v–163r (1335/5/8).

[33] ACA:C cr. Jaume II, box 57, no. 6974 (1322/3/21): "clamando."

[34] Compare C. Lévi-Strauss's discussion of "Instruments des ténèbres" in *Mythologiques II: du miel aux cendres* (Paris, 1966), pp. 348 ff., where noise is used to mark transitions in ritual performances. Lévi-Strauss specifically mentions medieval European Holy Week rituals, though not attacks against Jews.

[35] See n. 3, above. For a different and unpublished version of the same events, see ADG, Processos, no. 120, discussed briefly below, at n. 75.

give you so many stab wounds that it will be an evil day for you," and one of the canons drew his dagger.[36] The abbot of Saint Feliu of Girona, seeing this, restrained the canon and drew him back, and the two officials fled back to the court. Meanwhile, the rest of the officials saw that they were outnumbered and retreated back to the court.

.   .   .   .   .

During this first installment of the 1331 riot, the officials seem not to have expected too much trouble. They were lightly armed, confident enough of their authority that at one point the bailiff sent one of his men to disband a group of clerics. Official action was limited to confiscating weapons and ordering the groups, which tended to form in front of important religious buildings, to disband. Among the children and young clerics throwing stones, no one was arrested.

When conflict erupted in front of the cathedral, it began with words. The clerical attack itself was not as violent as at first appeared. For example, the bailiff was not stabbed, and the seemingly fatal knife blow to the head of one participant turned out to have been struck with the flat. The two officials who were cornered and threatened with death were allowed to flee. All the participants showed their intention to act violently: weapons were displayed, insults were shouted, people took up aggressive stances. These were action sequences that if carried through seriously would have resulted in severe injury to the officials. In fact, the actions were restrained, punches were pulled, and only minor injuries or humiliation resulted. The participants seem to have been following informal protocols, or rules of engagement, that prevented excessively brutal violence. In this sense, the confrontation between clergy and officials can be called "ritualized aggression."[37]

There are indications in the above account that the stoning of the *call* was, *for the Christians*, a ritual event as well. Virtually all of the participants in the stone throwing were clerics or from the retinues of clerics. These ranged from ten-year-old children to beneficed clergy, canons, and abbots. All the attacks occurred in front of religious buildings (the archdeacon's house, the bishop's court, the cathedral) fronting on the *call*. According to the clerics, the conflict began over a ritual transgression: the Jews refused to remain within their quarter during Holy Week.[38] The clerics thus presented themselves as enforcing the

[36]Millás and Batlle, "Un Alboroto," pp. 324–325/528, 531.

[37]For this formulation of ritualized aggression, see P. Marsh, E. Rosser, and R. Harré, *The Rules of Disorder* (London, 1978), pp. 24–27.

[38]Many of the witnesses in the 1302 inquest into a death during Holy Week riots in Girona stated that they believed the stones were thrown to keep Jews inside their *call*. Jews were required by both ecclesiastical and secular law to stay within their quarter during Holy Week. See Kriegel, *Les Juifs à la fin du Moyen Age*, p. 22; Millás and Batlle, "Un Alboroto," p. 299/503. See also ACA:C 384:101r

purity of a religious festival. Most suggestive is the cleric Vidal de Villanova's accusation against the two trapped officials that they had come to disturb the clerics' "offices," an offense which, Vidal threatened, would cost them their lives. For Vidal and his colleagues, stoning the *call* was an important part of the Easter service and the divine office.

The ritual, even ludic, aspect of the violence is evident in the terms contemporaries used for it. Both officials and clerics referred to various aspects of the events of Holy Thursday 1331 as *jochs*, that is, games, jokes, or plays. The bailiff was most explicit: "By my faith, sir, we are dealing with evil people. You see what a game the clerics are making for us, that they do not wish to be prevented by us from stoning the Jews." One of the clerics had already justified the clerical attack upon the *call* by complaining ironically, "You see what a beautiful game this is, that the Jews are still walking through the town."[39] The word *joch* was used to describe the reenactment of the Passion on Good Friday as well, as in the ledger entry for expenses "necessitated by the representation of the Good Friday games."[40] This vocabulary, imprecise as it is, reminds us that we are not far from the world of play and carnival invoked by Bakhtin in his treatment of "monkish pranks" (*joca monacorum*) and "Paschal laughter" (*risus paschalis*).[41] As testimony to the importance of fulfilling these offices and rituals, and the dangers inherent in failing to do so, consider the anxieties of the town council of Castellón de la Plana when their Corpus Christi procession was canceled because a local official had been excommunicated: "For they understood that our Lord God would not conserve their health nor multiply the fruits and harvests

---

(1321/4/22), in which Prince Alfonso ordered the prosecution of Jews of Vilafranca accused of violating this rule.

[39] Millás and Batlle, "Un Alboroto," pp. 314/518; 312/516.

[40] AMVil, no. 209, Clavería de Arnau Ayç, 1368–1369, fol. 18v, published in J. M. Doñate Sebastiá, "Aportación a la historia del teatro, siglos XIV–XVI," in *Martínez Ferrando Archivero. Miscelánea de estudios dedicados a su memoria* (Madrid, 1968), doc. no. 9. Though in each of these cases the meaning of *joch* is slightly different, there is clearly always a ludic element in its usage.

[41] M. Bakhtin, *Rabelais and His World* (Bloomington, IN, 1984), pp. 13 f., 84, and especially his treatment of the *Cena Cypriani* on pp. 286–289. The *Cena*, a text associated with Easter, is the account of a banquet to which a king invites the salient figures of sacred history. The characters at the banquet act, dress, and eat in accordance with their biblical roles (Judas, for instance, provides the silver; Jesus gets drunk on raisin wine [a play on *passus/passio*]). Each also brings the king a gift, and when some gifts are stolen, the king orders all the guests tortured (Jonah is thrown into the sea, Jesus is crucified). Guilt is assigned to Achan son of Carmi (not Hagar, as Bakhtin has it, p. 288), the same Achan who brought the curse of God upon the Israelites for his theft of an impure object in Joshua 7. He is delivered to the others, who execute him appropriately (e.g., Thecla tears his clothes off, David hits him with a stone, Eleazar transfixes him with a lance, etc.), bury him, and then return home. The point here is that the work presents sacred history more as drunken game than a deadly competition. (Its culmination in sacrifice will also be relevant to the argument below.) For the text, see *MGH, Poetae Latini aevi carolini*, vol. 4, pt. 2, ed. K. Strecker (Berlin, 1923), pp. 857–900, where some of the extant fourteenth-century Iberian manuscripts of the work are listed. For a fictional version of the *Cena* see U. Eco, *The Name of the Rose* (New York, 1984), pp. 517–524.

which had been commended to the earth."[42] To call these events an "office" or "ritual" is not to deny that they might be terrifying or brutal. They were, however, stylized, restrained, and significant.

The events of Holy Thursday 1331 did not end with the bailiff's flight. The bailiff asked the subvicar for support, and then, hearing that the *call* was again under attack, both returned with about twenty-five armed men to the cathedral. As the bailiff discussed the events with the noblewoman Elionore de Cabrera, who was also there, he heard a great noise and saw that his men were fighting with the clerics; they were striking each other with knives and throwing rocks. The clerics were shouting, "Kill them, kill them." One official entered the church while fleeing two clerics with knives. There some clerics tried to stab him, though one intervened on his behalf and he escaped. The attackers had yelled, "Kill him, kill him, for he is of the bailiff's company." The officials retreated, and the clerics locked themselves in the church. The hue and cry was raised, and the vicar arrived with his men to support the bailiff. Together the officials went to the cemetery, where they saw clerics among the tombs preparing stones to throw at them. At this point the sworn men of the city and other leading citizens came to support the royal officials. Finally, because of the great scandal that might result from a confrontation on holy ground, the officials returned to the court, declaring that the king would soon be in Girona and would settle this dispute. The vicar went again and spoke to the archdeacon and some canons; then the clergy came down from the tombs, and the citizens who had come to help the bailiff, along with other officials, went back to the city. Back at the court, they heard several reports that the *call* was being attacked, and each time found minor damage to the walls.

The protagonists are now more heavily armed, the stakes higher, but controls on the violence are still visible. Though the clerics chanted, "Kill them," when they actually cornered an official he was permitted to escape. At the point when serious injury seemed inevitable, the officials raised the hue and cry, calling all officials and the citizenry to their defense. The arrival of reinforcements did not result in a defeat for the clerics, however, who immediately took refuge in the church and demanded that the officials leave consecrated ground. With the emphasis shifted from a siege of the *call* to a siege of the cathedral, the parties spontaneously disbanded, and the resolution of the confrontation was put off for the future.

Each phase of the Girona riot had its own protocols and controls. During the first phase, which consisted of throwing rocks against the walls of the *call*, officials themselves were the main instrument of control, confiscating weapons that might cause severe injury and disbanding crowds. When, perhaps because of a

---

[42] The document, dated June, 16, 1409, is published in J. Sánchez Adell, "Castellón de la Plana en la baja edad media," *Boletín de la Sociedad Castellonense de Cultura* 54 (1978): 310–343, here pp. 335–336. Jews were represented in this procession: "Item an Anthoni Valenti, çabater, per uns scarpins de cuyr que de aquell compras per als juheus qui foren de la dita representacio, I sou" (p. 339).

misstep by an official, physical confrontation occurred, the actors emphasized aggressive actions and postures, but restrained themselves and one another from excessively violent behavior. Finally, at the very verge of chaos, the populace could intervene to avert the danger. Despite a narrative of considerable violence, virtually no serious injuries resulted from the riot of 1331.

This, then, was a ritual of escalating violence and excitement barely held in check. Controls could fail, or protocols be violated. The reaction of the bailiff of Girona when this occurred in 1320 is telling:

> Some people, in contempt of royal authority and against the announcement issued by order of Bernat de Olzeto, bailiff of the same city, threw rocks and harmed Jews of that city this past Good Friday. And when the said Bernat, as he ought, prevented them in this, these people, in even greater contempt of the royal eminence, rose up against the said bailiff, and seeking to kill him put him to flight . . . intending to inflict harm and an insidious death upon him. And when the same bailiff had the hue and cry raised throughout the city, no one came to help and defend him, so that the bailiff, frightened by the aforesaid, wishes to abandon his office.[43]

While the pattern followed by the 1331 riot in Girona seems to have been widespread, other patterns were possible. One such occurred in Barcelona in 1335.[44] With the knowledge and consent of the archdeacon of Lleida, tonsured and lay members of his household dug a secret tunnel into the Jewish *call* from a nearby house. The diggers were intimidated by the guards of the *call* and so did nothing on Holy Thursday and Good Friday. But on that Saturday, after the bell rang for divine service and "when the gates of the *call* stood open, with the guards, as is the custom, far away," they broke through in two holes large enough for two armed men to enter. Once through, they ran into the *call* and straight to a certain synagogue, where they smashed the lamps. Then they removed the Torah scrolls from their cabinet and injured a Jew who was present. After this they broke into a neighboring house, punched the couple living there and stole their money, smashed a coffer belonging to those Jews, and made off with a bag containing loan documents. Back in the streets, they screamed and yelled, fired slingshots at some Jews who came to resist them, and tried to excite the populace against the Jews. At this point the Jews raised the hue and cry, but

---

[43] ACA:C 406:59r–v (1320/4/5): ". . . cum quidam in contemptum dominationis regie ac contra praeconizationem factam ad mandatum Bernardi de Olzeto, baiuli eiusdem civitatis, dilapidarent et dampnificarent judeos ipsius civitatis die Veneris Sancta proxime praeterita, et dictus Bernardus sicut tenebatur ab hiis prohiberet eosdem ipsi in maiorem contemptum regie celsitudinis in dictum baiulum irruerunt, ipsumque fugando interficere voluerunt, et ad huc suam pravitatem augentes cominatur et procurant propose insidias mortem et dampnam irrogare eidem et quod ex nunc quamquam idem baiulus sonum de viafors emiti per civitatem fecisset, nullus ad ipsum iuvandum et deffendendum accessit, adeo quod idem baiulus perterritus ex predictis vult deserere officium supradictum." For a full transcription see Nirenberg, "Violence," pp. 345–347.

[44] The description of this event is drawn from ACA:C 530:162v–163r (1335/5/8).

none of the royal officials came to their aid, much to the displeasure of the king, who ordered judicial proceedings against the perpetrators.

This type of attack, too, had a history. In 1285 the Jews of Pina complained to King Peter that some Christians and Muslims of the town had penetrated into the synagogue and stolen some objects from the compartment where the Torah was kept. The date of the complaint suggests that the incident occurred during or just before Holy Week.[45] In their execution, such attacks differed from the Gironese model in that confrontation with the authorities was deliberately avoided. The breaching of the wall had of necessity to be clandestine if the attack was to attain its goal: the humiliation of the Old Law by the acolytes of the New. Once this was achieved, the yelling and screaming could begin. These attacks were also more dangerous for the Jews because they involved face-to-face confrontation. With its guards, tunnels, sorties, and walls, the 1335 documentation reads like an account of siege warfare, and so in some ways it was.

. . . . .

With these reconstructions of the riots in hand, we can ask what they resonated with, from what contexts they drew their meanings. One such context is obvious. Hence most analysis of Holy Week begins and ends with the statement that violence occurred because medieval Christians saw the Jews as deicides. "The medieval Christian believed that the Chosen People was responsible for the *deicide*. The Jews constantly suffered reproaches, insults, vexations and other excesses arising from this strange, anachronistic accusation, specifically on the most noted days of Holy Week."[46] But it is not enlightening, though it may be humane, to call these accusations strange and anachronistic. For contemporaries, deicide was not a matter of the distant past but an annual event.

Medieval reenactments of the Passion have received a good deal of critical attention, particularly from historians of the theater.[47] These representations generally receive the blame for whipping up the emotions of the mob, inciting the populace to attack the Jews.[48] Both Passion plays and the traditional forms of Holy Week violence that followed them can, however, be viewed in a differ-

[45] ACA:C 56:62v (1285/4/8) (= Régné no. 1335).

[46] Doñate and Magdalena, *Three Jewish Communities*, pp. 51–52 (emphasis in the original).

[47] For research on Catalan Passions, see J. F. Massip, *Teatre religiós medieval als països catalans* (Barcelona, 1984). For other regions, see the bibliography in *The Staging of Religious Drama in Europe and the Later Middle Ages*, ed. P. Meredith and J. Tailby (Kalamazoo, MI, 1983), pp. 15–32. The cathedral of Girona was a particularly active center of "colorful liturgical customs," including stagings of Easter cycles, and even re-creations of the stoning of St. Stephen by the Jews, complete with fake stones. See R. Donovan, *The Liturgical Drama in Medieval Spain* (Toronto, 1958), pp. 98–119.

[48] See, for example, Narbona, *Pueblo, poder y sexo*, p. 55, who sees Holy Week reenactments of the Passion unleashing a "semi-lynching." Cf. Delumeau, *La peur*, p. 279; H. Pflaum, "Les scènes de juifs dans la littérature dramatique du Moyen Age," *RdÉJ* 89 (1930): 115; Millás and Batlle, "Un Alboroto," p. 299/503; Lazar, "The Lamb and the Scapegoat," p. 53.

ent light, as ritualized agonistic events reenacting and encapsulating the foundational history of Jewish-Christian relations.

Good Friday Passion cycles were one of a number of medieval ceremonies that demanded the participation of Jews, either real or impersonated by Christians. Medieval account books and stage directions are full of references to such roles. Expenses for the Passion reenacted in Vilareal (Valencia) in 1376 included "masks for the Jews, which we had brought from Valencia by Mr. Johan Renau, nine sous. . . . *vayres* painted on paper for the use of the Rabbis, and the painting of the costume of the devil, and four masks for the devils, to the painter of Burriana, five sous."[49] For the festival of the Assumption in Tarragona, "first, the Jews are to build a beautiful pavilion, where they will be. Similarly Lucifer and the other devils are to build another."[50]

Of course there is no reason to believe that these parts were played by Jews: Lucifer was not played by Lucifer.[51] Nevertheless, these "Jews" represented for spectators the Jewish role in sacred history. When medieval Christians watched representations of the Passion, they witnessed the sacrificial act from which their history originated. They recognized that this history was affiliated with that of the Jews, that the Jews fulfilled a function in Christian genealogy and society. Far from demanding their excision from the body social, these ceremonies assigned the Jews a fundamental place in the Christian community. In this very restricted sense, Passion cycles could be termed (from the point of view of Christian spectators) "integrative."[52]

---

[49] AMVil, no. 214, Clavería de Arnau Bosch, 1375–1376, Papeles no. 24, published by Doñate, "Aportación a la historia del teatro," pp. 157–158.

[50] For the text of the Assumption drama, see J. Pié, "Autos Sagramentals del sigle XIV," *Revista de la Asociación Artístico-Arqueológica Barcelonisa* 1 (1896–1898): 673–683 and 726–744. The passage translated here is quoted in J. F. Massip, "Notes sobre l'evolució de l'espai escénic medieval als països catalans," *Acta historica et archaeologica mediaevalia* 5–6 (1984–1985): 142.

[51] Based on documentation from Vilareal, Doñate claimed that Jews participated in Passion plays. See his "Aportación a la historia del teatro," p. 158. D. Romano, though he first accepted this claim ("Figurantes judíos en representaciones sacras [Villareal, siglos XIV y XV]," *Sefarad* 29 [1969]: pp. 75–76), has since rejected it ("Judíos hispánicos y mundo rural," *Sefarad* 51 [1991]: 353–367, here p. 360n.30). Nevertheless, Jews did participate in other types of religious processions. The church council held in Valladolid in 1322 forbade the practice of bringing Jewish and Muslim musicians into churches to help celebrate nocturnal vigils. See Menendez Pidal, *Poesía juglaresca*, p. 97. In Avila a council condemned the practice, "monstrous to the body social," of Jews and Muslims dancing in Corpus Christi processions, and forbade priests to officiate at any funeral where they saw Jewish or Muslim women wailing or mourning. See A. García y García, "Jews and Muslims in the Canon Law of the Iberian Peninsula in the Late Medieval and Early Modern Period," *Jewish History* 3 (1988): 41–50, titles 7.6 and 7.2. The council was held in 1481 but repeated older material. On Jewish women as mourners in Christian funeral processions see *She'elot u-teshuvot bar Sheshet* (Responsa of R. Isaac ben Sheshet Perfet) no. 508 (for Zaragoza); Baer, *The Jews*, 1:313 (for Seville); E. Cantera Montenegro, "Actividades socio-profesionales de la mujer judía en los reinos hispanocristianos de la baja edad media," in *El trabajo de las mujeres en la edad media hispana*, ed. A. Muñoz Fernández and C. Segura Graiño (Madrid, 1988), p. 339.

[52] Compare B. Lincoln's analysis of "ancestor invocation and segmentary lineages" and "myth

Yet in contemporaries' understanding, the Jews' crime had not gone unpunished: of this both history and their immediate present were proof. Christians did not need to be theologians to know that the fall of Jerusalem and the initiation of the diaspora had been both divine vengeance and evidence of the immanence of Christian empire: they could read this in the numerous epics and apocrypha that sprang from Josephus's *De bello iudaico*, hear about it in stories drawn from these sources, and in some towns even see it reenacted in "plays of the destruction of Jerusalem."[53] Consider the Catalan *Destruction of Jerusalem* and *The Vengeance That Vespasian and His Son Titus Inflicted for the Death of Jesus Christ*. These chivalric epics, recently edited by Josep Hernando i Delgado, differ only slightly from the many other examples of the *Vindicta salvatoris* genre.[54]

In these epics Vespasian, pagan emperor of Rome and flower of chivalry, was afflicted with the cancer of leprosy by God's command.[55] Once cured by a relic of the Crucifixion, Vespasian swore that he would be baptized with his people, and embarked on the siege of Jerusalem. In the climactic battle the sun stood still, as it had done for Joshua and would do for Charlemagne, that the enemy might not find its escape in darkness. Tunnels and ditches were built against the walls of the city so that the Jews were trapped inside and began to die of starvation. It had been prophesied that Jerusalem would not fall until no stone remained upon another and a mother ate her own child from hunger.[56] To fulfill this latter clause, an angel visited an African queen who lived in Jerusalem and instructed her to eat her child. The odor of the roasting flesh was so sweet that it comforted all who smelled it.

---

and the construction of social boundaries" in his *Discourse and the Construction of Society* (Oxford, 1989), pp. 18–23.

[53]For a sense of the range of the topos in Iberian letters, see M. R. Lida de Malkiel, *Jerusalén: el tema literario de su cerco y destrucción por los romanos* (Buenos Aires, 1972). For plays of the fall of Jerusalem (though not specifically Iberian), see Pflaum, "Les scènes de juifs," p. 120; and most recently Wright, *The Vengeance of Our Lord*. There was also a Christian liturgical commemoration of the fall (which did not coincide with Holy Week), on which see A. Linder, "The Destruction of Jerusalem Sunday," *Sacris Erudiri* 30 (1987–1988): 253–292.

[54]Biblioteca de Catalunya, MS 710, *Destrucció de Jerusalem*, and MS 991, *La venjança que féu de la mort de Jhesuchrist Vespasià e Titus son fill*, edited by J. Hernando i Delgado, "La Destrucció de Jerusalem," in *Miscel.lània de Textos Medievals* 5 (1989): 1–116. These particular manuscripts are from the fifteenth century, but fourteenth-century versions exist, such as that published by P. Bofarull Mascaró, *Documentos literarios en la antigua lengua catalana (siglos XIV y XV)*, CoDoIn, vol. 13 (Barcelona, 1857), pp. 9–52.

[55]In Jewish traditions, which obviously interpret the fall of Jerusalem differently from Christian ones, God also inflicts illness upon the emperor, by sending a fly up Titus's nose to devour his brain as punishment for besieging Jerusalem and desecrating the Temple. See *Bereschit Rabba* 10; *Gittin* 56b; and I. Lévi, "La Mort de Titus," *RdÉJ* 15 (1887): 62–69.

[56]In this version the prophecy is attributed to Jesus upon his entry into Jerusalem on Palm Sunday, but compare Rupert of Deutz, *In Ieremiam prophetam commentariorum liber unus*, chap. 86, *PL* 167.1416 for an alternative attribution.

Pilate had ordered all the Jews to eat the treasure, gold, and jewels with which the city was filled, that they might not fall into the hands of the Romans. When the Romans entered the city, they seized all the Jews, and the emperor sold the Jews as the Jews had sold Jesus, though Jesus had cost thirty pennies, while Jews were thirty for a penny. One knight bought thirty Jews, brought them to his tent, and proceeded to disembowel them, but as he removed his sword from the body of the first Jew, the gold and silver the Jew had eaten poured out. All the knights then hurried to buy Jews from the king and disembowel them, until out of 80,000 Jews, only six pennyworth (180) remained: these the emperor kept for himself, so that in their descendants the passion of Jesus would be remembered whenever the Jews were seen. The walls of Jerusalem were torn down, and the surviving Jews were put aboard three ships in Acre, sixty to a ship, and set to the mercies of the wind. Because Jesus wished his passion remembered, and wanted the Jews to serve as examples for all of us, one boat came to Narbonne, another to Bordeaux, and the third to England.[57]

This account of the fall of Jerusalem presents the event as sacrifice, vengeance, and the foundation of Judeo-Christian history in the diaspora.[58] Like the Passion, vengeance needed to be re-created and remembered: "Present violences resonated with violences past and eternal, and a local topography transmuted into a sacred landscape: the familiar, reiterative astonishing miracle of ritual." The stoning of the Jewish quarter during Holy Week constituted this "miracle."[59]

This second unit of the Holy Week cycle was far from integrative. Its aim was to make brutally clear the sharp boundaries, historical and physical, that separated Christian from Jew.[60] A "theater of conquest," it reenacted the defeat and

[57] Like all of the elements of this narrative, the story of the three ships had a venerable pedigree in both Christian and Jewish tradition. One fourteenth-century Catalan variant maintained that since Titus had put no women aboard the ships, the male Jews had had to marry Muslim women, so that they were no longer real Jews but bastards with no claims to inherit the Jewish birthright. See J. Hernando i Delgado, "Un tractat anònim *Adversus Iudaeos* en català," in *Paraula i Història, Miscel·lània P. Basili Rubí* (Barcelona, 1986), p. 730. See also the older Latin polemic, edited by J. M. Millás Vallicrosa, "Un tratado anónimo de polémica contra los judíos," *Sefarad* 13 (1953): 3–34, here p. 28, where the Jews, aboard four ships in this version, take idolatrous women to wife. For a Jewish example of the tradition, see *Midrash rabbah Lamentations*, where the ships are loaded with Jewish captives bound for Roman brothels. Cf. also *Gittin* 57b.

[58] The divinely ordained cannibalism, the immolation of the captured Jews, and the fact that the Crusade was an offering of thanksgiving for the emperor's cure all suggest that the conquest of Jerusalem was a sacrifice as well as vengeance. Cf. R. Girard, "Generative Scapegoating," in *Violent Origins: Ritual Killing and Cultural Formation*, ed. R. G. Hamerton-Kelly (Stanford, 1987), p. 107.

[59] I. Clendinnen, "Ways to the Sacred: Reconstructing 'Religion' in Sixteenth Century Mexico," *History and Anthropology* 5 (1990): 119, writing, of course, of a very different context. For another example of stoning as sacrificial rite, see H. Hubert and M. Mauss, *Sacrifice: Its Nature and Function* (Chicago, 1968), p. 83.

[60] The importance of Holy Week riots in demarcating physical space should not be underestimated. In a city like Girona, where the Jewish quarter was surrounded by ecclesiastical properties,

humiliation of the Jews.[61] Yet it did so in a stylized and restrained fashion, with participation limited to the clergy.[62] If the Vengeance cycle was a reenactment of the "sacrificial crisis" at the foundation of the Judeo-Christian encounter, it was nevertheless a ritualized one, a "pugilistic event that evokes the rivalries inherent in the sacrificial crisis."[63] Read as a "ritual sacrifice," Holy Week violence served to reinstitute differences and emphasize boundaries while displacing violence from the interior of the community. By alluding to and containing the original act of vengeance at the foundation of Christian-Jewish relations in the diaspora, Holy Week attacks flirted with but ultimately avoided the repetition of that violence in contemporary society.[64]

Insofar as it concerned Jews, Christian Holy Week ritual contained at least two parts: the re-creation of the Passion, a reenactment of the sacrifice binding the two communities; and the stoning of the *call*, emphasizing vengeance, difference, and boundaries.[65] Neither of these called in any transparent way for the extermination of the Jews. Even the latter could be used to establish a common

---

stoning may have been a way of insisting on the maintenance of physical barriers (walls) that were breached and contested with increasing frequency in the course of urban development. For legal examples of such contestation in Girona, see, e.g., AHCG, cartes reials, box 1 (1293–1334), 1331/9/3 (= G. Escribà and M. Frago, *Documents dels jueus de Girona, 1124–1595* [Girona, 1992], no. 117); AHCG, Ordinacions dels Jurats, Lligall 4 (1340–1342), vol. 1340–1341, fol. 64r, 1341/7/23 (= ibid., no. 178); ADG, Pia Almoina, pergamins, Girona no. 187, 1345/4/26 (= ibid., no. 228). Further, the danger posed by Holy Week riots became the primary argument used by Jewish communities seeking permission to build walls around their neighborhoods, or to prevent Jews and Christians from perforating existing ones. See, e.g., ACA:C 491:105r–v (1328/3/12) and epilogue, n. 47, below.

[61] Compare R. Trexler, "We Think, They Act: Clerical Readings of Missionary Theatre in Sixteenth Century New Spain," in *Understanding Popular Culture: Europe from the Middle Ages to the Nineteenth Century*, ed. S. Kaplan (Mouton, 1984), pp. 189–227.

[62] Even as late as the eve of the massacres of 1391 the clergy still had a monopoly on Holy Week violence against the Jews in Girona. See ACA:C 1827:87v–88r, 88v–89r (1387/4/2) and ACA:C 1839:92r (1389/3/23), cited in Riera, "Els avalots del 1391," p. 111.

[63] R. Girard, *Violence and the Sacred* (Baltimore, 1977), p. 93. Girard believes that sacrifice evolved as a form of ritualized vengeance (p. 13). V. A. Kolve suggests that medieval Corpus Christi dramas had a competitive, gamelike quality in their portrayal of the crucifixion. See *The Play Called Corpus Christi* (Stanford, 1966), chap. 8.

[64] Following this interpretation of "ritual sacrifice," I disagree with Delumeau's claim (in *La peur*, p. 281, quoted above, n. 5) that Holy Week violence is a symptom of the transformation of "theological discourse" about Jews as Christ-killers into a generalized popular hatred of the Jews. If these attacks are in some sense a liturgical office, then they remain strictly within whatever Delumeau means by "theological discourse."

[65] Anthropologists have paid little attention to these types of contrapuntal rituals, in which "communitas" is succeeded by violence. In the modern Sierra de Alava (Basque country), inhabitants of some dozen villages that share pasture lands gather at a shrine to the Trinity, where each village hears mass separately, and then all attend a common mass. The next morning the youth of each village gather at the shrine and fight the youths of other villages. The violence is real, though it is governed by "sporting" rules. See C. Lisón Tolosana, *Invitación a la antropología cultural de España* (Madrid, 1980), p. 96.

historical foundation for Iberian Christian and Jewish culture, as when one Jewish chronicler began a chapter on the tribulations suffered by the Jews of Sepharad with Ferdinand I's desire to translate the bones of St. Isidore from Seville to Leon in the eleventh century, and used this as a segue into a legend of the destruction of Jerusalem. According to him, Titus was accompanied to Jerusalem by Isidore's father, the latter acting as representative of the king of Seville. While pillaging the city, Isidore's father found an old man shut up in a large house full of books, reading. The wise man had long ago foreseen the siege and gathered all these books together against that day. Marveling at his prophetic wisdom, Isidore's father brought the man back to Seville to be his son's tutor and built him a house there that, according to the chronicler, still stands. Here, the fall of Jerusalem and the resulting diaspora is treated as a *translatio sapientiae*, with displaced Jewish erudition and prophecy providing the foundation for the learning and prophetic skills of St. Isidore, a "founding father" of subsequent Iberian Christian culture. This was surely not a popular interpretation, but it serves as a reminder that even the fall of Jerusalem could be read in ways that stressed the common history of the two religious communities.[66]

Notwithstanding such idiosyncratic readings, as ritually reenacted in the violence of Holy Week the destruction of Jerusalem was meant to delimit the space for Jews in Christian culture, not expand it. If the use of the term "ritual" here seems disturbing, it is in part because we have been taught that ritual "tends to be inclusive, not exclusive, and seeks to bind rather than sunder. Many anthropological theorists have noted, despite their differing vocabularies or emphases, that participative drama seems to require harmony and good-will among participants for magico-religious efficacy."[67] In contrast, Inga Clendinnen has noted that "interludes of vigorous male action" (contests, battles, games) can be constitutive of sacred action, "however little such episodes square with our notions of sacred etiquette."[68] It was this sort of competitive action in which our stone-throwing clerics were engaged.

The competitive energy coursing through these "vigorous interludes" is one alien to our modern sporting sensibilities. Open-ended competition is obvious in the games of ball that raced up and down the streets of Valencia city on Christmas and other holidays.[69] It is not so evident in the Holy Week battles between clergy and officials, where a clear winner seldom emerged. And it

---

[66] *Sefer ha-Qabbalah* of Abraham bar Selomoh [of Torrutiel], trans. Y. Moreno Koch, *Dos crónicas hispanohebreas del siglo XV* (Barcelona, 1992), p. 95. Abraham, exiled from Spain in 1492, wrote his book in North Africa and completed it in 1510.

[67] T. Mitchell, *Violence and Piety in Spanish Folklore* (Philadelphia, 1988), p. 14.

[68] See "Ways to the Sacred," pp. 118 ff., which analyzes violence as transition marker in Meso-American ritual.

[69] Narbona, *Pueblo, poder y sexo*, pp. 46–47, on the ball games documented at the end of the fourteenth century, and on the violent "joch o solaz del Rey Passero appelat" played at Christmas time.

seems completely absent from those moments when the dominant majority ritually defeated a subordinate minority. In the Christian stoning of the Jewish *call*, for example (or in the Christians' defeat of Muslims in the festival battle of "Moors and Christians"),[70] the winners were preordained. Yet such ritualized and reiterated victories remained both necessary and competitive because the struggle was far from over: until the end of days all victories were insecure. Indeed, Christian competitive anxieties were never greater than during Holy Week and the period surrounding it.

The sharp increase in accusations of blasphemy against Jews during Passover, Purim, and, most especially, Easter is evidence of such feelings. A revealing one of many examples occurred during Holy Week 1367, in the village of Villanova de Cubells (province of Lleida), where a Christian youth was reading an account of the Passion. Vidal Afraym walked past, and the youth hailed him: "Look, Jew, what a joke [*joch*] your ancestors [*parents*] played on Jesus Christ." When Vidal asked what joke that was, he was told, "They crucified him," to which he responded, "In good faith, had I been there, I would have done so myself. . . !"[71] Vidal's story reflects the fact that at this time of year Jews were suspected of reenacting the Crucifixion, just as the Christians were doing, but with the opposite intentions. Hence some Jews of Sogorb were accused of molding the crucified Jesus out of bread dough and burning him in an oven.[72] In a world where past violences needed to be remembered, Christians tended to assume that Jewish ritual memory was as good as theirs.[73]

[70]Though the festival of "Moros i Crestians" is in some ways a Muslim parallel for Holy Week, it is not dealt with here because it is sparsely documented in the fourteenth century. For historical and anthropological treatments of this festival in Valencia see, inter alia, the *Actas del I congreso nacional de Fiestas de Moros y Cristianos (Villena 1974)* (Alacant, 1974); A. Salvà i Ballester, *Bosqueig històric i bibliogràfic de les Festes de Moros i Cristians* (Alacant, 1958); J. Amades, *Las danzas de Moros y Cristianos* (Valencia, 1966); and A. Ariño Villarroya, *Festes, rituals i creences* (Valencia, 1988), pp. 25–123.

[71]For the case of Vitalis, ACA:C 1708:123v (1367/7/23), in Baer, *Die Juden*, vol. 1, no. 285, p. 407. For a Jew of Biel charged during Holy Week with having (earlier) blasphemed by asserting that the Virgin Mary was an adulteress and Jesus a bastard magician, see ACA:C cr. Jaume II, box 87, no. 396 (1305/4/30) and ACA:C 137:5v (1305/9/29), in ibid., no. 157, p. 188.

[72]The original accusation was against Mosse, son of Jucef, a tailor of Sogorb. He seems to have fled, for an order was issued to return him dead or alive: ACA:C 246:172r (1321/2/17); 246:211r (1321/5/4). The accusation seems to have broadened to include others, since one Jew from the town took the precaution of obtaining a safe-conduct stating that he was *not* implicated: ACA:C 385:161r (1322/4/5).

[73]There is evidence (and this should not surprise us) that Jews could use ritual violence to criticize the Christians in whose lands they dwelled. An obvious example is Purim, on which see E. Horowitz, "The Rite to Be Reckless: On the Perpetuation and Interpretation of Purim Violence," *Poetics Today* 15 (1994): 9–54, esp. pp. 27–37; and for a late medieval Iberian example, S. Levy, "Notas sobre el 'Purim de Zaragoza,'" *Anuario de Filología* 5 (1979): 203–217. Compare ACA:C 86:6r (1291/7/30) and 90:12v (1291/8/28) (= Régné nos. 2380, 2385), where the Jewish community of Vilafranca is accused of "excesses" committed during Purim. But Christian concern on this score was doubtless amplified by the anxieties of the dominant about the resentments of the weak, a fear of, as George Eliot put it in *Daniel Deronda*, "the hidden rites of vengeance with which the persecuted have a dark vent for their rage."

Just as Christians could imagine Jews repeating the Crucifixion, they worried as well that the Jews might reenact the defense of their besieged "Jerusalem" against Christian attack by staging sorties and armed excursions during Holy Week. It is in this vein that we should interpret the accusation against some Jews of Zaragoza of building a tower onto their home so that they could watch services in the neighboring church, and of throwing meat bones from it onto the facade gallery of the church on Good Friday.[74] The same sense of a belligerent Judaism is evident in an alternative version of the 1331 Girona riots discussed above. In a separate lawsuit under ecclesiastical jurisdiction pursued by clerics against those very same royal officials whose testimony we have already heard, it is the Jews whose armed excursions seem to threaten even the Cathedral of Girona. Not surprisingly, this account denied the participation of any clerics other than schoolboys in the stoning of the Jewish quarter. Instead the blame was placed on the Jews, who, it was said, had opened the gates of the *call* and lounged about them bearing arms, thus violating the law. Other clerics added that the Jews had paid the bailiff to attack the cathedral, hiring him to avenge wrongs done them. Still others went further, testifying that the Jews had emerged armed from the *call* and marched to the stairs leading to the cathedral, intending to support the bailiff in his attack upon the clergy.[75] These clerical versions differed slightly from one another, but in this at least they all agreed: the Jews were not toothless enemies. This was an ongoing war, and once a year the Jews and their mercenaries needed to be defeated.

.   .   .   .   .

The claim that royal officials were mercenaries of the Jews was not an afterthought, a mere ink screen discharged as part of a legal defense. The connection between Jews and royal government was at the heart of Holy Week violence and accounts for some of its most stabilizing and its most subversive aspects at one and the same time. Some of the subversion is obvious. The opprobrium that the clerics heaped upon officials in 1331 ("He is of the bailiff's court: kill him, kill him") was extreme, much greater than that directed against the Jews,

[74] Açach Avençfora and his sons Vital and Abrahaym were the accused. The church in question was that of St. Lawrence. See ACA:C 393:4r (1326/9/5), in Baer, *Die Juden*, vol. 1, no. 147, p. 171. Muslims were also accused of displaying undue curiosity about what went on in Easter services. For a case in which several Muslims of Valencia were accused of concealing themselves in hoods in order to enter churches during Holy Week, see ACA:C 522:250v–251r (1330/1/20).

[75] ADG Procesos, no. 120 (1331). The manuscript contains partial testimony in the case, but no judgment. On the Jews' exit from the *call* bearing arms see fols. 1v, 3r (which lists their weapons, including lances and shields), 3v, 4v. For the claim that the bailiff was paid by the Jews to attack the clerics as revenge, see 4v: "Dicebatur enim tunc communiter quod dictus baiulus pro peccunia sibi data per judeos potiusquam pro justitia seu iniuria per aliquos facta judeis Gerunde fecit seu tractauit fieri dictam invasionem." The charge is repeated on the same folio. The clerics may have been referring to the customary bribes and remuneration paid by the Jews to royal officials in exchange for protection during Holy Week, on which see above.

and the citizens who intervened portrayed the conflict as one between court and clergy, not clergy and Jews ("It is evil, it is evil, that the court is treated this way"). Even in the many years when violence against officials did not erupt, the stoning of Jews contained implicit criticism of the king. We have seen how in *The Destruction of Jerusalem* the emperor claimed the remaining Jews and disposed of them as he willed. The Jews were his slaves.[76] In this, the epic conformed to medieval juridical reality. The Jews were the king's "cofre e tresor," "servi camera nostri" (our coffer and treasure, slaves of our chamber), and under royal protection. For any lord the ability to protect dependents was evidence of power, while infringements on that protection were a defiance of that power. This is what King John of England meant in his much-quoted edict forbidding attacks on Jews: "If I give my peace even to a dog, it must be kept inviolate."[77] Attacks upon the king's Jews were attacks on royal majesty, and time after time the Crown condemned them as such. One did not need to be a lawyer to understand this. A ban on violence against the "king's Jews" was proclaimed before Holy Week by town criers throughout the realm. When clerics attacked Jews during Holy Week, they knew full well that they were attacking the Crown. A clerical antiroyalist carnival was emerging within the privileged sphere of a sacred festival.

If attacks on Jews during Holy Week implied a criticism of the Crown, they also provided a forum for struggle between local elites. In the Gironese example, official intervention precipitated a battle in which the clerical hierarchy confronted royal officials, the municipal council, and the town's "leading men," the very people, incidentally, with a financial interest in the protection of the Jews.[78] This battle of the elites could even supplant "killing the Jews" as the focus of Holy Week violence. Events in Valencia provide a case in point.

In 1320, Jews from various areas of Valencia kingdom complained that Christians stoned them on Good Friday, and that officials were insufficiently watchful in protecting them. In 1321, the Jews of Valencia city again complained that their quarters were invaded during Holy Week. The king ordered them specially protected, since they were "camere nostre servos," and ordered

---

[76] The origins of Jewish "serfdom" in Vespasian's actions was noted in the Middle Ages by, among others, Eike von Repgow, author of the *Sachsenspiegel*. See S. Cassel, "Juden (Geschichte)," in Ersch and Gruber, *Allgemeine Encyklopädie*, 2d sec., vol. 27 (Leipzig, 1850), pp. 83–85. On the subject of Jewish serfdom in general, the best treatment is that of G. Langmuir, " 'Tanquam servi': The Change in Jewish Status in French Law about 1200," in *Les Juifs dans l'histoire de France*, ed. M. Yardeni (Leiden, 1980), pp. 25–54, reprinted in Langmuir, *Toward a Definition of Antisemitism* (Berkeley, 1990), pp. 167–194. For Spain see Baer, *The Jews*, 1:85–86.

[77] Quoted in C. Roth, *A History of the Jews in England* (Oxford, 1964), p. 33.

[78] Riera demonstrates the financial links between Jews and the municipal elite of Girona very nicely when discussing the events of 1391. See "Els avalots del 1391," pp. 98–99. For a detailed study of tensions between the city councillors and other sectors of society see C. Guilleré, *Diner, poder i societat a la Girona del segle XIV* (Girona, 1984), pp. 67–100. On p. 100 Guilleré asserts that these tensions led to the pogrom of 1391 against the Jews.

the gates of Caragol and the cemetery of the hospital closed during Holy Week to protect the Jews.[79]

By 1322 royal officials had had enough. I have found no record of a clerical attack on the Jews that year. If it occurred, it was probably overshadowed by the other events that took place during Holy Week. The *sagiones* of the criminal justice of Valencia, perhaps in their function as guardians of the Jews, argued with men of the bishop's family on Good Friday, though they parted without fatal violence. On Easter Sunday, the *sagiones* gathered before the bishop's palace, rang the bells, incited the populace, and then attacked the palace together with the mob, killing some of the bishop's men and injuring others.[80] Protocols that would barely restrain the violence in Girona in 1331 failed in the Valencia of 1322. The fact that the result was not a violent pogrom against the Jews, but rather unrestrained violence between local clerical and official elites, suggests that the dispute between secular and sacred, between monarchy and clergy, could be as large a component in Holy Week violence as the dispute between Church and Synagogue.

. . . . .

The events of 1331 in Girona, or 1322 in Valencia, are striking to us (and were recorded by contemporaries) because their violence, ritualized though it may have been, far exceeded the norm. Much more typical than these battles between adults were the juvenile festivities that so delighted the young Nicolas and cost him his life in 1302. An earlier observation bears repeating here: what is most conspicuous about Holy Week violence is its limits. In town after town, year after year, crowds of children hurled stones and insults at Jews and the homes of Jews without inciting broader riot.[81]

The integrity of these limits was due in large part, I believe, to the fact that the stoning of Jews during Holy Week was not only a game, but a children's game. The 1302 inquest in Girona, cited at the beginning of this chapter, makes clear the primary role of children and adolescents in the festivities. More specifically, this was a game for tonsured children, referred to in the documents as "clerics" and "students." Medieval towns abounded in such children. A great many parents tonsured their children to protect them from the severity of the civil courts, a shaving that was not tied to any consecration, though it signified an "inclination to the ecclesiastical condition" and was often linked to educa-

---

[79]ACA:C 170:295v (1320/12/4); ACA:C 171:155r (1321/1/13).

[80]ACA:C 174:207r (1322/4/5); ACA:C 175:69v (1322/5/13).

[81]These limits are especially striking in light of Peter Loizos's argument that "when forms of marriage between antagonistic groups are treated as unthinkable," restrictions on violence tend to be minimal. Recall chap. 5, and see his "Intercommunal Killing in Cyprus," *Man*, n.s., 23 (1988): 639–653, here p. 650.

tion in cathedral schools and universities.[82] These children were the only partic-ipants in Holy Week violence whose actions were fully protected by the ritual context in which they took place. This protection is explicit in the letter James II wrote to the Estudi General ("university") at Lleida forbidding doctors, poets, grammarians, and artists to dance dressed as Muslims or Jews during the festivi-ties for St. Nicholas and St. Catherine, but expressly allowing children (presum-ably students) under the age of fourteen to do so.[83] The participation of older clergy (as in 1331) may have been ritualized, but it was not "customary" or necessarily approved of. Moreover, even the children's liberties were temporally circumscribed, limited apparently to Holy Week. This is not to deny that clever strategists might seek to expand these boundaries. In Barcelona Jews were re-quired to swear a public oath in front of the Church of St. Just before suing a Christian debtor. Some debtors decided to gather crowds of young students (*scolares*) there to intimidate the Jews into foregoing the oath, leading on one occasion to the stoning of a Jew and of the bailiff. The king's reaction is instruc-tive. He not only forbade such activities but exempted the Jews from taking oath at St. Just at all, permitting them the safety of the vicar's court instead. It appears that the prerogatives of children were not easily manipulated by adults.[84]

Why children? I have no answers, only partial suggestions. Of course the legal immunities discussed above played a role,[85] but these may themselves have

[82]B. Geremek, *The Margins of Society in Late Medieval Paris* (Cambridge, 1987), pp. 136–147, here p. 136.

[83]The edict, dated 1300, is published by Villanueva, *Viaje literario*, 16:231. Cf. J.-R. Juliá Viñamata, "El estudio general de Lérida a finales del siglo XIV: Las reformas de Martín el Hu-mano," in *Miscel.lània Homenatge a Josep Lladonosa* (Lleida, 1992), pp. 323–348, here pp. 342 f. Students at Lleida also participated in direct violence against Jews. See, for example, the fight that took place in 1483 between the vicar's men and students attempting to stone the Jews, reported in J. Lladonosa i Pujol, *L'Estudi General de Lleida del 1430 al 1524* (Barcelona, 1970), pp. 85, 89, 172–173. See also idem, *Història de Lleida*, vol. 1 (Tàrrega, 1972), p. 671, where the Jews complain in 1420 that children regularly stone the walls of their quarter, though these are not stipulated as students.

[84]The fullest account of the affair is in ACA:C 437:130r–130v (1330/6/24): ". . . contra quendam judeum qui . . . venatur [sic] ad dictam ecclesiam et alios judeos qui ibi erant, scolares qui congregati erant ibidem, ad instantiam christiani, moti ex arrupto . . . et etiam contra Berengarium de Capellades, tunc baiulum Barchinone . . . irruerunt, eos lapidibus lapidando." Henceforth, the document continues, the Jews are not to be compelled to swear at St. Just. If this prejudices the church financially, compensation is to be worked out with the aljama. Cf. the brief mention of the document in Mutgé, *La ciudad de Barcelona*, p. 202. The court of the vicar is stipulated as the appropriate venue in order to avoid such incidents in the earlier ACA:C 434:263r–v (1329/7/1). Even earlier, ACA:C 433:33v (1328/10/15) forbids the gathering of students by debtors for the purposes of intimidating the Jews but does not mention this particular incident. Admittedly the later ACA:C 450:114v–115r (1332/2/24) calls into question the effectiveness of all previous, since even at this date the king is ordering officials to protect the Jews when they take their oaths at St. Just.

[85]Aside from the privilege of clergy tonsured children enjoyed, childhood then as today carried with it some diminished legal responsibilities, but these seem not to have been relevant to the issue

been partly predicated on social immunities. Children were "the raucous voice" of "the conscience of the community," a voice that could speak pure truth because it was thought to speak from outside the networks of social relations within which adults were caught and their utterances compromised.[86] As Girard would put it, children articulate most frankly a society's "persecutory mythopoesis."[87] Why this might be so is again unclear. Bruno Bettelheim has maintained that children's tendency toward polarization and projection represents a necessary stage in the process of psychic maturation. Only through this process of dividing the world into good and evil, then destroying the evil and rewarding the good, can children "sort out . . . contradictory tendencies" and gain the psychic stability to avoid being "engulfed by [the] unmanageable chaos" and ambiguities of adult life. According to this model, childhood clarity prepares one for the compromises and complexities of life in the world. If our tonsured children were involved in such a process, then this is yet another way in which Holy Week violence stabilized Jewish-Christian relations.[88]

An explanation grounded more in medieval than modern psychology might stress the relationship between childhood and memory. It is well known that in the early Middle Ages children were often made to act as witnesses to transfers of land and fealty. In an oral culture where memory was the sole guardian of contract, children had the advantage that, as Marc Bloch put it, "memory was . . . the more enduring the longer its possessors were destined to remain on this earth."[89] In Bloch's example, children might be hit or slapped to give them

---

at hand. See, e.g., *Furs de València* 2.13.6 (2:217), where minors (under the age of twenty) are not excused from the consequences of crime by reason of age unless they are seven years old or younger.

[86]Davis, "The Reasons of Misrule," in *Society and Culture*, p. 108, for the raucous voice. See also R. Trexler, "Ritual in Florence: Adolescence and Salvation in the Renaissance," in *The Pursuit of Holiness in Late Medieval and Renaissance Religion*, ed. H. Oberman and C. Trinkaus (Leiden, 1974), pp. 200–264; and idem, "From the Mouths of Babes: Christianization by Children in Sixteenth Century New Spain," in *Church and Community, 1200–1600* (Rome, 1987), pp. 549–573, for examples of children being taught by clerics to attack pagan religious ceremonies in Mexico.

[87]On the persecutory tendencies of children, see J. Caro Baroja on infantile "mythomania," *Las brujas y su mundo* (Madrid, 1961), pp. 310–313; idem, "Las brujas de Fuenterrabía," *Revista de Dialectología y Tradiciones Populares* 3 (1947): 200–204. Girard believes that children mimetically reproduce the persecutory fantasies of their environment and thus confirm them. See his *Des choses cachées depuis la fondation du Monde* (Paris, 1978), p. 171. See also Mitchell, *Violence and Piety*, pp. 66–70.

[88]B. Bettelheim identified children's destructive projections of good and evil as a necessary part of healthy cognitive development in *The Uses of Enchantment* (New York, 1975), pp. 7–10, 66 ff., 74–76, 144. His formulation is provocative here, though I doubt that the psychological model underlying it can easily be applied to the Middle Ages. It is worth the irony to note that in psychosocial terms, it was once fashionable to think of medieval society as a whole as caught in this "childlike" state of polarization and projection, and to use this as an explanation of medieval violence toward minorities (as some still do). Cf. T. J. Lears, *No Place of Grace: Antimodernism and the Transformation of American Culture* (New York, 1981), pp. 149–181.

[89]M. Bloch, *Feudal Society*, 2 vols. (Chicago, 1961), 1:114. Medieval theories abounded about the impressionability of children's minds and the ease with which they memorized.

something to remember the ritual by, to imprint what they were seeing indelibly on their minds. Violent games might be used to a similar effect. Note how children marked a contested boundary between the towns of Andújar and Jaén in 1470:

> On Monday 7 May the Constable assembled as many people as possible . . . concentrating particularly on securing a large number of youths and children. His objective was to beat the agreed bounds. . . . At the first landmark, which was a well, the Constable threw a lance inside it, then ordered a young aspiring knight to jump in fully dressed, and finally let the youths and children indulge in a water fight. At the next landmark the children played a game called "Mares in the Field" and then had a fist-fight until the Constable stepped in and parted them. At the third earthen landmark the youths and children . . . killed a ram, cut off its head, and buried the head in the middle of the landmark. At the fourth and final landmark the Constable organized a bullfight. . . . The express purpose of all these events was "to establish a memory so that in future times there would not be any doubt or debate about the said boundaries."[90]

In much the same way children and their Holy Week games may have served to beat the boundaries between Christian and Jew and to preserve them in memory.

Neither Bettelheim nor Bloch would object to calling these activities "educational," in the sense that they were intended to instill in children (and perhaps in the adult audience as well) a sense of the divisions that constituted their world. Educational too in that tonsured children may have participated in this violence as part of an apprenticeship, a step of their career path in which character could be proven and prestige gained. Like the youthful javelin-throwing games of future warriors,[91] Holy Week riots provided an age-specific way for young *tonsurati* to show their zeal. We can detect several roles among the participants in the Girona riot of 1331. Ten-year-olds threw stones and launched a multitude of minor attacks against the walls and gates of the *call*, fleeing upon detection. Older boys might lead such groups, or engage in exploits of limited

---

[90] A. MacKay, "Religion, Culture, and Ideology on the Late Medieval Castilian-Granadan Frontier," in *Medieval Frontier Societies*, ed. R. Bartlett and A. MacKay (Oxford, 1989), pp. 217–244, here 235–236. The events are recorded in *Hechos del condestable don Miguel Lucas de Iranzo*, ed. J. de Mata Carriazo (Madrid, 1940), pp. 425–431. For a study of games and ritualized violence in the *Hechos del condestable*, see L. Clare, "Fêtes, jeux et divertissements à la cour du connétable de Castille, Miguel Lucas de Iranzo (1460–1470): les exercices physiques," in *La fête et l'écriture: théâtre de cour, cour-théâtre en Espagne et en Italie, 1450–1530 (Colloque international: France-Espagne-Italie, 1985)* (Aix-en-Provence, 1987), pp. 5–32.

[91] Games long popular, and always dangerous. For the case of a youth accidentally killing another during such a game, see ACA:C 221:124r (1321/11/23). The accidental killing in Daroca ca. 1300 of a Christian boy by his Muslim playmate may have been similar. See T. del Campillo, *Documentos históricos de Daroca y su comunidad* (Zaragoza, 1915), no. 119, p. 378. For antique examples of such games and of such accidents, see Antiphon, *Tetralogies*, and Plutarch, *Pericles* 36.

daring, such as lighting a small fire beneath the gates. In Girona, as we have seen, this apprenticeship shaded into the careers of adult clerics, but the same stratification is evident even within the more brutal registers of a grown-up world. Some men participated in the ritual battles with officials, yelling and throwing stones. Among these, a handful were the most daring and aggressive, engaging in hand-to-hand combat and professing a willingness to kill their opponents, or perhaps executing bold sorties into the *call* in the quest for trophies. The senior clergy—archdeacons, abbots, and the like, men with no reputations to secure—provided the face-saving compromises and restraints that averted real bloodshed, pulling back the most aggressive and negotiating with the authorities. Participation in Holy Week games thus took place within a hierarchy of roles, as did participation in the mass, or any other clerical office. The hierarchy of ritualized violence need not, of course, overlap with those of other clerical offices. In this sense, the games could be termed an alternative "career" where prestige could be gained.[92]

It would be wrong, however, to see this career as part of a deviant subculture, the creation of frustrated youth alienated from mainstream clerical institutions by chronic underemployment, few opportunities for advancement, and a severing of ties with the secular world.[93] Men of such weight as canons and abbots do not normally partake in a culture of anomie. In Girona, it seems to me, and probably elsewhere in the Crown of Aragon, participation in Holy Week violence was part of mainstream clerical culture. It was indeed an "office." Through such participation the clergy rearticulated divine history, defined its sacral role, provided a critique of secular structures, and created a space for militant, even apostolic, Christianity. Holy Week violence belongs at the center, not the sordid margins, of clerical culture in the Crown of Aragon.

.   .   .   .   .

The previous pages depict Holy Week riots against Jews as a long-lived popular ritual of extraordinary persistence over centuries of Jewish life in Iberia (at least). They also stress a range of multiple meanings inherent in the violence, some of

[92]Compare, among groupings of soccer fans in England, the "Novices" (ages 9–12), the "Rowdies," and within the grouping of Rowdies, "Aggro Leaders," and finally, "Graduates." See P. Marsh, "Identity: An Ethogenic Perspective," in *Persons in Groups: Social Behavior as Identity Formation in Medieval and Renaissance Europe*, ed. R. Trexler (Binghamton, NY, 1985), pp. 25–27. This "career" (in Erving Goffman's sense) did not appear in practice to be as antithetical to the clerical calling as we might think. Clerics were in fact frequent participants in late medieval urban violence, both as individuals and in groups, and the retinues of bishops and abbots were a potent force in urban feuds.

[93]Such is the model suggested by Geremek, *The Margins*, p. 135. For a rapid overview of the sociological literature on "strain theories" of this type, see D. Downes, "The Language of Violence: Sociological Perspectives on Adolescent Aggression," in *Aggression and Violence*, ed. P. Marsh and A. Campbell (Oxford, 1982), pp. 30–33.

which we might call stabilizing, others the contrary. On the one hand, this clerical reenacting of foundational historical narratives, reinforcing of boundaries between groups, and ritualization of sacrificial violence all contributed to conditions that made possible the continued existence of Jews in a Christian society. On the other, Holy Week stonings can be read as a clerical gloss on *convivencia*, a warning that the toleration of Jews in a Christian society was not without its dangers and costs. It was also a comment on the nature of power, establishing as it did an opposition between uncorrupted sacred power and the many compromises of political and economic power. Both these latter readings emphasized choice and the existence of alternative models of society, what Victor Turner calls "anti-structure."[94] There would be moments (such as the advent of the Black Death and the massacres of 1391) when these alternatives achieved momentary and tragic dominance. Most of the time, however, they would only be adumbrated year after year by technicians of the sacred hurling stones at the walls of the *call*.

These conclusions have implications for the periodization of intolerance toward minorities in medieval Iberia and in Europe more generally. At a minimum, they ask us to question the traditional use by historians of episodes of violence in their attempts to periodize the ebb and flow of intolerance. In the historiography of Iberian Jews, for example, the fourteenth century marks what Baer called the "age of decline" in the Crown of Aragon, a decline graphed through points of violence like that of 1348, dropping inexorably to the massacres of 1391.[95] Those few Holy Week riots that have attracted the attention of historians have been used by them to connect these cataclysms, to give them a linearity they do not otherwise possess.

Such a seismic model makes little sense of Holy Week riots, in part because it ignores their rhythmic and ritualized aspect. Hubert and Mauss theorized long ago that the rhythmic time of repeatable rituals and the linear time of successions of events could coexist, and argued that rituals impose elements of rhythm and circularity on linear events at the same time that they draw meaning from them.[96] Further, the seismic model treats violence as oracle. Holy Week vio-

---

[94] "Anti-structure" represents "the latent system of potential alternatives from which novelty will arise when contingencies in the normative system require it," while "the normative structure represents the working equilibrium." V. Turner, *From Ritual to Theatre: The Human Seriousness of Play* (New York, 1982), p. 28, citing from B. Sutton-Smith, "Games of Order and Disorder" (paper presented to the Symposium on Forms of Symbolic Inversion, American Anthropological Association, Toronto, December 1972), pp. 18–19.

[95] Compare the imagery of A. MacKay, "The Jews in Spain during the Middle Ages," in *Spain and the Jews: The Sephardi Experience 1492 and After*, ed. E. Kedourie (London, 1992), pp. 33–50, here p. 33: "Morover, toward the end of the thirteenth century and during the fourteenth century *convivencia* broke down, and a rising tide of intolerance and persecution culminated in widespread and horrific massacres in 1391."

[96] Hubert and Mauss, "Étude sommaire," pp. 189–229.

lence was not predictive of future intolerance. It expressed a variety of alternative visions, but prophetic vision was not one of them. To treat Holy Week
riots as signs or symptoms of a linear march toward intolerance is to deny their
character as repeated, controlled, and meaningful rituals, and to ignore the possibility that violence can bind and sunder in the same motion. .

In much the same way, the persistence of this popular ritual undercuts the
well-known argument that an early medieval "Augustinian" tolerance toward
Jews was replaced by a harsher clerical intolerance which then spread to the
common people. According to this view, medieval attitudes toward Jews before
the late twelfth century were governed by an Augustinian paradigm that condemned the Jews but insisted on the importance of their presence within Christian society as living reminders of the Crucifixion, of Christ's victory, and of the
truth of the Christian version of sacred history.[97] This tolerant paradigm, we are
told, was replaced in high and later medieval polemics by an insistence that
medieval (rabbinic) Jews had strayed from the truth of their own ancient tradition, that they were irredeemably evil and inveterate enemies of Christendom,
and that they should be eliminated from the Christian community.[98]

Holy Week riots suggest that, while it may be true that the style of Christian
anti-Jewish polemic changed between the twelfth and fourteenth centuries,[99]
we should be cautious about overschematizing Christian-Jewish relations on the
basis of such evidence. We need to be less relentlessly bleak about the fate of
Augustinian tolerance in the later Middle Ages. It is in this period of what we
are told is its twilight that we find the greatest evidence for a widely distributed
clerical ritual which in good Augustinian fashion used the Jews to reenact the
triumphant place of Christianity in sacred history, while at the same time cir-
cumscribing for and assigning to the Jews a place in Christian society.[100] But
just as rumors of the Augustinian ideal's death have been exaggerated, so too
with accounts of its life. We should pause for breath in our panegyrics when we
realize that one of the most ancient, most popular, and clearest articulations of
the Augustinian paradigm in the Middle Ages turns out to be predicated on an
act of violence. It is this double register of rituals like the Holy Week stoning of

[97] This paradigm was most influentially articulated by Augustine of Hippo in the fifth century.
See his *De civitate Dei* 18.46, 20.29; *Enarrationes in Psalmos* 58.1.21–22; *Tractatus adversus Judeos*
42:51–67; and *Sermo* 200.2—texts cited constantly by medieval Christian writers on the Jews.

[98] The clearest exponent of this argument is J. Cohen in his *The Friars and the Jews: The Evolution
of Medieval Anti-Judaism* (Ithaca, NY, 1982).

[99] A shift well noted by A. Funkenstein, though he situates it differently than Cohen and draws
different conclusions. See his "Basic Types of Christian Anti-Jewish Polemics in the Middle Ages,"
Viator 2 (1971): 373–382; and idem, "Changes in the Patterns of Christian Anti-Jewish Polemic in
the Twelfth Century," *Zion* 33 (1968): 125–144 (in Hebrew).

[100] This increased volume of evidence in the late thirteenth and fourteenth centuries does not,
however, indicate increased incidence. It is primarily a function of the expanding record-keeping
abilities of secular and ecclesiastical authorities.

Jews that gives them their greatest value in explaining both *convivencia* and cata-clysm. The violence contained within them made possible both stasis and ex-plosive historical change. The same idioms that provided stability by ritualizing the sacrificial conquest of "Jerusalem" gave ritual form to the massacre of Jews in 1348 and 1391, and of Muslims in 1455, as we shall see in the epilogue.

Epilogue

THE BLACK DEATH AND BEYOND

BOTH PARTS of this book share as a goal the narrowing of the distance between "abnormal" and "normal," between cataclysmic violence and the everyday functional violence of a relatively stable society. Part One achieves this through its insistence on the location and contextualization of episodes of collective violence within political, economic, and cultural frameworks; Part Two by its emphasis on the systemic production of everyday violence between religious groups and the stabilizing function of that violence within society. Thus far, however, the relations between these two approaches remain implicit, with some difficulties unresolved. Part Two, for example, has to this point addressed the question of collective violence only indirectly. What relation do the violences of economic interactions, or of annual rituals, have to those of cataclysmic massacres? And Part One has, as medievalists will recognize, skirted the most famous outbreaks of cataclysmic violence against minorities on the Iberian Peninsula, those of 1348 and 1391. Are these events, which were of far greater virulence and scale than earlier ones, accessible by the same approaches? These questions, and the two parts of this book, converge here upon a study of the massacres that accompanied the advent of the Black Death in Europe in 1348.

More than any other event, the coming of the plague occupies a central space in premodern histories and periodizations of persecution. To Carlo Ginzburg, it represents the moment in which "obsession with conspiracy[,] . . . a thick sediment in the popular mentality," breaks to the surface, a critical point in the 1,500-year-long evolution of stereotypes that ends with the witches' Sabbath.[1] To others the sharp outbreaks of violence caused by the plague represent an end point of sorts, the logical consequence of centuries of accreted calumnies, fantasies, and stereotypes about the Jews.[2] It is this centrality that makes 1348 a fitting end to a discussion of violence against minorities, even if, as should be clear, the tragic events of that year are neither genesis nor telos of my narrative.

.   .   .   .   .   .

The appearance of the plague triggered attacks against groups as diverse as Jews, clerics, foreigners, beggars, pilgrims, and Muslims, in cities and towns through-

---

[1] *Ecstasies*, pp. 68, 74–76.

[2] E.g., Kriegel, *Les Juifs à la fin du Moyen Age*, pp. 32–38; Bauchau, "Science et racisme," pp. 28–29.

out Europe.[3] The phenomenon is almost universally treated as a general one. The sites of violence, from Cracow to Barcelona, are cataloged and subsumed into a single explanatory mechanism. We are told that the moment was one of "collective panic," a panic expressed in aggression toward the "other," particularly toward Jews.[4] The aggression itself is usually explained sparely, by allusion to psychosocial phenomena: "irrational," "fantasy," "unconscious," "projection." These are important concepts, but they could acquire explanatory sense only in the context of a medieval psychology that is never provided. The genealogy of the fantasies themselves, however, is the focus of a great deal of attention. Some historians have traced the "fantastic" stereotypes and accusations with which the violence was legitimated back to antiquity, and have described their elaboration in the intervening centuries, while others have argued at length over the proportional roles of "learned" and "popular" cultures in the crafting of these ideologies of persecution. I will take a more local approach, emphasizing the particularity of the Catalano-Aragonese experience, rather than focusing on pan-European characteristics.[5]

[3] The standard work on the events of 1348 and on later episodes of the plague is J. Biraben, *Les hommes et la peste en France et dans les pays européens et méditerranéens*, 2 vols. (Paris, 1975). For 1348 see 1:57–85. Several authors discuss the accusations of poisoning that arose in response to the plague. See most recently Ginzburg, *Ecstasies*, pp. 63–68. S. Guerchberg, "The Controversy over the Alleged Sowers of the Black Death in Contemporary Treatises on Plague," in *Change in Medieval Society*, ed. S. Thrupp (New York, 1964), pp. 208–224 (reprint and translation from *RdÉJ* 108 [1948]); and E. Wickersheimer, "Les accusations d'empoisonnements portées pendant la première moitié du XIVe siècle contre les lépreux et les Juifs; leurs relations avec les épidémies de la peste," *Comptes-rendus du 4e Congrès International de l'histoire de la médecine*, ed. Tricot-Roger and Laignel-Lavestine (Antwerp, 1927), pp. 76–83, remain indispensible. On poisoning accusations and attacks on Jews in the Crown of Aragon, see A. López de Meneses, "Una consequencia de la peste negra en Cataluña: el pogrom de 1348," *Sefarad* 19 (1959), pp. 92–131, 322–364. For Germany, see A. Haverkamp, "Die Judenverfolgungen zur Zeit des Schwarzen Todes im Gesellschaftsgefüge deutscher Städte," in *Zur Geschichte der Juden im Deutschland des späten Mittelalters und der frühen Neuzeit*, ed. A. Haverkamp (Stuttgart, 1981), pp. 27–93.

[4] "Collective panic" is from Delumeau, *La peur*, p. 98. H. Mollaret and J. Brossollet, in a passage often cited by students of the attacks upon the Jews, write: "Psychiatrists and sociologists understand how man reacts to anguish: by flight, aggression or projection. The plague inspired all three reactions." "La peste, source méconnue d'inspiration artistique," *Koninklijk Museum voor schone Kunsten, Jaarboek 1965*, as cited in Biraben, *Les hommes et la peste*, p. 57.

[5] Much work remains to be done on the course of the plague in the Iberian Peninsula. Besides the pages Biraben devotes to the subject, see J. Sobrequés Callicó, "La Peste negra en la península ibérica," in *Actas del I Simposio de Historia Medieval: La Investigación de la Historia Hispánica del siglo XIV, Problemas y Cuestiones* (Madrid and Barcelona, 1973), pp. 67–102; C. Verlinden, "La Grande Peste de 1348 en Espagne," *Revue Belge de Philologie et d'Histoire* 17 (1938): 103–146. On the plague in the lands of the Crown of Aragon, see A. López de Meneses, "Documentos acerca de la peste negra en los dominios de la Corona de Aragón," *Estudios de Edad Media de la Corona de Aragón* 6 (1956): 291–447; J. Gautier-Dalché, "La peste noire dans les états de la couronne d'Aragon," *Mélanges offerts à Marcel Bataillon par les Hispanistes français (Bulletin Hispanique* 54bis [1962]), pp. 65–80. Several local studies exist. See especially C. Guilleré, "La peste noire à Gérone (1348)," *Annals de L'Institut d'Estudis Gironins* 27 (1984): 87–161; idem, *Girona al segle XIV*, 2:162–189; Rubio,

The bubonic plague reached Barcelona and Girona in May of 1348, Valencia in June, and spread to other cities in the Crown of Aragon.[6] It did not come unannounced. King Peter IV, the Ceremonious, had already received a letter dated the 10th of April from the governor of Roussillon and Cerdanya, who had been informed by the *sénéchal* of Carcassonne and the vicar of Narbonne (both in France) about the pestilence raging there. The pestilence, wrote the governor, was spread by confessed poisoners and had killed a third of the people of Carcassonne, a "great infinity" of those in Narbonne, and half in certain towns of Roussillon.[7] The poisoners, it was said, traveled in the guise of pilgrims.

Municipal officials, too, had heard of the plague afflicting the south of France and written to their counterparts across the Pyrenees for information. Thus André Benedict, vicar of Narbonne, wrote directly to the sworn men of Girona, who had asked him what steps they could take to counter the disease; whether it had been spread by poison or by other causes; whether anyone had been arrested or had confessed to the crime; how such people had been punished; and at whose instigation they had committed the crime. André informed them that in the vicinity of Carcassonne and Narbonne one-quarter of the population had died, and that many poisoners, most of them paupers and beggars, had been captured together with their poisonous powders. Some confessed spontaneously, others under torture. None could name who had paid them to carry out the crime and given them the powders. It was widely believed, however, that this must have been some "enemies of the kingdom of France." The poisoners were dismembered in various ways, then burned. It was also believed by some that the pestilence was caused by the alignment of the planets. André himself favored the theory that the planets and poisons together had caused the deaths. Regardless of cause, he stressed that the illness was highly contagious: whenever one person died of it, the others in the household would perish within four days.[8]

Peste negra; J.-P. Cuvillier, "Les communautés rurales de la Plaine de Vich (Catalogne) aux XIIIe et XIVe siècles," *Mélanges de la Casa de Velázquez* 4 (1968): 73–106. See also the articles by various authors collected in the *VIII Congreso de Historia de la Corona de Aragón*, sec. II, vol. 1 (Valencia, 1969), pp. 9–103. The English language literature is restricted to M. Shirk, "The Black Death in Aragon, 1348–1351," *Journal of Medieval History* 7 (1981): 357–367; and idem, "Violence and the Plague in Aragón, 1348–1351," *Journal of the Rocky Mountain Medieval and Renaissance Association* 5 (1984): 31–39.

[6] Gautier-Dalché, "La peste noire dans les états de la couronne d'Aragon"; Biraben, *Les hommes et la peste*, 1:74–75; Guilleré, "La peste noire à Gérone," pp. 106–108.

[7] J. Coroleu, *Documents historichs catalans del siglo XIV* (Barcelona, 1899), pp. 69–70. For local studies on the effects of the plague in the south of France, see among others R. Emery, "The Black Death of 1348 in Perpignan," *Speculum* 42 (1967): 611–623; and for Jews, J. Shatzmiller, "Les juifs de Provence pendant la peste noire," *RdÉJ* 133 (1974): 457–480. See below for Peter's response to these letters.

[8] The letter is published by Villanueva, *Viaje literario*, 14:269–271, and by Guilleré, "La peste noire à Gérone," pp. 141–142. Several distinguished astrologers affiliated with Pope Clement VI's

Well before the plague reached Catalonia, municipal officials and (presumably) others were struggling to explain what had caused it. André's letter, in fact, represents only the barest sketch of both popular and learned theories (not necessarily so very different) about the workings of this deadly disease. For example, while the town council of Girona was writing to André, the council of Lleida asked advice from a local medical professor, Jacme d'Agramont. Jacme replied with a treatise called "Regimen for Preservation from Pestilence," dated April 24, 1348.[9] It was written in Catalan, not Latin, probably because, as its author stated, it was intended for popular consumption.

For Jacme, pestilence was "an unnatural shift in the air, either in its quality or in its substance, from which come corruptions and sudden deaths and diverse maladies into living things, in some specific regions, beyond what is customary in them." Thus did Jacme define "pestilence naturally understood." But there was a parallel, and equally important, "pestilence morally understood." This was "an unnatural shift of courage and of thought in people, from which come enmities and rancors, wars and robberies, destruction of places and deaths, in some specific regions, beyond what is customary in them." Both pestilences subverted the natural order of human relationships. Thus "pestilence naturally understood" turned good food into poison, so that things that normally "have the property of benefiting our body" acquire the "property of poisoning and killing."[10]

Jacme also believed that God could be the cause of universal plague, because of "our sins," though he followed most of his contemporaries in believing that the more immediate cause of such a plague resided in celestial and planetary alignments.[11] But Jacme stressed that plagues which were not "universal" could be caused by human agents, and he considered the possibility of such agency for the plagues raging across the mountains:

court at Avignon wrote prognostications based on an unusual conjuncture of the planets Saturn and Jupiter in 1345. Some of these were taken (immediately after the fact) to be predictions of the plague. See especially *Levi ben Gerson's Prognostication for the Conjunction of 1345*, ed. B. Goldstein and D. Pingree, *Transactions of the American Philosophical Society* 80, pt. 6 (1990): 3–8.

[9] *"Regiment de preservació de pestilència" de Jacme d'Agramont (s. XIV). Introducció, transcripció i estudi lingüístic*, ed. J. Veny i Clar (Tarragona, 1971), pp. 47–93. This treatise has received little attention. See J. Arrizabalaga's excellent article, "Facing the Black Death: Perceptions and Reactions of University Medical Practitioners," in *Practical Medicine from Salerno to the Black Death*, ed. L. García-Ballester et al. (Cambridge, 1994), pp. 237–288, which appeared as these pages were being revised. For references to the few treatments of Jacme's work, see p. 239n.7, to which add A.-C. Klebs, "A Catalan Plague Tract of April 24, 1348, by Jacme d'Agramont," in *Rapport du 6e Congrès International d'Histoire de la Médecine* (Antwerp, 1929), pp. 229–232. Jacme himself died in the first wave of the plague. See Lladonosa, *Història de Lleida*, 1:489, citing a document in which his widow seeks payment for the treatise from the town council.

[10] *"Regiment,"* pp. 52, 91. On food into poison and the inversion of order in nature, p. 53.

[11] Ibid., pp. 55–58, on sin, and 59–60 on the heavens and planets. Agramont provided an etymology for *pestilència* that assigned it the meaning "from the stars" (p. 55).

Deaths and pestilence can come into people for another reason, that is to say, through evil men, sons of the devil, who with diverse medicines and poisons corrupt foodstuffs with [their] very false ingenuity and wicked mastery, even though properly speaking such a mortality of people is not the pestilence of which we are speaking here, nevertheless I wished to mention it because we are now in a time when many deaths have occurred in some nearby regions, such as in Collioure, in Carcassonne, in Narbonne, and in the barony of Montpellier and in Avignon and in all Provence.[12]

Catalans thus had much to ponder as they waited for the disease to cross the mountains. Were they beset by both moral and natural plague? Surely the civil war embroiling the Crown constituted the former.[13] What were their sins? Who was a poisoner? And how could one know what poison was, in a time of universal pestilence? Finally, they could worry about the permeability of their own flesh to infection. If they had read Jacme d'Agramont (or Galen), they knew that temperament and lifestyle could affect their susceptibility to corruption of the humors. Had they eaten or drunk too much? Had too much sex? Taken too many baths?[14]

.   .   .   .   .

We can only imagine how the populations to the west of the Pyrenees felt as they waited for the plague to reach them, but the wait was not long. On or about the 2d of May, the plague reached Barcelona. In a matter of months, the city lost approximately 36 percent of its population of 42,000: some 15,000 souls.[15] Other cities in the Crown suffered comparable losses as the plague spread throughout the kingdom.[16] Awareness of these horrifying statistics is

[12] Ibid., p. 58. This was the explanation favored by Alfonso de Cordoba in his *Epistola et regimen de pestilentia*, written in Montpellier in 1348 or 1349. See the edition of K. Sudhoff, "Epistola et regimen Alphontii Cordubensis de pestilentia," *Archiv für Geschichte der Medizin* 3 (1909): 223–226.

[13] On the civil war and the unions of 1348 see chap. 1 and below.

[14] *"Regiment,"* pp. 65–66. On ideas of infection in Galen and Galenism, see V. Nutton, "The Seeds of Disease: An Explanation of Contagion and Infection from the Greeks to the Renaissance," *Medical History* 27 (1983): 1–34. These were moral, as well as physical, excesses. See P. Slack, "Responses to Plague in Early Modern Europe: The Implications of Public Health," *Social Research* 55 (1988): 433–453, here p. 437.

[15] The date and estimates for Barcelona are from Biraben, *Les hommes et la peste*, 1:198–218 (though he does not give a source for the date). On Valencia, where contemporaries estimated that 300–1,000 people perished each day, see Rubio, *Peste negra*, pp. 103–108. Guilleré, "La peste noire à Gérone," p. 115, gives an unusually low (and to my mind unconvincing) estimate of 14.25 percent. See also his *Girona al segle XIV*, 2:175–179. Attempts at statistical precision are in any event misplaced, since the sources cannot sustain them.

[16] For a recent summary in English of the demographic effects of the 1348 epidemic on Catalonia see Freedman, *The Origins of Peasant Servitude*, pp. 161–164. On p. 162 he writes, "Overall the most authoritative estimate for Catalonia is a loss of about 20 per cent of its population as a result of the epidemic, which followed a 5 per cent decline in the period from 1300–1347."

reflected in a contemporary tombstone: "In the year of Our Lord 1348, in which there was such mortality that scarcely one-quarter of humanity survived, died G. de Planils, archdeacon of the town, on the ninth day before the calends of August." This was not a crisis; it was a cataclysm.[17]

What place in this cataclysm did Christians ascribe to Muslims and Jews? Even within the outline of Jacme d'Agramont's economy of plague, one can imagine a variety of roles for minorities. They might have no role at all. Or, like Christians, their individual sins might have angered God. Perhaps their mere existence was the sin that angered God. Finally, they might (and this is the role stressed by all historians) be cast in the role of poisoners, as the direct source of the plague. In the Crown of Aragon, all these roles are attested except the last.

Very few statements linking Jews or Muslims in any way to the plague survive from the Crown of Aragon, although historians continue to accept the existence of poisoning accusations as a given.[18] There is in fact no textual evidence I know of indicating that Christians in the Crown accused religious minorities of spreading the plague through poison. This argument from silence is stronger than it may seem, because other types of accusations were indeed recorded. Peter the Ceremonious had been told by the governor of Roussillon and Cerdanya across the Pyrenees that the plague was spread by poison put in water and food, and sprinkled on "the benches on which men sit and put up their feet," and he took these accusations seriously enough to write the governor of the kingdom of Mallorca directing him to protect that kingdom from such poisoners. He wrote as well to the caretakers of his children, warning them of the poisoners and ordering them to move the princesses from Tarragona to Montblanc for greater safety.[19] But the king never connected religious minorities with his suspicions, and the issue of poisoning seems to have quickly vanished from the bureaucratic horizon.

Jews and Muslims are equally absent from nonroyal types of documentation, even as accusations against other groups survive. The governor's warning that the poisoners went about clad in the garb of pilgrims and religious, for example,

---

[17] The point is worth making, since historians of anti-Semitism have a tendency to call every period a "time of crisis." See, for example, *Anti-Semitism in Times of Crisis*, ed. S. Gilman and S. Katz (New York, 1991), p. 14. For the tombstone, see J. Serra Vilaró, *Santa Tecla la Vieja* (Tarragona, 1960), p. 301: "ANNO/ DNI.M.CCC/ XL. VIII. IN. QUO. FUIT. TANTA/ MORTALITAS. QUOD. VIX. QUARTA/ PARS. HOMINUM. REMANSIT/ IX. KLS. AUG. OBIIT. G. DE. PLA/ NILS. ARCHIDIACONUS. VILLE."

[18] E.g., most recently, Arrizabalaga, "Facing the Black Death," p. 256.

[19] ACA:C 1128:178r (1348/4/20), 179r (issued under secret seal). The king's concern for the princesses' health is again evident in 179v. López omits these from her otherwise admirable "Documentos," though she does publish the king's cover letter to the governor of Mallorca from 178r. The version of the governor of Roussillon's warning enclosed with this cover letter and omitted by López differs only slightly from that given by Coroleu, *Documents historichs*, pp. 69–70, which she cites in "Una consequencia," p. 95.

is echoed in the experience of two clerics traveling through Barcelona in May of 1348 on their way to the general chapter of their order. They were told that it was unsafe for them to travel because clerics were being seized on the suspicion "that men dressed as religious poisoned the waters and put potions in them." The clerics' story is preserved in a deposition presenting their excuses for their absence from the chapter.[20] I know of only one such accusation made against religious minorities in the Crown of Aragon, and it may be treated as the exception that proves the rule. In Mallorca a Muslim slave was suspected of poisoning the Christians. The captive "Turk" was accused of bathing in the sea, filling his mouth with seawater, then spitting it on the doors of various houses. He was also alleged to have threatened that if he was not freed, he would kill all the people of Alcudia. But the accusations found no purchase. Royal officials ruled that if the townsfolk wished to seize and try the Muslim, they should first compensate his owner. The citizens failed to raise the money, and there the matter ended.[21]

. . . . .

Nevertheless, Jews were attacked in Barcelona, Cervera, Lleida, Tàrrega, and perhaps in Girona, all in Catalonia.[22] Some of these attacks—Lleida, for example—were so slight as to leave barely a trace in the documentation. Others, like that of Tàrrega, in which three hundred Jews were killed, can only be described as massacres.

Details are scarce on the riots themselves, nearly nonexistent on the days preceding them. In Barcelona, commercial relations between Christians and Jews appear relatively stable from the advent of the plague in early May until the riot some two weeks later. Loan activity, for example, seems to have been normal in the first two weeks of May but ceased after Thursday, May 15, not to

---

[20]AHPG 4, no. 34, fols. 25r–v (1348/5/16): ". . . quamvis Barchinone illis fuisset, ut asseruerunt, intimatum quod sine magno periculo dictum iter facere non poterant, quia in locis pluribus licenter apparebantur homines ex toto expoliebantur et prescrutabantur et pro modica occasione capti tenebantur precipue religiosi, cum sacerdotalia facientes esset suspicio quod homines sub habitu religionis aquas inficiebant et potiones imponebant, ideo non erat securum alicui religioso iter illud accipere." The full text is published in Guilleré, "La peste noire à Gérone," pp. 142–143.

[21]AHM:LC 9:7r, 8v, 9r, 12v, all from April 1348. The documents are published and discussed in A. Santamaría Arández, "La peste negra en Mallorca," in *VIII Congreso de Historia de la Corona de Aragón*, sec. II, vol. 1 (Valencia, 1969), pp. 103–130, here pp. 110, 130.

[22]Cities where attacks are documented in the royal archives. A nineteenth-century historian believed that a peculiar riot took place in Girona (see below), and the chronicler Joseph Ha-Kohen added the towns of Tarragona and Solsona, but these places do not appear in the surviving documentation. For the documentation, see López, "Una consequencia," pp. 92–131, 322–364.

resume until the 26th and then at a very reduced pace.[23] It was on Saturday, the 17th, that the riot occurred. On that day, a funeral cortege was escorting a body through the plaza of St. James when some thatch fell from the walls of the Jewish *call*. Those in the funeral party abandoned the body and began to incite the populace.[24] They attacked the *call*, burned debt documents, and killed some twenty Jews.[25]

Similarly (though recorded with even less detail) in Cervera, where, according to Ha-Kohen, the rioters killed eighteen Jews and sacked houses.[26] In Tàrrega, on the "tenth day of the month of Av," mobs yelling, "Death to the traitors" attacked the Jewish quarter. According to Ha-Kohen they killed three hundred people.[27] In all these cases, as with so many acts of violence mediated through bureaucratic documents, we know much more about the administrative reaction than about the events themselves. Nevertheless, it is worth asking the question, why were the Jews attacked, if they were not accused of being poisoners?[28]

[23] As demonstrated by the number of loans (from Jews to Christians) inscribed in the records of the vicar's court, IMHB, Archive of the Veguer, Sec. 9, Legajo 7-B, fols. 45v–56v, for the month of May: 5/2:19 loans; 5/6:19; 5/12:13; 5/13:11; 5/15:6; 5/26:2; 5/28:3. No more loans are recorded until July 17. Compare the total of 73 loans recorded in May with a total of 182 in April (fols. 20r–45r): 4/1:6; 4/2:21; 4/3:8; 4/4:11; 4/7:18; 4/8:13; 4/9:11; 4/10:15; 4/11:18; 4/28:23; 4/29:25; 4/30:13. Data for the previous May do not exist. Guilleré has performed a more detailed analysis for Girona. See his "La peste noire à Gérone," pp. 98–102.

[24] ACA:C 653:83v (1348/6/3): ". . . cum hiis diebus cor[pus] cuiusdam deffuncti [. . .] nullos per plateam sancti Jacobi defferretur et a parte [calli ju]daici dicte civitatis quedam arundo mod[. . .] cecidisset, illi, qui dic[tum] defferebant deffunctum, dimisso corp[or]e antedicto, et [plu]res ali[i], populum concitando." Published in Baer, *Die Juden*, vol. 1, no. 232, pp. 327–328.

[25] The burning of the documents is widely attested. See, for example, ACA:C 887:45v (1348/7/14): ". . . plures ex ipsis judeis morti et occidati fuerint et plura ipsorum instrumenta debitoria capta et etiam lacerata," in López, "Documentos," no. 18, p. 307. The toll of twenty is given only by the chroniclers. See Ha-Kohen, ʿ*Emeq ha-Bakha*, p. 147. In other details, Ha-Kohen closely reflects archival accounts of the riots (see below, discussion of Tàrrega), so he may be accurate here.

[26] ʿ*Emeq ha-Bakha*, p. 148. Neither Duran, in *Referències documentals*, pp. 17–18 (giving the mistaken date of 1349), nor López, "Una consequencia," p. 110, has much to add to Ha-Kohen's account.

[27] Ha-Kohen, ʿ*Emeq ha-Bakha*, p. 148, for the date and death toll. The yell "muyren los traydors" is mentioned in ACA:C 658:52r–v (1349/12/23). The cry was generic and could be used in any attacks, whether on Jews or on Christians. In 1350, for example, three Christians were beaten and the wheat they were guarding stolen to the cry of "muyren los traydors." See ACA:C 666:185v–186r, cited by López, "Una consequencia," p. 116. A. MacKay and G. McKendrick discuss similar screams in "La semiología y los ritos de violencia: Sociedad y poder en la Corona de Castilla," *En la España Medieval* 11 (1988): 153–165, here p. 162. The date given by Ha-Kohen would have had resonance for his Jewish readers, for whom the 9th of Av was the traditional date upon which both Temples were destroyed. The month was consequently considered one of sorrow. See *Taʿanit* 4:6.

[28] Of these cities, only Lleida had a Muslim population of any significance, on which see Mutgé, *L'aljama*.

Contemporary Jews themselves asked this question in the years immediately following 1348, and the answer they arrived at merits serious consideration: "Without any reason they injure, harass, stone, and even kill the Jews living in the said kingdoms and lands [i.e., the Crown of Aragon], the said Christians declaring that because of the sins of the Jews there come mortalities and famines, and committing the said harms against the Jews so that the said pestilences might cease."[29] Jews were attacked not because they were poisoners, but because their sins precipitated the plague. There were a variety of mechanisms by which this could occur, not all of which implied criticism of the Jews as a group. Sin, even the sin of one individual, was thought to be enough to bring "divine punishment" in the form of plague. For this reason crimes were punished most severely when plague was felt to threaten. In 1379 the sworn men of Valencia wrote of a man who had committed "enormous crimes" that "it was publicly said that [the people] wondered if some great plague would not follow in the land, because of the injustice and impunity of this sin and others."[30] By extension, a number of immoral acts could bring down discipline upon the communities in which they were committed. Royal officials in Mallorca had this in mind when they attempted to forestall the pestilence of 1348 by banning gambling, swearing, working on Sundays, fishing for profit on holidays, and dressing ostentatiously.[31] In this context the sins of Muslims and Jews mattered, especially when they were compounded through commission with Christians. Thus in 1351 the bishop of Valencia wrote to the city council about the many sins committed in the Muslim and Jewish quarters of the city, since he feared lest "by their sins, our lord God all-powerful might wish to send pestilences about the land."[32] The bishop's complaint, that Christians were living in the Muslim and Jewish quarters, along with his suggestion that they be evicted, had

[29] From the partial transcription of a papal bull dated (by Simonsohn, *Apostolic See*, p. 405) January 21, 1356. The bull was one of the few results of an extraordinary cooperative effort undertaken by three of the richest Jews of Catalonia and Valencia in 1354. The (Hebrew) text of their accord, using slightly different language, states that whenever there was a plague or famine "the people . . . made the earth tremble with their cries of: 'all this is happening because of the sins of Jacob. Let us destroy this nation! Let us kill them!' " For the bull, see Simonsohn and also Baer, *Die Juden*, 1:358, who both follow the transcription given by Ribera and Asín, *Manuscritos arabes*, p. 240, no. 73. On the accord of 1354, see for the Hebrew version Baer, *Die Juden*, 1:348–359; and for a Catalan translation E. Feliu, "Els acords de Barcelona de 1354," *Calls* 2 (1987): 145–164. See also the "Guia per a una lectura comprensiva dels acords" by Jaume Riera appended to the translation, pp. 164–173. For a less accurate Hebrew version and an English summary, see L. Finkelstein, *Jewish Self-Government in the Middle Ages* (New York, 1924; reprint, Westport, CT, 1975), pp. 328–347.

[30] For the "enormous crimes" see Rubio, *Peste negra*, pp. 96–97, citing AMV, Ll.M., g³-4, fol. 115 (1379/10/13).

[31] Santamaría, "La peste negra en Mallorca," p. 114, citing AHM:LC 8:204v; AHM:LC 9:9v.

[32] The bishop's argument is in AMV, M.C., A-10, fol. 25 (1351/10/7). A similar argument was made before the council by Garcia deç Loriç a year and a half earlier (1350/3/4), in AMV, M.C., A-9, fol. 152.

repeatedly (and ineffectually) been made over the previous century. Now it took a new, though not necessarily more successful, form.[33] Note, however, that these fairly common concerns about sin were not claims about Jews (or Muslims) as a group. They did not call for the destruction of a "nation."

Joseph Ha-Kohen, living in Italy some two hundred years after the events, found the missing ingredient in an anachronistic but illuminating rewriting of his ancestors' analysis. Seeking to answer the question of motive behind the attacks of 1348, he had the Aragonese and Catalan Christians in his chronicle speak the following "unjust calumnies":

> "All this has occurred because of the sin of Jacob, for they have brought a mortal poison into the world; the guilt is theirs, and because of them the great tragedy that afflicts us has come upon us."[34]

Too good a historian to attribute an accusation of well poisoning to his subjects, but writing in the sixteenth century, long after a discourse of Jews as poisoners had crystallized, he turned the poisoning into an indirect act. Christians believed, he implied, that the plague, or the poisoning of the body social, was a product of the sinfulness of Jews as a group (i.e., of their rejection of Jesus?) and of their continued existence in the midst of Christian society, not of their individual actions. Hence the reiteration of distance between Jews and the rest of society, whether through sacrifice (see below), or less drastically, through stoning, was perceived as a remedy for plague. Here, for the first time in the Crown of Aragon, we can recognize the full brutal power of a fear of pollution centered on the Jews.

This interpretation is strengthened by an obscure incident that may or may not have occurred in Girona. No violence is documented for Girona in the Jewish chronicles, or in royal archives. But the mid-nineteenth-century historian Juan Cortada stated, without reference, that in 1348 the people of Girona exhumed the bodies from the Jewish graveyard and burned them publicly before attacking living Jews. It is unlikely that the murder of Jews would pass unnoticed by royal officials, but it is possible that the Jewish dead were exhumed and burned. If so, these bodies of dead Jews, obviously incapable of

---

[33] Compare the claims made about Muslim sins with Christians in 1335 described in chapter 4, n. 71. The king had most recently forbidden the cohabitation of Christians with Muslims in Valencia's Muslim quarter in May of 1346. See ARV, Real, no. 658, fols. 12r–v, published in *Cartas pueblas de las morerías valencianas y documentación complementaria*, ed. M. V. Febrer Romaguera (Zaragoza, 1991), no. 183. The earliest complaint is ACA:C 38:72r (1276), published in Roca, "Un siglo," doc. no. 5. The primary concern about such cohabitation was the possibility that it could lead to miscegenation.

[34] *'Emeq ha-Bakha*, p. 147. Ha-Kohen's account borrows from an earlier chronicle by Hayyim Galipapa, *'Emeq refaim*, who may have had access to the *takkanot* of 1354. Certainly the two formulations are very similar (e.g., "sins of Jacob").

"poisoning" in an active sense, were thought to be agents of pollution that needed to be destroyed.[35]

.   .   .   .   .

With this detailed narrative of events in hand, we can begin to ask the question of why the Jews were attacked in 1348 at a more general level. The general answer most commonly given is that the violence was a stereotypical medieval act of "scapegoating." This type of claim has been most clearly articulated recently by René Girard. In primitive societies, he writes, "contagious disease is not clearly distinguished from acute internal discord." In such societies plague is combated through a redefinition of the group. A scapegoat is identified, differentiated from the group, and attacked so that "insiders feel united as they never did before. They form a new and tighter inside. The alien threat displaces everything else; internal quarrels are forgotten. A new unity and comradeship prevails among those who, feeling attacked as a group, also feel they must defend themselves as a group."[36]

This common paradigm, whose best-known antecedents are in Freud and Durkheim, is useful in its insistence that violence has functional aspects which need to be incorporated into our understanding of social order. It is not, however, concerned with the processes by which difference is identified and maintained, nor does it ask how these processes are affected by the cultural and material structures of a particular place and time.[37] These questions have been

[35] J. Cortada, *Historia de España* (Barcelona, 1841), vol. 2 (= vol. 7 of *El mundo: historia de todos los pueblos*), p. 405. E. C. Girbal repeated Cortada's statement but confessed that, despite repeated investigations, he had found no documentary evidence to confirm it. See his *Los judíos en Gerona* (Girona, 1870), p. 21, reprinted in *Per a una història de la Girona jueva*, ed. D. Romano (Girona, 1988), 1:23–114, here p. 45. The notion that corpses which were not buried or burned could cause plague by putrefying the air was widespread. See Jacme d'Agramont, *"Regiment,"* p. 60. Compare the *Compendium de epidemia* composed by the faculty of medicine at Paris in 1348, ed. E. H. Rebouis, *Étude historique et critique sur la peste* (Paris, 1888), p. 82, discussing vapors from "mortuis corporibus non sepultis nec combustis." Authorities in Mallorca attempted to burn the bodies of early plague victims because they believed that burning was more effective than burial at preventing the spread of infection. The bishop, however, forbade the practice as against Christian doctrine. See Santamaría, "La peste negra en Mallorca," p. 109.

[36] The extended quotations are from Girard, "Generative Scapegoating," pp. 84, 90. On p. 87 Girard calls these events "some kind of collective madness that resulted in real events, in real 'scapegoating.'" For an example from a medievalist, see Delumeau, *La peur*, pp. 132–133. This model seems to me to derive from Durkheim's theory that deviance is defined and persecuted so as to reinforce the collective unity of the persecuting society. On Durkheim and deviance, see S. Lukes, *Durkheim: His Life and Work* (Harmondsworth, 1973), pp. 160 ff. In his contribution to H. Dagan's *Enquête sur l'antisemitisme* (Paris, 1899), pp. 59–63 ("Notes sur l'anti-semitisme"), Durkheim himself argued that attacks on Jews were scapegoating activities in unsettled economic or political conditions.

[37] For Girard, for example, the choice of a scapegoat is more or less random: "Generative Scapegoating," p. 85. See also his *Things Hidden since the Foundation of the World* (London, 1987)

left to those historians who, like R. I. Moore, have adapted the paradigm.[38] Following Mary Douglas, Moore sees the fear of pollution accreting along social boundaries as a result of anxiety about disparities of status and power, anxieties that focus on "those whose functions or value in a society give them much greater importance than is reflected in their status or influence." In medieval Europe, "the same anxieties are also easily identified in the fears projected against . . . groups which are clearly defined by race or caste as occupying an inferior position while performing essential functions. Such people present the danger that by asserting their real power they may subvert a social structure which is founded on the premise of their impotence."[39] Moore is interested in historicizing the structural conditions within which specific groups become the focus of anxiety about social purity and hence the target of rhetorics of pollution and persecution. He argues that the Jews, a despised minority, gain increasing economic and political power in the emerging states of the High Middle Ages.[40] They therefore become the targets of pollution anxiety and are attacked by Christians in an effort to reinforce the social structure. It is here, he suggests, that we may find the transformation of a tolerant to an intolerant Middle Ages, and the origins of the persecuting society in which we still dwell.

Historicized or not, these models are of limited utility in explaining the workings of a multiethnic society like that of the Crown of Aragon because their end point is the obliteration of difference. Even independent of a progressive historical narrative, the scapegoating paradigm identifies difference only in order to destroy it in the quest for ultimate unity. The inherent teleology here is heightened in a historicized version like Moore's, where scapegoating is married to an eschatological account of intolerance that terminates in exterminations medieval and modern.[41] Such a model is impoverishing in some obvious ways. First, with difference reduced to a transient stage on the way to identity, it becomes impossible to understand its importance in a (profoundly corporatist) society like that of the Crown of Aragon. Second, the model can recognize as

---

(trans. of *Des choses cachées*), pp. 26–27: "There is no telling what insignificant reasons will lead mimetic hostility to converge on one particular victim rather than on another. . . . The community satisfies its rage against an arbitrary victim."

[38] I am addressing Moore here because pollution and scapegoating are central to his model of the origins of a persecuting society. He himself, however, is not concerned with the plague, which postdates the period covered by his *Persecuting Society*. Ginzburg's adoption of the concept of scapegoating is less systematic than Moore's, though also problematic. See chap. 4, above.

[39] See Moore, *Persecuting Society*, chap. 3, "Purity and Danger," here pp. 100–101. D. Nelkin and S. Gilman stress that the location of blame for disease reflects "the line between insiders and outsiders, the 'pure' and the 'polluted,' the coreligionists and the sources of pollution." See their "Placing Blame for Devastating Disease," *Social Research* 55 (1988): 361–378, here p. 368.

[40] Whether this "power" of the inferior group is real or perceived is an issue not addressed by Moore, nor is he concerned with power other than the material sort. Thus he does not consider the "theological power" of Jews for a faith sprung in some sense *ex stirpe judaeorum*, and he does not see Christian "anxiety of influence" as a type of pollution fear.

[41] Cf. the conclusion to Moore's *Persecuting Society*, "The Enemy Destroyed," pp. 146–153.

significant only violence that seeks to destroy difference. It tells us little about everyday violence, about the limited and episodic nature of most attacks, or about the role of violence in the maintenance of minority-majority relations. Its explanatory potential is equally limited with respect to those cataclysmic events that it does recognize as significant, since it removes them from the contexts of more routine violences in which they are embedded and reads them in the light of linear narratives of extermination.

A great many aspects of the massacres that accompanied the plague make sense only if we reconnect them to the sublunary world of context, contingency, and functionality so resolutely ignored by the sorts of models described above. Consider that even in the first shock of 1348, the heightened fears of pollution elicited by the plague functioned within structures far more local than those addressed by traditional narratives, and followed lines of (quite transient) political loyalties. When the plague struck, the Crown of Aragon was embroiled in a bitter civil war, perhaps the most highly pitched moment in a long dispute among nobility, king, and municipalities. (The plague may even be said to have saved the king, for the *Unión* of Valencia that held him prisoner permitted his flight when the epidemic began.) Within this polarized geography of loyalty and rebellion, it is striking that the plague provoked violence against Jews only in the region most loyal to the Crown: in the promonarchical towns of Catalonia. Wherever antiroyalist forces had the upper hand, no Jews were attacked.[42] Context affected violence at even more local levels, in factors intrinsic to particular towns. In Cervera, the physical boundaries of the *call* had been disputed since the time of James II, and many Jews lived outside the Jewish quarter, among Christians.[43] Tàrrega, on the other hand, was a town split by faction. The bailiff of Tàrrega himself, as head of one faction, seems to have led the attack on the Jews. The attack and the inquest that followed mired the town in feud and vendetta for the next two years, with the faction of accusers and their witnesses opposing the accused.[44]

[42] Which is not to say that the armies of the union did not pillage Jews during their military campaigns against the royalists. They did, for example, sack the Jewish aljama of Morvedre, but this attack preceded the plague and had nothing to do with fears of pollution. See Zurita, *Anales de la Corona de Aragón*, 4:164 (8.33), sub 1348. Zurita did note that the civil war sharpened anxieties about Muslims, both Granadan and native, since it was feared that they might take advantage of the civil war to attack Christendom.

[43] Conflicts over the lack of segregation in Cervera date from the beginning of the century and continued into the 1340s. The account given by Duran, *Referències documentals*, pp. 16–17, is inadequate. See, among dozens of additional documents, ACA:C 173:163r (1321/7/6); 519:98v–99r (1328/5/9); 462:201r–v (1333/6/9). This may have contributed to tensions in the town. In 1346, at the request of the Jewish aljama, King Peter ordered the friar Pere dez Quo transferred from the convent at Cervera because he was agitating the populace against the Jews. See ACA:C 632:42v (1346/3/17), published in A. Rubió y Lluch, *Documents per l'historia de la cultura catalan mig-eval*, 2 vols. (Barcelona, 1921), 2:81.

[44] For the civil strife that erupted in Tàrrega over the murder of the Jews see López, "Una consequencia," pp. 116–117.

Consider, too, that far from severing cataclysm from stability, contemporaries (especially Jewish ones) spent a good deal of time discussing the ties that bound plague massacre to more traditional forms of violence like Holy Week riots. Some feared that the heightened violence of "sacrifice" during time of plague might spill over to its more ritualized Holy Week mode. At the request of the Jews, the king wrote to officials in Barcelona shortly before Holy Week 1349 that they should be especially vigilant that year, in light of the recent riots.[45] Indeed, initially these attacks may have been more violent than before the plague. In Jaca during Holy Week 1350, for example, a Christian guarding the Jewish quarter was killed by rioters. In Valencia that same year a *sagione* of the criminal justice was injured by a stone.[46] This assimilation of the two types of violence, cataclysmic and annual, to each other is implicit in the formulation chosen by the Jewish aljama of Teruel in its appeal of July 20, 1348, for enclosure and fortification. The aljama did not mention plague-related violence in its request. It stressed instead the danger from "injuries, violences, and offenses" aimed at Jews each Holy Week.[47] Similarly, the accord of 1354 followed its complaint that the Jews were stoned at every outbreak of plague with a criticism of "those more violent among the populace and their followers who think they are doing good work when they build towers and platforms around [the Jews] for Easter" in order to stone them.[48]

Such testimony serves to remind us that, even in cataclysm, we have not left the world of Holy Week riots. In that world the fears of pollution and the expiatory sacrifices ritually expressed in those more moderate events had been constrained and latent alternatives to a normative working equilibrium of coexistence. Now sacrifice (not excision) became a matter of urgent necessity for the survival of a social order beset by plague. The ritualized gestures of Holy Week

[45] ACA:C 654:128v–129r (1349/2/26), urging the leading men and ecclesiastics of Barcelona to defend the Jews with extra care, lest Holy Week invasions lead to deaths. The document is published in Baer, *Die Juden* vol. 1, no. 240, pp. 333–334.

[46] For events in Jaca, ACA:C 661:8v–9r. In Valencia the son of the deceased royal bailiff was a participant in the attack. See ACA:C 1064:80v–81r. There were, of course, also Holy Week riots in Girona. López, "Una consequencia," pp. 126–131, interprets all these events as evidence of increased anti-Semitism caused by the plague.

[47] ACA:C 887:37r, published by López, "Una consequencia," no. 4, pp. 323–324. Many Jews in Teruel lived scattered among Christians, and the enclosure of the aljama would probably have been opposed both by some of these Jews and by Christians living in predominantly Jewish areas, as it was in other towns in the Crown. B. Leroy, "Le royaume de Navarre et les juifs aux XIVe et XVe siècles: entre l'accueil et la tolerance," *Sefarad* 38 (1978): 261–292, here pp. 282 f., documents the conflicts occasioned by the enclosure of the Jewish quarter of Pamplona after a massacre. The conflicts of interest generated among both Jews and Christians by attempts to segregate and enclose Jewish neighborhoods (attempts sometimes promoted by the governing bodies of Jewish aljamas, not by Christian authorities) deserve further study. In any event, the arguments produced by the aljama of Teruel should be read in the context of such conflicts.

[48] Item 3 of the Barcelona accords of 1354, on which see n. 29 above.

riots needed to be heightened in the "sacrificial crisis" of 1348.[49] This was not the first time in Christian history that disease was cured by sacrifice. In the previous chapter we saw how the destruction of Jerusalem—the sacrificial crisis at the foundation of Jewish-Christian relations in the diaspora—was triggered by the leprosy God had inflicted upon the emperor Vespasian. Vespasian regained his health by avenging Christ's death. Some thirteen centuries later the coming of the plague as a divine punishment for the toleration of Christ's killers in Christian society was thought to demand a similar expiation: an expiation achieved by transforming the controlled mimesis of Holy Week stonings into the mimetic hysteria of the 1348 massacres.[50] But although they differed in stridency and despair, Holy Week riots and plague massacres were alike in that they were both part of the same violent mechanisms by which the Christian majority articulated the terms of coexistence and made it possible. Both partook of the double register of violence identified in the previous chapters; both were meant as much to reinforce the social order of this multireligious community as to shatter it. In the fourteenth-century Crown of Aragon, the violent definition and demarcation of difference reinforced the unity of various groups within the society at the same time that it maintained that society's potential for heterogeneity.

Even in times of plague and massacre, violence was a central and systemic aspect of the coexistence of majority and minorities. *Convivencia* was predicated upon violence; it was not its peaceful antithesis. Violence drew its meaning from coexistence, not in opposition to it. To call plague massacres (or Holy Week riots, miscegenation accusations, and the like) "intolerant" is therefore fundamentally to misconstrue the terms in which coexistence was articulated in medieval Iberia. Similarly, attempts to periodize through violence, to divide the medieval world into opposing categories of tolerance and intolerance, mutual interest versus mutual hostility, open society or closed, is to miss the dependence of the one upon the other.[51]

.   .   .   .   .

This book ends because it must. It ends with the plague of 1348 because to go further would require years of additional research. Still ahead are events of consequence: 1391, the largest slaughter of Jews in Iberian history, with thousands

---

[49] See chap. 7 for a brief discussion of "anti-structure" and for definition of the terms "ritual sacrifice" and "sacrificial crisis."

[50] See Girard, *Des choses cachées*, pp. 36, 46. (*Things Hidden*, pp. 22 and 30. E.g., p. 30: "There is no paradox in a disease that cures a disease. It is a question of augmenting the forces of destructive mimesis in order to channel them toward the sacrificial resolution.") See also his *To Double Business Bound: Essays on Literature, Mimesis and Anthropology* (Baltimore, MD, 1978), p. 136, on plague as a crisis of differentiation.

[51] See introduction.

killed and thousands more converted;[52] the later expulsions of hundreds of thousands of Jews and Muslims from Spain. . . . For me, at least, it is increasingly difficult to write of these events as symbolic products of a system of coexistence. So many men and women, thrust forth from their refuges by hands they had trusted, dragged in terror to have their throats slit by jeering, cheering mobs exulting in the unstoppable flow of their blood—what can their deaths have to do with *convivencia*? Confronted by such moments, one is tempted to embrace tolerance as a comparative ("this period was more tolerant than that one"), and to argue that 1348 represents a paradigm shift, an explosive transformation of ritualized violence in whose wake there emerges a world where the meanings and uses of violence are irrevocably altered, pushed toward univocal hatred, and leading with ever greater ease to extermination.

Such an embrace of linear narratives of escalating hatred is justified by despair, but it makes no better sense when applied to the period after the plague than it did in the period before. Of course this is not to say that events of the plague's magnitude did not change the possible meanings of violent acts like Holy Week riots. Few analysts interested in the relationship between symbolic systems and material or social structures would hesitate to ask what effects a change in the latter has on the former, or deny the importance of linear narratives in describing these effects. The annual Swazi Ncwala ceremonies provide a prominent example from the anthropological literature, since their historicization is now something of an industry in African studies. Originally a rather obscure fertility festival, in precolonial times the ceremony was given new prominence by King Mswati (r. 1839?–1865) in the aftermath of his suppression of a revolt, and represented a reaffirmation of the king's ideological and economic hegemony. As famously analyzed by Max Gluckman, later colonial versions of the same ceremony were ritual enactments of social conflict that increased group unity and stability. Finally, when performed on the eve of independence in 1966, the ceremony was interpreted as a manifestation of nationalism, demanding participation in a traditional idiom as a sign of allegiance and identity. The point is obvious. The interpretive field of symbolic acts, ritual or otherwise, is shaped and constrained by historical change.[53]

[52]The lack of an exhaustive study of these massacres is perhaps the greatest remaining gap in the historiography of Iberian Jewry. The sheer mass of documentation constitutes the greatest impediment: hundreds of thousands of documents survive for the period in the ACA alone. Jaume Riera i Sans has, however, published preliminary results from his years of research on the subject of 1391. See his "Els avalots del 1391," as well as his "Los tumultos contra las juderías de la Corona de Aragón en 1391," *Cuadernos de Historia: Anejos de la Revista Hispania* 8 (1977): 213–225. See also P. Wolff, "The 1391 Pogrom in Spain: Social Crisis or Not?" *Past and Present* 50 (1971): 4–18.

[53]See, in order of chronological focus: P. Bonner, *Kings, Commoners and Concessionaires: The Evolution and Dissolution of the Nineteenth-Century Swazi State* (Cambridge, 1983), pp. 48–49; M. Gluckman, *Order and Rebellion in Tribal Africa* (New York, 1963), pp. 110–136; H. Kuper, "A Royal Ritual in a Changing Political Context," *Cahiers d'études africaines* 12 (1972): 593–615; and for a synthesis and rereading of the problem and the ceremony, Lincoln, *Discourse and the Construc-*

It is safe to assume that the plague wrought many such changes on structures of power within the Crown, though we know little about them.[54] Some of these doubtless affected the ways in which arguments (violent or otherwise) about religious difference acquired meaning and "usefulness."[55] It seems, for example, that the demographic crisis which followed the plague affected ideologies of seigneury and serfdom. Lords, reacting to shortages of labor, attempted to define the servile status and restrict the freedoms of their peasants more sharply than had previously been the case, and met sharper resistance.[56] Muslims in particular suffered a degradation of status, and it is in this period that the image of the Muslim as exemplary (because compliant and exploitable) peasant solidified.[57] Such changes clearly affected the potential for violence. Only in their aftermath, for example, could Christian peasant rebellion against the seigneurial order meaningfully target Muslim peasants, as it did in the *Germanías* ("brotherhoods") of Valencia in 1521.[58] In cities, it appears that the plague sharpened differences in wealth, especially between lower classes and governing elites, and contributed to the emergence of a municipal rentier class increasingly dependent on interest from loans made to Jews and repaid by Jewish lending activity in rural hinterlands. These changes have been proposed as explanations for the 1391 riots in Girona, and they help to explain the predominant role of rural peasants in those attacks, as well as the relatively energetic attempts of municipal elites to protect the Jews.[59] It is even possible that the plague contrib-

---

tion of Society, pp. 53–74. For the most recent developments, see the forthcoming article by A. Kanduza, "The Revival of Incwala Ceremonies among the Ngoni of Zambia" (consulted in manuscript, 1992: my thanks to A. Odhiambo for the reference). By interpretive field I mean both that of contemporary participants and that of later analysts.

[54] The choice of the plague as linchpin of analysis here is to a certain extent arbitrary, since other events may have been equally significant. For example, contemporary Jews seeking to explain the massacres of 1391 considered the lengthy and ruinous "War of the Two Peters" between Castile and the Crown of Aragon a much more important factor in the deterioration of their position than the plague. See, e.g., the comment of Re'uven ben Nissim of Girona, published in A. Hershman, *Rab Ishaq Perfet* (in Hebrew) (Jerusalem, 1956), pp. 124–125, and translated into Catalan by Riera, "Els avalots del 1391," p. 156.

[55] I am not claiming that such changes were absolute. At any given performance interpretive responses could vary widely among spectators, a basic point of reader response criticism. But it is equally true that the same range of responses was not available to a "reader" of childrens' stonings in 1331 as to one in 1392.

[56] For the increasing restriction of freedoms, see Freedman, *The Origins of Peasant Servitude*, pp. 166–178. On polarization, Cuvillier, "Les communautés rurales," p. 94. These studies focus on Catalonia, where attempts to restrict Christian peasants were sharpest. The phenomenon differed in degree elsewhere in the Crown, but not in valence.

[57] See chap. 1.

[58] See introduction.

[59] For class polarization and conflict in Jewish communities, see chap. 1 and chap. 5. For Christian communities see especially Guilleré's work on Girona, *Girona al segle XIV*, 2:247–301. For his proposal that this polarization led to 1391: pp. 294–301. On the predominance of peasants among the attackers, see, inter alia, AHCG, Ordinacions dels Jurats, Lligall 7 (1389–1394), vol.

uted to changes in Catalano-Aragonese ideologies of kingship, ideologies with important implications for the meanings of violence against minorities, as we saw in Part One.[60]

None of these shifts, however, severed the connections between cataclysm and stability, or replaced the double register of violence with a univocal insistence on the extermination of minorities. Indeed, the affinities between Holy Week riots and massacre in 1391 are as striking as those in 1348. In Valencia, the killings and conversions of 1391 began in much the same way as Holy Week riots, with some fifty children marching with a flag (a white cross on a blue background) in procession around the Jewish quarter.[61] The same is true of an abortive attack on the Muslims of Valencia in 1399, when some twelve children on donkeys circled the Muslim quarter bearing a flag, or of the pillaging of the same aljama in 1455, which began when a procession of children celebrating the ascension of Alfonso de Borja to the papal throne scuffled with Mudejar children at the *moreria*'s gates over their unwillingness to genuflect and began chanting "let them convert or die."[62] Nor do the shifts seem to have given rhetorics of intolerance a new and transcendent virulence. Though in the years immediately following the plague Jewish communities expressed their worry that Holy Week ritual might now deform more readily into massacre, what is striking is how rarely this occurred. Very little differentiates the level of violence of

---

1391–1392, fol. 8r (1391/8/10), transcribed in J. de Chia, *Bandos y bandoleros en Gerona: Apuntes históricos desde el siglo XIV hasta mediados del XVII* (Girona, 1888), 1:174 f.

[60]Peter the Ceremonious and his son John I were increasingly attracted to French monarchical models and articulated more self-consciously than previous monarchs their special relations with divinity. Unfortunately I know of no work on this topic. For Peter's self-presentation, see his *Crònica*, passim, and J. Hillgarth's introduction to M. Hillgarth's translation, *Pere III of Catalonia*, 1:76–82. An increasingly sacral self-presentation is evident in royal coronation ceremonies. See Palacios, *La coronación de los reyes de Aragón*, pp. 245 ff. (compare, for example, Peter's ceremonial of ca. 1336 with that of 1353, or with that of his son John). King John even adopted the French title of *dauphin* for his firstborn in 1387. On the *dalfí* see J. Riera i Sans, "El dalfinat de Girona (1387–1388)," *Annals de l'Institut d'Estudis Gironins* 29 (1987): 105–128, here p. 107. As Infant, John occasionally adopted French techniques of self-representation vis-à-vis Jews, as in his prosecution of the aljama of Huesca on charges of Host desecration. As with the French case discussed in chap. 2, such actions raised much-needed revenues, but at the cost of creating space for ancient though heretofore little-used rhetorics of accusation against the Crown. For conflict between King Peter (well aware of this double bind) and his son on this subject, see J. Miret y Sans, "El procés de les hosties contra.ls jueues d'Osca en 1377," *Anuari de l'Institut d'Estudis Catalans* 4 (1911–1912): 59–80.

[61]Rubio, *Epistolari de la València medieval*, no. 103, pp. 269–271, transcribing AMV, LM 5, fols. 19r–20r, dated 1391/7/9. See also no. 104, transcribing fols. 23r–24r. According to municipal officials, the violence began after the Jews had closed the gates, trapping some of the children in the Jewish quarter, and the cry went up that the Jews were killing the children. Interestingly, the municipal officials used the term "pestilence" to refer to this outbreak of violent discord. Compare above and n. 36, on disease and internal discord.

[62]See Narbona, *Pueblo, poder y sexo*, p. 56. For the events of 1455, see Ruzafa, " 'Façen-se Cristians los moros o muyren!' " pp. 87–110, here p. 91–92. In both 1391 and 1455 municipal officials invoked the role of children as evidence that the attacks were not deliberate acts of adult rebellion.

the Holy Week riots that followed the plague from those preceding it: the Girona Holy Week riots of 1389 had more in common with the riots of 1331 than with the massacres of 1391 in that town. And successive waves of plague did not revive the violence. A century later, Jews could even become participants in processions to forestall plague, rather than being their targets.[63]

In short, there were clearly moments, such as 1348 and 1391, when rituals of violence were transformed in meaning, manifestation, and effect. We can even say that those moments indelibly altered the world in which they occurred, refiguring the field of meaning of their ritual lexicon. And yet such moments were themselves tightly bound in time and space. They were preceded, succeeded, surrounded, and structured by the kinds of violence upon which this book has focused: quotidian, strategic, controlled, and stabilizing. We cannot understand medieval violence against minorities if we study only moments of cataclysm and ignore this basic fact. Progressive narratives of persecution that focus on outbreaks of mass violence such as those of 1320, 1348, or 1391 repress the "abnormality" of such moments and ignore both their continuities and discontinuities with what precedes and follows them.[64] Such events were abnormal in that they shattered the symbolic vessels of the status quo and, with a terrible but transient clarity, revealed within them particular, sometimes obscure and minoritarian, visions of sacred and social history. These visions partook of the past and of the future, and transformed both, but not in a teleological way. For this reason the stringing together, no matter how elegant, of such episodes into a *longue durée* of persecuting mentalities can only leave unexplained the lengthy periods of complex, seemingly stable interaction that separate and produce them. Perhaps this is not so far from what Walter Benjamin meant when he wrote:

> History rests collected in a focal point, as formerly in the utopian images of thinkers. The elements of the end condition are not present as formless tendencies of progress but instead are embedded in every present as endangered, condemned, and ridiculed creations and ideas.[65]

[63] In 1449 the Jews of Seville marched in a procession asking for divine intercession to stop the plague, with the support of the archbishop of Seville or his officials. ASV, Reg. Vat. 389, fols. 136r–137r, published in Simonsohn, *Apostolic See*, pp. 930–932, no. 773.

[64] By abnormality I do not mean that the preconditions for their occurrence were not always present in normative conditions, but that, to use a linguistic metaphor, their articulation does not conform to the rules of conventional discourse. In this sense they are liminal.

[65] The quotation is from Benjamin's inaugural address to the Free Student League of Berlin in 1914, published in his *Gesammelte Schriften*, ed. R. Tieddemann and H. Schweppenhäuser, 7 vols. (Frankfurt, 1972–1989), here vol. 2, pt. 1, p. 75. The translation is from R. Wolin, *Walter Benjamin: An Aesthetic of Redemption* (New York, 1982), p. 49. Wolin discusses this conception of historical time on pp. 48–63. Of course Benjamin was speaking before the Holocaust, which transformed the stakes in making such a statement: "Auschwitz has changed the basis for the continuity of the conditions of life within history" (J. Habermas, *Eine Art Schadensabwicklung* [Frankfurt, 1987], p. 163). Indeed one of the purposes of this book has been to explore the consequences of this change for the historiography of premodern minorities.

BIBLIOGRAPHY OF WORKS CITED

T HIS bibliography contains full citations for printed works cited. Citations to biblical, Talmudic, Qur'ānic, and some Late Roman legal texts are omitted here, since they are given in the notes in standard abbreviated format. References to manuscript sources are given only in the notes. Additional sources may be found in the excellent bibliographies currently being compiled on Iberian religious minorities, such as that of Jaume Riera i Sans in the journal *Calls* 1–4 (1986–1990) on the Jews of Catalonia, or the ongoing bibliography of Iberian Islam begun by M. de Epalza, M. J. Paternina, and A. Couton in *Moros y moriscos en el Levante peninsular: Introducción bibliográfica* (Alicante, 1983), and continued in the pages of the journal *Sharq al-Andalus: Estudios Arabes*, no. 1 forward.

Abou-Zeid, A. "Honour and Shame among the Bedouins of Egypt" In *Honour and Shame: The Values of Mediterranean Society*, edited by J. Peristiany, pp. 245–259. London, 1965.

Abraham bar Selomoh (of Torrutiel). *Sefer ha-Qabbalah*. Translated by Y. Moreno Koch. In *Dos crónicas hispanohebreas del siglo XV*. Barcelona, 1992.

Abu'l-Ḥasan al-Mukhtār ibn al-Ḥasan Ibn Buṭlān. *Risāla fi Shirā al-Raqīq*. Edited by ʿAbd al-Salām Hārūn. Cairo, 1373/1954, pp. 354–358, 371–378. English translation in B. Lewis, *Islam*, vol. 2, *Religion and Society*. Oxford, 1987, pp. 243–251.

Abulafia, D. *A Mediterranean Emporium: The Catalan Kingdom of Majorca*. Cambridge, 1994.

Abumalham, M. "La conversíon según formularios notariales andalusíes: valoracíon de la legalidad de la conversíon de Maimónides." *Miscelánea de Estudios Arabes y Hebráicos* 34 (1985): 71–84.

Actas del III Congreso Internacional "Encuentro de las Tres Culturas." Edited by C. Carrete Parrondo. Toledo, 1988.

Actas del IV Congreso Internacional "Encuentro de las Tres Culturas." Edited by C. Carrete Parrondo. Toledo, 1988.

Actas del I Congreso Nacional de Fiestas de Moros y Cristianos (Villena 1974). Alacant, 1974.

Actas del I Simposio de Mudejarismo. Teruel, 1981.

Actas del III Simposio Internacional de Mudejarismo. Madrid, 1986.

Actas del V Simposio Internacional de Mudejarismo. Teruel, 1991.

African Political Systems. Edited by M. Fortes and E. Evans-Pritchard. London, 1940.

Aggression and Violence. Edited by P. Marsh and A. Campbell. Oxford, 1982.

Aizenberg, E. "*Una judía muy fermosa*: The Jewess as Sex Object in Medieval Spanish Literature and Lore." *La Corónica* 12 (1984): 187–194.

Alcuini epistolae. Edited by E. Dümmler. *MGH, Ep. Karolini*, vol. 2, 1895.

Alexander, P. *The Byzantine Apocalyptic Tradition*. Edited by D. deF. Abrahamse. Berkeley, 1985.

Alfonso de Cordoba. *Epistola et regimen de pestilentia*. Edited by K. Sudhoff, "Epistola et regimen Alphontii Cordubensis de pestilentia." *Archiv für Geschichte der Medizin* 3 (1909): 223–226.

Alford, V. *Pyrenean Festivals: Calender Customs, Music and Magic, Drama and Dance*. London, 1937.

Allmand, C. *The Hundred Years War: England and France at War c. 1300- c. 1450*. Cambridge, 1988.

Alphandéry, P. "Les croisades des enfants." *Revue de l'histoire des religions* 73 (1916): 259–282.

Alphandéry, P., and A. Dupront. *La Chrétienté et l'idée de croisade*. Vol. 2. Paris, 1959.

Amades, J. *Customari Català el curs de l'any*. 5 vols. 1950. Reprint, Barcelona, 1989.

———. *Las danzas de Moros y Cristianos*. Valencia, 1966.

Amador de los Ríos, J. *Historia social, politica y religiosa de los judíos de España y Portugal*. 2 vols. Madrid, 1875. Buenos Aires, 1943.

Amalric Auger. *Septima vita Joannis XXII*. In E. Baluze, *Vitae paparum Avenionensium*, edited by G. Mollat, 1:191–193. Paris, 1914.

Anderson, P. *In the Tracks of Historical Materialism*. Chicago, 1984.

Anti-Semitism in Times of Crisis. Edited by S. Gilman and S. Katz. New York, 1991.

Arendt, H. *Eichman in Jerusalem*. New York, 1963.

Ariño Villarroya, A. *Festes, rituals i creences*. Valencia, 1988.

Arnau de Vilanova. "Allocutio christiani, de hiis, que conveniunt homini secundum propriam dignitatem creature rationalis, ad inclitum dominum tertium Fredericum Trinacrie regem illustrem." Edited by J. Perarnau i Espelt, "*L'Allocutio Christini . . .* d'Arnau de Vilanova: Edició i estudi del text," *Arxiu de Textos Catalans Antics* 11 (1992): 1–135.

Arribas Palau, A. *La Conquista de Cerdeña por Jaime II de Aragón*. Barcelona, 1952.

Arrizabalaga, J. "Facing the Black Death: Perceptions and Reactions of University Medical Practitioners." In *Practical Medicine from Salerno to the Black Death*, edited by L. García-Ballester et al., pp. 237–288. Cambridge, 1994.

Asher ben Yeḥiel. *She'elot u-Teshuvot le-Harav Rabenu Asher ben Yeḥiel*. New York, 1954.

Asín Palacios, M. "Un tratado morisco de polèmica contra los judíos." In *Mélanges Hartwig Derenbourg*, pp. 343–366. Paris, 1909. Reprinted in *Obras escogidas*, 2:247–273. Madrid, 1948.

Assis, Y. T. "The Jews of Aragon under James II (1291–1327)." Ph.D. diss., Hebrew University, 1981 (in Hebrew).

———. *The Jews of Santa Coloma de Queralt*. Jerusalem, 1988.

———. "Juifs de France réfugiés en Aragon (XIIIe–XIVe siècles)." *RdÉJ* 142 (1983): 285–322.

———. "Sexual Behaviour in Mediaeval Hispano-Jewish Society." In *Jewish History: Essays in Honour of Chimen Abramsky*, edited by A. Rapaport-Albert and S. Zipperstein, pp. 25–59. London, 1988.

Atti del I° congresso storico Liguria-Catalogna (ottobre 1969). Bordighera, 1974.

Augustine. *De civitate Dei*. CC vols. 47–48. PL 41.13–804.

———. *Enarrationes in Psalmos*. CC vols. 38–40. PL 36.67–1028.

———. *Sermones*. PL 38–39.

———. *Tractatus adversus Judeos*. PL 42.51–64.

Aureum opus regalium privilegiorum civitatis et regni valentie. Edited by L. Alanya. Valencia, 1515. Facsimile edition, Valencia, 1972.

Babcock, B. *The Reversible World: Symbolic Inversion in Art and Society.* Ithaca, NY, 1978.

Bachrach, B. *Early Medieval Jewish Policy in Western Europe.* Minneapolis, 1977.

Baer, F./Y. *Galut.* Translated by R. Warshow. Lanham, MD, 1988.

———. *A History of the Jews in Christian Spain.* 2 vols. Philadelphia, 1978.

———. *Die Juden im christlichen Spanien.* 2 vols. Berlin, 1936. Reprint, London, 1970.

———. *Studien zur Geschichte der Juden im Königreich Aragonien während des 13. und 14. Jahrhunderts.* Berlin, 1913.

———. *Yisrael ba-ʿamim.* Jerusalem, 1955.

Bagby, A. "Alfonso X el Sabio compara moros y judíos." *Romanische Forschungen* 82 (1970): 578–583.

———. "The Jew in the *Cantigas* of Alfonso X el Sabio." *Speculum* 46 (1971): 670–688.

———. "The Moslem in the *Cantigas* of Alfonso X el Sabio." *Kentucky Romance Quarterly* 20 (1973): 173–207.

Bakhtin, M. *Rabelais and His World.* Bloomington, IN, 1984.

Balañà i Abadia, P. *Els Musulmans a Catalunya (713–1153).* Barcelona, 1993.

Baldwin, J. *The Government of Philip Augustus.* Berkeley, 1986.

Baluze, E. *Vitae paparum avenionensium.* Vol. 1. Edited by G. Mollat. Paris, 1914.

Barber, M. "Lepers, Jews and Moslems: The Plot to Overthrow Christendom in 1321." *History* 66 (1981): 1–17.

———. "The Pastoureaux of 1320." *Journal of Ecclesiastical History* 32 (1981): 143–166.

Barceló Torres, M. *Minoría islámicas en el país valenciano.* Valencia, 1984.

Barlow, F. "The King's Evil." *English Historical Review* 95 (1980): 3–27.

Basáñez, M. B. *La aljama sarracena de Huesca en el siglo XIV.* Barcelona, 1989.

Bauchau, B. "Science et racisme: les juifs, la lèpre et la peste." *Stanford French Review* 13 (1989): 21–35.

Beaune, C. "Messianesimo regio e messianesimo popolare in Francia nel XIII secolo." In *Poteri carismatici e informali: chiesa e società medioevali,* edited by A. Paravicini Bagliani and A. Vauchez, pp. 114–136. Palermo, 1992.

Beauvoir, S. de. *The Second Sex.* Translated by H. Parshley. New York, 1974.

Benjamin, W. *Gesammelte Schriften.* Edited by R. Tieddemann and H. Schweppenhäuser. 7 vols. Frankfurt, 1972–1989.

Bériac, F. "Comment les Bearnais consideraient les Crestians vers 1450–1500." In *Minorités et marginaux en France méridionale et dans la peninsule Ibérique (VIIe–XVIIIe siècles) (Actes du colloque de Pau, 27–29 mai, 1984),* pp. 55–70. Paris, 1986.

———. *Des lépreux aux cagots: recherches sur les sociétés marginales en Aquitaine médiévale.* Bordeaux, 1990.

———. *Histoire des lépreux au Moyen Age.* Paris, 1988.

———. "La persécution des lépreux dans la France méridionale en 1321." *Le Moyen Age* 93, no. 2 (1987): 203–221.

———. "Le vocabulaire de la lèpre dans l'ouest des pays de Langue d'Oc." *Annales du Midi* 96 (1984): 331–355.

Bériou, N., and F.-O. Touati. *Voluntate Dei Leprosus: les lépreux entre conversion et exclusion aux XIIème et XIIIème siècles.* Spoleto, 1991.

Berk, S. *Year of Crisis, Year of Hope: Russian Jewry and the Pogroms of 1881–1882.* Westport, CT, 1985.

Bernard Gui. *Tertia vita Joannis XXII.* In E. Baluze, *Vitae paparum Avenionensium,* edited by G. Mollat, 1:161–163. Paris, 1914.

Berner, L. "On Western Shores: The Jews of Barcelona during the Reign of Jaume I, 'el Conqueridor,' 1213–1276." Ph.D. diss., University of California, Los Angeles, 1986.

Bertran i Roigé, P. "Conflictes socials a Cervera, segons el llibre del batlle Antoni de Cabrera (1356–1357)." *Miscel.lània Cerverina* 6 (1988): 53–70.

———. "Els jueus en els llibres de batlle i cort de Cervera (1354–1357)." *Ilerda* 44 (1983): 189–205.

———. "El llibre del batlle reial de Lleida Ramon de Carcassona (1366–1369)." In *Miscel.lània Homenatge al Professor Salvador Roca i Lletjós*, pp. 157–186. Lleida, 1981.

Bettelheim, B. *The Uses of Enchantment*. New York, 1975.

Biale, D. *Power and Powerlessness in Jewish History*. New York, 1986.

Biraben, J. *Les hommes et la peste en France et dans les pays européens et méditerranéens*. 2 vols. Paris, 1975.

Bisson, T. *Fiscal Accounts of Catalonia under the Early Count-Kings (1151–1213)*. 2 vols. Berkeley, 1984.

———. *The Medieval Crown of Aragon: A Short History*. Oxford, 1986.

Blasco Martínez, A. "El adulterio de Doña Lumbre, judía de Zaragoza." *Michael* 11 (1989): 99–120.

———. "Avance de estudio de un caso de adulterio en la aljama de Zaragoza (siglo XIV)." *Proceedings of the Ninth World Congress of Jewish Studies, Division B*. Vol. 1, *The History of the Jewish People*, pp. 105–112. Jerusalem, 1986.

———. *La Judería de Zaragoza en el siglo XIV*. Zaragoza, 1988.

———. "Los judíos de Zaragoza en el siglo XIV: su evolución social." In *Minorités et marginaux en France méridionale et dans la peninsule Ibérique (VIIe–XVIIIe siècles) (Actes du colloque de Pau, 27–29 mai, 1984)*, pp. 177–201. Paris, 1986.

———. "Notarios mudéjares de Aragón (siglos XIV-XV)." In *Aragón en la Edad Media* 10–11 (1993): 109–133. (*Homenaje a la profesora emérita María Luisa Ledesma Rubio*.)

———. "La producción y comercialización del vino entre los judíos de Zaragoza (siglo XIV)." *Anuario de estudios medievales* 19 (1989): 405–449.

Bloch, M. *Feudal Society*. 2 vols. Chicago, 1961.

———. *The Historian's Craft*. New York, 1953.

———. *The Royal Touch: Sacred Monarchy and Scrofula in England and France*. Translated by J. E. Anderson. London, 1973.

Blumenkranz, B. "Augustin et les juifs, Augustin et le judaïsme." *Recherches Augustiniennes* 1 (1958): 225–241.

———. *Die Judenpredigt Augustins: Ein Beitrag zur Geschichte der jüdisch-christlichen Beziehungen in den ersten Jahrhunderten*. Basel, 1946.

———. *Le Juif medieval au miroir de l'art Chrétien*. Paris, 1966.

Bofarull, F. de. "Jaime I y los judíos." In *Congrés d'Historia de la Corona d'Aragó, dedicat al rey en Jaume I i la seva época*, pp. 818–943. Barcelona, 1913.

———. "Los judíos malsines." *Boletín de la Real Academia de Buenas Letras de Barcelona* 6 (1911): 207–216.

Bofarull, M. de. *El registro del merino de Zaragoza el caballero don Gil Tarin, 1291–1312*. Zaragoza, 1889.

Bofarull Mascaró, P. *Documentos literarios en la antigua lengua catalana (siglos XIV y XV)*. CoDoIn, vol. 13. Barcelona, 1857.

Boix Pociello, J. "Montclús: una aljama jueva a la capçalera del Cinca." *Occidens* 1 (1985): 19–23. (*Homenatge a J. Lladonosa*.)

Bonfil, R. *Jewish Life in Renaissance Italy*. Berkeley, 1994.

Bonner, P. *Kings, Commoners and Concessionaires: The Evolution and Dissolution of the Nineteenth-Century Swazi State*. Cambridge, 1983.

Boswell, J. *Christianity, Social Tolerance and Homosexuality: Gay People in Western Europe from the Beginning of the Christian Era to the Fourteenth Century*. Chicago, 1980.

———. *The Kindness of Strangers: The Abandonment of Children in Western Europe from Late Antiquity to the Renaissance*. New York, 1988.

———. *The Royal Treasure: Muslim Communities under the Crown of Aragon in the Fourteenth Century*. New Haven, 1977.

Boulay, J. du. "The Blood: Symbolic Relationships between Descent, Marriage, Incest Prohibitions and Spiritual Kinship in Greece." *Man*, n.s., 19 (1984): 533–556.

Bourdieu, P. *Outline of a Theory of Practice*. Translated by R. Nice. Cambridge, 1977.

———. "The Sentiment of Honour in Kabyle Society." In *Honour and Shame: The Values of a Mediterranean Society*, edited by J. Peristiany, pp. 191–243. London, 1965.

Bramon, D. *Contra moros y judíos*. Barcelona, 1986.

Brann, R. *The Compunctious Poet: Cultural Ambiguity and Hebrew Poetry in Muslim Spain*. Baltimore, 1991.

Brodman, J. *Ransoming Captives in Crusader Spain: The Order of Merced on the Christian-Islamic Frontier*. Philadelphia, 1986.

Brody, S. *The Disease of the Soul: Leprosy in Medieval Literature*. Ithaca, NY, 1974.

Broszat, M., et al. *Alltagsgeschichte der NS-Zeit: Neue Perspektive oder Trivilisierung?* Munich, 1984.

Brown, E.A.R. "Philip V, Charles IV, and the Jews of France: The Alleged Expulsion of 1322." *Speculum* 66 (1991): 294–329.

———. "Subsidy and Reform in 1321: The Accounts of Najac and the Policies of Philip V." *Traditio* 27 (1971): 399–430.

Brundage, J. "Intermarriage between Christians and Jews in Medieval Canon Law." *Jewish History* 3 (1988): 25–40.

———. *Law, Sex, and Christian Society in Medieval Europe*. Chicago, 1987.

———. "Marriage and Sexuality in the Decretals of Pope Alexander III." In *Miscellanea Rolando Bandinelli Papa Alessandro III*, edited by F. Liotta, pp. 59–83. Siena, 1986.

———. "Prostitution in the Medieval Canon Law." *Signs: Journal of Women in Culture and Society* 1 (1976): 825–845.

———. "Prostitution, Miscegenation and Sexual Purity in the First Crusade." In *Crusade and Settlement*, edited by P. Edbury, pp. 57–65. Cardiff, 1985.

———. "Rape and Marriage in the Medieval Canon Law." *Revue de Droit Canonique* 28 (1978): 62–75. (*Etudes offertes à J. Gaudemet.*)

Buc, P. "David's Adultery with Bathsheba and the Healing Power of the Capetian Kings." *Viator* 24 (1993): 101–120.

al-Bukhārī, Muḥammad bin Ismāʿīl bin al-Mughīrah. *Ṣaḥīḥ*. Edited and translated by M. Muhsin Khan. 9 vols. Beirut, n.d.

Burman, T. *Religious Polemic and the Intellectual History of the Mozarabs*. Leiden, 1994.

Burns, R. I. "The Crusade against Al-Azraq: A Thirteenth-Century Mudejar Revolt in International Perspective." *American Historical Review* 93 (1988): 80–106.

———. *Islam under the Crusaders: Colonial Survival in the Thirteenth-Century Kingdom of Valencia*. Princeton, 1973.

———. "The Language Barrier: The Problem of Bilingualism and Muslim-Christian

Interchange in the Medieval Kingdom of Valencia." In *Contributions to Mediterranean Studies*, edited by M. Vassallo, pp. 116–136. Malta, 1977.

Burns, R. I. *Medieval Colonialism: Postcrusade Exploitation of Islamic Valencia*. Princeton, 1975.

——. *Muslims, Christians, and Jews in the Crusader Kingdom of Valencia: Societies in Symbiosis*. Cambridge, 1984.

——. "Muslims in the Thirteenth Century Realms of Aragon: Interaction and Reaction." in *Muslims under Latin Rule: 1100–1300*, edited by J. M. Powell, pp. 57–102. Princeton, 1990.

——. "Renegades, Adventurers and Sharp Businessmen: The Thirteenth-Century Spaniard in the Cause of Islam." *Catholic Historical Review* 58 (1972): 341–366.

——. "Social Riots on the Christian-Moslem Frontier: Thirteenth-Century Valencia." *American Historical Review* 66 (1961): 378–400.

Bussi, E. "La condizione giuridica dei musulmani nel diritto canonico." *Rivista di storia del diritto italiano* 8 (1935): 459–494.

Butler, J. *Gender Trouble: Feminism and the Subversion of Identity*. New York, 1990.

Cabaniss, A. "Bodo-Eleazar: A Famous Jewish Convert." *Jewish Quarterly Review* 43 (1953): 313–318.

Cabestany Fort, J. "El cronicó de Guillem Mascaró: l'autor i l'obra." *Estudís Universitaris Catalans* 24 (1980): 115–122.

Cabré i Pairet, M. "Formes de cultura femenina a la Catalunya medieval." In *Més enllà del silenci: les dones a la història de Catalunya*, edited by M. Nash, pp. 31–52. Barcelona, 1988.

Caesarius of Arles. *Sermones*. Edited by G. Morin. Maretioli, 1937.

Camarena Mahiques, J. *Colección de documentos para la historia de Gandía y su comarca*. Gandía, 1959–1961.

Campillo, T. del. *Documentos históricos de Daroca y su comunidad*. Zaragoza, 1915.

Cantelar Rodríguez, F. *El matrimonio de herejes: Bifurcación del impedimentum disparis cultus y divorcio por herejía*. Salamanca, 1972.

Cantera Montenegro, E. "Actividades socio-profesionales de la mujer judía en los reinos hispanocristianos de la baja edad media." In *El trabajo de las mujeres en la edad media hispana*, edited by A. Muñoz Fernández and C. Segura Graiño, pp. 321–345. Madrid, 1988.

Cantigas de Santa María de Don Alfonso el Sabio. Edited by the Real Academia. 2 vols. Madrid, 1889.

Cantor, N. *Inventing the Middle Ages: The Lives, Works, and Ideas of the Great Medievalists of the Twentieth Century*. New York, 1991.

Carboneres, M. *Picarones y alcahuetas, ó la mancebía de Valencia*. Valencia, 1876. Reprint, 1978.

Cardaillac, L. *Moriscos y cristianos: un enfrentamiento polemico (1492–1640)*. Madrid, 1977.

Carmen Peris, M. "La prostitución valenciana en la segunda mitad del siglo XIV." In *Violència i marginació en la societat medieval* (= *Revista d'Història Medieval* 1 [1990]), 179–199.

Caro Baroja, J. "Las brujas de Fuenterrabía." *Revista de Dialectología y Tradiciones Populares* 3 (1947): 189–204.

——. *Las brujas y su mundo*. Madrid, 1961.

——. "Honour and Shame, a Historical Account of Several Conflicts." In *Honour and*

Shame: The Values of a Mediterranean Society, edited by J. Peristiany, pp. 79–139. London, 1965.

Carpenter, D. "Alfonso el Sabio y los moros: algunas precisiones legales, históricas y textuales con respecto a *Siete Partidas 7.25.*" *Al-Qanṭara* 7 (1986): 229–252.

———. *Alfonso X and the Jews: An Edition and Commentary on* Siete Partidas 7.24 "De los judíos." *(Modern Philology* 115.) Berkeley, 1986.

———. "Fickle Fortune: Gambling in Medieval Spain." *Studies in Philology* 85 (1988): 267–278.

———. "Minorities in Medieval Spain: The Legal Status of Jews and Muslims in the *Siete Partidas.*" *Romance Quarterly* 33 (1986): 275–287.

Carreras y Candi, F. "Ordinacions urbanes de bon govern a Catalunya (segles xiii a xviii)." *Boletín de la Real Academia de Buenas Letras de Barcelona* 11 (1923–1926): 293–335, 365–431; and 12 (1926–1928): 37–63, 121–153, 189–208, 286–295, 368–380, 419–423, 520–533.

Carta de población de la ciudad de Santa María de Albarracín. Edited by C. Riba y Garcia. Zaragoza, 1915.

Cartas pueblas de las morerías valencianas y documentación complementaria. Edited by M. V. Febrer Romaguera. Zaragoza, 1991.

Carter, D. *Scottsboro: A Tragedy of the American South.* Rev. ed. Baton Rouge, 1979.

Casas i Nadal, M. "El *Liber iudeorum* de Cardona (1330–1334)." *Miscel.lània de Textos Medievals* 3 (1985): 121–345.

———. "La litúrgia en una canònica de la diòcesi d'Urgell a l'edat mitjana: Sant Vicenç de Cardona." In *Miscel.lània Homenatge a Josep Lladonosa,* pp. 218–244 Lleida, 1992.

Cassel, S. "Juden (Geschichte)." In Ersch and Gruber, *Allgemeine Encyklopädie,* 2d sec., vol. 27. Leipzig, 1850.

Castro, A. *España en su historia: cristianos, moros, y judíos.* 2d ed. Barcelona, 1983.

"Cena Cypriani." Edited by K. Strecker. *MGH, Poetae Latini aevi carolini* vol. 4.2, pp. 857–900. Berlin, 1923.

Chalmeta, P. "Le passage à l'Islam dans al-Andalus au Xe siècle." In *Actas del XII Congreso de la U.E.A.I. (Málaga, 1984),* pp. 161–183. Madrid, 1986.

Chavel, H. D. *Kitvei Rabenu Moshe ben Naḥman.* Vol. 1. Jerusalem, 1964.

Chazan, R. *Church, State and Jew in the Middle Ages.* New York, 1980.

———. *Medieval Jewry in Northern France: A Political and Social History.* Baltimore, 1973.

Chejne, A. *Islam and the West: The Moriscos.* Albany, 1983.

Chia, J. de. *Bandos y bandoleros en Gerona: Apuntes históricos desde el siglo XIV hasta mediados del XVII.* Vol. 1. Girona, 1888.

Chrétien, H. *La prétendu complot des juifs et lépreux en 1321.* Châteauroux, 1887.

Chronica Adefonsi Imperatoris. Edited by L. Sanchez Belda. Madrid, 1950.

The Chronicle of Muntaner. Vols. 1–2. Translated by Lady Goodenough. The Hakluyt Society, 2d ser., vols. 47, 50. London, 1920–1921; Liechtenstein, 1967.

Chronicon Girardi de Fracheto. In *Recueil des historiens des Gaules et de la France,* 21:1–70. Paris, 1855.

Chronique de Saint-Denis. In *Recueil des historiens des Gaules et de la France,* 20:654–724. Paris, 1840.

Chronique latine de Guillaume de Nangis de 1113 à 1300 avec les continuations de cette chronique de 1300 à 1368. Edited by H. Géraud. Vol. 2. Paris, 1843.

Chronique parisienne anonyme de 1316 à 1339 précédée d'additions à la chronique française dite de Guillaume de Nangis (1206–1316). In *Mémoires de la Société de l'Histoire de Paris et de l'Ile-de-France* 11 (1884).

Chronographia regum Francorum. Vol. 1. Edited by H. Moranvillé. Paris, 1891.

Clare, L. "Fêtes, jeux et divertissements à la cour du connétable de Castille, Miguel Lucas de Iranzo (1460–1470): les exercices physiques." In *La fête et l'écriture: théâtre de cour, cour-théâtre en Espagne et en Italie, 1450–1530 (Colloque international: France-Espagne-Italie, 1985)*, pp. 5–32. Aix-en-Provence, 1987.

Clendinnen, I. "Ways to the Sacred: Reconstructing 'Religion' in Sixteenth Century Mexico." *History and Anthropology* 5 (1990): 105–141.

Código de las costumbres escritas de Tortosa. Edited by R. Foguet and J. Foguet Marsal. Tortosa, 1912.

Cohen, G. "The Song of Songs and the Jewish Religious Mentality." In *The Samuel Friedland Lectures, 1960–1966*, pp. 1–21. New York, 1966.

Cohen, J. *The Friars and the Jews: The Evolution of Medieval Anti-Judaism.* Ithaca, NY, 1982.

Cohen, M. "Islam and the Jews: Myth, Counter-Myth, History." *Jerusalem Quarterly* 38 (1986): 125–137.

———. "The Neo-Lachrymose Conception of Jewish-Arab History." *Tikkun* 6, no. 3 (May–June 1991): 55–60.

———. *Under Crescent and Cross: The Jews in the Middle Ages.* Princeton, 1994.

Cohn, N. *Europe's Inner Demons.* London, 1975.

———. *The Pursuit of the Millennium.* Rev. ed. New York, 1970.

———. *Warrant for Genocide: The Myth of the Jewish World-Conspiracy and the Protocols of the Elders of Zion.* New York, 1967.

La colección canonica hispana. Vol. 4, *Monumenta Hispaniae Sacra*, edited by G. Martínez Díez and F. Rodríguez. Madrid, 1984.

La colección canonica hispana. Vol. 5, *Concilios Hispanos: segunda parte*, edited by G. Martínez Díez and F. Rodríguez. Madrid, 1992.

Compayré, C. *Études historiques et documents inédits sur l'Albigeois, le Castrais et l'ancien diocèse de Lavaur.* Albi, 1841.

Compendium de epidemia Edited by E. H. Rebouis. *Étude historique et critique sur la peste.* Paris, 1888.

VIII Congreso de Historia de la Corona de Aragón ii.1. Valencia, 1969.

Constitutiones concilii quarti lateranensis una cum commentariis glossatorum. Edited by A. García y García. *Monumenta Iuris Canonici*, Corpus glossatorum, vol. 2. Vatican City, 1981.

Conte Cazcarro, A. *La aljama de Moros de Huesca.* Huesca, 1992.

Contel Barea, C. *El císter zaragozano en los siglos XIII y XIV: Abadia de Nuestra Señora de Rueda de Ebro.* 2 vols. Zaragoza, 1977.

Corbella i Llobet, R. *L'aljama de jueus de Vic.* Vic, 1909. Reprint, 1984.

Coroleu, J. *Documents historichs catalans del siglo XIV.* Barcelona, 1899.

Cortada, J. *Historia de España.* 2 vols. Barcelona, 1841 (= vols. 6–7 of *El Mundo: historia de todos los pueblos*).

Coulet, N. "De l'intégration à l'exclusion: la place des juifs dans les cérémonies d'entrée solennelle au moyen age." *Annales: ESC* 34 (1979): 672–683.

———. "Les juifs en Provence au bas moyen-age: les limites d'une marginalité." In

Minorités et marginaux en France méridionale et dans la peninsule Ibérique (VIIe–XVIIIe siècles) (Actes du colloque de Pau, 27–29 mai, 1984), pp. 203–219. Paris, 1986.

Coulson, N. J. *A History of Islamic Law.* Edinburgh, 1964.

Coulton, G. G. *The Friar's Lantern.* London, 1906.

Curto i Homedes, A. *La intervenció municipal en l'abastament de blat d'una ciutat catalana: Tortosa, segle XIV.* Barcelona, 1988.

Cutler, A. "Innocent III and the Distinctive Clothing of Jews and Muslims." *Studies in Medieval Culture* 3 (1970): 92–116.

Cutler, A., and H. Cutler. *The Jew as Ally of the Muslim: Medieval Roots of Anti-Semitism.* Notre Dame, IN, 1986.

Cuvillier, J.-P. "Les communautés rurales de la Plaine de Vich (Catalogne) aux XIIIe et XIVe siècles." *Mélanges de la Casa de Velázquez* 4 (1968): 73–106.

Dahan, G. *Les intellectuels chrétiens et les juifs au moyen âge.* Paris, 1990.

Daniel, N. *Islam and the West: The Making of an Image.* Edinburgh, 1962.

Davis, N. Z. *Society and Culture in Early Modern France.* Stanford, 1975.

"De duodecim abusiuis saeculi." In *Texte und Untersuchungen zur Geschichte der altchristlichen Literatur*, ser. 3, vol. 4, edited by S. Hellmann, pp. 1–62. Leipzig. 1909.

De excidio urbis Hierosolymitanae libri quinque. PL 15.1962–2206.

De glorioso rege Ludovico Ludovici filio. In *Vie de Louis le Gros par Suger, suivie de l'histoire du roi Louis VII: collection des textes pour servir à l'étude et à l'enseignement de l'histoire*, edited by A. Molinier. Paris, 1887.

Delumeau, J. *La peur en occident (XIVe–XVIIIe siècles).* Paris, 1978.

Demaitre, L. "The Description and Diagnosis of Leprosy by Fourteenth-Century Physicians." *Bulletin of the History of Medicine* 59 (1985): 327–344.

———. *Doctor Bernard de Gordon: Professor and Practitioner.* Toronto, 1980.

Denny, F. *An Introduction to Islam.* 2d ed. New York, 1994.

Derrida, J. "Plato's Pharmacy." In *Dissemination*, translated by B. Johnson, pp. 61–156. Chicago, 1981.

Devic, C., and J. Vaissete. *Histoire générale de Languedoc.* Vol. 9. Edited by A. Molinier. Toulouse, 1885.

Diepgen, P. *Die Theologie und der ärztliche Stand.* Vol. 1. Berlin, 1922.

Dinur, B. *Yisrael ba-Golah.* Vol. 2. Tel Aviv, 1969.

Documents pontificaux sur la Gascogne d'après les Archives de Vatican: pontificat de Jean XXII. Vol. 1. Edited by L. Guerard. Paris, 1896.

Domínguez Ortiz, A., and B. Vincent. *Historia de los moriscos.* Madrid, 1978.

Doñate Sebastiá, J. M. "Aportación a la historia del teatro, siglos XIV–XVI." In *Martínez Ferrando Archivero. Miscelánea de estudios dedicados a su memoria*, pp. 149–164. Madrid, 1968.

Doñate Sebastiá, J. M., and J. R. Magdalena Nom de Déu. *Three Jewish Communities in Medieval Valencia.* Jerusalem, 1990.

Donovan, R. *The Liturgical Drama in Medieval Spain.* Toronto, 1958.

Douglas, M. *Natural Symbols: Explorations in Cosmology.* New York, 1982.

———. *Purity and Danger: An Analysis of the Concepts of Pollution and Taboo.* Boston, 1966.

———. "Witchcraft and Leprosy: Two Strategies of Exclusion." *Man*, n.s., 26 (1991): 723–736.

Downes, D. "The Language of Violence: Sociological Perspectives on Adolescent Aggression." In *Aggression and Violence*, edited by P. Marsh and A. Campbell, pp. 27–46. Oxford, 1982.

DuCange. *Glossarium ad scriptores mediae et infimae latinitatis*. Vol. 4. Paris, 1733.

Duplès-Agier, H. "Ordonnance de Philippe le Long contre les lépreux (21 juin 1321)." *Bibliothèque de l'Ecole des chartes*, 4th ser., 3 (1857): 265–272.

Duran y Sanpere, A. *Llibre de Cervera*. Tarrega, 1972.

———. *Referències documentals del call de juheus de Cervera. Discursos llegits en la "Real Academia de Buenas Letras" de Barcelona*. Barcelona, 1924.

Durkheim, E. *De la division du travail social: études sur l'organization des sociétés supérieures*. Paris, 1893.

———. *The Division of Labour in Society*. New York, 1964.

———. "Notes sur l'anti-semitisme." In H. Dagan, *Enquête sur l'antisemitisme*, pp. 59–63. Paris, 1899.

Dyer, C. *Standards of Living in the Later Middle Ages*. Cambridge, 1989.

The Early English Version of the Gesta Romanorum. Edited by Sidney J. H. Herrtage. Early English Text Society, e.s., no. 33. London, 1879.

Echániz Sans, M. "Las Mujeres de la Orden Militar de Santiago: el monasterio de Sancti Spiritus de Salamanca (1268–1500)." 4 vols. Ph.D. diss., University of Barcelona, 1990.

Eco, U. *The Name of the Rose*. New York, 1984.

Eiximenis, F. *Lo Crestià*. Edited by A. Hauf. Barcelona, 1983.

Emery, R. "The Black Death of 1348 in Perpignan." *Speculum* 42 (1967): 611–623.

Epalza, M. de. *Fray Anselm Turmeda (Abdallah Al-Taryuman) y su polemica islamo-cristiana*. Madrid, 1994.

———. *Jésus otage: Juifs, chrétiens et musulmans en Espagne (VIe–XVIIe s.)*. Paris, 1987.

Epstein, I. *Studies in the Communal Life of the Jews of Spain*. 2d ed. New York, 1968.

Epstein, L. *Marriage Laws in the Bible and the Talmud*. Cambridge, MA, 1942.

———. *Sex Laws and Customs in Judaism*. New York, 1948.

Escribà i Bonastre, G., and M. Frago i Pérez. *Documents dels jueus de Girona, 1124–1595*. Girona, 1992.

España Sagrada, teatro geográfico-histórico de la iglesia de España. Edited by E. Flórez et al. 58 vols. Madrid, 1747–1918.

Fattal, A. *Le statut légal des non-musulmans en pays d'Islam*. Beirut, 1958.

Fay, H. M. *Histoire de la lèpre en France: lépreux et cagots du Sud-Ouest*. Paris, 1910.

Feierman, S. *Peasant Intellectuals: Anthropology and History in Tanzania*. Madison, WI, 1990.

Feldman, L. *Josephus and Modern Scholarship (1937–1980)*. Berlin, 1984.

———. *Josephus, a Supplementary Bibliography*. New York, 1986.

Feliu, E. "Els acords de Barcelona de 1354." *Calls* 2 (1987): 145–164.

Ferrer i Mallol, M. T. *Les aljames sarraïnes de la governació d'Oriola en el segle XIV*. Barcelona, 1988.

———. *La frontera amb l'islam en el segle XIV: Cristians i sarraïns al país valencià*. Barcelona, 1988.

———. *Organització i defensa d'un territori fronterer: La governació d'Oriola en el segle XIV*. Barcelona, 1990.

———. *Els sarraïns de la Corona Catalano-Aragonesa en el segle XIV: segregació i discriminació*. Barcelona, 1987.

Fiaschini, G. "Genovesi e Catalani nel basso Medioevo: un problema storiografico aperto." In *Atti del I° congresso storico Liguria-Catalogna (ottobre 1969)*, pp. 572–601. Bordighera, 1974.

Field, D. *Rebels in the Name of the Tsar*. Boston, 1976.

Finke, H. *Acta Aragonensia*. 3 vols. Berlin, 1908–1922.

Finkelstein, L. *Jewish Self-Government in the Middle Ages*. New York, 1924. Reprint, Westport, CT, 1975.

Flor del tesoro de la belleza: Tratado de muchas medicinas o curiosidades de las mujeres. Edited by J. de Olañeta. Barcelona, 1981.

Font Rius, J. M. "La carta de seguridad de Ramon Berenguer IV a las morerías de Ascó y Ribera del Ebro (siglo XII)." In his *Estudis sobre els drets i institucions locals en la Catalunya medieval*, pp. 561–576. Barcelona, 1985.

Fori Antiqui Valentiae. Edited by M. Dualde Serrano. Valencia, 1967.

Foucault, M. "Nietzsche, Genealogy, History." In *Language, Counter-Memory, Practice*, edited by D. Bouchard, pp. 139–164. Ithaca, NY, 1977.

Fraade, S. *From Tradition to Commentary: Torah and Its Interpretation in the Midrash Sifre to Deuteronomy*. Albany, 1991.

Freedman, P. "Cowardice, Heroism and the Legendary Origins of Catalonia." *Past and Present* 121 (1988): 3–28.

———. *The Origins of Peasant Servitude in Medieval Catalonia*. Cambridge, 1991.

Freud, S. "On the Universal Tendency to Debasement in the Sphere of Love," in vol. 11 of *The Standard Edition of the Complete Psychological Works of Sigmund Freud*, translated and edited by J. Strachey, pp. 177–190. London, 1957.

El Fuero de Teruel. Edited by J. Castañé Llinás. Teruel, 1991.

El Fuero latino de Teruel. Edited by J. Caruana Gomez de Barreda. Teruel, 1974.

Los Fueros de Aragón según el manuscrito 458 de la biblioteca Nacional de Madrid. Edited by G. Tilander. Lund, 1937.

Funkenstein, A. "Basic Types of Christian Anti-Jewish Polemics in the Middle Ages." *Viator* 2 (1971): 373–382.

———. "Changes in the Patterns of Christian Anti-Jewish Polemic in the Twelfth Century." *Zion* 33 (1968): 125–144 (in Hebrew).

Furs de València. Edited by G. Colón and A. Garcia. 5 vols. to date. Barcelona, 1970–1990.

García-Arenal, M. "Los moros en las Cantigas de Alfonso X el Sabio." *Al-Qanṭara* 6 (1985): 133–151.

———. "Rapports entre groupes dans la péninsule ibérique: la conversion de juifs à l'islam (XIIe–XIIIe siècles)." In *Minorités Religieuses dans l'Espagne Médiévale, Revue du Monde Musulman et de la Méditerranée* 63–64 (1992): 91–101.

García-Ballester, L., M. McVaugh, and A. Rubio Vela. *Medical Licensing and Learning in Fourteenth-Century Valencia*. Philadelphia, 1989.

García Cárcel, R. *Las Germanías de Valencia*. Barcelona, 1975.

García y García, A. "Jews and Muslims in the Canon Law of the Iberian Peninsula in the Late Medieval and Early Modern Period." *Jewish History* 3 (1988): 41–50.

Gargallo Moya, A. "La carta-puebla concedida por el Temple a los moros de Villastar (1267)." In *Actas del III Simposio Internacional de Mudejarismo*, pp. 209–220. Madrid, 1986.

Gautier-Dalché, J. "La peste noire dans les états de la couronne d'Aragon." In *Mélanges offerts à Marcel Bataillon par les Hispanistes français*, pp. 65–80. (*Bulletin Hispanique* 54 bis [1962].)

Génestal, R. *Le Privilegium fori en France du décret de Gratien à la fin du XIV siècle*. Bibliothèque des Hautes Etudes. Sciences Religieuses, vol. 35. Paris, 1921.

Geremek, B. *The Margins of Society in late Medieval Paris*. Cambridge, 1987.

Giddens, A. "Action, Subjectivity, and the Constitution of Meaning." In *The Aims of Representation: Subject / Text / History*, edited by M. Krieger, pp. 159–174. New York, 1987.

———. "Hermeneutics and Social Theory." In *Hermeneutics: Questions and Prospects*, edited by G. Shapiro and A. Sica, pp. 215–231. Amherst, MA, 1984.

Gil García, M. P. "Conflictos sociales y oposición étnica: La comunidad mudéjar de Crevillente, 1420." In *Actas del III Simposio Internacional de Mudejarismo*, pp. 305–312. Teruel, 1986.

Ginzburg, C. *Ecstasies: Deciphering the Witches' Sabbath*. New York, 1991.

———. *Myths, Emblems, Clues*. London, 1986.

Ginzburg, C., et al. "Saccheggi rituali: premesse a una ricerca in corso." *Quaderni storici* 65 (1987): 615–636.

Girard, R. *Des choses cachées depuis la fondation du Monde*. Paris, 1978.

———. "Generative Scapegoating." In *Violent Origins: Ritual Killing and Cultural Formation*, edited by R. G. Hamerton-Kelly, pp. 73–148. Stanford, 1987.

———. *Things Hidden since the Foundation of the World*. London, 1987.

———. *To Double Business Bound: Essays on Literature, Mimesis and Anthropology*. Baltimore, 1978.

———. *Violence and the Sacred*. Baltimore, 1977.

Girbal, E. C. *Los judíos en Gerona*. Girona, 1870. Reprinted in *Per a una història de la Girona jueva*, edited by D. Romano, 1:23–114. Girona, 1988.

Glick, T. "The Ethnic Systems of Premodern Spain." *Comparative Studies in Sociology* 1 (1978): 157–171.

———. *Islamic and Christian Spain in the Early Middle Ages: Comparative Perspectives on Social and Cultural Formation*. Princeton, 1979.

Gluckman, M. *Analysis of a Social Situation in Modern Zululand*. Rhodes Livingstone Paper 28. Manchester, 1958.

———. *Custom and Conflict in Africa*. Oxford, 1956.

———. *Order and Rebellion in Tribal Africa*. New York, 1963.

Goitein, S. *A Mediterranean Society: The Jewish Communities of the Arab World as Portrayed in the Documents of the Cairo Geniza*. Vol. 4, *Daily Life*. Berkeley, 1983.

Gomez Zorraquino, J. I. "Consecuencias económicas de la expulsión de los moriscos aragoneses: los censales." *Actas del III Simposio Internacional de Mudejarismo*, pp. 269–275. Teruel, 1986.

González Antón, L. *Las Uniones aragonesas y las Cortes del reino (1283–1301)*. 2 vols. Zaragoza, 1975.

Goodman, J. *Stories of Scottsboro*. New York, 1994.

Graboïs, A. "La royauté sacrée au xiie siècle: manifestation de propagande royale." In *Idéologie et propagande en France*, edited by M. Yardeni, pp. 31–41. Paris, 1984.

Graullera, V. "Los hostaleros del burdel de Valencia." In *Violència i marginació en la societat medieval* (= *Revista d'Història Medieval* 1 [1990]), 201–213.

Grayzel, S. *The Church and the Jews in the Thirteenth Century*. Philadelphia, 1933.

————. "The Confession of a Medieval Jewish Convert." *Historia Judaica* 17 (1955): 89–120.

Green, M. "Women's Medical Practice and Health Care in Medieval Europe." *Signs: Journal of Women in Culture and Society* 14 (1989): 434–473.

Gross, R. "Registering and Ranking of Tension Areas." In *Confini e regioni: il potenziale di sviluppo e di pace delle periferie*, pp. 317–28. Trieste, 1973.

Gual Camarena, M. "Los mudéjares valencianos en la época del Magnánimo." In *IV Congreso de Historia de la Corona de Aragón*, 1:467–494. 1959.

Guallart de Viala, A. *El derecho penal histórico de Aragón*. Zaragoza, 1977.

Guerchberg, S. "The Controversy over the Alleged Sowers of the Black Death in Contemporary Treatises on Plague." In *Change in Medieval Society*, edited by S. Thrupp, pp. 208–224. New York, 1964. Reprint and translation from *RdÉJ* 108 (1948).

Guerreau, A., and Y. Guy. *Les cagots du Béarn: recherches sur le développement inégal au sein du système féodal européen*. Montrouge, 1988.

Guichard, P. "Un seigneur musulman dans l'Espagne chrétienne: le 'rais' de Crevillente (1243–1318)." *Melanges de la Casa de Velázquez* 9 (1973): 283–334.

Guillaume de Chartres. *De vita et miraculis Sancti Ludovici*. In *Recueil des historiens des Gaules et de la France*, 20:28–44. Paris, 1840.

Guilleré, C. *Diner, poder i societat a la Girona del segle XIV*. Girona, 1984.

————. "Les finances de la Couronne d'Aragon au debut du XIVe siècle (1300–1310)." In *Estudios sobre renta, fiscalidad y finanzas en la Cataluña bajomedieval*, edited by M. Sánchez Martínez, pp. 487–507. Barcelona, 1993.

————. *Girona al segle XIV*. 2 vols. Girona, 1993–1994.

————. "La peste noire à Gérone (1348)." *Annals de l'Institut d'Estudis Gironins* 27 (1984): 87–161.

Gutiérrez, R. *When Jesus Came the Corn Mothers Went Away: Marriage, Sexuality, and Power in New Mexico, 1500–1846*. Stanford, 1991.

Gutwirth, E. "Hispano-Jewish Attitudes to the Moors in the Fifteenth Century." *Sefarad* 49 (1989): 237–261.

Habermas, J. *Eine Art Schadensabwicklung*. Frankfurt, 1987.

Hagerty, M. *Los libros plúmbeos del Sacromonte*. Madrid, 1980.

Hahn, S. *The Roots of Southern Populism*. Oxford, 1983.

Hall, J. D. *Revolt against Chivalry: Jessie Daniel Ames and the Women's Campaign against Lynching*. New York, 1979.

Harvey, L. P. *Islamic Spain, 1250 to 1500*. Chicago, 1990.

Haverkamp, A. "Die Judenverfolgungen zur Zeit des Schwarzen Todes im Gesellschaftsgefüge deutscher Städte." In *Zur Geschichte der Juden im Deutschland des späten Mittelalters und der frühen Neuzeit*, edited by A. Haverkamp, pp. 27–93. Stuttgart, 1981.

Hechos del condestable don Miguel Lucas de Iranzo. Edited by J. de Mata Carriazo. Madrid, 1940.

Helgaud de Fleury. *Vie de Robert le Pieux*. Edited by R.-H. Bautier and G. Labory. *Sources d'histoire médiévale* 1. Paris, 1965.

Henneman, J. *Royal Taxation in Fourteenth Century France: The Development of War Financing 1322–1356*. Princeton, 1971.

Herde, P. "Christians and Saracens at the Time of the Crusades: Some Comments of Contemporary Canonists." *Studia Gratiana* 12 (1967): 359–376.

Hernando i Delgado, J. "La Destrucció de Jerusalem." *Miscel.lània de Textos Medievals* 5 (1989): 1–116.

———. "Realidades socioeconómicas en el *Libro de las Confesiones* de Martín Perez: usura, justo precio y profesión." *Acta Historica et Archaeologica Mediaevalia* 2 (1981): 93–106.

———. "Un tractat anònim *Adversus Iudaeos* en català."In *Paraula i Història, Miscel.lània P. Basili Rubí*. Barcelona, 1986.

Hershman, A. *Rab Ishaq Perfet*. Jerusalem, 1956 (in Hebrew).

Hertz, R. *"Death" and "the Right Hand."* Translated by R. Needham and C. Needham. Glencoe, IL, 1960.

Hillgarth, J. *The Spanish Kingdoms*. Vol. 1. Oxford, 1976.

Hinojosa, E. "Mezquinos y exaricos." In *Homenaje a Codera*, pp. 523–531. Zaragoza, 1904.

Hinojosa Montalvo, J. *The Jews of the Kingdom of Valencia: From Persecution to Expulsion, 1391–1492*. Jerusalem, 1993.

Histoire générale de Languedoc. Edited by J. Vaissète et al. 2nd ed. 16 vols. Toulouse, 1872–1904.

Historiae de excidio Hierosolymitanae urbis Anacephalaeosis. PL 15.2206–2218.

Hocart, A. M. *Kings and Councillors: An Essay in the Comparative Anatomy of Human Society*. Edited by R. Needham. Chicago, 1970.

Hodes, M. "Sex across the Color Line: White Women and Black Men in the Nineteenth Century American South." Ph.D. diss., Princeton University, 1991.

Horowitz, C. *Tosefta ʿAtiqta*. Pt. 5. Frankfurt, 1890.

Horowitz, E. "The Rite to Be Reckless: On the Perpetuation and Interpretation of Purim Violence." *Poetics Today* 15 (1994): 9–54.

Hubert, H., and M. Mauss. "Étude sommaire de la représentation du temps dans la religion et la magie." In idem, *Mélanges d'histoire des religions*, pp. 189–229. Paris, 1929.

———. *Sacrifice: Its Nature and Function*. Chicago, 1968.

Ibn Adret, Solomon b. Abraham, *Sheʾelot u-teshuvot (Responsa)*, 7 vols. Jerusalem, 1965–1970.

Ibn Buṭlan, Abuʾl-Ḥasan al-Mukhtār ibn al-Ḥasan. *Risāla fi Shirā al-Raqīq*. Edited by ʿAbd al-Salām Ḥārūn. Cairo, 1373/1954.

Ibn Qayyim al-Jawziyya. *Aḥkām ahl al-dhimma*. Edited by Ṣubḥī Ṣāliḥ. Pt. 1. Beirut, 1983.

Ibn Verga, Solomon. *Chébet Jehuda (La vara de Judá) de Salomón Ben Verga*. Translated by Francisco Cantera Burgos. Granada, 1927.

———. *Shevet Yehudah*. Jerusalem, 1947.

Idoate, F. *Documentos sobre agotes y grupos afines en Navarra*. Pamplona, 1973.

Isaac b. Sheshet Perfet. *Sheʾelot u-teshuvot bar Sheshet (Responsa)*. Vilna, 1878.

Jacme d'Agramont. *"Regiment de preservació de pestilència" de Jacme d'Agramont (s. XIV). Introducció, transcripció i estudi lingüistic*. Edited by J. Veny i Clar. Tarragona, 1971.

Jacquart, D., and C. Thomasset. *Sexuality and Medicine in the Middle Ages*. Princeton, 1988.

Jacques de Vitry. *Exempla ex sermonibus vulgaribus*. Edited by Crane. London, 1890.

Jay, M. "Force Fields. Songs of Experience: Reflections on the Debate over *Alltagsgeschichte*." *Salmagundi* 81 (1989):. 29–41.

Jean XXII (1316–34). Lettres secrètes et curiales relatives à la France. Edited by A. Coulon. Vol. 2. Paris, 1906.

Jean de Saint-Victor. *Prima vita Joannis XXII.* In E. Baluze, *Vitae paparum avenionensium,* edited by G. Mollat, vol. 1. Paris, 1914.

Jeanselme, E. "Comment l'Europe au Moyen Age se protégea contre la lèpre." *Bulletin de la Société Française d'Histoire de la Médecine* 25 (1931): 1–155.

Johnston, J. *Race Relations in Virginia and Miscegenation in the South, 1776–1860.* 1937. Amherst, MA, 1970.

Jordan, W. C. *The French Monarchy and the Jews: From Philip Augustus to the Last Capetians.* Philadelphia, 1989.

———. *Louis IX and the Challenge of the Crusade.* Princeton, 1979.

———. "Problems of the Meat-Market of Beziers 1240–1247: A Question of Anti-Semitism." *RdÉJ* 135 (1976): 31–49.

Les Journaux de Trésor de Charles IV. Edited by J. Viard. Paris, 1917.

Die Judenpogrome in Russland. 2 vols. Cologne, 1910.

Juliá Viñamata, J.-R. "El estudio general de Lérida a finales del siglo XIV: Las reformas de Martín el Humano." In *Miscel.lània Homenatge a Josep Lladonosa,* pp. 323–348. Lleida, 1992.

Kalonymos b. Kalonymos. *Even Bohan.* Lemberg, 1865.

Kanduza, A. "The Revival of Incwala Ceremonies among the Ngoni of Zambia." Unpublished manuscript.

Kant, I. "Idea for a Universal History with a Cosmopolitan Purpose." Edited by H. Reiss. In *Kant's Political Writings,* pp. 41–53. Cambridge, 1970.

———. "On the Common Saying: 'This May Be True in Theory, But It Does Not Apply in Practice.'" Edited by H. Reiss. In *Kant's Political Writings,* pp. 61–92. Cambridge, 1970.

———. "Perpetual Peace: A Philosophical Sketch." Edited by H. Reiss. In *Kant's Political Writings,* pp. 93–130. Cambridge, 1970.

Kapferer, B. *Legends of People, Myths of State: Violence, Intolerance, and Political Culture in Sri Lanka and Australia.* Washington, DC, 1988.

Karras, R. "Holy Harlots: Prostitute Saints in Medieval Legend." *Journal of the History of Sexuality* 1 (1990): 3–32.

———. "The Regulation of Brothels in Later Medieval England." *Signs: Journal of Women in Culture and Society* 14 (1989): 399–433.

Kassin, L. "A Study of a Fourteenth-Century Polemical Treatise *Adversus Judaeos.*" Ph.D. diss., Columbia University, 1969.

Katz, J. *Exclusiveness and Tolerance: Studies in Jewish-Gentile Relations in Medieval and Modern Times.* Oxford, 1961.

Kershaw, I. "The Great Famine and Agrarian Crisis in England, 1315–1322." *Past and Present* 59 (1973): 3–50.

Klebs, A.-C. "A Catalan Plague Tract of April 24, 1348, by Jacme d'Agramont." In *Rapport du 6e Congrès International d'Histoire de la Médecine,* pp. 229–232. Antwerp, 1929.

Ha-Kohen, Joseph. *Emeq Ha-Bakha de Yosef Ha-Kohen.* Translated by Pilar Leon Tello. Madrid, 1964.

———. ʿ*Emeq ha-Bakha.* Edited by M. Letteris and S. Luzzatto. Cracow, 1895.

Kolve, V. A. *The Play Called Corpus Christi*. Stanford, 1966.

Kovel, J. *White Racism: A Psychohistory*. 2d ed. New York, 1984.

Kriegel, M. *Les Juifs à la fin du Moyen Age dans l'Europe méditerranéenne*. Paris, 1979.

———. "Mobilisation politique et modernisation organique: les expulsions des juifs au bas moyen âge." *Archives des sciences sociales et des religions* 46 (1978): 5–20.

———. "Un trait de psychologie sociale dans les pays méditerranéens du bas moyen age: le juif comme intouchable." *Annales: ESC* 31 (1976): 326–330.

Kristeva, J. *Powers of Horror: An Essay in Abjection*. Translated by L. Roudiez. New York, 1982.

Kritzeck, J. *Peter the Venerable and Islam*. Princeton, 1964.

Kuper, H. "A Royal Ritual in a Changing Political Context." *Cahiers d'études africaines* 12 (1972): 593–615.

Lacarra, J. M. "Introducción al estudio de los mudéjares aragoneses." In *Actas del I Simposio Internacional de Mudejarismo*, pp. 17–28. Madrid-Teruel, 1981.

———. "Introducción al estudio de los mudéjares aragoneses." *Aragón en la Edad Media* 2 (1979): 7–22.

Lactantius. *Liber de mortibus persecutorum*. PL 7:189–276.

Laeuchli, S. *Power and Sexuality: The Emergence of Canon Law at the Synod of Elvira*. Philadelphia, 1972.

Laistner, M. *Thought and Letters in Western Europe, A.D. 500–900*. New York, 1931.

Laliena Corbera, C. "La adhesión de las ciudades a la Unión: poder real y conflictividad social en Aragón a fines del XIII." *Aragón en la Edad Media* 8 (1989): 319–413.

Lang, B. *Act and Idea in the Nazi Genocide*. Chicago, 1990.

Langlois, C.-V. "Registres perdus des archives de la Chambre des comptes de Paris." *Notices et extraits des manuscrits de la Bibliothèque nationale et autres bibliothèques* 40 (1917): 33–399.

———. *La vie en France au Moyen-âge*. Rev. ed. Vol. 4. Paris, 1928.

Langmuir, G. "Majority History and Postbiblical Jews." In *Toward a Definition of Antisemitism*, pp. 21–41. Berkeley and Los Angeles, 1990.

———. " 'Tanquam servi': The Change in Jewish Status in French Law about 1200." In *Les Juifs dans l'histoire de France*, edited by M. Yardeni, pp. 25–54. Leiden, 1980. Reprinted in Langmuir, *Toward a Definition of Antisemitism*, pp. 167–194. Berkeley and Los Angeles, 1990.

Lapeyre, H. *Géographie de l'Espagne morisque*. Paris, 1959.

Larenaudie, M. "Les famines en Languedoc aux XIVème et XVème siècles." *Annales du Midi*, 1952, pp. 27–39.

Lavergne, G. "La persécution et la spoliation des lépreux à Périgueux en 1321." In *Recueil de Travaux offerts à M. Clovis Brunel*, 2:107–113. Paris, 1955.

Laws of the Alamans and Bavarians. Translated by T. J. Rivers. Philadelphia, 1977.

Lazar, M. "The Lamb and the Scapegoat: The Dehumanization of the Jews in Medieval Propaganda Imagery." In *Anti-Semitism in Times of Crisis*, edited by S. Gillman and S. Katz, pp. 38–80. New York, 1991.

Lazard, L. "Les juifs de Touraine." *RdÉJ* 17 (1888): 210–234.

Lazarus-Yafeh, H. "Is There a Concept of Redemption in Islam?" In *Some Religious Aspects of Islam*. Leiden, 1981.

Lears, T. J. *No Place of Grace: Antimodernism and the Transformation of American Culture*. New York, 1981.

Ledesma Rubio, L. "El libro de cuentas del merinado de Jaca (años 1387–1399)." *Aragón en la Edad Media* 1 (1977): 133–174.

Leges Visigothorum. Edited by K. Zeumer. *MGH, Leges* 1. Hanover, 1902.

Le Goff, J. "Le mal royal au moyen âge: du roi malade au roi guérisseur." *Mediaevistik* 1 (1988): 101–109.

Lehugeur, P. *Histoire de Philippe le Long, roi de France (1316–22)*. Paris, 1897.

Leroy, B. *The Jews of Navarre*. Jerusalem, 1985.

———. "Recherches sur les Juifs de Navarre à la fin du Moyen Age." *RdÉJ* 140 (1981): 319–432. Reprinted in Spanish as "Los judíos de Navarra al final de la edad media," in M. García Arenal and B. Leroy, *Moros y judíos en Navarra en la baja edad media*, pp. 143–257. Madrid, 1984.

———. "Le royaume de Navarre et les juifs aux XIVe et XVe siècles: entre l'accueil et la tolérance." *Sefarad* 38 (1978): 261–292.

Lévi, I. "La Mort de Titus." *RdÉJ* 15 (1887): 62–69.

Levi ben Gerson's Prognostication for the Conjunction of 1345. Edited by B. Goldstein and D. Pingree. *Transactions of the American Philosophical Society*, vol. 80, pt. 6 (1990).

Lévi-Provençal, É. *Séville musulmane au début du XIIe siècle: le traité d'Ibn ʿAbdun sur la vie urbaine et les corps de métiers*. Paris, 1947.

Lévi-Strauss, C. *The Elementary Structures of Kinship*. Edited by R. Needham. Translated by J. H. Bell, J. R. von Sturmer, and R. Needham. Boston, 1969.

———. *Mythologiques II: du miel aux cendres*. Paris, 1966.

Levy, S. "Notas sobre el 'Purim de Zaragoza.'" *Anuario de Filología* 5 (1979): 203–217.

Lewis, B. "An Anti-Jewish Ode: The Qasida of Abu Ishaq against Joseph ibn Nagrella." In *Salo W. Baron Jubilee Volume*, edited by S. Liebermann, 2:657–668. Jerusalem, 1974.

———. *Islam: From the Prophet Muhammad to the Capture of Constantinople*. 2 vols. Oxford, 1987.

———. *The Jews of Islam*. Princeton, 1984.

Leyes de moros del siglo XIV. Edited by P. de Gayangos. In *Memorial Histórico Español*, 5:1–246. Madrid, 1853.

Lida de Malkiel, M. R. *Jerusalén: el tema literario de su cerco y destrucción por los romanos*. Buenos Aires, 1972.

Lincoln, B. *Discourse and the Construction of Society*. Oxford, 1989.

Linder, A. "The Destruction of Jerusalem Sunday." *Sacris Erudiri* 30 (1987–1988): 253–292.

———. *The Jews in Roman Imperial Legislation*. Detroit, 1987.

Lisón Tolosana, C. *Invitación a la antropología cultural de España*. Madrid, 1980.

Little, L. *Religious Poverty and the Profit Economy in Medieval Europe*. Ithaca, NY, 1978.

Lladonosa i Pujol, J. *L'Estudi General de Lleida del 1430 al 1524*. Barcelona, 1970.

———. *Història de Lleida*. Vol. 1. Tàrrega, 1972.

Llibre de les ordinacions de Torroja. Edited by J. Torné i Cubells and E. M. Vallejo i Fidalgo. Tarragona, 1989.

Llibre del batlle reial de Barcelona Berenguer Morey (1375–1378). Edited by J. M. Casas Homs. Barcelona, 1976.

Loizos, P. "Intercommunal Killing in Cyprus." *Man*, n.s., 23 (1988): 639–653.

López de Meneses, A. "Una consequencia de la peste negra en Cataluña: el pogrom de 1348." *Sefarad* 19 (1959): 92–131, 322–364.

López de Meneses, A. "Documentos acerca de la peste negra en los dominios de la Corona de Aragón." *Estudios de Edad Media de la Corona de Aragón* 6 (1956): 291–447.

———. "Documentos culturales de Pedro el Ceremonioso." *Estudios de Edad Media de la Corona de Aragón* 5 (1952): 669–771.

Lourie, E. "Anatomy of Ambivalence: Muslims under the Crown of Aragon in the Late Thirteenth Century." In *Crusade and Colonisation.*

———. "Complicidad criminal: un aspecto insolito de convivencia judeo-cristiana." In *Actas del III Congreso Internacional "Encuentro de las Tres Culturas,"* edited by C. Carrete Parrondo, pp. 93–108. Toledo, 1988. Reprinted in *Crusade and Colonisation.*

———. *Crusade and Colonisation: Muslims, Christians and Jews in Medieval Aragon.* Variorum Collected Studies 317. Aldershot, 1990.

———. "Free Moslems in the Balearics under Christian Rule in the Thirteenth Century." *Speculum* 45 (1970): 624–649. Reprinted in *Crusade and Colonisation.*

———. "Jewish Moneylenders in the Local Catalan Community, c. 1300: Vilafranca del Penedés, Besalú and Montblanc." *Michael* 11 (1989): 33–98.

———. "Jewish Participation in Royal Funerary Rites: An Early Use of the *Representatio* in Aragon." *Journal of the Warburg and Courtauld Institutes* 45 (1982): 192–194. Reprinted in *Crusade and Colonisation.*

———. "Mafiosi and Malsines: Violence, Fear and Faction in the Jewish Aljamas of Valencia in the Fourteenth Century." In *Actas del IV Congreso Internacional "Encuentro de las Tres Culturas,"* edited by C. Carrete Parrondo, pp. 69–102. Toledo, 1988. Reprinted in *Crusade and Colonisation.*

———. "A Plot Which Failed? The Case of a Corpse Found in the Jewish *Call* of Barcelona (1301)." *Mediterranean Historical Review* 1 (1986): 187–220.

de Lozoya, Marqués. *La moreria de Segovia.* Madrid, 1967.

Lucas, H. S. "The Great European Famine of 1315, 1316 and 1317." *Speculum* 5 (1930): 341–377. Reprinted in *Essays in Economic History,* edited by E. M. Carus-Wilson, 2:49–72. London, 1954–1966.

Luce, S. "Catalogue des documents du Trésor des chartes relatifs aux juifs sous le règne de Philippe le Bel." *RdÉJ* 2 (1881): 15–72.

Lukes, S. *Durkheim: His Life and Work.* Harmondsworth, 1973.

Lukes, S., and A. Scull. *Durkheim and the Law.* Oxford, 1984.

MacKay, A. "The Jews in Spain during the Middle Ages." In *Spain and the Jews: the Sephardi Experience 1492 and After,* edited by E. Kedourie, pp. 33–50. London, 1992.

———. "Religion, Culture, and Ideology on the Late Medieval Castilian-Granadan Frontier." In *Medieval Frontier Societies,* edited by R. Bartlett and A. MacKay, pp. 217–244. Oxford, 1989.

MacKay, A., and G. McKendrick. "La semiología y los ritos de violencia: Sociedad y poder en la Corona de Castilla." *En la España Medieval* 11 (1988): 153–165.

McVaugh, M. *Medicine before the Plague: Practitioners and Their Patients in the Crown of Aragon, 1285–1345.* Cambridge, 1993.

Madero, M. *Manos violentas, palabras vedadas: la injuria en Castilla y León (siglos XIII-XV).* Madrid, 1992.

Magdalena Nom de Déu, J. R. "La aljama judía de Segorbe en un 'responsum' de Rabí Ishaq bar Séset Perfet." *Boletín de la Sociedad Castellonense de Cultura* 59 (1983): 385–393.

————. "Delitos de los judíos de Aragón a inicios del siglo XIV (1310 a 1312): Aportación documental." *Anuario de Filología* 5 (1979): 219–227.

Maimon, Moses ben. *The Code of Maimonides, Book Five: The Book of Holiness.* Translated by L. Rabinowitz and P. Grossman. Yale Judaica Series, vol. 16. New Haven, 1965.

Maitland, F. "The Deacon and the Jewess: or, Apostasy at Common Law." In his *Collected Papers*, edited by H. Fisher, 1:385–406. Cambridge, 1911.

Malti-Douglas, F. *Woman's Body, Woman's Word: Gender and Discourse in Arabo-Islamic Writing.* Princeton, 1991.

Mansi, G. D. *Sacrorum conciliorum nova et amplissima collectio.* Paris, 1901–1927.

————. *Sacrorum oecumenicorum conciliorum nova et amplissima collectio.* Vol. 25. Venice, 1782.

Marcus, J. *The Jew in the Medieval World: A Source Book (315–1791).* New York, 1969.

Marmon, S. "Concubinage, Islamic." In *Dictionary of the Middle Ages*, 3:527–529. New York, 1983.

Marquette, J. B. "Les Albret: le rôle politique." *Cahiers du Bazadais* 41 (1978): 377–536.

Marsh, P. "Identity: An Ethogenic Perspective." In *Persons in Groups: Social Behavior as Identity Formation in Medieval and Renaissance Europe*, ed. R. Trexler, pp. 17–30. Binghamton, NY, 1985.

Marsh, P., E. Rosser, and R. Harré. *The Rules of Disorder.* London, 1978.

Masiá, A. "Aportaciones al estudio de los 'pastorellos' en la corona de Aragón." In *Homenaje a Millás-Vallicrosa*, 2:9–30. Barcelona, 1956.

————. *Jaume II: Aragó, Granada i Marroc.* Barcelona, 1989.

Massip, J. *La gestació de les costums de Tortosa.* Tortosa, 1984.

Massip, J. F. "Notes sobre l'evolució de l'espai escénic medieval als països catalans." *Acta historica et archaeologica mediaevalia* 5–6 (1984–1985): 129–159.

————. *Teatre religiós medieval als països catalans.* Barcelona, 1984.

Maubourguet, J. M. *Le Périgord méridional des origines à l'an 1370.* Cahors, 1926.

Mauss, M. *The Gift: The Form and Reason for Exchange in Archaic Societies.* Translated by W. D. Halls. New York, 1990.

————. "Gift, gift." In *Mélanges Charles Andler.* Strasbourg, 1924.

Mayordomo Font, R. "Notas históricas sobre la carnicería de la aljama sarracena de Tortosa (siglo XIV)." In *Homenatge a la memòria del prof. Dr. Emilio Sáez*, pp. 223–231. Barcelona, 1989.

Menache, S. "The King, the Church, and the Jews." *Journal of Medieval History* 13 (1987): 223–236.

Menendez Pidál, R. *Poesia juglaresca y origenes de las literaturas romanicas.* Madrid, 1957.

Mérindol, C. de. "Mouvements sociaux et troubles politiques à la fin du Moyen Age: essai sur la symbolique des villes." In *Actes du 114e Congrès National des Sociétés Savantes*, pp. 267–302. Paris, 1989.

Merrick, J. *The Desacralization of the French Monarchy in the Eighteenth Century.* Baton Rouge, LA, 1990.

Més enllà del silenci: les dones a la història de Catalunya. Edited by M. Nash. Barcelona, 1988.

Meyerson, M. "Comparative Perspectives on Muslims and Jews in Christian Spain." Paper presented at the Midwest Medieval History Conference, Ohio State University, October 1990.

Meyerson, M. *The Muslims of Valencia in the Age of Fernando and Isabel: Between Coexistence and Crusade.* Berkeley, 1991.

————. "Prostitution of Muslim Women in the Kingdom of Valencia: Religious and Sexual Discrimination in a Medieval Plural Society." In *The Medieval Mediterranean: Cross-Cultural Contacts.* Medieval Studies at Minnesota 3, edited by M. J. Chiat and K. L. Reyerson, pp. 87–95. St. Cloud, MI, 1988.

Millás Vallicrosa, J. M. "Un tratado anónimo de polémica contra los judíos." *Sefarad* 13 (1953): 3–34.

Millás Vallicrosa, J. M., and L. Batlle Prats. "Un Alboroto contra el call de Gerona en el año 1331." *Sefarad* 12 (1952): 297–335. Reprinted in *Per a una història de la Girona jueva,* edited by D. Romano, 2:501–541. Girona, 1988.

Minorités et marginaux en France méridionale et dans la peninsule Ibérique (VIIe–XVIIIe siècles) (Actes du colloque de Pau, 27–29 mai, 1984). Paris, 1986.

Miret y Sans, J. "Le massacre des juifs de Montclus en 1320: épisode de l'entrée des pastoureaux dans l'Aragon." *RdÉJ* 53 (1907): 255–266.

————. "El procés de les hosties contra.ls jueues d'Osca en 1377." *Anuari de l'Institut d'Estudis Catalans* 4 (1911–1912): 59–80.

Mitchell, T. *Violence and Piety in Spanish Folklore.* Philadelphia, 1988.

Mollaret, H., and J. Brossollet. "La peste, source méconnue d'inspiration artistique." *Koninklijk Museum voor schone Kunsten, Jaarboek 1965.*

Mollat, M., and P. Wolff. *Ongles bleus, Jacques et Ciompi: les révolutions populaires en Europe aux XIVe et XVe siècles.* Paris, 1970.

Monroe, J. *Hispano-Arabic Poetry: A Student Anthology.* Berkeley, 1974.

Moore, B., Jr. *Injustice: The Social Bases of Obedience and Revolt.* White Plains, NY, 1987.

Moore, R. I. *The Formation of a Persecuting Society.* Oxford, 1987.

————. "Heresy as Disease." In *The Concept of Heresy in the Middle Ages (Eleventh–Thirteenth C.),* edited by W. Lourdaux and D. Verhelst, pp. 1–11. The Hague, 1976.

Moreira, J. *Del Folklore Tortosí.* Barcelona, 1934.

Morel-Fatio, A. "Notes et documents pour servir à l'histoire des Juifs des Baléares sous la domination aragonaise du XIIIe au XVe siècle." *RdÉJ* 4 (1882): 31–56.

Moreno Koch, Y. *Dos crónicas hispanohebreas del siglo XV.* Barcelona, 1992.

Muldoon, J. *Popes, Lawyers, and Infidels: The Church and the Non-Christian World, 1250–1550.* Philadelphia, 1979.

Mutgé Vives, J. *L'aljama sarraïna de Lleida a l'edat mitjana: aproximació a la seva historia.* Barcelona, 1992.

————. *La ciudad de Barcelona durante el reinado de Alfonso el Benigno (1327–1336).* Barcelona, 1987.

Myers, D. " 'From Zion will go forth Torah': Jewish Scholarship and the Zionist Return to History." Ph.D. diss., Columbia University, 1991.

Nadich, J. *Jewish Legends of the Second Commonwealth.* Philadelphia, 1982.

Narbona Vizcaíno, R. *Pueblo, poder y sexo. Valencia medieval (1306–1420).* Valencia, 1992.

————. "Violencias feudales en la ciudad de Valencia." In *Violència i marginació en la societat medieval (= Revista d'Història Medieval* 1 [1990]), pp. 59–86.

Nelkin, D., and S. Gilman. "Placing Blame for Devastating Disease." *Social Research* 55 (1988): 361–378.

Niederhellmann, A. *Arzt und Heilkunde in den Frühmittelalterlichen Leges.* Berlin, 1983.

Nieto Fernández, A. "Hermandad entre las aljamas de moros y las villas de la goberna-ción de Orihuela en el siglo XV." *Primer Congreso de Historia del País Valenciano*, 2:749–760. Valencia, 1980.

Nirenberg, D. "Les juifs, la violence, et le sacré." *Annales: HSS* 50 (1995): 109–131.

———. "Maria's Conversion to Judaism." *Orim: A Jewish Journal at Yale* 2 (1984): 38–44.

———. "Muslim-Jewish Relations in the Fourteenth-Century Crown of Aragon." *Viator* 24 (1993): 249–268.

———. "Violence and the Persecution of Minorities in the Crown of Aragon: Jews, Lepers and Muslims before the Black Death." Ph.D. diss., Princeton University, 1992.

Nutton, V. "The Seeds of Disease: An Explanation of Contagion and Infection from the Greeks to the Renaissance." *Medical History* 27 (1983): 1–34.

O'Callaghan, J. F. "The Mudejars of Castile and Portugal in the Twelfth and Thirteenth Centuries." In *Muslims Under Latin Rule: 1100–1300*, edited by J. M. Powell, pp. 11–56. Princeton, 1990.

Ollich i Castanyer, I. "Aspects econòmics de l'activitat dels jueus de Vic, segons els *Libri iudeorum* (1266–1278)." *Miscel.lània de Textos Medievals* 3 (1985): 1–118.

Omont, M. "Mémorial de l'inquisition d'Aragon à la fin du XIVe siècle." *Bibliothèque de l'Ecole des Chartes* 66 (1905): 261–268.

Orcástegui, C., and E. Sarasa. "El libro-registro de Miguel Royo, merino de Zaragoza en 1301: una fuente para el estudio de la sociedad y economía zaragozanas a comienzos del siglo XIV." *Aragón en la Edad Media* 4 (1981): 87–156.

———. "Miguel Palacín, Merino de Zaragoza en el siglo XIV." *Aragón en la Edad Media* 1 (1977): 51–131.

Ordonnances des rois de France de la troisième race. Edited by E.-J. Laurière et al. 21 vols. Paris, 1723–1849.

Otis, L. *Prostitution in Medieval Society: The History of an Urban Institution in Languedoc.* Chicago, 1985.

Pakter, W. *Medieval Canon Law and the Jews*. Ebelsbach am Main, 1988.

Palacios Martín, B. *La Coronación de los reyes de Aragón, 1204–1410*. Valencia, 1975.

Pareja, F. "Un relato morisco sobre la vida de Jesús y María." *Estudios Eclesiásticos* 34 (1960): 859–871.

Parkes, J. *The Conflict of the Church and the Synagogue*. London, 1934.

Pateman, C. *The Sexual Contract*. Stanford, 1988.

Patterson, O. *Slavery and Social Death: A Comparative Study*. Cambridge, MA, 1982.

Pegg, M. "Le corps et l'autorité: la lèpre de Baudouin IV." *Annales: ESC* 45 (1990): 265–287.

Perarnau i Espelt, J. "L'*Allocutio Christini* d'Arnau de Vilanova." *Arxiu de Textos Catalans Antics* 11 (1992): 7–135.

——— "El procés inquisitorial barceloní contra els jueus Janto Almuli, la seva muller Jamila i Jucef de Quatorze (1341–1342)." *Revista Catalana de Teologia* 4 (1979): 309–353.

Pere III of Catalonia (Pedro IV of Aragón): Chronicle. Translated by M. Hillgarth. Edited by J. Hillgarth. 2 vols. Toronto, 1980.

Pérez Santamaría, A. "El hospital de San Lazaro o Casa dels Malalts o Masells." In *La pobreza y la asistencia a los pobres en la Cataluña medieval*, edited by M. Riu, 1:77–115. *Anuario de Estudios Medievales*, anejo 9. Barcelona, 1980.

Perles, J. R. *Salomo b. Abraham b. Adereth. Sein Leben und seine Schriften.* Breslau, 1863.

Perlmann, M. "The Medieval Polemics between Islam and Judaism." In *Religion in a Religious Age,* edited by S. D. Goitein, pp. 103–138. Cambridge, MA, 1974.

Persons in Groups: Social Behavior as Identity Formation in Medieval and Renaissance Europe. Edited by R. Trexler. Binghamton, NY, 1985.

Pflaum, H. "Les scènes de juifs dans la littérature dramatique du moyen-âge." *RdÉJ* 89 (1930): 111–134.

Pichon, G. "La lèpre et le péché: Étude d'une représentation médiévale." *Nouvelle revue de Psychanalyse* 38 (1988): 147–157.

Pié, J. "Autos Sagramentals del sigle XIV." *Revista de la Asociación Artístico-Arqueológica Barcelonisa* 1 (1896–1898): 673–683 and 726–744.

Piles Ros, L. *Estudio documental sobre el Bayle General de Valencia.* Valencia, 1970.

Pilosu, M. *La donna, la lussuria e la chiesa nel medioevo.* Genoa, 1989.

Pinto, G. *Il libro del biadaiolo: Carestia e annona a Firenze della metà del '200 al 1348.* Florence, 1978.

Pistarino, G. "Genova e Barcellona: incontro e scontro di due civiltà." In *Atti del I° congresso storico Liguria-Catalogna (ottobre 1969),* pp. 81–122. Bordighera, 1974.

Pitt-Rivers, J. *The Fate of Shechem, or the Politics of Sex: Six Essays in the Anthropology of the Mediterranean.* Cambridge, 1977.

Plato, *Theaetetus.* In *Collected Dialogues,* edited by E. Hamilton and H. Cairns, pp. 845–919. Princeton, 1963.

La pobreza y la asistencia a los pobres en la Cataluña medieval. Edited by M. Riu. 2 vols. *Anuario de Estudios Medievales,* anejos 9 and 11. Barcelona, 1980–1982.

Poliakov, L. *The Aryan Myth: A History of Rascist and Nationalist Ideas in Europe.* New York, 1974.

———. *The History of Anti-Semitism.* London, 1965.

Pospisil, L. *The Ethnology of Law.* 2d ed. Menlo Park, CA, 1978.

Prakash, G. *Bonded Histories: Genealogies of Labor Servitude in Colonial India.* Cambridge, 1990.

The Prose Salernitan Questions. Edited by B. Lawn. London, 1979.

Pullan, B. *The Jews of Europe and the Inquisition of Venice, 1550–1670.* Totowa, NJ, 1983.

al-Qarāfī, Aḥmad ibn Idrīs. *Al-ajwiba al-fākhira ʿan al-asʾila al-fājira.* In the margins of ʿAbd al-Raḥman Bachajī Zādeh, *Al-fāriq bayn al-makhlūq waʾl-khāliq.* Cairo, 1322/1904.

Radcliffe-Brown, A. Preface to *African Political Systems,* edited by M. Fortes and E. Evans-Pritchard. London, 1940.

Recueil des historiens des Gaules et de la France. Edited by M. Bouquet et al. 24 vols. Paris, 1738–1904.

Le registre de l'inquisition de Jacques Fournier, 1318–25. Edited by J. Duvernoy. 3 vols. Toulouse, 1965.

Registres du Trésor des chartes, I: Règne de Philippe le Bel. Edited by R. Fawtier. Paris, 1958.

Reglá Campistrol, J. *Estudios sobre los moriscos.* 3d ed. Valencia, 1974.

Régné, J. *History of the Jews in the Crown of Aragon.* Edited by Y. T. Assis and A. Gruzman. Jerusalem, 1978.

———. "Rapports entre l'inquisition et les juifs d'après le mémorial de l'inquisiteur d'Aragon (fin du XIVe siècle)." *RdÉJ* 52 (1906): 224–233.

Reif, S. "What Enraged Phineas?: A Study of Numbers 25:8." *Journal of Biblical Literature* 90 (1971): 200–206.

Reworking the Past: Hitler, the Holocaust, and the Historians' Debate. Edited by P. Baldwin. Boston, 1990.

Ribera y Tarragó, J. "La enseñanza entre los musulmanes españoles." In his *Disertaciones y opúsculos*, 1:229–359. Madrid, 1928.

Ribera y Tarragó, J., and M. Asín Palacios. *Manuscritos Arabes y Aljamiados de la Biblioteca de la Junta*. Madrid, 1912.

Riches, D. "The Phenomenon of Violence." In *The Anthropology of Violence*, edited by D. Riches, pp. 1–27. Oxford, 1986.

Riera i Sans, J. "Els avalots del 1391 a Girona." In *Jornades d'història dels jueus a Catalunya*, pp. 95–159. Girona, 1987.

———. "La Catalunya jueva del segle XIV." *L'Avenç* 25 (March 1980): 52–55.

———. "La conflictivitat de l'alimentació dels jueus medievals (segles XII–XV)." In *Alimentació i societat a la Catalunya medieval*, pp. 295–311. Barcelona, 1988.

———. "El dalfinat de Girona (1387–1388)." *Annals de l'Institut d'Estudis Gironins* 29 (1987): 105–128.

———. "Guia per a una lectura comprensiva dels acords." *Calls* 2 (1987): 164–173.

———. "Jafudà Alatzar, jueu de València (segle XIV)." *Revista d'Història Medieval* 4 (1993): 65–100.

———. "Supuestos agotes vascos en Monzón." *Príncipe de Viana* 36 (1975): 465–470.

———. "Los tumultos contra las juderías de la Corona de Aragón en 1391." *Cuadernos de Historia: Anejos de la Revista Hispania* 8 (1977): 213–225.

Rivière-Chalan, V. *La marque infâme des lepreux et des christians, sous l'Ancien Régime*. Paris, 1978.

Roca Traver, F. *El justicia de Valencia, 1238–1321*. Valencia, 1970.

———. "Un siglo de vida mudéjar en la Valencia medieval (1238–1338)." *Estudios de Edad Media de la Corona de Aragón* 5 (1952): 115–208.

Rodríguez, A. *Leyendas aljamiadas y moriscas sobre personajes bíblicos*. Madrid, 1983.

Le Roman de Perceval. Edited by W. Roach. Geneva, 1956.

Romano, D. "Conversión de judíos al Islam." *Sefarad* 36 (1976): 333–337.

———. "Figurantes judíos en representaciones sacras (Villarreal, siglos XIV y XV)." *Sefarad* 29 (1969): 75–76.

———. *Judíos al servicio de Pedro el Grande de Aragón (1276–1285)*. Barcelona, 1983.

———. "Los judíos en los baños de Tortosa." *Sefarad* 40 (1980): 57–64.

———. "Judíos hispánicos y mundo rural." *Sefarad* 51 (1991): 353–367.

——— "Musulmanes residentes y emigrantes en la Barcelona de los siglos XIV–XV." *Al-Andalus* 41 (1976): 49–88.

———. "Prorrata de contribuyentes judíos de Jaca en 1377." *Sefarad* 42 (1982): 3–39.

Romeu Alfaro, S. "Los fueros de Valencia y los fueros de Aragón: jurisdicción Alfonsina." In *Anuario de Historia del Derecho Español* 42 (1972): 75–115.

Ronsard, P. de. *Oeuvres Complètes* (La Pléiade). 2 vols. Paris, 1950.

Roper, L. " 'The Common Man', 'the Common Good', 'Common Women': Gender and Meaning in the German Reformation Commune." *Social History* 12 (1987): 1–21.

———. "Discipline and Respectability: Prostitution and the Reformation in Augsburg." *History Workshop* 19 (1985): 3–28.

Rosen, L. *Bargaining for Reality: The Construction of Social Relations in a Muslim Community.* Chicago, 1984.

Rossiaud, J. *Medieval Prostitution.* Translated by L. Cochrane. Oxford, 1988.

Roth, C. "European Jewry and the Dark Ages: A Revised Picture." *Hebrew Union College Annual* 23 (1950–1951): 151–169.

———. *A History of the Jews in England.* Oxford, 1964.

Roth, N. "The Jews in Spain at the Time of Maimonides." In *Moses Maimonides and His Times.* Studies in Philosophy and the History of Philosophy 19, edited by E. L. Ormsby, pp. 1–20. Washington, DC, 1989.

———. "The Jews of Spain and the Expulsion of 1492." *Historian* 55, no. 1 (Fall 1992): 17–30.

———. *Jews, Visigoths, and Muslims in Medieval Spain: Cooperation and Conflict.* Leiden, 1994.

———. "1992 and Its Mythology: A Warning." *Jewish Spectator* 55, no. 4 (Spring 1991): 26–30.

Rothkrug, L. "Peasant and Jew: Fears of Pollution and German Collective Perceptions." *Historical Reflections / Réflexions Historiques* 10 (1983): 59–77.

Rubin, G. "The Traffic in Women: Notes on the 'Political Economy' of Sex." In *Toward an Anthropology of Women,* edited by R. Reiter, pp. 157–210. New York, 1975.

Rubió y Lluch, A. *Documents per l'historia de la cultura catalan mig-eval.* 2 vols. Barcelona, 1921.

Rubio Vela, A. *Epistolari de la València medieval.* Valencia, 1985.

———. *Peste negra, crisis y comportamientos sociales en la España del siglo XIV: La ciudad de Valencia (1348–1401).* Granada, 1979.

———. *Pobreza, enfermedad y asistencia hospitalaria en la Valencia del siglo XIV.* Valencia, 1984.

Ruiz, T. "Une royauté sans sacre: la monarchie castillane du bas moyen age." *Annales: ESC* 39 (1984): 429–453.

Rupert of Deutz. *In Ieremiam prophetam commentariorum liber unus.* PL 167.1363–1419.

Ruzafa García, M. " 'Façen-se Cristians los moros o muyren!' " In *Violència i marginació en la societat medieval* (= *Revista d'Història Medieval* 1 [1990]), 87–110.

Sabean, D. *Power in the Blood: Popular Culture and Village Discourse in Early Modern Germany.* Cambridge, 1984.

Sackur, E. *Sybyllinische Texte und Forschungen.* Halle a.d.S., 1898. Reprint, Torino, 1963.

Sahlins, M. *Islands of History.* Chicago, 1985.

Sahlins, P. *Boundaries: The Making of France and Spain in the Pyrenees.* Berkeley, 1989.

Saige, G. *Les juifs du Languedoc antérieurement au XIVe siècle.* Paris, 1881.

Sáinz de la Maza, R. *La orden de Santiago en la Corona de Aragon (II): La encomienda de Montalbán bajo Vidal de Vilanova (1327–1357).* Zaragoza, 1988.

Salarrullana de Dios, J. "Estudios históricos acerca de la ciudad de Fraga: la aljama de judíos de Fraga." *Revista de Archivos, Bibliotecas y Museos,* 3ª epoca, año 23, 40 (1919): 69–90, 183–206, 431–446.

———. "Estudios históricos acerca de la ciudad de Fraga: la aljama de moros de Fraga." *Revista de Archivos, Bibliotecas y Museos,* 3ª epoca, año 26, 42 (1921): 361–381, 491–512, and 43:19–44, 197–234, 354–374.

Salvà i Ballester, A. *Bosqueig històric i bibliogràfic de les Festes de Moros i Cristians.* Alacant, 1958.

Sanahuja, P. "El monestir de Santa Clara de Cervera." *Estudis Franciscans* 47 (1935): 301–333, 457–482.

Sánchez Adell, J. "Castellón de la Plana en la baja edad media." *Boletín de la Sociedad Castellonense de Cultura* 54 (1978): 310–343.

Sánchez-Albornoz, C. *España: un enigma histórico.* 2 vols. Buenos Aires, 1956.

Sánchez Martínez, M. "La Corona de Aragón y el Reino Nazarí de Granada durante el siglo XIV: Las bases materiales y humanas de la cruzada de Alfonso IV (1329–1335)." Ph.D. diss., University of Barcelona, 1974.

———. "La fiscalidad real y las aljamas catalano-aragonesas en el primer tercio del siglo XIV." *Acta Historica et Archaeologica Mediaevalia* 3 (1982): 93–142.

———. "Mallorquines y Genoveses en Almeria durante el primer tercio del siglo XIV: El proceso contra Jaume Manfré." *Miscel.lània de Textos Medievals* 4 (1988), *La frontera terrestre i marítima amb l'islam*, pp. 103–162.

Sans i Travé, J. M. *El procés dels Templers catalans.* 2d ed. Lleida, 1991.

Santamaría Arández, A. "La peste negra en Mallorca." In *VIII Congreso de Historia de la Corona de Aragón* II.1, pp. 103–130. Valencia, 1969.

Santiago-Otero, H. "The *Libro declarante*: An Anonymous Work in the Anti-Jewish Polemic in Spain." *Proceedings of the Tenth World Congress of Jewish Studies, Division B.* Vol. 2, edited by D. Assaf, pp. 77–81. Jerusalem, 1990.

Santiago-Otero, H., and K. Reinhardt. "Escritos de polémica antijudía en lengua vernácula." *Medievalia* 2 (1993): 185–195.

Santillana, D. *Istituzioni di diritto musulmano malichita con riguardo anche al sistema sciafiita.* 2 vols. Rome, 1925–1938.

Santos Otero, A. de. *Los Evangelios Apócrifos.* Madrid, 1984.

Saperstein, M. *Decoding the Rabbis: A Thirteenth-Century Commentary on the Aggadah.* Cambridge, MA, 1980.

Schacht, J. *An Introduction to Islamic Law.* Oxford, 1964.

Schiffman, L., and M. Swartz. *Hebrew and Aramaic Incantation Texts from the Cairo Genizah.* Sheffield, 1992.

Schneider, J. "Of Vigilance and Virgins: Honor, Shame and Access to Resources in Mediterranean Societies." *Ethnology* 10 (1971): 1–24.

Schreckenberg, H. *Rezeptionsgeschichtliche und textkritische Untersuchungen zu Flavius Josephus.* Leiden, 1977.

Schreiner, M. "Die apologetische Schrift des Salomo b. Adret gegen einen Muhammedaner." *Zeitschrift der Deutschen Morgenländischen Gesellschaft* 48 (1894): 39–42.

Scott, J. *Domination and the Arts of Resistance: The Hidden Transcript.* New Haven, 1990.

Secall i Güell, G. *La comunitat hebrea de Santa Coloma de Queralt.* Tarragona, 1986.

Sedgwick, E. *Between Men: English Literature and Male Homosocial Desire.* New York, 1985.

Seed, P. *To Love Honor and Obey in Colonial Mexico: Conflicts over Marriage Choice, 1574–1821.* Stanford, 1988.

Septimus, B. " 'Better under Edom Than under Ishmael,' the History of a Saying." *Zion* 47 (1982): 103–111 (in Hebrew).

Septimus, B. *Hispano-Jewish Culture in Transition: The Career and Controversies of Ramah.* Cambridge, MA, 1982.

――――. "Hispano-Jewish Views of Christendom and Islam." Unpublished paper.

――――. "Piety and Power in Thirteenth Century Catalonia." In *Studies in Medieval Jewish History and Literature,* edited by I. Twersky, pp. 197–230. Cambridge, MA, 1979.

Sermo de sacrilegia. PL, Supplementum, 4.969–973.

Serra Ruiz, R. *Honor, honra e injuria en el Derecho medieval Español.* Murcia, 1969.

Serra Vilaró, J. *Santa Tecla la Vieja.* Tarragona, 1960.

Shatzmiller, J. "Les juifs de Provence pendant la peste noire." *RdÉJ* 133 (1974): 457–480.

――――. *Shylock Reconsidered: Jews, Moneylending, and Medieval Society.* Berkeley, 1990.

Shirk, M. "The Black Death in Aragon, 1348–1351." *Journal of Medieval History* 7 (1981): 357–367.

――――. "Violence and the Plague in Aragón, 1348–1351." *Journal of the Rocky Mountain Medieval and Renaissance Association* 5 (1984): 31–39.

Shmueli, E. *Seven Jewish Cultures: A Reinterpretation of Jewish History and Thought.* New York, 1990.

Sifre: A Tannaitic Commentary on the Book of Deuteronomy. Translated by R. Hammer. New Haven, 1986.

Simmel, G. "Conflict." In *"Conflict" and "The Web of Group-Affiliation,"* translated by K. Wolff, pp. 11–123. London, 1955.

Simonsohn, S. *The Apostolic See and the Jews. Documents: 492–1404.* Toronto, 1988.

――――. *History of the Jews in the Duchy of Mantua.* Jerusalem, 1977.

Slack, P. "Responses to Plague in Early Modern Europe: The Implications of Public Health." *Social Research* 55 (1988): 433–453.

Sobrequés Callicó, J. "La Peste negra en la península ibérica." In *Actas del I Simposio de Historia Medieval: La Investigación de la Historia Hispánica del siglo XIV, Problemas y Cuestiones,* pp. 67–102. Madrid and Barcelona, 1973.

Southern, R. *The Making of the Middle Ages.* New Haven, 1953.

Spiegel, G. " 'Defense of the Realm': Evolution of a Capetian Propaganda Slogan." *Journal of Medieval History* 3 (1977): 115–133.

The Staging of Religious Drama in Europe and the Later Middle Ages Edited by P. Meredith and J. Tailby. Kalamazoo, MI, 1983.

Stalls, W. C. "Jewish Conversion to Islam: The Perspective of a *Quaestio*." *Revista Española de Teología* 43 (1983): 235–251.

Stallybrass, P., and A. White. *The Politics and Poetics of Transgression.* Ithaca, NY, 1986.

Steinschneider, M. *Polemische und apologetische Literatur in arabischer Sprache.* Leipzig, 1877.

Stern, S. M. "Rationalists and Kabbalists in Medieval Allegory." *Journal of Jewish Studies* 6 (1955): 73–86.

Stillman, N. "Myth, Countermyth, and Distortion." *Tikkun* 6, no. 3 (May–June 1991): 60–64.

Stow, K. *Alienated Minority: The Jews of Medieval Latin Europe.* Cambridge, MA, 1992.

Strathern, M. *The Gender of the Gift: Problems with Women and Problems with Society in Melanesia.* Berkeley, 1988.

Strayer, J. "The Costs and Profits of War: The Anglo-French Conflict of 1294–1303."

In *The Medieval City*, edited by H. Miskimin, D. Herlihy, and A. Udovitch, pp. 269–291. New Haven, 1977.

———. *The Reign of Philip the Fair*. Princeton, 1980.

Suma de los principales mandamientos y devedamientos de la ley y çunna por don Içe de Gebir. . . . Edited by P. de Gayangos. In *Memorial Histórico Español*, 5:247–421. Madrid, 1853.

Sutton-Smith, B. "Games of Order and Disorder." Paper presented to the Symposium on Forms of Symbolic Inversion, American Anthropological Association, Toronto, December 1972.

Taylor, C. "French Assemblies and Subsidy in 1321." *Speculum* 43 (1968): 217–244.

TeBrake, W. *A Plague of Insurrection: Popular Politics and Peasant Revolt in Flanders, 1323–1328*. Philadelphia, 1993.

Thomas of Chobham. *Summa confessorum*. Edited by F. Broomfield. *Analecta Mediaevalia Namurcensia* 25. Louvain, 1968.

Thompson, E. P. "The Moral Economy of the English Crowd in the Eighteenth Century." In *Customs in Common*, pp. 185–258. London, 1991. Reprinted from *Past and Present* 50 (1971).

———. "The Moral Economy Reviewed." In *Customs in Common*, pp. 259–351. London, 1991.

Tischendorf, C. *Evangelia Apocrypha*. Leipzig, 1876.

Toaff, A. *Il vino e la carne: Una comunità ebraica nel Medioevo*. Bologna, 1989.

Torres Fontes, J. "La hermandad de moros y cristianos para el rescate de cautivos." In *Actas del I Simposio de Mudejarismo*, pp. 499–508. Teruel, 1981.

Torró, J. "Sobre ordenament feudal del territori i trasbalsaments del poblament mudèjar: La *Montanea Valencie* (1286–1291)." *Afers* 7 (1988–1989): 95–124.

Touati, F.-O. "Facies leprosorum: réflexions sur le diagnostic facial de la lèpre au Moyen Age." *Histoire des Sciences Médicales* 20 (1986): 57–66.

———. "Histoire des maladies, histoire total?" *Sources. Travaux historiques* 13 (1988): 3–14.

Un tratado Catalán medieval de derecho islámico: el llibre de la çuna e xara dels moros. Edited by C. Barceló. Córdoba, 1989.

Trevisa's Dialogus inter Militem et Clericum, Sermon by FitzRalph and þe Bygynnyng of þe World. Edited by A. Perry. Early English Text Society, vol. 167. London, 1925.

Trexler, R. "From the Mouths of Babes: Christianization by Children in Sixteenth Century New Spain." In *Church and Community, 1200–1600*, pp. 549–573. Rome, 1987.

———. "Ritual in Florence: Adolescence and Salvation in the Renaissance." In *The Pursuit of Holiness in Late Medieval and Renaissance Religion*, edited by H. Oberman and C. Trinkaus, pp. 200–264. Leiden, 1974.

———. "We Think, They Act: Clerical Readings of Missionary Theatre in Sixteenth Century New Spain." In *Understanding Popular Culture: Europe from the Middle Ages to the Nineteenth Century*, edited by S. Kaplan, pp. 189–227. Berlin, 1984.

Turner, V. *From Ritual to Theatre: The Human Seriousness of Play*. New York, 1982.

Ubieto, A. *Historia de Aragón*. Vol. 1, *Divisiones Administrativas*. Zaragoza, 1983.

Usque, Samuel. *Consolaçam as Tribulaçoes de Israel*. Ferrara, 1552.

———. *Consolation for the Tribulations of Israel*. Translated by M. A. Cohen. Philadelphia, 1965.

Utrilla Utrilla, J., and J. C. Esco Samperiz. "La población mudéjar en la Hoya de Huesca (siglos XII y XIII)." In *Actas del III Simposio Internacional de Mudejarismo*, pp. 187–208. Teruel, 1986.

Vajda, G. "Un chapitre de l'histoire du conflit entre la kabbale et la philosophie: la polémique anti-intellectualiste de Joseph ben Shalom Ashkenazi de Catalogne." *Archives d'histoire doctrinale et littéraire du Moyen Age*, 1957, pp. 45–144.

———. "Juifs et Musulmans selon le Ḥadīt." *Journal Asiatique* 229 (1937): 57–127.

Valdeón Baruque, J. *Los conflictos sociales en el reino de Castilla en los siglos XIV y XV.* Madrid, 1975.

———. *Los judios de Castilla y la revolucion Trastamara.* Valladolid, 1968.

Van D'Elden, S. C. "Black and White: Contact with the Mediterranean World in Medieval German Narrative." In *The Medieval Mediterranean: Cross-Cultural Contacts.* Medieval Studies at Minnesota 3, edited by M. Chiat and K. Reyerson, pp. 112–118. St. Cloud, MN, 1988.

Vendrell de Millás, F. "En torno a la confirmación real, en Aragón, de la pragmatica de Benedicto XIII." *Sefarad* 20 (1960): 1–33.

Verlinden, C. *L'esclavage dans l'Europe Médiévale.* Vol. 1, *Péninsule Ibérique-France.* Bruges, 1955.

———. "La Grande Peste de 1348 en Espagne." *Revue Belge de Philologie et d'Histoire* 17 (1938): 103–146.

Viajes de extranjeros por España y Portugal. Vol. 1. Edited by J. García Mercadal. Madrid, 1952.

Vicens Vives, J. *Manual de história económica de España.* 4th ed. Barcelona, 1965.

Vidal, J.-M. "L'Émeute des pastoureaux en 1320: Lettres du pape Jean XXII; déposition du Juif Barac devant l'Inquisition de Pamiers." *Annales de Saint-Louis-des-Français: publication trimestrielle des études et travaux des chapelains* 3 (1898): 121–174.

———. "Le messire de Parthenay et l'Inquisition (1323–1325)." *Bulletin historique et philologique*, 1913, pp. 414–434.

———. "La poursuite des lépreux en 1321 d'après des documents nouveaux." *Annales de Saint-Louis-des-Français: publication trimestrielle des études et travaux des chapelains* 4 (1900): 419–478.

Vides de sants rosselloneses. 3 vols. Edited by C. Maneikis Kniazzeh and E. Neugaard. Barcelona, 1977.

Viguera, M. *Aragón Musulman: La presencia del Islam en el Valle del Ebro.* Zaragoza, 1988.

Villanueva, J. *Viaje literario a las Iglesias de España.* 22 vols. Madrid, 1803–1852.

St. Vincent Ferrer. *Sant Vincent Ferrer: Sermons.* Vols. 3–6. Edited by G. Schib. Barcelona, 1975–1988.

———. *Sermons.* Vol. 1. Edited by J. Sanchis Sivera. Barcelona, 1932.

Vincke, J. *Documenta selecta mutuas civitatis arago-cathalaunicae et ecclesiae relationes illustrantia.* Barcelona, 1936.

———. *Zur Vorgeschichte der Spanischen Inquisition: Die Inquisition in Aragon, Katalonien, Mallorca und Valencia während des 13. und 14. Jahrhunderts, Beiträge zur Kirchen- und Rechtsgeschichte.* Vol. 2. Bonn, 1941.

Vinyoles, T.-M. "L'esdevenir quotidià: treball i lleure de les dones medievals." In *Més enllà del silenci: les dones a la història de Catalunya*, edited by M. Nash, pp. 73–89. Barcelona, 1988.

Voltaire, F.-M. *Lettres philosophiques.* Paris, 1964.

Wacholder, B. Z. "Attitudes towards Proselytizing in the Classical Halakah." *Historia Judaica* 20, no. 2 (1958): 77–96.

Walter of Wimborne. *The Poems of Walter of Wimborne.* Edited by A. G. Rigg. Toronto, 1978.

Weakland, J. "Pastorelli, Pope, and Persecution: A Tragic Episode in 1320." *Jewish Social Studies* 38 (1976): 73–76.

Weber, M. *Law in Economy and Society.* New York, 1967.

White, H. "Historical Emplotment and the Problem of Truth." In *Probing the Limits of Representation: Nazism and the "Final Solution,"* ed. S. Friedlander, pp. 37–53. Cambridge, MA, 1992.

Wickersheimer, E. "Les accusations d'empoisonnements portées pendant la première moitié du XIVe siècle contre les lépreux et les Juifs; leurs relations avec les épidémies de la peste." *Comptes-rendus du 4ᵉ Congrès International de l'histoire de la médecine,* ed. Tricot-Roger and Laignel-Lavestine, pp. 76–83. Antwerp, 1927.

Wiegers, G. *Islamic Literature in Spanish and Aljamiado: Yça of Segovia (fl. 1450), His Antecedents and Successors.* Leiden, 1994.

Williams, R. *Marxism and Literature.* Oxford, 1977.

Wolf, A. "Los *Fori Aragonum* de 1247 y el Vidal Mayor." *Anuario de Historia del Derecho Español* 53 (1983): 178–203.

Wolff, P. "The 1391 Pogrom in Spain: Social Crisis or Not?" *Past and Present* 50 (1971): 4–18.

Wolfram von Eschenbach: Parzival: Studienausgabe. Edited by K. Lachmann. Berlin, 1965.

Wolin, R. *Walter Benjamin: An Aesthetic of Redemption.* New York, 1982.

Wright, S. *The Vengeance of Our Lord: Medieval Dramatizations of the Destruction of Jerusalem.* Toronto, 1989.

Wyatt-Brown, B. *Southern Honor: Ethics and Behavior in the Old South.* New York, 1982.

Yehuda ben Asher, R. *Zikhron Yehuda.* Berlin, 1846.

Yerushalmi, Y. *Assimilation and Racial Anti-Semitism: The Iberian and the German Models.* Leo Baeck Memorial Lecture 26. New York, 1982.

———. "The Inquisition and the Jews of France in the Time of Bernard Gui." *Harvard Theological Review* 63 (1970): 317–376.

———. "Messianic Impulses in Joseph ha-Cohen." In *Jewish Thought in the Sixteenth Century,* edited by D. Cooperman, pp. 460–487. Cambridge, MA, 1983.

———. *Zakhor: Jewish History and Jewish Memory.* Seattle, 1982.

Young, I. *Justice and the Politics of Difference.* Princeton, 1990.

Zacour, N. *Jews and Saracens in the Consilia of Oldradus de Ponte.* Toronto, 1990.

Zurita, J. *Anales de la Corona de Aragón.* Edited by A. Canellas López. 9 vols. Zaragoza, 1967–1986.

INDEX